MORAL DISCOURSE

in a Pluralistic World

This book is dedicated to my maternal grandmother,

MARY CHRISTINA (GRIFFIN) EVE

in memory of her fiery spirit and cheerful wisdom

Banish wisdom, discard knowledge,
And the people will be benefited a hundredfold.
Banish human kindness, discard morality,
And the people will be dutiful and compassionate.
Banish skill, discard profit,
And thieves and robbers will disappear.
If when these three things are done they find life
too plain and unadorned,
Let them have accessories;
Give them simplicity to look at,
the Uncarved Block to hold,
Give them selflessness and fewness of desires.

—Tao Tê Ching

MORAL DISCOURSE

in a Pluralistic World

DANIEL VOKEY

UNIVERSITY OF NOTRE DAME PRESS

Notre Dame, Indiana

Manufactured in the United States of America

Library of Congress Cataloging-in-Publication Data
Vokey, Daniel.
Moral discourse in a pluralistic world / Daniel Vokey.
p. cm.
Includes bibliographical references and index.
ISBN 0-268-03466-4 (alk. paper)
1. Ethics. 2. Pluralism (Social sciences)—Moral and
ethical aspects. I. Title.
BJ1012.V655 2001
170'.42—dc21   2001000524

∞ *This book is printed on acid-free paper.*

Contents

Preface

In this book, I show how—contrary to the claims of moral sceptics—it is possible for people from very different moral traditions to argue productively about the issues that divide them. Along the way, I venture to analyse, critique, and reconstruct Alasdair MacIntyre's account of the rationality of traditions; chart the epistemological middle ground between objectivism and relativism; outline a coherent conceptual framework for moral intuitionism; and restore the traditional association between the beautiful and the good. My hope is that, by clarifying the ways in which genuine agreement on moral issues can be pursued through moral discourse, this book will help address some of the political, social, and environmental problems resulting from unresolved moral conflict. Agreement on some core of fundamental moral values is necessary, I believe, for justice and democracy to flourish.

The arguments in this book first took form as a doctoral dissertation in the Philosophy of Education Program of the Ontario Institute for Studies in Education at the University of Toronto (OISE/UT). Those arguments were sharpened by astute comments from my supervisor, Dwight Boyd; from other members of my committee, Dieter Misgeld, Deanne Bogdan, and Ronald de Sousa; and from the examiners, Wayne Sumner and Alasdair MacIntyre. The dissertation also benefited from the kindness of other faculty and students at OISE/UT—most especially Barbara Appelbaum, Alan Cantor, Jim Cunningham, Claudia Eppert, and Stella Gaon—who questioned my assumptions and shared their ideas, thereby broadening my intellectual horizons.

All of these generous souls must be exempted, of course, from any responsibility for the errors in which I persist.

The crux of this book's argument against moral scepticism lies in its characterization of intrinsic moral goodness. In defending that characterization against anticipated objections, I draw freely from the conceptual resources of Mahāyāna Buddhism. For my introduction to the buddhadharma I am indebted to the past and present teachers of the Karma Kagyü and the Nyingma lineages, and most particularly to Chögyam Trungpa Rinpoché. I am indebted also to my instructors and friends at Shambhala International for their guidance and companionship on the path of meditation. I owe a special debt of thanks to Chris Elliott, Charles Davis, and Anne Bruce for setting my feet on that path.

Through the many years during which this book has been written, I have been blessed by the support of family and friends. Joyce and Lyle Morton, Bessie Silver, and many others made me welcome when I sought respite in Lunenburg County. Patricia and Denis Eve, Trudy and Edgar Eve, and Lauretta and Brydon Horwood all conspired to remind me that there is more to life than book learning. Dorothy Vokey, my mother, has helped me in a thousand ways, not least through providing the inspiration of her strength of spirit. One of my few regrets in connection with this book is that my father, Wilfred Vokey, did not live long enough for me to share it with him. He worked very hard to give me the educational opportunities that he was denied.

My partner, Charlene Morton, has provided moral and dietary fibre to sustain me through the ups and downs of the writing process. I continue to benefit from her insight, wry humour, and tender heart.

Those who I have mentioned and many others I have not named—but not forgotten—have contributed much to this book. My heartfelt thanks to all.

Introduction

The man pulling radishes
pointed the way
with a radish.
                    —Issa

My intent in writing this book is very simple: I want to further the cause of greater cooperation within and among nation-states and the peaceful resolution of conflict. We lack sufficient agreement to deal adequately with the grave problems facing the planet and its inhabitants, problems such as poverty and environmental destruction.[1] The persistence of opposing views on such issues as how the earth's natural resources should be developed and by whom increases the chances that disagreement will be resolved through force. As recent wars have dramatically demonstrated, armed conflict within or among nation-states not only obstructs the cooperation we require to respond adequately to human suffering and ecological degradation, it contributes to those very conditions. Poverty and the deterioration of natural and social environments in turn offers fertile ground for violence.

To provide for the possibility of greater cooperation and peaceful resolution of conflict, this book describes how people in a pluralistic world could arrive at a convergence of rival moral points of view. To say more about why I want them to converge and how I will promote that possibility, I will explain what I mean by *moral points of view*.

1

PRACTICAL JUDGMENTS AND MORAL POINTS OF VIEW

As I use the term, *practical judgments* are choices among alternatives in some concrete context of practice. Practical judgments can be influenced by moral values and, as Bernard Williams (1985, 5–18) argues, there is more than one kind of moral value. *Moral judgments* attribute moral value to something in pronouncing it morally right or morally wrong, morally good or morally bad. Moral value could be attributed to objects, events, states of affairs, attitudes, actions, principles, policies, or people, whether past, present, or future. The large question of how moral values might be differentiated from other values is a topic for later discussion. Here, I will only note that we commonly designate as *moral* those values that we believe *ought* to take priority over other considerations in guiding action (however we interpret the force of *ought* in that context).

Practical and moral judgments are not made in a vacuum. They are conditioned by beliefs, attitudes, interests, norms, and priorities that influence and in turn are influenced by the practices in which we engage. Using a visual metaphor, we could say that practical and moral judgment take place within a horizon corresponding to a moral point of view. Bernard Lonergan captures well the meaning of the term *horizon* as I use it here:

> Horizons . . . are the structured results of past achievement and, as well, both the condition and the limitation of further development. They are structured. All learning is, not a mere addition to previous learning, but rather an organic growth out of it. So all our intentions, statements, deeds, stand within contexts. To such contexts we appeal when we outline the reasons for our goals, when we clarify, amplify, qualify our statements, or when we explain our deeds. Within such contexts must be fitted each new item of knowledge and each new factor in our attitudes. What does not fit, will not be noticed or, if forced on our attention, it will seem irrelevant or unimportant. Horizons then are the sweep of our interests and of our knowledge; they are the fertile sources of further knowledge and care; but they also are the boundaries that limit our capacities for assimilating more than we already have attained. (Lonergan 1973, 237)

As I use it, then, the term *moral point of view* is a short-handed way of referring to the sets of beliefs, attitudes, interests, norms, and priorities that condition (but do not determine) practical and moral judgment. Moral points of view typically include implicit or explicit beliefs about what should count as a moral value; that is, why certain kinds of considerations should take precedence over others in deciding what to do.

More will be said about moral points of view in later chapters, but three further aspects of the notion should be mentioned here. First, our decisions and actions typically are consistent with the background assumptions and commitments that constitute our moral standpoint and corresponding horizon. A moral point of view may thus be heuristically defined as the set of beliefs, attitudes, interests, norms, and priorities that would, if known, help explain why we choose and act in the way we do.[2]

Second, the standpoint and corresponding horizon that is implicit in practical judgments involves more than what can be formulated as a set of beliefs. I use the term *moral theory* (also *moral framework* and *scheme of moral beliefs*) to refer to the results of efforts to make explicit the assumptions and commitments that condition particular practical judgments. Moral theories systematize those elements of a moral point of view that can be expressed in propositional form.

Third, agreement on more than moral values is required for social cooperation. Consider an example from education. Legislation on public schooling usually enshrines the basic principle of respect for persons, which is generally derived from the judgment that persons are intrinsically worthy of respect. Teachers can agree that gender stereotyping is contrary to this principle and that it causes harm to both its targets and its perpetrators without necessarily agreeing on broad policies to eliminate gender bias from public schools. They might agree that all students should be treated equally, for instance, but disagree on whether or not this entails treating all students the same. They might thus disagree when, if ever, it is legitimate to restrict classes to students of one or the other sex. Even when teachers agree on broad policies, they might consciously or unconsciously interpret them in different ways. For instance, teachers might share a commitment to discussing with their students how gender stereotypes are reproduced, but devote more class time or less to the topic depending upon their other educational priorities. They might agree that language can reproduce

patriarchal norms but disagree on whether or not it is acceptable to address girls and boys together as "guys." Even two teachers with similar
guidelines for avoiding sexist language and behaviour in the classroom
can interact with students differently, for if one has more background
in and commitment to gender issues than the other, then their unequal
levels of interest will affect which student behaviours they do and do
not notice as requiring correction.

To take a different example, you and I might agree that world hunger
is a problem but still have very different ideas about what we could and
should do about it corresponding to contrary assumptions about the
root causes of poverty. My general point is that practical judgment is
conditioned by a complex interaction of beliefs, attitudes, interests,
norms, and priorities such that achieving greater social cooperation requires, not just a wider consensus on moral values, but also some convergence of our moral points of view.

MORAL TRADITIONS AND MORAL SCEPTICISM

We do not develop our moral points of view in isolation, but in social
contexts shaped by one or more moral communities. By definition, let
us say, a moral community is the present embodiment of a moral tradition, which could be a predominantly religious, philosophical, and/or
political tradition such as Christianity, Judaism, Buddhism, Marxism,
liberalism, or feminism in all their variations. Within the communities
corresponding to these traditions, there is enough commonality among
moral points of view for productive debate on moral issues. In pluralistic societies, however, different moral communities embodying rival
moral traditions articulate these issues in different and incompatible
terms.[3] As Alasdair MacIntyre points out, this plurality of moral points
of view results in an inability to resolve conflict on moral issues through
rational argument. The persistence of disagreement on fundamental
moral issues has resulted in widespread *moral scepticism*, the belief that
moral conflict is impossible to resolve in a rational way.[4]

MacIntyre did not mean to suggest that all members of modern societies are also members of a moral community. Indeed, he attributes
a large part of the inconclusive character of contemporary moral debates to the fact that many people are not committed to any tradition

of moral enquiry and practice—and perhaps do not even appreciate that different traditions exist—with the consequence that their arguments juxtapose fragments from incompatible moral perspectives. The inability to reach agreement in modern societies and associated moral scepticism is a consequence of the *breakdown* as much as the plurality of moral communities and traditions.

Moral scepticism is my target in this book.[5] I see at least five reasons to be concerned about it. The first reason is that, to the extent it is widespread, scepticism about reaching agreement on moral issues rationally undermines hopes for resolving conflict peaceably. For if it is widely held to be true that moral commitments are ultimately a matter of personal choice or social convention, then not only could appeal to such concepts as "respect for human rights" be seen as just another strategic means for promoting partial interests, but the very distinction between strategic and non-strategic means of resolving conflict would be erased. MacIntyre makes a similar point: "emotivism entails the obliteration of any genuine distinction between manipulative and non-manipulative social relations."[6] Of course, it is possible to deny that consensus on moral values is achievable and still advocate the resolution of conflict through dialogue. For example, Habermas (1975, 111) distinguishes between agreement based on recognition of truly generalizable norms identified through rational discourse and compromise reached through negotiation of interests. The problem with situations in which the motivation to resolve conflict through negotiation is based solely upon a calculation of interests is that they are inherently unstable, for one would expect any party to abandon negotiation as soon as they believed it was in their interests to do so. This strategy for avoiding conflict is particularly unstable where the avoidance of strategic and instrumental action is contingent upon the maintenance of a balance of power.

A second and related reason to be concerned about moral scepticism is that we live in a global context of oppression.[7] Virtually all human interactions—including those in homes, schools, workplaces, political offices, courts of law, and places of worship—are adversely affected by unequal and unjust relations of political power, cultural privilege, and economic opportunity. This oppression is systemic in the sense that unjust relations are reinforced by social structures such as language, religion, public education, the economic order, the legal system, and the family. Inequality is perpetuated by the efforts of those in positions of privilege to maintain and enhance their advantages through strategic and instrumental means. Inequality is also perpetuated by the internalization—by both the privileged and the victimized—of oppressive attitudes, beliefs, and behaviours.[8]

So long as there is the expectation that the exercise of political power and legal authority be legitimated on grounds that admit of truth, beliefs about what kinds of truth claims are justifiable bear on political issues in a number of important ways.[9] For example, the question of *how* power and authority are properly legitimated is at least in part an epistemological one (Bernstein 1983, 155–156). The relationship between power and knowledge works in both directions: those in privileged positions can determine or at least influence what kinds of knowledge or "forms of discourse" enjoy social recognition. However they may come to have social force, our beliefs about what does and does not count as knowledge can limit the kinds of arguments that we will recognize as valid in public debate. On this view, challenging moral scepticism is important because doubting or denying the possibility of moral knowledge undermines the force of moral objections to oppression.[10]

Moral scepticism is not the only epistemological position that can undermine moral objections to oppression. Even if we recognize some forms of moral knowledge and argument as valid, we might discount other ways of arriving at and defending moral convictions to the extent they do not conform to our dominant conceptions of morality and/ or of knowledge. For example, J. B. Elshtain (1981) has shown how political debate in the Western liberal tradition has been characterized by a separation between public and private domains. Within this tradition, arguments must conform to a formal understanding of rationality (as opposed to a substantive one) in order to be admitted to the public domain. Elshtain argues that inequalities of power in modern liberal capitalist societies are served by this split between public and private domains, for it has the effect of excluding from public debate moral arguments grounded in the experiences of oppression of particular social groups.[11] On essentially epistemological grounds, then, the moral convictions of particular communities can be deemed irrelevant to the formation of public policy.[12] Hence, my interests in social cooperation and social justice extend to a concern with the philosophical limitations—and corresponding political consequences—of strictly formal definitions of morality.

A third reason to be concerned about moral scepticism is the difficulty it presents to those who wish to affirm the moral value of *multiculturalism*, defined as the right of distinct moral communities to exist and the corresponding obligation of other moral communities to respect that right (Boyd 1989b, 11–12). How could commitment to multiculturalism be justified? I see two possibilities. One would be to argue that there is no rational way to establish that one moral community's views are more valid or true than conflicting views, and conclude that no particular community's moral viewpoint should be privileged over any other's. However, such moral scepticism would seem to lead into a dead end: those who accepted this argument could not coherently promote multiculturalism if that value was only affirmed within their own particular moral traditions, because to do so would privilege their corresponding moral points of view, and hence be self-contradictory. In other words, those who profess moral scepticism cannot coherently introduce multicultural social policies until agreement exists across distinct moral communities on the value of multiculturalism. But if it is true that there is no rational way to judge between the claims of conflicting moral communities, then it is highly unlikely that the legitimate conditions for multicultural policies would ever be achieved.

The other possibility I see would be to affirm the value of multiculturalism on the grounds that those moral points of view that do so are more rationally defensible than those moral perspectives that do not. For people who affirmed the moral value of multiculturalism as rationally defensible, there would be no necessary contradiction involved in introducing multicultural social policies in a pluralistic state. I hasten to add, however, that those who believe that their point of view is a good approximation to moral truth need not feel compelled to impose it on others. It is unlikely that efforts to implement multicultural social policies would be successful if the value of multiculturalism was widely rejected. Therefore, those committed to preserving distinct moral communities would seem to be also committed to working towards enough of a convergence of moral points of view that the value of multiculturalism would be widely shared and publicly defensible.

A fourth reason to be concerned about moral scepticism is that, in a world where technologies are multiplying and resources dwindling, complex moral issues arise on every hand. I find myself at loss for an adequate response to many such issues when rival moral perspectives suggest incompatible courses of action, and I am unable to find good reasons for adopting one point of view over another. I expect that a convergence of moral viewpoints and values would increase the chances that our practical judgments will be *right*. I do not know what the chances are of even a partial convergence of moral points of view, but I think agreement across moral traditions is unlikely to occur so long as it is generally believed that it cannot be reached in a rational way.

A fifth reason to be concerned about moral scepticism is that it undermines moral education. I define *moral education* broadly to include all deliberate efforts to promote moral maturity, which in turn can be heuristically defined as the ability to make sound practical judgments. On this definition, moral education encompasses such social practices as psychotherapeutic treatments, consciousness-raising seminars, anti-racist workshops, public lectures, multicultural programs, ecological fairs, spiritual disciplines, and even academic conferences on moral philosophy. There are many different ways of conceiving and promoting moral maturity corresponding to the wide variety of moral traditions in our pluralistic world. The same is true within more formal educational contexts: there are many different theoretical frameworks for moral education programs corresponding loosely to the variety of metaethical positions current in moral philosophy.[13]

Moral scepticism undermines moral education in two ways. One, as Dwight Boyd has argued (1989a, 83–89), moral education requires that moral judgments be open to correction with reference to justifiable standards, and this is what moral subjectivists deny. If we do not understand how judgments of value can be objective, or lack confidence that such objectivity is possible, we are unlikely to undertake efforts to foster moral development. Two, so long as we are unable to reach agreement across moral points of view, we will be left with educational initiatives based upon different sets of assumptions that may produce incoherent, if not contradictory, results. As Fernhout (1989) argues, moral education programs based upon the assumptions of a liberal secular humanist would likely have different methods and objectives than programs based upon the assumptions of a committed Catholic. Neither approach would likely cohere with the efforts of a Marxist feminist, or perhaps a Nietzschean genealogist, to encourage personal and social responsibility. So long as efforts to promote moral maturity disagree on their basic starting points, then, there is a real possibility that they will be working at cross-purposes. This suggests that some convergence of moral points of view is desirable if efforts to promote moral maturity are to have positive effects on a socially significant scale.

This objective of moving towards shared assumptions does not include or entail the elimination of different practices of moral education, or even the elimination of all conflicts among them. I believe that healthy social and cultural environments are—like natural environments—characterized by diversity, and that there should be room for dissension within educational, social, political, and other frameworks or sets of agreements. I do not believe that working towards some convergence of competing moral perspectives is necessarily incompatible with the goal of preserving moral diversity. On the contrary, if such diversity is to be preserved, some way of achieving moral consensus would be helpful—and possibly even required.[14] As I have already suggested, a viable multicultural society is one whose members genuinely value pluralism. Tolerating diversity out of fatigue and/or a recognition of fallibility is not the same as having good reasons for judging diversity to be desirable for its own sake. Thus, if the existence of diverse moral communities is to be preserved within a larger social context, then it could only help if the members of that larger social group (whether or not they identified with some particular cultural or moral community) shared some agreement on the moral value of diversity and on what kinds of social policies would best serve to preserve it. Furthermore, if the value of diversity is to be upheld, there must be some shared agreement on why it is legitimate to restrict those individuals or communities wishing to oppose it.[15]

The objective of preserving diversity raises the general question of how much consensus is required, and on what issues, to allow for social cooperation *and* for the coexistence of diverse points of view. I do not think this question can be settled *a priori* for particular educational, social, political, religious, or other contexts. I do think that efforts to build consensus should not be undertaken in such a way that they become another source of conflict. Perhaps the best answer is pragmatic rather than philosophical: we should pursue the convergence of moral points of view until activities harmful to the environment have ceased, injustice has ended, wars have stopped, and everyone is safe and has enough to eat.

MORAL DISCOURSE

Borrowing (and interpreting) a phrase from MacIntyre, I use *moral enquiry and practice* (or *moral enquiry* for short) to refer to all of the activities involved in the search for a satisfactory moral point of view. What those activities are will become clearer throughout the book. What I want to emphasize here is that moral enquiry includes assessing the strengths and limitations of alternative moral viewpoints in comparison to one's own. To refer to the collection of processes involved in assessing moral points of view I use the term *moral discourse*. To argue for the possibility of productive moral discourse is thus to argue, against the conclusions of moral sceptics, that it is possible to resolve conflict among moral points of view in a rational way.

I appreciate that the word *rational* has negative connotations for some people, because it can imply an abstract, disembodied form of argument that excludes appeal to feelings or concrete experience. However, what I have in mind in speaking of resolving conflict or reaching agreement in a rational way is simply an open exchange of reasons for and against opposing points of view. I do not wish to prejudge what processes should be involved in moral discourse or what should and should not count as "good reasons" in support of moral commitments. I speak of resolving conflict rationally to distinguish it from securing agreement through coercion or deceit. Similarly, I speak of a convergence of moral viewpoints to distinguish it from agreement reached through the imposition of a dominant ideology.

The arguments for moral scepticism may be classified as semantic, epistemological, or ontological. A review of those arguments will introduce the specific tasks I undertake in this book.

Semantic arguments

Semantic arguments for moral scepticism are based upon logical analyses of moral language, particularly moral judgments. There are two main varieties of semantic arguments, which (following R. M. Hare

1981, 208ff.) may be referred to respectively as descriptive and non-descriptive subjectivism. Descriptive subjectivism understands moral claims to be statements about people's states of minds, for example, their attitudes of approval or disapproval. True moral claims are subjective, from this point of view, because they are not knowledge of "objective" things or events; that is, they are not knowledge of what is intersubjectively observable or of what exists independently of human thoughts, feelings, and desires. Non-descriptive subjectivism (or emotivism) understands moral utterances not as *statements about* but as *expressions of* states of mind.[16] Interpreted in this way, moral utterances are not objective because they are not knowledge of any kind. In other words, emotivism denies that moral utterances can be true or false on the grounds that moral utterances do not function to make truth claims.

I will *not* consider either descriptive or non-descriptive variations of moral subjectivism in this book. There are two reasons for this. First, existing versions of these positions have been sufficiently refuted that further argument is unnecessary.[17] Second, linguistic or logical analyses are not in themselves sufficient to resolve disagreements about the epistemological status of moral judgments. I am not saying that such analyses are irrelevant or unhelpful. I am saying only that analyses of the meaning of moral language cannot by themselves resolve the issue of moral scepticism, because how moral terms are used varies according to moral point of view.[18] Logical analyses must therefore either beg the question by limiting what counts as the correct use of moral terms to what is consistent with one particular moral perspective or end up with conflicting views. Accordingly, although analyses of moral language may illuminate the relationships among different interpretations of moral claims and the kinds of evidence required to support those claims, they cannot provide conclusive grounds for deciding among alternative interpretations.[19] For these reasons, I will proceed on the understanding that there are no conclusive logical or linguistic grounds for denying that moral judgments can be true or false.

Epistemological arguments
Epistemological arguments for moral scepticism are based upon claims about the limitations either of all forms of knowledge or of moral judgment in particular. Generally, epistemological arguments for moral scepticism are strong versions of moral relativism. Moral relativists deny

or strongly doubt the existence of universally valid standards according to which moral judgments may be decisively judged true or false.[20] It is important to note that moral relativists (in this sense of the term) need not be moral sceptics. One of my tasks in this book is to explain how moral judgments can be relative as well as objective.[21]

One form of relativism does entail moral scepticism, as I have defined it, and this is *framework relativism*. The claims of this position may be summarized as follows:

1. All judgments are made, interpreted and evaluated—and accepted, modified, or rejected—with reference to the assumptions and practices of particular frameworks.
2. At least some of these distinct frameworks are incommensurable, and there is no neutral "meta-perspective" from which their relative merits could be assessed.
3. It follows from (1) and (2) that there is no rational way to justify one among conflicting judgments, if those judgments are made within incommensurable frameworks.[22]

Framework relativism allows that reaching agreement on moral values is possible among those who share the same moral perspective, for particular moral judgments can be evaluated "relative to" the framework internal to that point of view. However, it denies that we can assess the respective strengths and limitations of rival moral points of view, or resolve conflict among them in a rational way, so long as they are incommensurable. Framework relativism thus maintains that efforts to reach agreement must break down when participants recognize they are arguing from incommensurable standpoints. Because framework relativism rules out the possibility of productive moral discourse, my primary task in this book is to identify processes through which and criteria with respect to which advocates of rival moral traditions can assess the strengths and limitations of their respective moral points of view *even when they are incommensurable.*

Ontological arguments

Ontological arguments for moral scepticism deny that there are any moral facts to be known outside the ones constructed by individuals or social groups. Ontological arguments are employed by moral subjectivists, who reject the possibility of productive moral discourse on the grounds that moral values "are not part of the fabric of the world" (Mackie 1977, 15). There are two basic forms of argument for this position. The argument from "queerness" observes the difficulty of saying what it is that true moral judgments could be knowledge *of*, and concludes that moral judgments must be subjective, because "if there were objective values, then they would be entities or qualities or relations of a very strange sort, utterly different from anything else in the universe" (Mackie 1977, 38). Any advocate of moral discourse must explain *why* moral points of view might be expected to converge. Accordingly, my second task in this book is to give some account of what makes moral judgments true or false beyond the thoughts, feelings, and desires of the person or persons making the claim. This ontological question of what is known in true moral judgments is closely related to the epistemological question of what kinds of evidence would constitute "good reasons" in moral discourse.

The second form of argument for moral subjectivism submits that the non-existence of "objective" moral facts is the best explanation for the diversity of moral points of view and for the persistent inability of those representing different viewpoints to reach agreement.[23] Any advocate of moral discourse must give some reason why previous efforts to achieve convergence of moral viewpoints have not been successful. In other words, a case for the possibility of productive moral discourse must include a different explanation for persistent moral conflict than the sceptical one. Therefore, my third task is to explain how the possibility of true moral judgments is compatible with the facts of moral diversity and disagreement.

It is open to moral sceptics to argue that moral discourse is theoretically but not practically possible: the obstacles to a convergence of moral points of view might be more psychological, political, or economical than philosophical. I would agree that talking can be of little use when conflict is rooted in aggression or fear. Therefore, although a full account is more than I can provide, I will identify some of the conditions under which moral discourse has at least the potential to be productive. A partial convergence of moral points of view would not guarantee an easy or quick end to conflict in many cases, but it might restrict the exercise of force and so keep the hope of peaceful resolution alive.

To summarize, in this book I undertake the following four tasks:

1. to identify processes through which and criteria with respect to which advocates of incommensurable moral traditions might assess the strengths and limitations of their moral points of view;
2. to give some account of what makes moral judgments true or false beyond the thoughts, feelings, and desires of the person or persons making the claim;
3. to explain how the possibility of true moral judgments is compatible with the facts of moral diversity and disagreement; and
4. to identify some of the conditions under which moral discourse has potential to be productive.

As Frankena observes: "There is not space to debate everything" (1973, xvi). The scope of my topic places a limit upon how deeply I can go into many philosophical topics. With this in mind, I build whenever possible upon the work of those who have and are developing positions compatible with my own. Generally, in such cases, I summarize the relevant points of the supporting position and refer the reader to the original texts for a more thorough discussion.

In particular, I develop my characterization of moral discourse among rival moral points of view through a critical appropriation of Alasdair MacIntyre's account of the rationality of traditions of enquiry. I have chosen to focus on MacIntyre's work because his position is close to my own in many respects. We both attribute moral scepticism in large part to the unnecessarily limited conceptions of reason and morality current in liberal moral philosophy, of which recourse to purely formal moral arguments is symptomatic. At the same time, my response to moral scepticism differs from MacIntyre's in ways that I hope are instructive. In any event, there is much that I can build upon in MacIntyre's publications: his arguments have been developed over many years, and are supported with extensive textual and historical analyses.[24]

As a consequence of my focus on MacIntyre's work, I offer little discussion of positions within rival traditions such as Humean empiricism, Kantian deontology, utilitarianism, social contract theory, feminist ethics, and neo-pragmatism. The conclusions presented in this book must therefore be understood as provisional. This notwithstanding, the reader familiar with (and perhaps sympathetic to) the perspectives I have mentioned might discover that I have developed my arguments with at least some of their potential concerns in mind.

My case against moral scepticism proceeds in two parts. Chapters one, two, and three describe how it is possible for advocates of incommensurable traditions of enquiry to reach agreement in a rational way on the strengths and limitations of their respective points of view. The first three chapters thus present a general response to the challenge of framework relativism. Chapters four, five, six, and seven explore how this "generic" account of productive discourse applies specifically to the moral domain. The last four chapters challenge the subjectivist position that moral values are nothing more than personal preferences or social conventions. My hope is that, by clarifying the senses in which moral judgment can be objective, this book will contribute to productive moral discourse in a pluralistic world.

CHAPTER ONE

The Rationalism-Relativism Debate

"Hallo!" said Piglet, "What are *you* doing?"

"Hunting," said Pooh.

"Hunting what?"

"Tracking something," said Winnie-the-Pooh very mysteriously.

"Tracking what?" said Piglet, coming closer.

"That's just what I ask myself. I ask myself What?"

"What do you think you'll answer?"

"I shall have to wait until I catch up with it," said Winnie-the-Pooh. "Now, look here." He pointed to the ground in front of him. "What do you see there?"

"Tracks," said Piglet. "Paw-marks." He gave a little squeak of excitement. "Oh Pooh! Do you think it's a—a—a Woozle?"

"It may be," said Pooh. "Sometimes it is, and sometimes it isn't. You never can tell with paw-marks."

—A. A. Milne, *The World of Pooh*

BEYOND OBJECTIVISM AND RELATIVISM

Richard Bernstein has argued that much of the outstanding philosophical work of the later twentieth century shares a common interest in moving beyond objectivism and relativism. *Objectivism* refers to "the basic conviction that there is or must be some permanent, ahistorical matrix or framework to which we can ultimately appeal in determining the nature of rationality, knowledge, truth, reality, goodness, or rightness" (Bernstein 1983, 8). According to Bernstein, objectivism is motivated by what he calls "the Cartesian anxiety," which is based on a seductive either/or assumption. The assumption is that *either* our beliefs about what is true and right can be given solid foundations in the form of universally valid standards for rational assessment, *or* we shall fall into an intellectual and moral chaos "where nothing is fixed, where we can neither touch bottom nor support ourselves on the surface."[1] In its desire for certainty, objectivism is closely related to *foundationalism*, which is the project of establishing unshakable grounds for belief.

In Bernstein's terms, *relativism* refers to a conviction that the meaning of and standards for such fundamental ideals as "rationality, knowledge, truth, reality, goodness, or rightness" are internal and peculiar to some particular "conceptual scheme, theoretical framework, paradigm, form of life, society, or culture" (Bernstein 1983, 8). The relativist is profoundly suspicious of the objectivist's desire for universal standards, for the relativist fears that claims to universality will inevitably serve to privilege one particular and limited point of view over others. Thus, while objectivists tend to see challenges to universal standards of rational judgement as a threat to truth, justice, and stability, relativists see attempts to fix absolute standards as stifling, dogmatic, and ultimately oppressive.[2]

As Bernstein notes, objectivism today is rarely considered to be a viable position: foundationalism is widely discredited.[3] Most contemporary theorists would accept both that the standards used in rational judgment have changed through history and that no set of standards is absolutely and universally true. At the same time, many contemporary theorists cannot accept framework relativism as an alternative to objectivism. If it were true, as framework relativism asserts, that the standards of rational assessment internal to particular conceptual schemes cannot themselves be rationally justified, then beliefs and values would become arbitrary in the last analysis. In addition, rational argument would be possible only within frameworks, and not among them. For theorists unwilling to accept these conclusions, the search for middle ground between objectivism and relativism is a search both for non-circular and non-foundational forms of justification for standards used in rational judgment *and* for a way of assessing the relative strengths and limitations of competing conceptual schemes that does not require a universally applicable, framework-neutral, non-historically conditioned standpoint.[4]

I have already noted that the term *rationality* has negative connotations for some people. This is particularly true for postmodernists. It has been associated with such things as the efforts of Western European white males to promote the patriarchal capitalist project of global domination through the hegemony of uncontextualized disciplinary practices.[5] This suspicion of the discourses of reason and rationality is not without justification. Nevertheless, partly because I do not wholly share these negative associations, and partly to be consistent with similar reviews, I shall use the term *rationalists* to refer collectively to the diverse assortment of theorists searching for middle ground between objectivism and relativism—even though some of the theorists in question might object to being called a rationalist. And, similarly, while acknowledging that (a) not all relativists are framework relativists,[6] (b) not all framework relativists hold compatible positions (or even wish to be known as relativists),[7] and (c) the belief that frameworks are incommensurable does not necessarily entail framework relativism, I shall in the interests of brevity use the term *relativists* to refer collectively to those who conclude from one or another interpretation of incommensurability that it is impossible to justify the standards of rational judgment and corresponding conceptual schemes that are internal to competing communities of enquiry. In other words, I shall use *relativists* as short for *radical framework relativists*.

The rationalist-relativist debate persists in various guises within the methodological literature of the natural sciences, the social sciences, and the humanities—including education, history, aesthetics, literary criticism, and ethics. A recurring theme on the rationalist side of the debate is that framework relativists have an unnecessarily narrow view of what should count as rational justification. It is claimed that the relativist is caught within the same false either/or as the objectivist: *either* there are universal and absolute standards of justification, *or* there can be no evaluation of competing frameworks. Rationalists typically conclude that the way to move beyond objectivism and relativism is to contest the limited view of rationality unproblematically assumed by both objectivists and relativists, and to provide a broader and more accurate account of how justification actually proceeds.[8] On their side, relativist critiques of attempts to move beyond objectivism and relativism typically claim that the rationalists in question have failed to grasp the full extent of the incommensurability of rival frameworks. Rationalists are often accused of being thinly disguised objectivists who falsely universalize their particular and context-bound reason-giving practices.[9]

The rationalist-relativist debate has been particularly vigorous within the philosophy of natural science. This is due in part to the common modern belief that scientific practice is our best example of rational activity. It is due in part to the notoriety enjoyed by Thomas Kuhn's *The Structure of Scientific Revolutions*, which has provided a focus for much of the debate. For this reason, many of the examples I cite in this chapter will be drawn from the literature on Kuhn's work. On the whole, however, the philosophical issues are the same whether the competing frameworks in question are rival conceptual schemes, scientific paradigms, disparate cultures, diverse forms of life, or historical traditions of enquiry. Therefore, there is much to be learned from the debates among competing accounts of scientific rationality that is relevant to understanding how the strengths and limitations of incommensurable moral points of view could be assessed.

In what follows, I will consider three different ways in which frameworks are said to be incommensurable. In each case, I will take a closer look at how relativists argue from a particular understanding of incommensurability to the conclusion that disagreement among competing conceptual schemes cannot be resolved in a rational way. In each case, I will also discuss how responses to the relativist arguments enrich our understanding of what it means to be rational, which will begin to chart the middle ground between objectivism and relativism.

DIFFERENT RULES: THE INCOMMENSURABILITY OF METHODS

One conception of commensurability holds that the rationally superior among competing claims and theoretical perspectives within a given domain can be identified by following a single set of rules:

> By "commensurable" I mean able to be brought under a set of rules which will tell us how rational agreement can be reached on what would settle the issue on every point where statements seem to conflict. These rules tell us how to construct an ideal situation, in which all residual disagreements will be seen to be "noncognitive" or merely verbal, or else merely temporary—capable of being resolved by doing something further. (Richard Rorty 1979, 316, cited in Bernstein 1983, 61)

To conceive commensurability in this way is to equate rationality with the strict observance of method. For example, on one view of science, all empirical disputes are commensurable because (a) they all concern matters of fact, and (b) all disputes over matters of fact may be decisively resolved by following scientific method, understood as rules for acquiring and evaluating evidence.[10]

Thomas Kuhn and others have vigorously disputed this understanding of science. If rational enquiry is a matter of following rules of evidence, they claim, then science is not a rational process (Bernstein 1983, 53–61, 71–73, 85–86; Feyerabend 1978, 64–65). It is a mistake to equate scientific enquiry and rule-following for at least three reasons. First, there is no agreement on the one correct scientific method: scientific communities operating under different paradigms employ different procedures for constructing and evaluating evidence (Laudan 1984, 25; 1990, 96–97; Nola 1988, 17–18). Second, whatever the sets of rules or procedures used, they are not sufficient to decide decisively among conflicting empirical claims or theoretical perspectives. In other words, rational choice among competing scientific theories is *underdetermined* by methodological rules. Third, not only do they use a variety of methodological procedures, and not only do they supplement those rules with other considerations in choosing among theories, but successful scientists also actually ignore or violate what are accepted as the canons of scientific method (Feyerabend 1978, 13; Laudan 1984, 16).

Rationalist responses to these and similar arguments have generally not disputed the limitations of method narrowly conceived.[11] Rather, they have argued that rational enquiry—scientific and otherwise—involves more than simply following rules. From this point of view, methodological procedures are properly understood as a guide to, not as a substitute for, rational judgment. Deciding *which* of accepted methods is appropriate to the investigation of a given question, problem, or topic is itself a matter of judgment. Thus, to grant the existence and fallibility of different methods for constructing and evaluating evidence is to give up, not rationality, but certainty. As Kuhn (1977, 326) observes, most philosophers of science have abandoned the search for a set of methodological rules or procedures that would guarantee correct results. At the same time, however, those same philosophers— Kuhn included—have not necessarily abandoned the attempt to describe how scientific enquiry is a rational process.[12]

Practical Rationality

Of what does rational judgment consist, if not of following rules? This question has contributed to a revival of interest in Aristotle's account of practical rationality, or *phronēsis*. There is, of course, no consensus on "the" correct interpretation of Aristotle's remarks on practical rationality. However, for many authors a canonical interpretation of Aristotle is not necessary, for they do not wish to take his account of *phronēsis* as authoritative. Rather, their intent is to develop and even revise Aristotle's account in the interests of a more accurate understanding of what makes a judgment rational than the narrow view challenged by relativists.[13] The way in which different authors characterize practical rationality varies according to their particular interests. Such differences notwithstanding, the following summary represents points of convergence:

Paradigmatically, practical rationality is concerned with questions of what is to be done and so its deliberations conclude in an action or a commitment to act. However, practical rationality also refers more generally to the capacity for evaluating multiple factors in a concrete situation. Thus, in Aristotle's terms, *phronēsis* is the ability to combine a variety of considerations in sound practical judgment.

What is an adequate, correct, or true practical judgment is determined in part by the antecedent beliefs, interests, norms, and priorities of the persons involved, and partly by the specific demands of the particular context (Nussbaum and Sen 1989, 310). Consequently, the exercise of practical rationality has a social dimension. This is not only because matters requiring practical judgment will often involve more than one person, but also because the beliefs, interests, norms, and priorities that are brought to practical deliberation—and that are in part definitive of the situation and its actors—are collectively negotiated, interpreted, and re-interpreted. Thus, persons who are practically rational know what assumptions and commitments are shared within a social context. Also, they typically exercise both imagination and empathy to appreciate the particular values and perspectives involved in specific matters requiring judgment. In this sense, sound practical judgment demands engagement in, as opposed to complete detachment from, human affairs (Bernstein 1983, 147; Nussbaum 1986b, 190–192).

In its context-sensitive judgments, *phronēsis* mediates between the abstract and the concrete, the universal and the particular. This mediation does not take the form of the application of independently established general rules, procedures, standards, principles, definitions, or other criteria. Rather, the particular and the universal are *co-determined* in practical judgments (Allen 1989, 365–366; Bernstein 1983, 54, 156–157; *WJ*, 116–117).

The distinctive features of practical rationality can be clarified by comparison to other forms of reasoning. For example, Aristotle distinguishes *phronēsis* from *epistēmē*, or theoretical knowledge. *Epistēmē* is concerned with the universal and invariant features of experience, and so yields demonstrably certain generalizations. However, the judgments of *phronēsis* are neither certain nor context-independent, for they concern the particular and variable contexts of actual practice. More recently, many authors have contrasted the value-laden process of practical reasoning to *technical rationality*, which reduces decision-making on practical and moral issues to the application of scientific theory.[14]

The distinctive features of practical rationality can be illustrated by the following fictional scenario: A student at a university accuses a professor of sexual harassment. According to the university's procedures for dealing with such accusations, a committee with representation from students, faculty, and administration is struck to review the case. The committee's terms of reference are open-ended, so its members begin their deliberations by discussing what information on the particular features of the case they must collect in order to render a satisfactory judgment. They debate the relevance of the histories, motivations, characters, and previous encounters of the people involved; the consequences of different courses of action by the committee for each person; other definitions of harassment; and the precedents set by previous committees and their judgments. The committee decides to interview the student, the professor, and all witnesses to the incident. To this task they assign committee members who are thought likely to appreciate the different perspectives of the persons being questioned.

The committee reconstructs the incident from multiple and somewhat inconsistent accounts. There is consensus that the incident as reconstructed is appropriately characterized as sexual harassment under the definition in the university regulations, but not under the definition in provincial legislation. Initially, there is considerable divergence in the responses recommended by the members of the committee according to their varied interests, which include (a) to see justice served through a public reprimand of the professor, (b) to see justice served through compensation to the student, (c) to be seen as sensitive to public opinion about the case and thereby minimize bad publicity for the university, (d) to protect themselves by following the letter of the law, (e) to minimize harm to both the accuser and the accused, and (f) to set a proper precedent for subsequent cases. Some of the disagreement is based on the committee members' conflicting interpretations of the rather ambiguous university regulations surrounding harassment; some is based on their differing views on the extent to which sexual harassment is prevalent at the university and the best means to prevent it. The committee members eventually reach agreement on their recommendations after many long conversations both within and without committee meetings, and after consulting a variety of empirical studies on sexual and other forms of harassment. The recommendations are generally perceived as fair by the wider university community, and the judgment helps establish for that community both (a) what will and will not count as sexual harassment, and (b) what responses to harassment are appropriate.

This process of arriving at a judgment exemplifies the exercise of practical rationality in a number of ways. First, the process was prompted by a specific situation that required choice among alternative courses of action. Second, a crucial part of the process was deciding whether or not to name the incident sexual harassment. That decision was informed by existing guidelines and precedents, but also represented a judgment about how the guidelines should be interpreted. In this way, the general guidelines and specific incident were co-determined. Third, the conclusion of the process was a judgment precisely because certainty was not possible, given that the members of the committee had to decide what information regarding the case was relevant and how it should be interpreted. At the same time, the judgment was not arbitrary, but was supported with reasons and evidence. Fourth, the process made demands on the people involved to balance competing interests and to appreciate diverse perspectives. As such, it required commitment to such ideals as fairness, openness, and consensus, and to corresponding norms for group process. Fifth, the judgment was rational in a way that did not exclude but incorporated the particulars of the situation and the social context, including the university community's varied values concerning harassment.

According to Bernstein, there is a growing consensus that the process of scientific enquiry is more like the exercise of practical rationality than simple induction or deduction.

> Central to this new understanding is a dialogical model of rationality that stresses the practical, *communal* character of rationality in which there is choice, deliberation, interpretation, judicious weighing and application of "universal criteria," and even rational disagreement about which criteria are relevant and most important. (Bernstein 1983, 172)

Indeed, some authors argue that practical reasoning should be the model for all rational enquiry (Allen 1989, 359). At the same time, those who argue for *phronēsis* as a valid form of rational judgment recognize that it has limitations. In particular, the successful exercise of practical rationality presupposes a community defined in part by shared beliefs, attitudes, interests, norms, priorities, and practices—for it is these shared assumptions and commitments that partially define what makes particular practical judgments count as reasonable.[15] For example, in the preceding scenario, reaching consensus was contingent upon a shared commitment to dialogue, a common respect for empirical research, and a reasonable degree of consensus on what should and should not be considered harassment. Consequently, while it is plausible that practical rationality can supplement rule-following to provide for reasoned agreement within a scientific community on the merits of a particular scientific claim or theory, it is not clear how *phronēsis* could decide among scientific methods that represent the divergent beliefs, attitudes, interests, norms, priorities, and practices of different scientific paradigms. Similarly, accounts of practical rationality might accurately represent how people arrive at judgments on specific moral issues, but such accounts do not show that *phronēsis* could justify the moral values employed in its deliberations, or assess the relative strengths and limitations of competing moral points of view.[16]

To summarize: In response to the charge that choice among competing claims, theories, or paradigms is not rational because it is underdetermined by methodological procedures, rationalists have proposed that judgment need not be based on universally accepted sets of rules, standards, or principles in order to be rational. As Bernstein (1983, xi) puts it:

Each of them opens the way to a more historically situated, non-algorithmic, flexible understanding of human rationality, one which highlights the tacit dimension of human judgment and imagination and is sensitive to the unsuspected contingencies and genuine novelties encountered in particular situations.

Modern reconstructions of Aristotle's notion of *phronēsis* have underlined the social and context-bound nature of reasoning, and in particular how the exercise of practical rationality presupposes a community with at least some shared beliefs, attitudes, interests, norms, priorities, and practices.

DIFFERENT "WORLDS," DIFFERENT "TRUTHS": THE INCOMMENSURABILITY OF MEANING

The second category of debates over the meaning and implications of incommensurability contains three (at least) overlapping sets of relativist arguments and rationalist responses, each with its own extensive literature. The first set of arguments centres on the notion of conceptual schemes and is concerned with such questions as "What exactly is a conceptual scheme?" "Can there be more than one, and how would we know?" and "In what way is the existence of objects of knowledge relative to schemes?" The second set of arguments centres on competing theories of truth and is concerned with such questions as "What could it mean to say that something is true?" "In what ways is truth correctly understood to be relative?" and "What is the truth status of the claims upon which relativist conclusions themselves depend?" The third set of arguments deals with theories of translation and raises such questions as "Under what conditions, and to what extent (if at all), is translation possible?" and "How can we *know* (if at all) when translation is successful?" Each of these three sets of rationalist-relativist disputes concerns one or more steps on the route to framework relativism by way of *incommensurability of meaning.*

The Five-Step Route to Relativism

The first step towards relativism by way of arguments appealing to the incommensurability of meaning is to claim that beliefs are necessarily expressed in the terms of an interrelated set of concepts—that is, in the terms of a theoretical framework or conceptual scheme, broadly defined.[17] From this point of view, the objects of belief are *constructed*: "What it means to be an object at all, what it means to have properties, and what sorts of properties an object may have vary as a function of the structure of human language, knowledge, or action" (Okrent 1984, 347). When groups of people misunderstand each other because they use different conceptual frameworks to interpret their experience— women and men, perhaps—we say that they "speak different languages."[18] When groups of people construct the objects of their beliefs through the languages of different conceptual schemes, we could say that they "live in different worlds."[19]

The second step towards relativism is to observe that the kind of things that are candidates for being true or false are precisely the beliefs that are necessarily formulated in the terms of one or another conceptual scheme. On a correspondence understanding of truth, truth claims function to represent some particular feature or aspect of the way things are. Accordingly, the proper way to evaluate truth claims is to determine whether what is claimed to be true does correspond to what is actually so. However, to evaluate the truth of propositions in this way would seem to require the ability to describe the way things are independently of our beliefs, in order to compare one with the other. This is precisely what the constructivist view of knowledge denies. On this view, our descriptions of the way things are—and perhaps also our very perceptions—always rely upon the language of one or another conceptual framework.[20] Consequently, a particular proposition is only judged true or false relative to features of "the world" as it is constructed through the terms of one or another conceptual scheme.

Another way of making this point is by way of the relationship of meaning to truth. On most accounts of this relationship, the meaning of a proposition is tied to its truth conditions such that understanding a claim entails understanding what it would mean for that claim to be true. In order for a belief to be a candidate for being true or false, there must be a conceptual framework in terms of which the difference between it being true and merely being believed to be true can be conceived. For example, if the proposition "human beings are intrinsically worthy of respect" is to be a candidate for being true or false, then there must be a way of conceiving the difference between this claim being true and only being believed to be true.[21] Again, then, to question whether or not some particular claim or belief is true *presupposes* a context of meaning established in part by a community of enquiry's conceptual scheme.[22]

This understanding of the relationship of meaning to truth does entail a kind of relativism of truth claims to languages or conceptual schemes, but not the kind of framework relativism that worries rationalists.[23] The third step on the route to that sort of full-blown relativism is to maintain that the conceptual schemes used by different groups of people can be incommensurable in the sense that some or even all of the terms of one framework have no equivalents in the other. Relativist arguments based on claims about incommensurability of meaning thus point either to the *failure* (partial or full) or to the *indeterminacy* of translation between frameworks. On the view of the relationship between truth and meaning presented above, if two claims have different truth conditions, then they refer to, signify, or mean different things, and vice versa. It follows that, so long as a claim in one scheme is made in terms that have no equivalents in a second scheme, then that claim cannot be understood—much less judged true or false—from the point of view of the second scheme.

The existence of frameworks with non-equivalent terms does not in itself entail framework relativism. The fourth step required is that the incommensurable schemes in question be understood as rivals: that is, as mutually exclusive ways of making sense of the *same* domain of human experience.[24] If not understood as rivals, incommensurable schemes could be regarded as simply different and perhaps even complementary ways of looking at the world; and no interesting conclusion about relativity of truth would follow from the fact that they lack equivalent terms.

To arrive at framework relativism requires one final step: the claim that, if rival conceptual schemes exhibit incommensurability of meaning, then they cannot in principle be compared and evaluated.[25] This is the relativist position the rationalist abhors: that no compelling reasons can be given to prefer one among alternative ways of constructing the world, one among competing conceptions of truth, or one among rival sets of standards for rational judgment.

In what follows, I will take a closer look at the arguments on both sides of the rationalist-relativist debates about incommensurability of meaning. Along the way, I will present suggestions for resolving some of the disputes in order to defend a conception of relative truth.

Conceptual Schemes Revisited

One rationalist response to arguments for framework relativism has been to challenge the intelligibility of the notion of incommensurable conceptual schemes. The first problem with the notion is the wide variety of candidates put forward for the role of that to which truth claims are supposedly relative. The list of candidates includes belief systems, categorical schemes, constellations of absolute presuppositions, cultures, disciplinary matrixes, dogmas, forms of life, ideologies, historical epochs, language games, linguistic frameworks, modes of discourse, paradigms, perspectives, practices, point of views, research programs, social classes, societies, systems of thought, theories, traditions, and *Weltanschauungen* or world views.[26] Before the issue of their commensurability or incommensurability can be resolved, *conceptual schemes* must be defined in a way that differentiates them from other kinds of frameworks or sets of agreements.

My suggestion here is that particular truth claims be understood as embedded or "nested" within progressively broader sets of shared assumptions, meanings, commitments, and practices. For example, someone pursuing a Kohlbergian research program might claim that a particular person is at a Stage Four level of reasoning about issues of justice. This specific claim presupposes Kohlberg's *theory* of moral development, that is, the description of stages of justice-reasoning that he and others have formulated to explain observed differences in moral judgment. Kohlberg's theory is part of a larger *conceptual scheme* or *theoretical framework,* an interrelated set of beliefs about the moral domain that includes (for example) the claim that morality is separate from ethics. It this larger scheme of background beliefs that explains why Kohlberg's research focuses upon justice-reasoning to the exclusion of other aspects of morality.

Kohlberg's conceptual scheme is itself part of a cognitive-developmental psychological *paradigm.* The cognitive-developmental paradigm posits the existence of invariant stages of reasoning, is guided by the metaphor of healthy biological development, is committed to the validity of quantitative empirical research methodologies, and has a history of using structured or semi-structured interviews. Cognitive-develop-mental psychology in turn presupposes a modern version of the mech-anistic *world view* with its associated assumptions about human nature.[27] Variations on the mechanistic view of the world can be located histori-cally as emerging within a Western *tradition* of empirical science that explores the metaphor of cosmos as machine—accompanied, perhaps, by *narratives* that promise human progress through the discovery and application of theoretical knowledge. Variations on the mechanistic world view also can be located within concrete *forms of social life*, com-prising patterns of economic relations: political, legal, and educational institutions; cultural practices; and artistic endeavour.[28]

Claims, theories, conceptual schemes, paradigms, world views, tra-ditions, cultures, languages, social practices, and institutions can all be understood as products of human attempts to make sense of and bring order to their experience. Because any particular claim presupposes not one but many sets of meanings, more than one set of meanings must be understood before specific claims are fully comprehended. In this way, fully comprehending a particular truth claim is like under-standing a particular organism through grasping its interrelationships with other species in its local ecosystem, *and* understanding that local ecosystem—whether pond, forest, desert, or estuary—through appre-ciating its interrelationships with larger ecosystems, and so on. A his-torical perspective is also required, because local, regional, and even global environments do not persist as static systems, but change in re-sponse to internal and external influences. Analogously, fully compre-hending the meaning and implications of a particular claim requires that it be located within broader sets of meanings which themselves change over time. Of course, to understand the *full* background con-text of shared meanings for every claim is impractical, if not impossible. How much of the context of a particular claim needs to be understood is itself a matter of the context in which the claim occurs.

On the analysis I have just presented, shared beliefs differ in the de-gree to which they are in the foreground or the background of a particular enquiry. I will reserve *theory* or *theories* to refer to an interre-lated set of claims—such as Kohlberg's account of the stages of moral development—intended to resolve problems identified as important within some domain of human experience. I will reserve *conceptual scheme* and *theoretical framework* to refer to the background beliefs that establish how such domains are conceived and what problems or issues take priority. Defined in this way, a particular conceptual scheme is part of, but not coextensive with, the set of shared attitudes, interests, norms, priorities, and practices that constitutes a particular paradigm of enquiry.[29]

Incommensurability of Meaning Revisited

Once conceptual schemes are defined, making a case for framework relativism requires some way of identifying *which* frameworks are incommensurable. Three different ways of conceiving incommensurability of meaning among frameworks have been proposed: as full failure, as partial failure, or as indeterminacy of translation. Each way can be challenged. Davidson (1982, 1989) rules out the first possibility, arguing that the idea of full failure of translation between conceptual schemes cannot be formulated in a meaningful way. He reasons that, if the utterances of another person or group are completely unintelligible, then there are no grounds for affirming that they represent an alternative conceptual scheme. Conversely, to understand the sense-making activities of another person or group sufficiently to describe those activities correctly as the use of an alternative conceptual scheme presupposes that some of their utterances and cognitive practices are somewhat intelligible in our terms. Davidson's arguments thus rule out complete failure of translation between schemes simply by definition: "The meaninglessness of the idea of a conceptual scheme forever beyond our grasp is due not to our inability to understand such a scheme or to our other human limitations; it is due simply to what we mean by a system of concepts" (Davidson 1989, 160; also Hacking 1982, 61).

The notion of complete indeterminacy of translation among schemes is vulnerable to a similar objection: how we could know that *all* efforts at translation between two particular conceptual frameworks will *always* be indefinite or uncertain? One relativist argument is that translation is always indeterminate because it is always conceivable that, for any given utterance or set of utterances, there could be a number of equally coherent but mutually exclusive translations.[30] This argument fails to convince for two reasons. First, it implies that we can only have confidence in an interpretation—or any other judgment, for that matter—if we can *prove* beyond doubt that the interpretation is uniquely correct, and this expectation is unrealistic.[31] Second, it is open to arguments parallel to Davidson's against full failure of translation: if *all* translation is indeterminate, then there are no grounds for concluding that the utterances of another group represent the use of a rival conceptual scheme. For these reasons, arguments claiming the indeterminacy of *all* translation are insufficient to establish the existence of incommensurable conceptual schemes.

The third way of conceiving incommensurability of meaning between schemes is partial failure of translation: some terms from one conceptual framework can be rendered in the terms of another, some cannot. In general, rationalists have agreed that it is possible to identify conceptual schemes that fit this description (Laudan 1990, 122). However, they have also argued that failure of translation in this sense *does not* in itself rule out understanding or even comparison across frameworks. Incommensurability *does not* necessarily entail incomparability because we are not necessarily limited to any one particular language, theoretical framework, or conceptual scheme, but are capable of learning or inventing new ones.[32] Indeed, the very claim that two languages or conceptual frameworks contain non-equivalent terms *presupposes* that someone has understood and compared them both, each in its own terms.[33] Moreover, it is possible in at least some cases to render the meanings of incommensurable frameworks in each other's terms by expanding their respective vocabularies and other conceptual resources (Laudan 1990, 125). Because of this, to recognize that translation can partially fail between two schemes does not in itself result in any robust form of framework relativism.

Rivalry Revisited

A different rationalist challenge to the intelligibility of the notion of incommensurable schemes observes that it presupposes a distinction between the *form* supplied by alternative frameworks and the *content* they organize in different ways. In the original way of making the distinction, conceptual schemes were understood as imposing form upon the world as it is prior to human sense-making activities.[34] However, relativists themselves have argued that, because our experience of the world is the product of our sense-making activities, the concept of the world "as it is" is "nearly empty."[35] This point is similar to the conclusion that, because all linguistic description of human experience is to some degree "theory-laden," the distinction between "observation sentences" and "theory sentences" cannot be maintained.[36]

To forestall these counter-arguments, relativists must formulate the notion of rival conceptual schemes without presupposing the possibility of unmediated description of what exists in an experience-independent way. A variety of formulations have been put forward.[37] In each case, the content or "input" that alternative schemes of beliefs conceptualize in different ways is the "output" of previous human sense-making activities. In some cases, although it is granted that all observations are human constructs, it is claimed that there is a range of experiences that virtually all humans share by virtue of living on the same planet, using the same senses, and having similar concerns. It is these shared experiences that make understanding and partial translation among frameworks possible—the differences between cultures notwithstanding.[38] This formulation of conceptual schemes allows that "what is" exists prior to and independently of human sense-making activities, while granting that propositional knowledge is based only upon human experience.

Horton (1982, 282ff.) introduces a distinction between *primary theory* and *secondary theories* to recover what was useful and true in his original distinction between observational and theoretical languages. In Horton's terms, primary theory refers to commonsense assumptions about how the world of everyday experience works and the kinds of things to be found there:

> Primary theory gives the world a foreground filled with middle-sized (say between a hundred times as large and a hundred times as small as human beings), enduring, solid objects. These objects are interrelated, indeed interdefined, in terms of a "push-pull" conception of causality, in which spatial and temporary contiguity are seen as crucial to the transmission of change. . . . Finally, primary theory makes two major distinctions amongst its objects: first, that between human beings and other objects; and second, that between self and others. (Horton 1982, 228)

According to Horton, the basic framework provided by primary theory "does not differ very much from community to community or from culture to culture," although some cultures will develop particular aspects of the framework in more detail than others.

Since the scope of explanation of primary theory's "push-pull" version of causation is limited, secondary theories are developed to explain the features of human experience that primary theory cannot account for. One commonality among the very different kinds of secondary theories developed within human history—Horton contrasts traditional African witchcraft to modern Western science—is the "postulation of a 'hidden' or 'underlying' realm of entities and processes of which the events of everyday experience, as described in primary-theory terms, are seen as surface manifestations."[39] Different secondary theories postulate different invisible entities and processes: souls and curses in one case and quarks and natural laws in another. It is at the level of secondary theories that incommensurability arises because of the different sets of postulated invisible entities and processes. However, because these entities and processes are formulated to explain what the limited causal vision of primary theory cannot, secondary theories remain "indebted to and/or dependent upon" the shared world of everyday experience:

> Development of ideas as to the character of the "hidden" realm is based on the drawing of analogies with familiar everyday experiences as described in primary-theory terms. . . . Once the causal regularities governing this hidden realm have been stated, their implications for the world as described in primary-theoretical terms are spelled out by a process akin to translation, guided by a "dictionary" which correlates aspects of the "hidden" world with aspects of the "given." (Horton 1982, 230)

By showing how secondary theories are related to primary theory, Horton's account provides one way of understanding how alternative conceptual schemes can be competing but incommensurable explanations of the same domain of experience.[40] His account also provides a framework in which at least partial success in translation between frameworks is plausible. It reinforces the point that incommensurability of meaning among rival conceptual schemes does not in itself entail the relativist conclusion that their respective strengths and limitations cannot be rationally compared.[41]

Truth Revisited

A key point of contention in the rationalist-relativist debates over in-commensurability of meaning is in what sense, if any, truth is relative if we accept a constructivist view of knowledge.[42] There are two issues here. First, if truth claims are necessarily formulated in the terms of one conceptual scheme or another, and there is no way to describe "the way things actually are" other than in the terms of a conceptual scheme, then it is not clear how claims could be considered more or less "true" in a correspondence sense. Because of this difficulty with correspondence theories, framework relativists typically propose co-herence theories of truth in which beliefs are determined to be true or false according to how well they fit with other propositions within the same framework, scheme, or point of view. According to these theo-ries, belief is not constrained by a language-independent reality but by the desire for consistency among beliefs within a scheme.[43]

Second, if what the term *truth* means is *internal to* one or another conceptual scheme, and if meaning is necessarily tied to truth condi-tions, then it is logically impossible for schemes themselves to be can-didates for being true or false. In other words, it has been argued that conceptual schemes cannot be true or false because they are the sets of meanings that must be assumed for particular claims to be candi-dates for truth.[44]

Rationalists are quick to object that any suggestion that truth is in-ternal to frameworks immediately runs into its own logical difficulties. For one thing, the claim "truth is relative" cannot mean that the same sentence A is true in conceptual scheme X but false in conceptual scheme Y. For on the understanding that meaning is tied to truth con-ditions, if the truth conditions for two sentences of the same form are different, then they necessarily refer to different things. Thus, even if they use the same words, sentence A is referring to one thing in con-ceptual scheme X and to another in conceptual scheme Y. W. Newton-Smith (1982, 107) provides an example: The utterance "grass is good to smoke" may be false in a hay field, and true in a hippie commune, but its meaning and truth conditions are different in each context. The rationalist conclusion is that, if relativists wish to argue for such an in-terpretation of the relativity of truth, then they must furnish another understanding of meaning.[45]

"Truth is relative" also cannot mean that a claim is true simply by virtue of being coherent with other beliefs. This position is self-defeating, because then relativism (for example) would only be true for relativists. The essential problem with coherence theories of truth is that they collapse the distinction between something being true and only being believed to be true, which inevitably leads to incoherent conclusions.[46] Framework relativists cannot dispense with truth, because the arguments they put forward require that at least some of their claims be accepted as true in a non-relativistic way (Mandelbaum 1982, 34). Because the practice of philosophical argument implicitly invokes truth as an ideal, relativists are often accused of performative self-contradiction.

My suggestion here is that correspondence and coherence theories be seen as *complementary*: the former understood as theories of truth and the latter as theories of justification. From the conventional point of view, experience is the outcome of interaction between an organism and its environment. And, even while it is granted that the contents of experience are not directly caused by the environment, human perceptions—sights, sounds, smells, tastes, and other sensations—function in part to "represent" aspects of the environment that are relevant to human interests.[47] Similarly, the *truth claims* that are expressed in the terms of conceptual schemes—including primary and secondary theories, in Horton's terms—function at least in part to represent and explain what exists, whether in a mind-dependent or mind-independent way.[48] In this context, *justification* can be understood as a social process mediated by language, in which truth claims are accepted, modified, or rejected *with reference to human experience*, including other beliefs.

Truth refers to the status of claims that adequately represent the way things actually are. For example, the claim that there is an environment that exists independently of human experience is *true* if there actually is such an environment. That claim is *justified* to the extent it can be successfully argued that belief in an experience-independent world overall makes more sense out of our experience than any form of subjective idealism (W. Newton-Smith 1982, 114ff.). In this way, a constructivist view of knowledge is not necessarily incompatible with the distinction between truth and justified belief.[49]

It was earlier proposed that one or another conceptual scheme is required for there to be beliefs that are candidates for being true or false.

This proposal does not entail the conclusion that accepting a scheme's assumptions guarantees that the particular claims made in its terms will be true (Okrent 1984, 348; also Elgin 1989, 89). For example, to claim that a certain person is at a Stage Four level of justice-reasoning presupposes Kohlberg's theory. However, to accept that claim as meaningful and significant does not establish it as true. This is consistent with the understanding that theories such as Kohlberg's are intended to represent aspects of the way things are prior to and independently of the activity of constructing conceptual frameworks.

With regard to the issue of whether or not frameworks themselves can be judged true or false: All that is required for a particular conceptual scheme to be a candidate for being true or false is another framework in the terms of which there is a distinction between the first conceptual scheme being true and only being believed to be true.[50] The arguments for framework relativism themselves presuppose such a distinction, because framework relativism requires that its own conceptual scheme be true, and not merely the product of relativist imaginations. Thus there is no logical reason why a conceptual scheme—even when it is a theory about the nature of truth—cannot be judged true or false according to how well it coheres with our experience.

Lonergan (1973, 34–35) provides a distinction relevant to understanding how *truth* can be both internal to and independent of particular theoretical frameworks. In Lonergan's terms, the *notion* of truth refers to a critical scepticism manifest in such questions as "Is this *really* the case?" The notion of truth is thus equivalent to the *intention* of truth, and as such is prior to and independent of particular *theories* or *definitions* of truth formulated in the terms of philosophical systems. Lonergan argues that, because the intention of truth is prior to and independent of particular theories of truth, it is still meaningful to ask of any particular theory of truth—"Is this *really* the case?" Justice provides an analogous example. On the one hand, what is and is not just is defined by the laws and procedures of particular legal systems. On the other hand, it can still be meaningfully asked whether or not particular legal systems are themselves just. Similarly, it is always logically possible to ask whether particular standards, practices, or traditions of rational judgment are themselves reasonable. Because the dynamic intentionality manifest in such questioning is distinct from how the notions are defined in particular schemes, *truth*, *justice*, and *rationality* are (to borrow Putnam's terms) transcendent as well as immanent criteria of judgment.

To summarize: Truth is relative in the sense that the meaning and truth conditions of particular claims are established, in part, by their corresponding conceptual schemes.[51] Truth is also relative in the sense that truth claims are evaluated with reference to human experience. However, truth is not relative in the sense that the same claim can be true in one framework and false in another. Nor is truth relative in the sense that adopting particular schemes or frameworks will guarantee that the empirical truth conditions for particular claims are satisfied. Finally, although what *truth* means is necessarily formulated in the terms of one or another theoretical framework, it is still possible to ask whether or not conceptual schemes are themselves true. A constructivist view of knowledge is compatible both (a) with at least some correspondence theories of truth and (b) with frameworks themselves being candidates for being judged true or false.[52]

Incomparability Revisited

Relativists may grant the logical possibility of assessing the relative strengths and limitations of competing conceptual schemes and still deny the feasibility of such evaluation. For example, they might concede that there is a "world" independent of experience and at the same time argue that it does not provide grounds for preferring one among theoretical constructs.[53]

> Nature can be patterned in different ways: it will tolerate many different orderings without protest. . . . No particular ordering is intrinsically preferable to all others, and accordingly none is self-sustaining. Specific orderings are constructed not revealed, invented not discovered, in sequences of activity which however attentive to experience and to formal consistency could have been otherwise. (Barnes and Bloor, cited in Nola 1988, 13)

One difficulty with this idea is that it is inconsistent with the purpose for which at least some conceptual schemes are developed: to represent actual features of our experience more accurately than existing alternatives. Moreover, if our experience is such that it tolerates incompatible schemes, then it is not clear how schemes would be rivals, or why incommensurability among them would matter. However, the chief difficulty with this idea is that some conceptual schemes do get rejected as failures: Some beliefs and belief systems—geocentric as opposed to heliocentric cosmologies, for example—are deemed to be less accurate representations of the natural or social environments than their alternatives. Again, although experience can only be talked about in the terms of one or another conceptual scheme, it seems reasonable to conclude that something independent and prior to those schemes is "talking back" when acting on assumptions leads to totally unexpected and perhaps disastrous consequences.[54] The notion of true as opposed to false beliefs can thus arise not from a comparison between beliefs and "the world" as it is independently of our experience, but from the relative success and failure of our beliefs in accounting for experience and in guiding practice. Keller, for example, explains that

> I invoke the term "nature" to refer not to any particular representations of reality, but to that which pre-exists us as cultural, linguistic beings, and accordingly, that provides a kind of ultimate (although perhaps not "absolute") resistance to the free invention of culturally specific imagination. The fact is that not all theories or representations are equally durable, or equally satisfying. And an important, even undeniable, aspect of the contraction of scientific theories is their responsiveness to what I call the "recalcitrance of nature." None of this is to say that it is possible to achieve anything one could reasonably call "truth," but only that scientists can and do sometimes discard theories because of their failure to provide efficacious guides to the interactions we engage in with the world I call "nature"—i.e., with those non-symbolic objects with which we live even though they can never be adequately named. (Keller 1989, 150–151; cf. WJ, 356–357)

Others have offered similar arguments that conceiving schemes of beliefs as free-floating constructions unconstrained by experience contradicts our usual practices of enquiry.[55] Consequently, in *some* cases our experience might tolerate conflicting explanations, but in other contexts it might provide decisive grounds for favouring one conceptual scheme over others.

A different relativist argument is that truth claims made in the untranslatable terms of two incommensurable frameworks are not referring to the same thing or appealing to the same evidence. For example, even when they use the same terms such as *mass, space,* and *time,* scientists working within the paradigm of Newtonian classical mechanics define these terms in ways that are incommensurable with the definitions used within Einstein's relativity theory. Consequently, the results of Newtonian and Einsteinian experiments cannot be compared in any straightforward way to demonstrate the predictive superiority of one theoretical framework over the other.[56] Kuhn uses the analogy of different languages to suggest how incommensurability of meaning between conceptual schemes can make comparison of their claims very difficult:

> Some words in the basic as well as in the theoretical vocabularies of the two theories . . . do function differently. These differences are unexpected and will be discovered and localized, if at all, only by repeated experience of communication breakdown. . . . The same limits make it difficult, or, more likely, impossible for an individual to hold both theories in mind together and compare them point by point with each other and with nature. (Kuhn 1977, 338)

Some relativists conclude that, because there is no neutral or framework-independent language in which the claims of incommensurable schemes can be faithfully represented, their truth claims cannot be compared without presupposing the validity of one or the other rival scheme. Again, however, to grant that some of the claims made within schemes cannot be rendered *either* in the other's terms *or* in the terms of a neutral framework does not mean that such incommensurable schemes cannot be compared. It means only that the two schemes have to be appreciated in their own terms. Contrary to Kuhn, that such comparison of schemes in their own terms is possible is demonstrated in the actual practice of science and other forms of rational enquiry: In at least some cases, claims from incommensurable schemes are evaluated without requiring "either that there is a set of universal, ahistorical criteria of theory comparison, or that there is a theory-free language for describing predictions" (Brown 1983, 22; cf. Kuhn 1977, 339). The lack of equivalent terms might make point by point comparisons of the particular claims of incommensurable frameworks difficult. But this does not justify the conclusion that the overall strengths and limitations of those frameworks cannot be appreciated and assessed (Laudan 1977, 140–146).

To speak of evaluating the relative merits of incommensurable schemes brings us to a final relativist argument in the "incommensurability of meaning" category. This argument begins with the affirmation of *holism:* "the philosophical doctrine which asserts that a number of different, apparently distinct elements are so integrally related that they must be considered, evaluated, or be seen to be as a whole rather than as separable atomic bits" (Okrent 1984, 353). *Justificational holism* asserts that, because individual claims take their meaning from their corresponding scheme of beliefs, frameworks must be evaluated as wholes. Relativists have attempted to argue from justificational holism to *epistemological behaviourism,* a view that frameworks are supported only by other sets of propositions or claims, on the grounds that "facts" or "states of affairs" can only cause, not justify, propositions. As Okrent argues (1984, 354–357), epistemological behaviourism is equivalent to the coherence theory of truth and is vulnerable to the same objections. Whatever validity holistic theories of meaning or justification might have, they provide no grounds for denying that the relative strengths and limitations of incommensurable schemes can be assessed.[57]

Understanding across Frameworks: The Hermeneutical Circle

To this point, my review of the rationalism-relativism debate supports a position that partial failure of translation among rival conceptual schemes does not necessarily rule out their comparison. This position suggests that a necessary first step in the assessment of a framework incommensurable to one's own is to appreciate it *in its own terms.* Thus, a key point in the rationalist response to incommensurability of meaning arguments for framework relativism has been to reject the idea that we are trapped within any particular scheme of beliefs or point of view.

> Just as the individual is never simply an individual, because he is always involved with others, so too the closed horizon that is supposed to enclose a culture is an abstraction. The historical move-

ment of human life consists in the fact that it is never utterly bound to one standpoint, and hence can never have a truly closed horizon. (Gadamer, cited in Bernstein 1983, 167; see also 90–92 re. Karl Popper's rejection of the *Myth of the Framework*.)

One positive outcome of the stress relativists have placed on the differences and disjunctions among distinct points of view is that rationalists have taken a closer look at how those operating within incommensurable frameworks can actually come to understand each other. Descriptions of how understanding is reached across linguistic, cultural, historical, or other differences converge on a "back and forth" or *dialectical* process often called the *hermeneutical circle*. This process involves two (at least) distinct dialectical movements. One is the movement back and forth in understanding a rival scheme of beliefs between using some understanding of the whole to illuminate the part, and using some understanding of the parts to illuminate the whole. The other dialectic is the movement back and forth between using one's own point of view to understand the other, and then using the rival point of view (as best understood) to illuminate one's own. In both cases the dialectical process is open-ended: all judgments are open to revision contingent upon further insight or information.

In discussing versions of the hermeneutical circle important to Kuhn, Feyerabend, Geertz, and Taylor, Bernstein (1983, 131–139) emphasizes that it is *not* necessary to forget or negate one's assumptions in order to understand another point of view. On the contrary, existing frameworks or perspectives are the necessary starting point:

A false picture is suggested when we think that our task is to leap out of our own linguistic horizon, bracket all our preunderstandings, and enter into a radically different world. Rather the task is always to find the resources within our own horizon, linguistic practices, and experience that can enable us to understand what confronts us as alien. And such understanding requires a dialectical play between our own preunderstandings and the forms of life that we are seeking to understand. It is in this way that we can risk and test our own prejudices, and we can not only come to understand what is "other" than us but also better understand ourselves. (Bernstein 1983, 173)

Those who advocate some variation of the hermeneutical circle do not claim that it will necessarily always lead to genuine understanding across differences. The dialectical process of reaching understanding is not infallible because it depends both upon qualities of character and upon abilities that people possess in varying degrees. For example, if we are to enter genuinely into the hermeneutical process, we must be open to the possibility that our own point of view is mistaken or incomplete. While such openness does not require that we begin by negating our assumptions or "prejudices," it does require that we recognize them as such "and in so doing strip them of their extreme character."[58] Similarly, we are more likely to make the effort to comprehend new perspectives that initially may seem foreign or strange if we start with the assumption that the other point of view will have its own validity and coherence. Furthermore, in addition to such important attitudes, we need the qualities of patience, attentiveness, intelligence, empathy, and imagination to appreciate unfamiliar perspectives (Bernstein 1983, 91, 137; Kuhn 1977, xii; *WJ*, 166–167).

Many people have observed that participating in a dialectical encounter with a genuinely different perspective contains the potential for greater self-understanding. This is because the beliefs we use to interpret our experience may be so taken for granted that they are invisible until brought to light by contrast with alternative conceptual schemes. Further, engaging in dialectic might lead to—indeed, require—a process of self-transformation. This is because learning to understand a framework incommensurable to one's own will involve learning to see things—*including oneself*—in a new way. Seeing oneself in that new way might reveal limitations or biases in one's point of view that, once recognized, must be corrected. This need for self-renewal might be experienced on *both* sides of a dialectical exchange, if that encounter gives rise to a more complete perspective that builds on the best of both competing points of view. Hence, Feyerabend talks about the process of *open exchange* among those representing different viewpoints as potentially leading to a transformation of all participants:

> The participants get immersed into each others' ways of thinking, feeling, perceiving to such an extent that their ideas, perceptions, world views may be entirely changed—they become different people participating in a new and different tradition. (Feyerabend 1978, 29).

Similarly, Bernstein (1983, 143–144) describes Gadamer's notion of a *fusion of horizons* as "an ongoing and open dialogue or conversation" whereby our own perspective may be "enlarged and enriched." In each case, incommensurability of meaning among points of view is not seen as an unsurmountable obstacle to understanding, but as an opportunity for self-knowledge and self-transformation for those willing to risk an encounter with the unfamiliar.

To summarize: The relativist claim that some competing conceptual schemes are characterized by incommensurability of meaning survives rationalist objections in at least this form: schemes of beliefs interpret the same domain of human experience in different terms, some of which have no equivalents in the alternative schemes. We have seen that if any robust form of relativism is to follow from incommensurability of meaning between two schemes, then they must be rivals in some sense and there must be no way in which their respective strengths and limitations can be rationally assessed. However, we have also seen that partial failure of translation between schemes does not necessarily rule out understanding, comparison, and evaluation across differences. On the contrary, as more than one rationalist has observed, the problem of relativism is felt most keenly when those using one conceptual scheme understand those using another well enough to realize that the second group's scheme represents a real alternative to their own.

> It is precisely our understanding of other languages and other cultures that persuades us of the existence of incommensurability with respect to fundamental premises of forms of reasoning. . . . The possibility of evaluative incommensurability arises precisely when untranslatability is overcome. In fact, it seems to me that the most powerful evidence for evaluative incommensurability arises, not when we fail to make another culture intelligible to us, but precisely when we make it intelligible enough to realize that their fundamental concepts, beliefs, and modes of justification are different from ours.[59]

As this quotation observes, when incommensurability of meaning is overcome, "the possibility of evaluative incommensurability arises." What "evaluative incommensurability" is, how it arises, and whether or not a case for relativism can be made from it, are topics of the third category of rationalist-relativist debates.

DIFFERENT OBJECTIVES, DIFFERENT PROBLEMS:
THE INCOMMENSURABILITY OF STANDARDS

Traditions and Communities of Enquiry

The context for this third category of debates over incommensurability is a shift in focus from theoretical frameworks to the traditions of enquiry that develop, revise, and reformulate conceptual schemes over time.

> In the philosophy of science, and more generally in contemporary analytic epistemology, we have witnessed an internal dialectic that has moved from the preoccupation (virtually an obsession) with the isolated individual term, to the sentence or proposition, to the conceptual scheme or framework, to an ongoing historical tradition constituted by social practices—a movement from logical atomism to historical dynamic continuity. . . . We are now aware that it is not only important to understand the role of tradition in science as mediated through research programs or research traditions but that we must understand how such traditions arise, develop, and become progressive and fertile, as well as the ways in which they can degenerate.[60]

A tradition of enquiry is embodied in a historical succession of communities of enquiry. As noted in the discussion of practical rationality, members of a community of enquiry share a set of interrelated beliefs, attitudes, interests, norms, priorities, and practices. This shared *paradigm* is the common ground that makes rational debate productive in any particular form of enquiry, whether philosophical, literary, historical, scientific, or moral. For example, within communities of scientific enquiry there is some consensus not only on what conceptual schemes are appropriate to specific domains of experience, but also on what the aims of their scientific discipline should be, what problems are significant, what heuristic models are helpful in conceiving solutions, what methods of enquiry are sound, and what standards or criteria should be used in evaluating theories and claims (Laudan 1977, 78–93; 1984, 68–69). In addition, because they share the same tradition, members of a community of enquiry draw upon a common history of customary practices, exemplary figures, notable achievements, and significant failures. They also generally pursue their investigations in similar concrete contexts of practice—universities or research institutions, for instance—which shape the direction and form of their enquiry through such things as administrative structures and reward systems.[61]

From this description, it is clear that the shared beliefs, attitudes, interests, norms, and priorities that differentiate distinct communities of enquiry are not always stated explicitly, but are often implicit in accepted practices, heuristic models, current exemplars, and historical narratives.[62] It is difficult, if not impossible, to capture all of a community of enquiry's implicit assumptions and commitments in language, much less in logical propositions or rules. This is particularly the case for those shared agreements that are embodied in images, models, and exemplars. For example, Kuhn shows how science students learn how to see resemblances between "apparently disparate problems" through studying a scientific community's collection of exemplary problems and solutions. Acquiring the ability to see new problems as similar to familiar ones teaches students both what abstract generalizations are relevant to those new problems and how to relate them to experience. As Kuhn has observed, then, becoming a member of a community of enquiry involves not only absorbing facts and arguments but also tacitly learning to *see* in new ways. Similarly, MacIntyre shows how the meaning of abstract moral concepts within a particular tradition of enquiry is learned in part through concrete images and exemplars passed on in oral or written histories, which illustrate how those moral concepts are properly applied.[63]

It is important to recall here that it is by virtue of their implicit and explicit shared assumptions that members of a community of enquiry agree both on what kinds of problems are significant and on what kinds of solutions to those problems are adequate. When they are learned and used in a tacit way, these agreements might only come to conscious awareness when they are called into question.[64] Even explicit beliefs may be so taken for granted that, rather than being recognized as the commitments held at some stage in the development of a particular tradition, they are simply assumed to be true. The dependence of enquiry upon these underlying assumptions and commitments sets the stage for relativist arguments that appeal to evaluative incommensurability.

Evaluative Incommensurability

With the shift in focus from conceptual schemes to traditions of enquiry there is a shift in the grounds for framework relativism from incommensurability of meaning to evaluative incommensurability. Two communities of enquiry are said to exhibit evaluative incommensurability when there is sufficient overlap in their beliefs, attitudes, interests, norms, priorities, and practices for them to understand each other as rivals, but insufficient overlap for them to evaluate each other's theories and other conceptual resources according to the same set of criteria. For example, evaluative incommensurability can arise when rival communities have different conceptions of the proper nature and aims of their kind of enquiry. This is because, given their different objectives, they will assign highest priority to the solution of different problems. In turn, because they differ on which problems are most important to solve, they will arrive at incompatible evaluations of the strengths and limitations of their respective theoretical frameworks.

According to Doppelt (1982, 118–119), it is just this kind of evaluative incommensurability that characterizes rival Kuhnian paradigms of scientific enquiry. For, in Kuhn's account of scientific revolutions, rival paradigms have incompatible definitions of their scientific discipline and its proper objectives. Accordingly, their theoretical frameworks place emphasis on different sets of observations, or interpret the same set of observations in incompatible ways. Similarly, because each scientific community places emphasis on solving different problems, each community "implicitly defines standards of scientific adequacy favouring its achievements and research program and unfavourable with respect to the work of its rivals."[65]

To produce framework relativism, this characterization of evaluative incommensurability must be supplemented with two additional claims. The first is the claim that *all* practices of reasoning and rational justification—of presenting, understanding, evaluating, and accepting or rejecting arguments and conclusions—presuppose a set of beliefs, attitudes, interests, norms, priorities, and practices that have developed within the history of some tradition of enquiry. To return to the visual metaphor: the claim is that all reasoned judgments and evaluations are made from one or another historically and socially conditioned point of view and corresponding horizon. There is no such thing as a "neutral" perspective on a problem or issue. If this is correct, it follows that *there are no standards or criteria for rational judgment except those developed within one or another tradition.*

The second claim is that if there are no standards of rational assessment external to or independent of traditions of enquiry, then the standards internal to traditions cannot themselves be vindicated without some form of circular reasoning. The argument concludes that all rational assessment is relative because its standards derive from assumptions, attitudes, interests, norms, priorities, and practices that cannot themselves be justified. In other words, there can be no evaluation of the relative merits of the schemes of belief of rival communities of enquiry that does not in some way take the background assumptions of one tradition for granted. Consequently, if recognizing the role that a tradition's shared assumptions and commitments play in evaluation and judgment is not to lead to the sort of relativism rationalists abhor, then some way of vindicating those agreements is required.[66]

The same question arises with reference to the relation of meaning and truth. The shift in focus from conceptual schemes to traditions has included a realization that the meaning of truth claims is often fixed, not just by the languages, but also by the tacit agreements shared within social groups.[67] In other words, for members of a group to agree on truth conditions for particular kinds of truth claims requires more than a shared conceptual scheme. It also requires that everyone understands the connection between words and experience in more or less the same way. Such shared understandings are the unquestioned background of communication, and it is doubtful that they could all be brought to conscious awareness and objectified in propositional form. The relativist concludes that practices of formulating and justifying truth claims presuppose tacit agreements that cannot be fully articulated, much less vindicated. Again, then, if agreement that truth conditions for particular kinds of claims have been fulfilled is not to be considered conditional upon arbitrary agreements, there must be some way of establishing confidence in the unspoken understandings presupposed in such judgments.

To summarize: the debate between those who would affirm and those who would deny the possibility of assessing the strengths and limitations of incommensurable points of view becomes focused on this question: *"How, if at all, can the beliefs, attitudes, interests, norms, priorities, and practices shared by members of a community of enquiry be justified in a non-circular way and non-foundational way, if there is no standpoint for justification outside of a tradition?"*

CHAPTER TWO

The Rationality of Traditions

A pearl goes up for auction. No one has enough,
so the pearl buys itself.

—Rumi

Alasdair MacIntyre recognizes that rival communities of enquiry can
exhibit both incommensurability of meaning and evaluative incommensurability. He also acknowledges—indeed, insists—both that there
are no standards for rational judgment that are not internal to socially
and historically conditioned traditions and that the standards shared
across rival communities of enquiry are not sufficient to resolve the issues which divide them (*WJ*, 166, 329–335, 348, 351). MacIntyre thus
agrees with framework relativists insofar as they affirm that there is no
tradition-independent meta-perspective from which to assess rival conceptual schemes. However, he argues that relativistic conclusions follow from the lack of a neutral meta-perspective only if we accept the
Enlightenment's distrust of tradition and the associated ideal of context-independent rational justification:

> It was a central aspiration of the Enlightenment, an aspiration the
> formulation of which was itself a great achievement, to provide for
> debate in the public realm standards and methods of rational jus-
> tification by which alternative courses of action in every sphere of
> life could be adjudged just or unjust, rational or irrational, en-
> lightened or unenlightened. So, it was hoped, reason would dis-
> place authority and tradition. Rational justification was to appeal

to principles undeniable by any rational person and therefore independent of all those social and cultural particularities which the
Enlightenment thinkers took to be the mere accidental clothing
of reason in particular times and places. (*WJ*, 6)

MacIntyre submits that the Enlightenment preoccupation with context-independent justification has obscured the true rationality of traditions. He describes the rationality of traditions as a historical and
dialectical process through which members of a community of enquiry
can justify their shared conceptual scheme, and assess its strengths and
limitations relative to those of their rivals, in a non-circular and non-
foundational way. Against Enlightenment assumptions, then, MacIntyre argues that there is no need to search for a standpoint outside of
a tradition. In this chapter, I summarize MacIntyre's account of the
rationality of traditions to provide a basis for responding to framework
relativism.

DIALECTICAL JUSTIFICATION: INTERNAL DEBATES

MacIntyre claims that the background agreements shared within communities of enquiry are not arbitrary commitments but are—at least in
part—the outcome of ongoing debates both within and among historical traditions. Communities of enquiry thus embody histories of
conflict as well as of agreement. Indeed, depending upon how its arguments evolve over time, a tradition may splinter into antagonistic
groups or reform out of previously adversarial factions.

> A tradition is an argument extended through time in which cer-
> tain fundamental agreements are defined and re-defined in terms
> of two kinds of conflict: those with critics and enemies external to
> the traditions who reject all or at least key parts of those funda-
> mental agreements, and those internal, interpretative debates
> through which the meaning and rationale of the fundamental
> agreements come to be expressed and by whose progress a tradi-
> tion is constituted. Such internal debates may on occasion destroy
> what had been the basis of common fundamental agreement, so
> that either a tradition divides into two or more warring compo-
> nents, whose adherents are transformed into external critics of

each other's positions, or else the tradition loses all coherence and fails to survive. It can also happen that two traditions, hitherto independent and even antagonistic, can come to recognize certain possibilities of fundamental agreement, and reconstitute themselves as a single, more complex debate. (*WJ*, 12; see also *AV*, 222)

According to MacIntyre's account, there are two kinds of arguments that are used in a tradition's internal debates. In the first kind, *demonstration* or deduction, argument is *from* first principles *to* conclusions. In the second kind, the first principles required for demonstration are established *dialectically*. Dialectical justification—like the dialectical process of coming to understand an unfamiliar language or point of view—incorporates two "back and forth" movements. The first is the back and forth movement between first principles and the specific conclusions that they entail: "So in the construction of any demonstrative science we both argue *from* what we take, often rightly, to be subordinate truths *to* first principles . . . as well as from first principles *to* subordinate truths" (*WJ*, 175, cf. 100–101, 118, *TRV*, 88). The second is the back and forth movement between different sets of first principles and implications, in which each is examined to determine its success in withstanding arguments and objections arising from each of the other positions (*WJ*, 8, 91, 118, 224, 252, 360). MacIntyre claims that, through these two kinds of dialectical argument, one set of first principles can be vindicated as being part of a scheme of beliefs that is overall more coherent and defensible than existing alternatives.

> Progress in rationality is achieved only from a point of view. And it is achieved when the adherents of that point of view succeed to some significant degree in elaborating ever more comprehensive and adequate statements of their positions through the dialectical procedure of advancing objections which identify incoherences, omissions, explanatory failures, and other types of flaw and limitation in earlier statements of them, of finding the strongest arguments available for supporting those objections, and then of attempting to restate the position so that it is no longer vulnerable to those specific objections and arguments. (*WJ*, 144)

According to MacIntyre, this twofold process of dialectical justification is *internal* to a community of enquiry and corresponding point of view.

This is because, in evaluating the relative merits of the competing theories that develop the implications of rival sets of first principles, dialectical argument presupposes "a shared conceptual framework, a shared conception of what constitutes a central problem, and shared view of how data are to be identified" (*WJ*, 252; cf. 134, 205). MacIntyre thus reiterates that first principles, and the dialectical arguments that support them, are always accepted or rejected from the perspective of one or another tradition and its current paradigm of enquiry.

> In systematizing and ordering the truths they take themselves to have discovered, the adherents of a tradition may well assign a primary place in the structures of their theorizing to certain truths and treat them as first metaphysical or practical principles. But such principles will have had to vindicate themselves in the historical process of dialectical justification. . . . Hence such first principles are not self-sufficient, self-justifying epistemological first principles. They may indeed be regarded as both necessary and evident, but their necessity and their evidentness will be characterizable as such only to and by those whose thought is framed by the kind of conceptual scheme from which they emerge as a key element, in the formulation and reformulation of the theories informed by that historically developing conceptual scheme. (*WJ*, 360)

MacIntyre's proposal that the justification of first principles is internal to a tradition would seem to reinforce the conclusions of framework relativists. However, he claims that dialectical argument can also serve to vindicate the conceptual scheme shared by members of a community of enquiry—*and* their associated standards for rational assessment—in a non-circular and non-foundational way. How is this possible?

In MacIntyre's account, every tradition of enquiry begins with the unquestioned beliefs, institutions, and practices of some contingent historical and social context (*WJ*, 354; *TRV*, 116). At some point in its history, its shared agreements are called into question, "sometimes by being challenged from some alternative point of view, sometimes because of an incoherence identified in the beliefs, sometimes because of a discovered resourcelessness in the face of some theoretical or practical problem, sometimes by some combination of these" (*TRV*, 116;

cf. Laudan, 1977, 54–64). This precipitates what MacIntyre terms an *epistemological crisis,* "a systematic breakdown of enquiry in the face of a certain set of intractable problems within a particular scheme of belief" (*TRV,* 120; cf. *WJ,* 361–362). The inability to make progress within a particular conceptual scheme results in a loss of confidence in all or a significant part of its assumptions. MacIntyre claims that, in order to resolve such a crisis, the adherents of a tradition must be able to reformulate their shared scheme of beliefs in a way that meets the following three criteria:

> First, this in some ways radically new and conceptually enriched scheme, if it is to put an end to the epistemological crisis, must furnish a solution to the problems which had previously proved intractable in a systematic and coherent way. Second, it must also provide an explanation of just what it was which rendered the tradition, before it had acquired these new resources, sterile or incoherent or both. And third, these first two tasks must be carried out in a way which exhibits some fundamental continuity of the new conceptual and theoretical structures with the shared beliefs in terms of which the tradition of enquiry had been defined up to this point. (*WJ,* 362, cf. 79–80, 327, 354–356; *TRV,* 116)

According to MacIntyre, then, "It is with respect of their adequacy or inadequacy in their responses to epistemological crises that traditions are vindicated or fail to be vindicated" (*WJ,* 363; *TC,* 9). This applies to the shared beliefs of that tradition taken as a whole, or to some particular portion of them that has been called into question. In particular, MacIntyre contends that the standards and procedures of rational justification shared within a tradition of enquiry "emerge from and are part of a history in which they are vindicated by the way in which they transcend the limitations of and provide remedies for the defects of their predecessors within the history of that same tradition" (*WJ,* 7). Thus, in MacIntyre's account, the justification of a community of enquiry's scheme of beliefs is never a matter of showing that they cannot be denied by any rational person whatsoever. It is a matter of showing that they are the best of existing alternatives for addressing a tradition's *problematic;* that is, the issues and problems considered of central importance to a tradition at one or more stages of its development:

Every such tradition, to some significant degree . . . has within itself at each stage a more or less well-defined problematic, that set
of issues, difficulties, and problems which have emerged from its
previous achievements in enquiry. Characteristically, therefore,
such traditions possess measures to evaluate their own progress or
lack of it, even if such measures necessarily are framed in terms of
and presuppose the truth of those central theses to which the tradition gives its allegiance. (*WJ*, 167, cf. 8, 144, 361; *RPP*, 199–200;
TRV, 100, 116)

As MacIntyre characterizes the rationality of traditions, the evaluation
and justification of a tradition's scheme of beliefs *is* thus relative to its
interests, represented by its current problematic. At the same time, this
relativity-to-interests does not guarantee that ongoing enquiry will con-
firm that tradition's current conceptual framework. Further investigation could reveal that framework to be internally incoherent or to be
inadequate with respect to that tradition's objectives. For as MacIntyre
is careful to explain, his claim that a tradition of enquiry's *standards* for
assessing truth claims are justified historically, relative to the previous
standards that have emerged within that tradition, does not entail a belief that the *truth* itself to which enquiry aspires is also historical, or relative to a tradition's point of view:

There is nothing paradoxical at all in asserting that from within
particular traditions assertions of universal import may be and are
made, assertions formulated within the limits set by the conceptual, linguistic, and argumentative possibilities of that tradition, but
assertions which involve the explicit rejection of any incompatible claim, advanced in any terms whatsoever from any rival standpoint. So within every major cultural and social tradition we find
some distinctive view of human nature and some distinctive conception of the human good presented as *true*. And although these
claims to truth are supported within different traditions by appeal to rival and often de facto incommensurable standards of rational justification, no such tradition is or can be relativistic either
about the truth of its own assertions or about the truth. (*PRC*, 295;
cf. *WJ*, 356-359; *TRV*, 121–122, 200–201; *ITC*, 113–115)

NARRATIVE AND DIALECTIC

MacIntyre draws a number of related implications from his account of the process of justification that is internal to traditions of enquiry. One implication is that, because resolving an epistemological crisis involves identifying previously unrecognized limitations, incoherences, or inadequacies in a conceptual scheme, "to have passed through an epistemological crisis successfully enables the adherents of a tradition of enquiry to rewrite its history in a more insightful way" (*WJ*, 363). A second implication is that it is only with the benefit of hindsight that a tradition is able to recognize that it has successfully passed through an epistemological crisis (*WJ*, 363). Consequently, "the history of all successful enquiry is and cannot but be written retrospectively" (*TRV*, 150). A third implication is that the beliefs shared within a community of enquiry, and the arguments used to support and defend those agreements, are only adequately understood when seen in their proper historical context (*WJ*, 9, 12–13, 144, 205, 258). That is to say, a community of enquiry's shared assumptions are only fully appreciated and vindicated through a narrative reconstruction of the history of the interests, issues, problems, practices, accomplishments, and debates that resulted, over time, in those agreements (*SH*, 461; *AV*, 268–269; *WJ*, 23, 143–144). It is in this way that justification is *historical* as well as dialectical:

> Thus the notion of a tradition embodies a . . . theory of knowledge according to which each particular theory or set of moral or scientific beliefs is intelligible and justifiable—insofar as it is justifiable—only as a member of an historical series. (*AV*, 146)
>
> To appeal to tradition is to insist that we cannot adequately identify either our own commitments or those of others in the argumentative conflicts of the present except by situating them within those histories which made them what they have now become. (*WJ*, 12–13).

It follows, on MacIntyre's account, that to participate in a tradition is to find a place in its narratively reconstructed history and a role to play in its ongoing enquiry. To become a full member of a particular tradition is thus to learn, not only how to narrate the history of its arguments, but also how to take those arguments up as one's own.

> To be an adherent of a tradition is always to enact some further stage in the development of one's tradition; to understand another tradition is to attempt to supply, in the best terms imaginatively and conceptually available to one—and later we shall see what problems can arise over this—the kind of account which an adherent would give. And since within any well-developed tradition of enquiry the question of precisely how its history up to this point ought to be written is characteristically one of those questions to which different and conflicting answers may be given within the tradition, the narrative task itself generally involves participation in conflict. (*WJ*, 11; cf. *SH*, 461; *TRV*, 65, 201–202)

To recapitulate: The rational superiority of a new formulation of a tradition's scheme of beliefs—including, perhaps, a new formulation of its standards of rational assessment—consists in its ability to "remedy the defects, transcend the limitations, and extend the reach of the tradition of which it is so far the best outcome" (*TRV*, 125). Thus, on MacIntyre's view, a community of enquiry's framework of beliefs is vindicated to the extent it has, through successive reformulations, provided the conceptual resources for resolving epistemological crises. Crises are resolved, not only through conceptual innovation, but also through the construction of a narrative that enables each member of a tradition of enquiry

> to understand *both* how he or she could intelligibly have held his or her original beliefs *and* how he or she could have been so drastically misled by them. The narrative in terms of which he or she first understood or ordered experiences is itself made into the subject of an enlarged narrative. (*EC*, 455; cf. 460, 467)

Accordingly, to justify a community of enquiry's conceptual scheme is to provide a narrative reconstruction of the history of the corresponding tradition, showing how innovations at each new stage in its development resulted in formulations of their agreements that corrected the defects of previous stages as they came to light. When members of a tradition of enquiry are sufficiently self-reflective to appreciate how their shared scheme of beliefs has developed through successive reformulations, their narrative reconstruction of its history could include retrospective accounts of previous justificatory narratives (*WJ*, 383; *TRV*, 150–151). It could also include retrospective accounts of the transformations that occurred in the language(s) of that tradition, that is, of the linguistic innovations that were required to express the new ideas introduced at each of its stages of development (*WJ*, 383–384).

DIALECTICAL JUSTIFICATION: EXTERNAL DEBATES

From his characterization of the historical and dialectical process whereby traditions can justify their schemes of beliefs, MacIntyre draws a number of conclusions concerning the possibility of productive debate between incommensurable traditions of enquiry. Such external debates are less straightforward than internal arguments because, by definition, incommensurable traditions conceive and pursue their enquiry within very different conceptual frameworks, and so address themselves to very different sets of problems (*WJ*, 328–329). Nonetheless, MacIntyre holds that encounters between rival and incommensurable schemes can be productive—under certain conditions. His first point is that the adherents of a mature tradition properly recognize that dialectical enquiry is an ongoing process, and that the conclusions reached through dialectic should therefore be kept open to revision in the light of new developments or discoveries (*WJ*, 100–101, 172; *TRV*, 88–89). This is precisely because a mature tradition has, by definition, successfully emerged from one or more epistemological crises. Its adherents have already experienced the rejection of older assumptions and beliefs in favour of more recent formulations of its agreements, which proved to be more adequate in addressing its outstanding issues and problems. A mature tradition therefore will recognize that its current conceptual scheme—including its definition of truth and standards of rational assessment—might also be supplanted by more adequate formulations.[1]

MacIntyre's second point is that a tradition's recognition of its limitations properly results in an openness to the possibility that the conceptual resources of an incommensurable tradition might be more adequate to its issues and problems than its own (*WJ*, 388). This is particularly the case when a community of enquiry is experiencing an epistemological crisis that the resources of its own point of view have been inadequate to resolve.

> We have already noticed that central to a tradition-constituted enquiry at each stage in its development will be its current problematic, that agenda of unsolved problems and unresolved issues by reference to which its success or lack of it in making rational progress toward some further stage of development will be evaluated. At any point it may happen to any tradition-constituted enquiry that by its own standards it ceases to make progress. Its hitherto trusted methods of enquiry have become sterile. Conflicts over rival answers to key questions can no longer be settled rationally. Moreover, it may indeed happen that the use of the methods of enquiry and of the forms of argument, by means of which rational progress had been achieved so far, begins to have the effect of increasingly disclosing new inadequacies, hitherto unrecognized incoherences, and new problems for the solution of which there seem to be insufficient or no resources within the established fabric of belief. (*WJ*, 361–362, cf. *TRV*, 120; *ITC*, 117)

In such cases, one or more adherents of that community of enquiry might make the effort to appreciate another tradition's point of view in its own terms and conclude that, *by their own standards*, the rival perspective is superior to their own. Not only does the new perspective allow for a solution to their crisis that was unavailable within their own tradition, it also enables them to understand in retrospect the limitations that had made progress within their theoretical framework unattainable (*AV*, 276–277; *WJ*, 387–388; *TRV*, 118–120, 146). MacIntyre concludes that one tradition's scheme of beliefs is justifiably held to be rationally superior to that of a rival tradition when it can provide both (a) better solutions to the central issues and problems of its rival by their own standards, and (b) better explanations than its rival of their respective strengths and limitations.

> Just as a later stage within that tradition is held superior to an earlier stage only if and insofar as it is able to transcend the limitations

and failures of that earlier stage, limitations and failures by the standards of rationality of that earlier stage itself, so the rational superiority of that tradition to rival traditions is held to reside in its capacity not only for *identifying* and *characterizing* the limitations and failures of that rival tradition as judged by that rival tradition's own standards—limitations and failures which that rival tradition itself lacks the resources to explain or understand—but also for *explaining* and *understanding* those limitations and failures in some tolerably precise way. (*TRV*, 180–181, my italics; see also 4–5, 120, 125; *WJ*, 172, 362; *ITC*, 117–118; *PPI*, 78–79)

In this way, narrative plays a key role in external as well as internal debates (*WJ*, 403). Adherents of competing communities of enquiry may each attempt to provide a narrative account of its rational superiority that is overall more coherent and plausible than the comparable accounts offered by its rivals. Or, perhaps the competing narratives are constructed by those members of one community who are attempting to evaluate the conceptual resources of their own point of view against those of alternative positions. In either case, the relative merits of the rival schemes of beliefs are evaluated from the perspective of one or another tradition. This evaluation is not circular in a vicious way, because there is no guarantee that a conceptual scheme will emerge as superior according to its own standards of rational assessment. MacIntyre thus understands his account of the rationality of traditions as refuting the relativist claim that debate among incommensurable perspectives will necessarily be inconclusive because each will be vindicated by its own standards of rational adequacy (*WJ*, 364-366, 387–388).

MacIntyre is careful to add that there are no guarantees that the encounter between members of rival communities of enquiry will result in agreement on the relative strengths and limitations of their respective conceptual frameworks. This is first because a fair comparison between two incommensurable schemes requires that both rival traditions be understood and evaluated in their own terms, and adherents of one or both traditions may be unwilling or unable to appreciate the other point of view. According to MacIntyre, to understand a second tradition in its own terms, the members of the first tradition must learn to speak the "language-in-use" of the members of the second tradition as a "second first language." For someone to learn another tradition's language-in-use as a second first language requires "a work of the imagination whereby the individual is able to place him- or herself imaginatively within the scheme of belief inhabited by those whose allegiance is to the rival tradition, so as to perceive and conceive the natural and social worlds as they perceive and conceive them" (*WJ*, 394–395). Learning to imaginatively adopt the perspective of another tradition, particularly one incompatible with one's own, is not impossible, but it is difficult:

> It requires a rare gift of empathy as well as intellectual insight for the protagonists of such a tradition to be able to understand the theses, arguments, and concepts of their rival in such a way that they are able to view themselves from such an alien standpoint and to recharacterize their own beliefs in an appropriate manner from the alien perspective of the rival tradition. (*WJ*, 167)

For the members of one tradition to appreciate the perspective of another requires that they possess *and exercise* such empathy and insight. In other words, their dedication to truth must outweigh their attachment to their own beliefs, such that they are willing to acknowledge the rational superiority of a competing view should that acknowledgment be warranted.

MacIntyre adds that even if adherents of one or both of two competing communities are willing and able to appreciate the other perspective in its own terms, it may still occur that neither will be convinced of the rational superiority of the other. There may be sufficient divergence in the issues and problems that each holds to be central that each will consider its own conceptual scheme more coherent and overall defensible than that of its rival (*AV*, 277; *WJ*, 328, 366, 370). In such cases, neither community of enquiry will be clearly better than its rival at resolving the rival's own difficulties.

One of the important implications MacIntyre draws from his account of the rationality of traditions is that *how* we engage in debate should vary according to whether or not those with whom we are arguing give allegiance to the same tradition of enquiry as our own. He identifies four possibilities (*TRV*, 145–147; cf. *WJ*, 394–396). In dealing with those people who as yet have no allegiance to a tradition, and so have no standpoint from which to advance and evaluate arguments, we should postpone debate until they are educated into one or another community of enquiry. In arguing with those who share allegiance to our tradition, our debates will properly include appeal to shared assumptions and first principles. In arguing with those who give their allegiance to another tradition, and who are willing and able to understand an incommensurable point of view, we should compare the relative coherence and explanatory power of the alternative frameworks with respect to the issues and problems identified as outstanding within each tradition's problematic. Finally, when dealing with those who are "systematically unable" to grasp the limitations of their position and who claim that it is only other communities of enquiry whose members suffer from "ideological blindness," our response will properly include the construction and evaluation of competing accounts of systemic bias. MacIntyre argues that "for one view to have emerged from its encounter with another with its claim to superiority vindicated it must first have rendered itself maximally vulnerable to the strongest arguments which that other and rival view can bring to bear against it" (*TRV*, 181). Consequently, any tradition's claim to rationality is put in doubt to the extent that it consistently exempts its fundamental beliefs from critical assessment.

CONVERGING VIEWS

Debate within a variety of contexts is converging upon a view of the justification of conceptual schemes and the evaluation of rival frameworks that is consistent with MacIntyre's account of the rationality of traditions. For one thing, there is a growing appreciation that both the Enlightenment's distrust of tradition is misplaced and the associated attempts to provide context-free justification are unnecessary. According to Bernstein (1983, 130), Gadamer, like MacIntyre, believes that "All reason functions *within* traditions."

> The understanding of reason and rationality itself undergoes a subtle transformation in Gadamer's work. For he rejects the oppositions that have been so entrenched since the Enlightenment— between reason and tradition, reason and prejudice, reason and authority. Reason is not a faculty or capacity that can free itself

from its historical context and horizons. Reason is historical or situated reason which gains its distinctive power always within a living tradition. For Gadamer this is not a limitation or deficiency of reason, but rather the essence of reason rooted in human finitude. (Bernstein 1983, 37)

For such theorists, to grant that the relative validity of competing interpretations or explanations is evaluated with respect to a historically and socially conditioned point of view in itself entails no relativist conclusions.[2]

There is also a growing number of theorists arguing that the evaluation of the conceptual schemes of competing communities of enquiry involves the narrative reconstruction of the histories of their internal and external debates. For example, Weinert (1984, 389–390) states that "all arguments and propositions are embedded in a *tradition*, and thus are dependent on preexisting principles, modes of argumentation, choice of acceptable problems, available techniques and tools." At the same time, he argues that incommensurable sets of such agreements can be compared by locating them within a process of historical transformation. This process of transformation is precisely the dialectical development of new forms of argument and new ways of conceiving problems to surpass the limitations of previous perspectives. Weinert concludes that

Accepting the existence of incommensurable viewpoints both on the synchronic and diachronic level neither excludes those viewpoints being comparable (consequently, they compete) nor does it rule out one viewpoint being judged superior, in some specifiable sense, to an alternative approach, with respect to some well-defined area. (Weinert 1984, 388)

Similarly, in his review of the positions of Richard Rorty, Kuhn, and Lakatos, Bernstein (1983, 67–68) argues that the emergence of new sets of assumptions within communities of scientific enquiry can be understood retrospectively as happening for "good reasons." Furthermore, that later conceptions of scientific rationality can retrospectively be seen to be superior to earlier ones requires no reference to neutral, permanent, and context-free standards of rationality. Laudan (1977,

193–194) argues specifically that evaluating the systems of ideas of competing scientific research traditions necessarily requires a historical study of their respective resources for solving empirical and conceptual problems.

Bernstein (1983, 167–169), Laudan (1984, 80–82) and MacIntyre (*EC*, 469–470) all observe that the dialectical evaluation of competing conceptual schemes entails an implicit if not explicit understanding that what is intended in narrative reconstructions of the debates within and among traditions is historical truth, as well as intelligibility. This notwithstanding the fact that the relative accuracy of competing histories will itself be a matter of debate, because there are no accounts of what has happened in the past that are not themselves historically and socially conditioned (Bernstein 1983, 73–74; *WJ*, 332–333; *TRV*, 117–118, 151). In the same way that we cannot step outside of our experience to compare our descriptions of the world to what is prior to experience, we cannot step out of the present to compare our accounts with what "really happened." Thus, Krausz argues that just as there are no theory-independent "facts" or "observations" that will serve to resolve disputes among rival scientific theories, there are no narrative-independent "events" that will serve to determine which of competing histories is "true": "Events (or, more precisely, descriptions of events) are not the raw material out of which narratives are constructed; rather an event is an abstraction from a narrative."[3] However, in the same way that rival scientific theories are evaluated, not just with respect to the single facts "picked out" by their conceptual schemes, but also with respect to their overall coherence and explanatory power, so too narratives are properly evaluated through a dialectical comparison with competing narratives (Krausz 1984, 402). And again, that the criteria according to which rival narratives are evaluated derive from the interests of some historically and socially conditioned tradition entails no relativist conclusions.

> Alternative competing narratives are compared and judged according to such values as accuracy, consistency, scope, simplicity, fruitfulness, comprehensiveness, cogency, openness to further narratizing, or the like. And these meta-theoretical values are non-foundationally articulable within the terms of the historian-critic's own historic place. (Krausz 1984, 402)

To summarize: MacIntyre argues that the conceptual scheme shared by members of a community of enquiry can be justified, but not in the context-independent way anticipated by the Enlightenment conception of rationality. Justification always presupposes a context of problems and issues arising within one or another particular historical tradition, for a scheme of beliefs is vindicated by its ability to transcend the limitations of previous schemes. Thus "to provide the rational justification for any thesis or theory always involves the telling of a story that places the theory to be evaluated in relation to its predecessors" (*TC*, 10). On this view, the inability of communities of enquiry to provide context-free justification for their agreements—justification, that is, that would be accepted by all rational persons whatsoever—reveals a failure not of the rationality of traditions but of the Enlightenment conception of rational justification. In MacIntyre's eyes, then, the quest for context-free rationality is futile.[4] At the same time, his claim that assessment is context-dependent does not entail the relativistic conclusion that a community of enquiry's scheme of beliefs is always justified in a circular manner. This is because dialectical arguments can result in compelling reasons for the members of one community of enquiry to grant the rational superiority of a rival conceptual scheme *according to their own standards of rational adequacy.*

Looking Back, Looking Ahead

Chapter one ended with the question "How, if at all, can the beliefs, attitudes, interests, norms, priorities, and practices shared by members of a community of enquiry be justified, if there is no standpoint for justification outside of a tradition?" MacIntyre has argued that, because the assumptions and commitments shared within a tradition of enquiry emerge from its internal and external debates, it is through narrative reconstructions of the history of those debates that a community's scheme of beliefs—including its theories of truth and rationality—is vindicated. Because MacIntyre's account of dialectical argument within and among traditions requires no reference to universal or context-free rational principles, it provides a good beginning to understanding how the strengths and limitations of incommensurable points of view can be evaluated in a non-circular and non-foundational way. At the same time, his account of the rationality of traditions leaves important questions unaddressed. For example, MacIntyre claims that a community of enquiry's scheme of beliefs is justified if it proves adequate to that tradition's evolving problematic. The significance of those problems and issues *presupposes* the fundamental agreements constitutive of that tradition (*WJ*, 167). On MacIntyre's own definition, rival traditions are characterized by mutually exclusive sets of fundamental agreements. Consequently, as the proponents of framework relativism observe, competing communities of enquiry typically consider different problems to be significant and so typically affirm the relative superiority of their scheme of beliefs according to their own standards of rational adequacy. How is it, then, that one tradition's theoretical framework could prove more adequate to the problems of its rivals than their own conceptual schemes? What must be assumed if it is reasonable to expect that dialectical debate among members of rival and incommensurable traditions of enquiry will lead to the convergence of their competing points of view?

CHAPTER THREE

The Search for Wide Reflective Equilibrium

Life can only be understood backwards, but it must be lived forwards.

—Kierkegaard

This chapter has three sections. In section one, I raise questions about MacIntyre's description of the rationality of traditions in order to identify aspects of his work that need clarification if the problem of framework relativism is to be adequately addressed. To provide the needed clarification, I present in sections two and three an expanded account of non-circular and non-foundational justification both by systematizing what I see as implicit in MacIntyre's texts and by integrating ideas from my own and other work on related topics. Section two illustrates the relationships among paradigms of enquiry, world views, and ways of life; section three reframes the historical and dialectical process of justification as a search for wide reflective equilibrium.

THE RATIONALITY OF TRADITIONS: FURTHER QUESTIONS

How Are Traditions Differentiated?

I have shown how, according to MacIntyre, a tradition of enquiry's conceptual framework is justified to the extent its successive reformulations continue to provide the resources for the resolution of epistemological crises arising within that tradition's ongoing investigations. In encounters between rival traditions, the members of one or both of the corresponding communities of enquiry assess the capabilities of each competing scheme of beliefs to address the issues and problems outstanding within their tradition at its current stage of historical development. As part of this dialectical process, competing conceptual schemes are compared to determine which is best able to explain and to overcome what the rival traditions recognize by their own standards to be their limitations and failures.

MacIntyre's characterization of dialectical argument presupposes that it is possible to differentiate one rival tradition of enquiry from another. However, he provides no clear answer to the question of *how many* or *what kinds* of "fundamental agreements" constitute a tradition of enquiry. Neither does he specify how many or what kinds of disagreements would serve to differentiate rival traditions. For, on the one hand, MacIntyre describes the conflict *internal* to traditions as extending to the most fundamental issues:

> For it is not merely that different participants in a tradition disagree; they also disagree as to how to characterize their disagreements and as to how to resolve them. They disagree as to what constitutes appropriate reasoning, decisive evidence, conclusive proof. A tradition then not only embodies the narrative of an argument, but is only to be recovered by an argumentative retelling of that narrative which will itself be in conflict with other argumentative retellings. (*EC*, 461; cf. *SH*, 90–92; *AV*, 221–222, 260; *WJ*, 43; *TRV*, 12)

On the other hand, MacIntyre describes members of rival traditions as sharing some standards of rational argument—for example, "in according a certain authority to logic"—and as sharing some understanding of their common subject matter (*AV*, 51–52; *WJ*, 351, 359). Consequently, it is not clear in MacIntyre's account how much or what kinds of conflict would serve to differentiate disputes *within* from disputes *between* traditions. This is particularly an issue for religious and philosophical traditions of enquiry that over hundreds or even thousands of years have crossed geographical, political, ethnic, linguistic, and cultural boundaries. For instance, it seems very much open to question whether the conflict between Augustinian and Thomistic Catholic theologies is properly understood as within or as between traditions (cf. *WJ*, 326–327).

Similar questions arise from MacIntyre's insistence that, on the one hand, a tradition may be said to survive epistemological crises only if some "core of shared belief, constitutive of allegiance to the tradition" is retained in the shift from earlier to later conceptual schemes (*WJ*, 356). On the other hand, he also allows that later conceptual and theoretical structures can in at least some ways be "radically new," exhibiting a "radical discrepancy" with previous beliefs. For example, later formulations of a tradition of enquiry's agreements can include new conceptions of both its objectives and its methods:

> Among the beliefs and belief-presupposing practices which are subject to reformulation as a rationally mature tradition moves through its various stages may be, and characteristically are, both those which concern what it is to evaluate beliefs and practices as more or less rational, what truth is and how rationality and truth are connected, and those which concern the theoretical and practical goals toward which at each stage those participating in that particular tradition are directing themselves. (*TRV*, 116)

It is therefore not clear how much or what kind of continuity is required between successive reformulations of a scheme of beliefs and the corresponding communities of enquiry, if they are to be properly located within the *same* tradition.

Questions also arise concerning *how many* of a tradition's fundamental agreements someone can reject and still legitimately consider him or herself a member of that tradition. Aquinas' appropriation of elements of Aristotle's ethics is a case in point. MacIntyre describes Aquinas as continuing a tradition which up to that time had received its definitive formulation by Aristotle. Indeed, in contrast to other medieval thinkers, Aquinas is judged a "strict Aristotelian" (*AV*, 178). At the same time, because Aquinas rejects Aristotle's conception of the human *telos*, MacIntyre acknowledges that key aspects of Aquinas' ethics, epistemology, and metaphysics are alien to Aristotle's overall conceptual scheme (*AV*, 174–177). These differences provide reasonable grounds for understanding Aquinas as originating—or at least representing—a set of agreements that are *rival to* the Aristotelian scheme of beliefs. In such cases, MacIntyre provides no guidelines for judging which or how many fundamental agreements are definitive of a tradition such that they must be accepted before someone can be truly said to represent that tradition's point of view.

With regard to the "continuity through change" question: MacIntyre does propose that it is with respect to a tradition's problematic that the progress or lack of progress of later over earlier stages is identified (*WJ*, 361; *RPP*, 199–200). Perhaps, then, continuity between later and earlier formulations of a tradition's beliefs is provided by its agenda of unresolved issues and problems. The difficulty with this is MacIntyre's claim that later stages in a tradition of enquiry are superior to earlier ones in part because they include a more adequate description of its final goal. I would expect that the issues and problems considered most important by a tradition of enquiry would change along with the formulation of "radically new" conceptual schemes and "conceptually richer" accounts of its proper objective (*WJ*, 80). Moreover, if problems are important enough to provide a standard of progress within a tradition of enquiry, I would expect that a persistent inability to solve them would be sufficient to provoke an epistemological crisis. Conversely, if later stages of a tradition are superior to earlier ones by virtue of resolving epistemological crises, then later stages must include solutions to the problems and issues once given priority within that tradition. It would therefore seem that issues and problems can provide continuity only between two historically adjacent formulations of a tradition's beliefs, and not between the entire historical development of that tradition.[1] Moreover, even if two conceptual schemes can be related as respectively more and less able to address the same set of problems, this still leaves unanswered how much continuity is required between two historically adjacent formulations of a tradition's beliefs if the later formulation's resolution of the earlier one's epistemological crisis is properly understood as an innovative development (rather than a rejection or radical transformation) of that tradition.

Similar arguments could be made against any suggestion that the continuity of a tradition is provided by the texts they hold to be authoritative. For any such suggestion would beg the question of how much agreement is required in the interpretation of those texts for continuity to be affirmed through reformulations of that tradition, since interpretation of even those works considered authoritative can vary widely within, as well as among, traditions (*WJ*, 231, 288, 354–355, 383; cf. *AV*, 165; *TRV*, 84–85). Similarly, given that rival traditions consider at least some of the same texts to be authoritative, to suggest that a tradition is defined by its canon begs the question of *how many* texts must be shared between two groups if they are to count as belonging to the same tradition.

On one model of their relationship, some of a tradition's beliefs are more important or "central" than others. In this model, the rejection or radical reformulation of a tradition's core beliefs represents its demise or transformation into a new tradition. By definition, in other words, *core beliefs* are those which must be retained if a tradition is to retain its integrity and identity. On another model, all of the commitments of a tradition are open to revision, and only some portion of the total must be retained for the tradition or paradigm to be considered to survive change (Swoyer 1982, 97–98). MacIntyre's use of the phrase "core of shared beliefs" indicates that he favours the former model (*WJ*, 356). Perhaps, then, a tradition maintains continuity through its conceptual reformulations, and is differentiated from its rivals, by some nucleus of sacrosanct beliefs. Unfortunately, while MacIntyre does say that "some elements of present theory or belief may be such that it is difficult to envisage their being abandoned without the tradition as a whole being discarded" (*AV*, 146–147), this does not explain how the core of a particular tradition's beliefs could be identified. Furthermore, MacIntyre's own description of the degree of conflict within traditions strongly suggests that adherents of the same tradition will not always agree upon which of their shared beliefs must be retained through its evolution, and MacIntyre does not explain how such disputes could be resolved.

A useful perspective on these questions concerning the identities and boundaries of traditions is, I believe, implicit in MacIntyre's position. He is clear that his account of the rationality of traditions is self-referring; that is, that his account is itself part of a particular historical tradition (*PRC*, 295). It is consistent with this view to say that, like other frames of reference or systems of classification based on judgments of sameness and of difference, distinctions among traditions of enquiry are human constructions drawn according to specific assumptions, interests, and priorities. It follows that the boundaries between rival traditions and communities of enquiry do not exist "out there" in any absolute sense. This does not mean that boundaries are necessarily groundless, arbitrary, or beyond dispute.[2] It does mean that there is no context-independent way of deciding how much or what kind of change in a tradition's beliefs is sufficient to represent its demise or transformation. The narrative which provides for continuity between earlier and later formulations of a tradition's "fundamental agreements" is always constructed—and challenged or accepted—from one or another historically situated point of view. In the same way, judgments that conflicts are internal to a community of enquiry or are between two rivals are always made from one or another tradition's perspective. This is consistent with MacIntyre's point that two communities of enquiry may agree that they are rivals without necessarily being able to agree on how to characterize each other or the nature of the rivalry (*TC*, 6; *WJ*, 350–351).

That the boundaries between traditions will vary according to who is drawing them and why suggests that who is considered "inside" and who "outside" a community of enquiry may vary from issue to issue. MacIntyre himself suggests that "the relationships which can hold between individuals and a tradition are very various, ranging from unproblematic allegiance through attempts to amend or redirect the tradition to large opposition to what have hitherto been its central contentions" (*WJ*, 326). Thus, a person's relation to a tradition might be characterized both by ambiguity and by ambivalence. Rather than categorizing people as members of one or another community of enquiry, or none at all, it might be more accurate to locate them as somewhere between the "fringe" and "centre" of a tradition of enquiry, or as inhabiting the intersection of two or more traditions—particularly in modern societies where competition among traditions accelerates their development, making their boundaries more fluid.[3]

Conceiving membership in traditions of enquiry as context-dependent has a number of advantages. For example, it allows that we may align ourselves with a tradition with respect to certain issues, but distance ourselves from it with respect to others. It also reinforces the understanding that we are not necessarily limited to only one perspective, but can imaginatively inhabit rival points of view. Conceiving membership as context-dependent also allows for considerable variation in how communities of enquiry are defined. Depending upon the kind and the scope of enquiry under consideration, membership in a community and corresponding tradition of enquiry could mean participation in a school or university class, affiliation with a scientific or professional association, engagement in one of the many forms of artistic expression, allegiance to an abstract philosophical position, solidarity with an emancipatory political movement, or commitment to the study and practice of a religious tradition. This is consistent with MacIntyre's passing remark that a tradition's beliefs "may inform only a limited part of the whole community's life or be such as concern its overall structure and indeed its relation to the universe" (*WJ*, 356).

Recognizing that boundaries between traditions of enquiry are not absolute allows that even rival points of view may share considerable "common ground." For example, without minimizing their disputes, Thomist and Augustinian theologians may come to appreciate the extent of their shared assumptions when arguing with adherents of Protestant denominations (cf. *TC*, 11). In turn, even members of historically antagonistic Jewish, Christian, and Muslim groups may realize they have much in common when compared to non-theistic religious communities. And so forth: through interfaith dialogue, theistic and non-theistic contemplatives may discover profound areas of commonality in their shared respect for spirituality (Walker 1987). MacIntyre argues at length that there are no tradition-independent or tradition-neutral criteria for rational assessment (*WJ*, 334–346). Yet he himself suggests that representatives of rival traditions within the same historical context can share broad areas of agreement, which shape the form and objectives of enquiry in important ways (*AV*, 51–53, 135, 140, 142, 222, 248–250, 276; *WJ*, 243, 350, 359, 387). As I will discuss below, it is their common ground that makes productive debate possible—in a way that MacIntyre does not fully explore—among traditions that exhibit both incommensurability of meaning and evaluative incommensurability.

Finally, and perhaps most importantly, recognizing that boundaries among and allegiances to traditions are not absolute may help to avoid the kind of insider/outsider dynamics that obstructs understanding and productive debate. Indeed, if MacIntyre is correct about the extent of disagreement among individuals that is compatible with their being members of the same tradition, labelling someone a "liberal" or a "communitarian" (for example) may do as much to obscure as to identify her or his fundamental commitments. Recognizing that we argue from one or another point of view internal to a tradition is potentially liberating in its rejection of any claims to or assumptions of an interest-free rationality, for such claims can serve an ideological function. In other words, to challenge the notion of "rationality as such" protects against one tradition's understanding of rationality becoming the unquestioned norm against which others are evaluated and found wanting. At the same time, recognizing that traditions and their boundaries are human constructions undermines any tendency to define people exclusively in terms of their membership within a particular community, whether of enquiry or otherwise.[4]

Only Rivals? A Schema of Possibilities

A second set of questions concerns MacIntyre's references to competing claims of rival schemes of belief as both incommensurable and logically incompatible. The rival claims are *incommensurable* in the sense that some of the key terms in which they are expressed lack equivalents in the opposing scheme (incommensurability of meaning), *and* in the sense that their validity is warranted by different standards of rational judgment (evaluative incommensurability). The rival claims are *incompatible* in the sense that accepting the applicability of the terms of one conceptual scheme entails rejecting the applicability of the terms of the other (*AV*, 244–246; *WJ*, 351, 380; *ITC*, 109–110). The first question here is whether or not the relationship between the truth claims of incommensurable schemes is properly understood to be one of logical incompatibility. The second question is whether or not rival incommensurable schemes are always mutually exclusive. To address these questions requires a closer look both at (a) the possible relationships among claims made within different conceptual schemes or theoretical frameworks and (b) the relationship between theoretical frameworks and what they conceptualize in their particular terms.

To begin with the second item first: I find it useful to think of the relation of a theory to some domain of human experience on the analogy of the relation of a map to the territory it represents. A map may be accurate without including every detail of the corresponding territory. Rather, according to different purposes—for example, crossing a continent by canoe versus by car or by aircraft—different maps of the same area will select different features of the social and natural environment to represent. Using such different kinds of maps will, quite appropriately, draw attention to some features of that environment and not others. Maps differ with respect not only to *what* is represented but also with respect to *how*. Different systems of representation—for example, different combinations of colours, text, and symbols—are used to depict aspects of the environment relevant to particular purposes. Even the same kinds of maps are constructed to very different scales. Similarly, when choosing which aspects of human experience to explain and in what detail, those constructing a theory make trade-offs between simplicity, accuracy, and generalizability according to the intentions of a given context (Weick 1979; cf. Aristotle *Nicomachean Ethics* 1107a28–31, henceforth *NE*). Thus, the same domain of human experience can support a variety of theories constructed according to the different interests and perspectives of distinct schemes of beliefs.

With regard to the second item: *how* conceptual schemes are related varies according to whether the truth claims of their associated theories are related compatibly, incompatibly, paradoxically, obliquely, genetically, antagonistically, or complementarily.[5] The first three of these kinds of relationship hold between claims that are formulated in terms either of the same scheme or of commensurable schemes. The last four hold between claims formulated in the terms of frameworks that exhibit partial incommensurability of meaning.

Claims are *compatible* when they can be integrated within a coherent theoretical framework. Some claims might be logically deduced from others, they might all be stipulated first principles, they might be conclusions of related sets of premises, or they might be empirically supported propositions. Conversely, claims are *incompatible* when they entail a logical contradiction. As Bernstein argues (1983, 82–83; 1991, 87; cf. *ITC*, 109–110), only those claims that share a "common *logical* framework" can be incompatible in the strict sense of the term. By definition, then, when the beliefs of two distinct conceptual schemes are related compatibly, those schemes could be integrated into one coherent framework; in part, perhaps, by identifying terms within each scheme having equivalent meanings.

Claims are related *paradoxically* when they are logically incompatible *and* practice requires the affirmation of both.[6] Some paradoxes are understood to indicate limitations in existing theories or beliefs that could eventually be eliminated either through further enquiry (*MD*,

377–378, 380–381) or through a shift to a more adequate perspective.[7] Other paradoxes might be understood to indicate the inherent limitations of bivalent logical frameworks: human experience may not necessarily be bound by the rule of the excluded middle.[8] That is to say, in at least some contexts it might be necessary to replace or expand "either/or" with "both/and" thinking. Christian theology would seem to include paradoxical claims of this second kind; for example, the doctrines that God is both one and three, and that Jesus is both fully human and fully divine. By definition, because paradoxically related claims are logically incompatible, they are advanced either within one conceptual scheme or within two commensurable frameworks.

Claims are related *obliquely* when they are neither logically compatible nor logically contradictory, and yet concern the same domain of experience. Claims expressed in the incommensurable terms of schemes *formulated to serve different interests* are related in this way.[9] For example, it is easy to imagine different people describing the same series of dramatic performances in very different terms, according to technical, historical, literary, ethical, or other concerns. This category of relationships among truth claims is included to allow for the possibility that the complete description and explanation of some domains of human experience will require a variety of perspectives which cannot be integrated into one logically coherent framework. Komesaroff (1986, 270) makes a similar suggestion: "a complete elucidation of one and the same object may require diverse points of view which defy a unique description." To judge that two claims or schemes are related obliquely leaves open the possibility that a theoretical framework will eventually be constructed within which they will be seen to be logically compatible or incompatible. In the short term, however, when the beliefs of two conceptual schemes are related obliquely, even if they prove difficult to integrate theoretically they could coexist as alternative perspectives on a given domain of experience appropriate to different interests.

Claims are related *genetically* when one *sublates* the other in the sense of "at once negation, preservation, and overcoming or synthesis" (Bernstein 1983, 84).

> What sublates goes beyond what is sublated, introduces something new and distinct, puts everything on a new basis, yet so far from interfering with the sublated or destroying it, on the contrary needs

it, includes it, preserves all its proper features and properties, and
carries them forward to a fuller realization within a richer context.
(Lonergan 1973, 241)

This is the relationship of claims made within later stages to those made
within earlier stages of some developmental process. Later stages in a
developmental process, like later stages in a tradition, exhibit some
continuity with earlier stages while remedying their defects. For example, the different forms of justice-reasoning described in Kohlberg's
cognitive-developmental theory of moral judgment are related genetically because later perspectives lead to the reformulation of moral concepts in a way that resolves moral dilemmas that were intractable at
earlier stages. This means that later stages of development are understood to be addressing what is in some sense the same issue, problem,
or interest as earlier stages, although how that issue, problem, or interest is conceptualized will necessarily have changed. It is because of
the conceptual innovation associated with shifting to a more adequate
perspective that there can be some degree of incommensurability between earlier and later stages of a developmental process or a tradition
of enquiry. Because the later stages are by definition more adequate
than earlier stages, when the beliefs of two conceptual schemes are related genetically, the developmentally advanced scheme could simply
replace the other perspective.

Claims are related *antagonistically* when they (a) are expressed in incommensurable terms, (b) concern the same domain of human experience, (c) are formulated to serve the same or very similar interests,
and (d) represent pragmatically irreconcilable perspectives. In Mac-
Intyre's account, this is the relationship which necessarily holds between the claims of two rival traditions of enquiry.

Genuinely to adopt the standpoint of a tradition thereby commits
one to its view of what is true and false and, in so committing one,
prohibits one from adopting any rival standpoint. . . . The multiplicity of traditions does not afford a multiplicity of perspectives
among which we can move, but a multiplicity of antagonistic commitments, between which only conflict, rational or nonrational, is
possible. (*WJ*, 367–368, cf. 394–395)

For MacIntyre, it is not that those committed to one tradition's standpoint cannot adopt *any* claims from a rival perspective, but that they must reject the rival perspective's scheme of beliefs considered as a whole.

Contrary to MacIntyre, I do not believe that it is either necessary or helpful to rule out the possibility that adherents of rival schemes of beliefs could adopt the opposing perspective—even when they recommend mutually exclusive courses of action in some particular situations. The complexity of such domains of human endeavour as science, literary criticism, politics, or education can require successful practitioners to draw from a repertoire of incommensurable theoretical perspectives.[10] That is to say, it might not be possible either to derive or to justify all elements of successful practice with reference to one logically coherent theoretical framework. For example, it is at least conceivable that no one theory of justice could adequately capture all of the considered moral intuitions about what actions are just in particular circumstances.[11] In such cases, the claims or judgments corresponding to the particular actions are related *complementarily*, because they are expressed in incommensurable terms and yet each represents a useful perspective on the *same* domain of experience with the *same* or very similar interests. Again, in such contexts, the need to employ incommensurable frameworks could be interpreted as temporary; as eliminable through the development of a new conceptual scheme that integrates the insights of two previously incommensurable points of view. Or, the need for incommensurable frameworks might be interpreted as permanent, given the limitations of language. In any case, when the beliefs of two conceptual schemes are related complementarily, the schemes could coexist as part of a repertoire of possible perspectives on a given domain of experience, if only in the short term.

It is quite possible, of course, that different truth claims associated with two broad schemes of beliefs will be related in a variety of ways. The outcome of the encounter between two such comprehensive schemes could be some complex combination of integration, co-existence, mutual rejection and/or mutual transformation. Again, Kohlberg's cognitive-developmental framework for studying moral development comes to mind as an example; in this case, specifically for its partial rejection, partial adoption, and partial reinterpretation of the *ethics of care* psychological framework propounded by Gilligan (Kohlberg 1984,

338–370). MacIntyre himself provides an excellent example of the complex relationships that can exist between the claims of two rival and incommensurable traditions in his examination of how Aquinas integrated elements from the Aristotelian and Augustinian traditions of enquiry into a new synthesis (*WJ*, 164–208, esp. 188; *TRV*, 105–148).

To allow that members of two incommensurable communities of enquiry can in some cases adopt each other's beliefs and perspectives, in whole or in part—*even when* they cannot be integrated into a logically coherent synthesis and can have mutually exclusive implications for practice—might seem to be a minor point. However, my concern here is to avoid situations where adherents of rival traditions divide into hostile camps, each believing they have nothing to learn from the other. Such strident polarization is too often evident in contemporary moral and political debates. MacIntyre is a strong advocate of learning from people who have views different from one's own: "In the search for our good, everyone is a potential teacher and has therefore to be treated as one from whom I still may have to learn" (*RVG*, 10; cf. *WJ*, 388). Even so, I worry that tendencies towards polarization are reinforced by his suggestion that one conceptual scheme could eventually represent the "single true view" of some particular domain of human experience (*TRV*, 66). Hence, I think it important to acknowledge explicitly that "rival" incommensurable schemes can be related in a variety of ways— obliquely, genetically, and even complementarily—and not just antagonistically.

Consider the implications for the practice of dialectic. As characterized by MacIntyre, dialectical argument presupposes that holding a belief to be true entails holding logically incompatible beliefs to be false. Because holding two logically incompatible beliefs is seen as a weakness, one important consideration in comparing competing conceptual schemes is their *internal* logical coherence. MacIntyre does not consider when—if ever—exceptions to the law of non-contradiction could be made to allow for paradoxical beliefs within a given framework or scheme. He also seems to reject the possibility that the perspective of one conceptual scheme could usefully be supplemented by the perspective of an incommensurable framework, for he states, "to claim that such an overall scheme of concepts and beliefs is true is to claim that no fundamental reality could ever be disclosed about which it is impossible to speak truly within that scheme" (*TRV*, 122, cf. 66–67;

WJ, 358; *FP*, 31–32, 34; *PRC*, 295). Similarly, he suggests that drawing upon the resources of incommensurable traditions inevitably results in a "fundamental incoherence" that is counterproductive (*WJ*, 397). Accordingly, for MacIntyre, the only satisfactory outcome of dialectic involves the elimination of incommensurability between schemes or frameworks, either through the emergence of one as more overall defensible than the other or through the construction of a new scheme that combines the conceptual resources of both in a logically compatible way.

Against MacIntyre, I have proposed that practitioners can be justified in adopting—at least temporarily—other perspectives that round out their own. For one example, Thurman (1991, 60–63) shows how Tibetan culture draws upon three incompatible theoretical frameworks because each contributes to successful practice in a given context. For another, some feminists adopt postmodernist theories of multiple identities that deny the existence of a singular self in order to resist essentialism, while at the same time retain liberal discourses on equal rights based on respect for "persons" to ground their objections to women's oppression. These examples suggest that, in the dialectical evaluation of two incommensurable schemes of beliefs, expectations of logical coherence may need to be tempered by considerations of practical utility.

It is important to note that accepting the necessity in certain contexts of adopting two or more incommensurable conceptual frameworks is not the same thing as accepting logical contradictions *within* a theory. Furthermore, to grant that members of a community of enquiry could be justified in adopting incommensurable or even logically incompatible beliefs does not exempt them from the expectation of having an overall coherent point of view. This expectation could be accommodated if that tradition included an understanding of why, and under what conditions, logically incompatible but practically complementary truths could be allowed, and even anticipated.

Dialectical Justification: Is Resolving Epistemological Crises Enough?

A third set of questions concerns MacIntyre's description of the role of epistemological crises in the development and justification of traditions. To begin with, contrary to what MacIntyre sometimes suggests (*WJ*, 366), it is not clear that its ability to resolve an epistemological crisis is in itself sufficient to justify the selection of one reformulation of a tradition's conceptual scheme over others. For this criterion offers little guidance in situations where there exist two or more reformulations which resolve a crisis in mutually exclusive ways. MacIntyre himself has observed that epistemological crises arise because a tradition's scheme of beliefs has encountered one or more *different kinds* of difficulties: "It may be an incoherence within the established beliefs or an impotence in the face of new questions which have arisen or an encounter with some alternative mode of understanding" (*TC*, 9; cf. *WJ*, 354–355; *TRV*, 116). If a scheme of beliefs can suffer from different kinds of limitations or failures, then there are different criteria by which the relative superiority of possible alternatives will be assessed, and *these may conflict*. For example, of two rival positions formulated to resolve a crisis, one may be more internally consistent, the other more productive in generating solutions to recognized problems. How is the choice of one new scheme over its alternatives rationally defensible in such situations? This problem could arise not only when the competing schemes are two possible reformulations of one tradition's beliefs, but also when they represent the frameworks of rival traditions.

Again, a helpful perspective on this problem is implicit in MacIntyre's own work. MacIntyre claims that progress or lack of progress in enquiry is evaluated with respect to one or another tradition's problematic, that "more or less well-defined . . . set of issues, difficulties, and problems which have emerged from its previous achievements in enquiry" (*WJ*, 167; cf. 346). I think it consistent with this view to say that rival schemes of belief—whether emerging within or encountered outside a community in crisis—are properly evaluated with respect to one or another tradition's understanding of its fundamental intentions. For it is at least partly on the basis of its intentions that a tradition deems certain issues and problems to be most significant. Indeed, a problem is only a problem to individuals or groups in relation to their interests, aims, and objectives. This interpretation is consistent with MacIntyre's comments that the adequacy of representations is "always relative to some specific purpose of mind" (*WJ*, 357), and that the relevance of particular problems derives in part from their place within a larger system of thought and practice (*TRV*, 149).

On this interpretation of MacIntyre's position, showing how it contains the resources to resolve epistemological crises is only one—albeit important—part of justifying a tradition's scheme of beliefs. A conceptual scheme can also receive support from every other success it enjoys in furthering the intentions for which it was originally developed. Similarly, a new formulation of a tradition's fundamental agreements might have to be justified not simply as a solution to a particular epistemological crisis, but as overall more adequate to that tradition's intentions than alternative solutions. A community of enquiry's intentions can inform the evaluation of the relative strengths and limitations of two possible reformulations of its conceptual scheme—even if each resolves an epistemological crisis in a different way—because whether coherence or fruitfulness or some other criteria should take precedence will depend in part on the form of enquiry in question. Of course, even so, it might be the case that there are no "knockdown" arguments for the superiority of one proposed reformulation of a scheme of beliefs over an alternative: it might be necessary to explore both avenues of enquiry further.

On What Grounds Can Traditions Be Expected to Converge?

To claim that justification and assessment should be relative to one or another tradition's understanding of its fundamental intentions raises further questions, including that raised at the end of the previous chapter. It was there observed both (a) that a tradition's standards of rational adequacy derive from its background framework of beliefs, which determines the problems that take priority (*WJ*, 167), and (b) that rival traditions are characterized by mutually exclusive sets of fundamental agreements, which generally result in evaluative incommensurability. How, then, is it possible that one tradition's theoretical framework could prove more adequate to a rival's problems than its own?

The answer to this question is related to how a tradition is able to maintain continuity through radical reformulations of its conceptual framework. To explain: I have mentioned that, in MacIntyre's account, later stages of a tradition of enquiry include a "conceptually richer and more detailed" characterization of its final goal, a better conception "of what it would be to have completed the enquiry." Following Aristotle, MacIntyre refers to the final goal or *telos* of an enquiry as its *archē*. The *archē* of a particular form of enquiry is the set of first principles from which it would be possible to deduce "every relevant truth concerning the subject matter of the enquiry" (*WJ*, 80–81; cf. 100; *FP*, 27–30). He suggests that it would only be possible to conceive accurately an enquiry's *telos* when that enquiry is "substantially complete"; that is, when a completely satisfactory set of first principles has been formulated. And only from the perspective afforded by achieving this final goal would it be possible to describe correctly what was lacking in earlier conceptions of a particular form of enquiry and its *archē:*

> The *archē* will . . . afford an understanding of why each of the successive stages by which it was approached was distinct from it as well as a characterization of the specific type of error that would have been involved in mistaking each of these stages of the completion of the enquiry. For each of the stages will have been marked both by less and less partial insight and yet also by a continuing one-sidedness. Only from the standpoint of the completion of the enquiry, of a final and fully adequate conception of the *archē*, is such one-sidedness left behind. (*WJ*, 80; cf. 128)

Kohlberg's theory again serves as a case in point. For Kohlberg, Boyd, and Levine (1990) have argued that it is necessary to define a sixth and final stage of moral development in order to provide a perspective from which (a) earlier forms of justice-reasoning can be recognized as progressively more adequate stages in the *same* developmental sequence, and (b) limitations in earlier conceptions of justice can be identified.

MacIntyre leaves open whether or not it would be possible to achieve a complete and final perspective upon the subject matter of a particular form of enquiry. His own account of how first principles are approached through dialectic and of how dialectic is always incomplete suggests a negative answer to this question (*WJ*, 100–101, 172, 361; *FP*, 39–40, 45–46; *FG*, 261). Even so, MacIntyre claims that a community of enquiry's ongoing pursuit of its *archē* can function to challenge the one-sidedness of any particular perspective (*WJ*, 81; *FP*, 40).

What MacIntyre leaves implicit in this account is that *recognizing* later formulations of a community of enquiry's final goal as more complete or otherwise adequate than earlier ones *presupposes* a dynamic intentionality that persists throughout changes in a tradition's conceptual scheme. It is this underlying interest that provides for continuity between the distinct stages of a developmental process. Kohlberg's theory of moral development requires just such a dynamic intentionality to provide continuity through its stages, because it proposes that we can recognize reasoning at the next higher stage as providing a solution to our current dilemmas about what is morally right, even when the higher stages involve substantially different conceptions of justice.[12] It was just such a dynamic intentionality that was invoked to explain how *truth, justice*, and *rationality* can refer to transcendent as well as immanent criteria of evaluation. On this view, the adequacy of successive reformulations of a scheme of beliefs is assessed relative to the fundamental intentions of a particular tradition of enquiry, *even though those intentions are only imperfectly understood at each stage of their conceptualization.*[13]

This distinction between a tradition of enquiry's fundamental intentions and its evolving conceptions of those intentions provides for answers to a number of questions about justification. First, there are two distinct ways in which one conceptual scheme can demonstrate its advantages relative to another. One way is for the first conceptual scheme to provide solutions to problems considered important within the second scheme, but on which that second scheme had made no significant progress. The other way is for the first conceptual scheme to show that those problems can be simply avoided, rather than solved, because they arise from a fundamental misconception within the second scheme of its fundamental intentions. In other words, *the first conceptual scheme provides a way of understanding the goal of a particular form of enquiry which those using the second scheme can recognize as a more accurate and productive way of conceiving their own fundamental intentions.* In this way, those working within one community of enquiry can be justified in adopting the conceptual scheme of another, even if that new scheme provides no solutions to problems that they previously considered to be of central significance (cf. *WJ*, 328–329, 348; *FG*, 256).

Second, MacIntyre maintains that, because there are no tradition-independent viewpoints, a tradition's progress can only be *evaluated* from the point of view of one or another tradition. It is important that this not be understood as saying that a tradition only *makes progress* from the point of view of one or another tradition, for this would be equivalent to collapsing truth into warranted assertability. This point is consistent with MacIntyre's (*PRC*, 297) claim that rival traditions compete precisely because they intend the *truth* about the subject matter of their enquiry, where truth is understood to be distinct from justified belief.

It was argued in chapter one that, although one or another conceptual scheme is required for there to be claims that are candidates for being true or false, adopting a scheme's language does not in itself guarantee that particular claims made in its terms are true, because those claims concern what exists prior to and independently of the practices of enquiry. Similarly, evaluating a tradition's conceptual scheme presupposes one or another interest or set of related interests, but undertaking enquiry in accordance with a tradition's interests does not guarantee that its scheme of beliefs will prove adequate to either conceptualizing or satisfying its fundamental intentions. This is because the satisfaction of a tradition's intentions can be constrained by what exists prior to and independently of its practices, even granted that what so exists can only be described in the terms of one or another particular conceptual scheme.

Third, to grant that the same fundamental intention can be conceptualized in significantly different ways, some of which are more adequate than others to the accomplishment of that intention, explains how two traditions can be rivals even though their respective schemes of belief are sufficiently different to engender evaluative incommensurability. They are rivals by virtue of a common intentionality that each defines in the terms of its particular conceptual scheme. *It is their common intentionality which provides for the possibility that dialectical debate will result in the convergence of rival points of view.*

How Can Agreements Other than Explicit Beliefs Be Justified?

A fourth set of questions concerns whether or not dialectical debate is in itself sufficient to justify a particular tradition's point of view, or to appreciate and assess incommensurable perspectives. These questions arise from MacIntyre's use of *conceptual scheme* and related terms (for example, conceptual framework, conceptual structures, conceptual resources, scheme, scheme of beliefs, and framework of beliefs). I have used *conceptual scheme* and *theoretical framework* to refer to sets of assumptions that are or could be objectified in propositional form. These background beliefs help establish which problems and issues are most important to address, and so help define the criteria against which competing theories are evaluated (cf. *WJ*, 134, 252; *RPP*, 199–200). As I define it, then, a conceptual scheme is part of, not coextensive with, the attitudes, interests, norms, priorities, and practices that together constitute a community of enquiry's paradigm and corresponding point of view.

In contrast, although he observes that traditions of enquiry are always embodied in social institutions and practices and always involve normative attitudes and commitments (*WJ*, 372–373), MacIntyre generally speaks as if a tradition's point of view is shaped entirely by, or is equivalent to, a scheme of beliefs that is or could be explicitly formulated in propositional form.[14] If this were true, then it is more plausible to grant that the rational superiority of one point of view over alternative perspectives could be demonstrated through MacIntyre's dialectical debate, in which explicitly formulated theses are challenged and defended (*WJ*, 134, 144, 172, 360, 364–365; cf. *TRV*, 125). Conversely, *if a tradition's point of view involves more than its explicit beliefs, and cannot be wholly objectified in propositional form, then its justification and assessment could well require more than dialectical argument alone.*

Three features of tradition-informed enquiry indicate that an elaboration of MacIntyre's account of dialectical argument is required if the rationality of traditions is to be accurately characterized. First, a tradition's tacit assumptions shape the form, priorities, and outcome of enquiry as much as its explicit assumptions and commitments.[15] Consequently, those agreements must also be capable of justification or the conclusions of enquiry are open to charges of being arbitrary or irrational. How, then, if at all, can a community of enquiry's implicit agreements—particularly those carried in images, models, exemplars, narratives, and practices—be justified? How can the relative superiority of one community's tacit knowledge over another be demonstrated?

Second, it is by no means self-evident that a community of enquiry's attitudes, interests, norms, and priorities can be equated with, reduced to, or even wholly explained in terms of that community's explicit beliefs. For while a community of enquiry's priorities could be explained as following from their beliefs about the way things are and the way they should be, those beliefs could also be explained as serving that community's priorities. Similarly, it cannot simply be assumed that the scheme of beliefs directing a particular form of enquiry will determine the corresponding community's attitudes or interests. Whether rightly or wrongly, a community of enquiry's attitudes and interests could well affect what its members are predisposed to consider as worthy of serious investigation, and so affect what they believe.[16] How, then, if attitudes, interests, norms, and priorities also shape a community's perspective, can they be justified and/or critically assessed in a non-circular and non-foundational way?

Third, all particular forms of enquiry—whether analytic, hermeneutical, or empirical—originate and develop within larger contexts of belief and practice. For example, I have briefly indicated how Kohlberg's theoretical framework is embedded within broader sets of shared assumptions and commitments that are themselves located within a particular cultural history. Histories of science and technology show in more detail how enquiry has been and continues to be shaped by the assumptions embedded in ways of life, such as the root metaphors that are so basic and pervasive as to be generally below the threshold of conscious awareness. MacIntyre (*WJ*, 389–390; cf. *PRC*, 292) himself argues that particular positions can only be fully appreciated, challenged, and defended in the context both of their larger background schemes and of the history through which those schemes have evolved. How, then, is the conceptual scheme of a particular form of enquiry related to the larger sets of assumptions and commitments in which it is embedded? What role do those larger contexts play in non-foundational justification and in the assessment of rival points of view?

To address these and other questions about justification requires a better understanding of the interrelationships among a community of enquiry's explicit beliefs, tacit assumptions, attitudes, interests, norms, priorities, and practices. I will therefore proceed to my own characterization of non-foundational justification by way of a preliminary look at the interrelationships between world views and ways of life.

WORLD VIEWS AND WAYS OF LIFE

As I use the term, a *world view* is a set of beliefs about the fundamental nature of things. In that sense, a world view is roughly equivalent to what others have called a *Weltanschauung* (Kearney 1984, 28), a *theory of existence* (Sprigge 1985, 9), or a *vision of reality* (Greene 1981). World views range in scope and sophistication from simple sets of unarticulated assumptions to comprehensive ontological theories. Implicitly or explicitly, world views typically include beliefs about the origin, history, and structure of the cosmos; the kinds of objects that exist in the world; the kinds of relationships that hold among those objects; and the nature of humans and their place in the world order. Together with associated images, these ontological beliefs generally function as part of an unquestioned background to thought and action, only recognized as assumptions when something renders them problematic. World views may thus be considered a kind of broad conceptual scheme or theoretical framework, although I have reserved these latter terms for less comprehensive sets of beliefs directing some particular form of enquiry.

The relationships between the world views of individuals and that of their culture(s), between successive world views held by individuals or by cultures, between a world view and individual or collective behaviour, and even between distinct beliefs within a world view, are all complex.[17] Speaking generally, however, a social group's fundamental ontological assumptions shape and are shaped by such things as their attitudes towards the world, their broad interests, their corresponding norms and priorities for living, and the practices of their concrete socio-historical context. In other words, images of and beliefs about the world tend to form a coherent and mutually supporting whole with a corresponding way of life, where *way of life* refers to a broad constellation of attitudes, interests, norms, priorities, and practices within a specific socio-historical context.[18] Levin (1986, 280), for example, characterizes a way of life as "a way of being in the world, a way of relating to other people and groups and to the natural environment, and a sense of what is most important in life as well as a sense of one's project(s) in life." A way of life thus refers both to a social group's shared meanings and values and to how those meanings and values are given concrete expression in day to day life. As I use the term, then, *a way of life* is roughly equivalent to what MacIntyre refers to as *a form of social life*.

The relationship between a world view and a way of life is analogous to the relationship between a conceptual scheme and the attitudes, interests, norms, priorities, and practices of the corresponding paradigm of enquiry. That relationship is *not* one of logical or causal necessity. The "fit" between world views and ways of life, and that between the different aspects of a way of life, is not that "tight": Different sets of beliefs about the world can be compatible with the same way of life, and the same set of beliefs can be compatible with different ways of life. This "looseness" of fit notwithstanding, an individual's or culture's most basic attitudes, interests, norms, priorities, and practices must make sense in the context of their fundamental beliefs about the world. For example, MacIntyre remarks that "metaphysical nominalism sets constraints upon how the moral life can be achieved. And, conversely, certain kinds of conceptions of the moral life exclude such nominalism" (*TRV*, 138). Generally, then, commitment to a particular world view encourages us to adopt ways of life that fit well with our basic ontological assumptions, while commitment to a particular way of life supports our acceptance of some world views and not others.

The Mechanistic World View

The interrelationships between world views and ways of life can be illustrated with reference to mechanistic ontological assumptions.[19] To begin with, the mechanistic world view provides a good example of how explicit ontological beliefs are associated with certain images or root metaphors. In this case, the fundamental image or metaphor is that of a machine: like a machine, the world is seen to consist of different parts defined by their functional relationships—how they fit or work together. Historically, mechanistic images have been related to conceptual frameworks that conceive "reality" as the interaction of discrete particles in absolute time and space according to universal and invariant laws. Indeed, the mechanistic world view came to dominate European intellectual life in part because of the immense success of Newton's classical physics.

The mechanistic view of the world is deterministic, materialistic, reductionistic, and atomistic. It is deterministic in that

> The original configuration of the particles in the universe was accidental and now is accidental, in the sense that it could have been otherwise. But, and this is the important point, once the configuration is set, given the laws that govern particle interaction, events inexorably follow. (Kilbourn 1980, 38; see also Pepper 1942, 196–197, 207–208)

An image which captures this view of determinism is the billiard table where, even though the location of the balls may be random, once the properties of the table and the direction and momentum of the cue ball are known, all subsequent interactions can be predicted with certainty. The mechanistic world view is materialistic and reductionistic in the sense that everything—including human thought and action—can be explained in terms of the predetermined interaction of physical particles.[20] It is atomistic in the sense that everything can be broken down into simple, discrete components. An associated image here is the clock, whose workings are explained by its constituent parts and their interrelationships.[21]

Three further characteristics of the world conceived in mechanistic terms are particularly worthy of note. One: all events (except perhaps the first one), including human behaviours, can be explained in terms of an unbroken chain of causes and their necessary effects. Hence, when purposes, choices, or reasons are employed in explanations of human behaviours, they are interpreted in terms of necessary cause and effect relationships (cf. AV, 82–84). Two: because the world is reducible to quantitative relationships among material particles, the qualities humans apprehend are understood to have no "objective" significance, but belong to the realm of merely "subjective" experience.[22] Three: because the world order is accidental and contingent, it is seen to be without inherent meaning or purpose (Pepper 1942, 197). The mechanistic universe is thus wholly indifferent, if not actually hostile, to human interests and desires.[23]

What ways of life make sense given this view of the world? Mechanistic assumptions are compatible with an instrumental attitude towards the world because, once it is believed that it has no inherent meaning or purpose, it makes sense to assume that the world, like a machine, exists to be used. Similarly, once it is believed that the world is indifferent or hostile to human intentions, it makes sense to try and bring it under control. In a mechanistic world, control is achieved through "discovering" the cause-effect relationships that govern interaction of its parts. Therefore, given the mechanistic assumption that all interaction is law-governed, it makes sense to attempt to maximize control by developing theoretical knowledge of all domains of human experience. Indeed, those who inhabit a mechanistic world can dream of formulating a theoretical framework which explains everything about everything in terms of necessary cause and effect relationships. In the same vein, given mechanistic assumptions, it makes sense to assign priority to the application of theoretical knowledge to social, political, and economic ends.[24]

World Views, Research Paradigms, and Communities of Enquiry

What is the relationship between a world view and a particular paradigm of enquiry? As the discussion above already suggests, the ontological assumptions shared by members of a community of enquiry influence the conceptual schemes they employ, the images and analogies they use, the attitudes they hold, the interests they pursue, the methodological norms they observe, and the priorities they assign in particular forms of enquiry. In this way, the assumptions and commitments shared within a community of enquiry can be understood, at least to some degree, as the *application* of a world view to a particular domain of human experience.[25] It is only reasonable that how an individual or group would attempt to understand their environment (including themselves) would be shaped by their beliefs both about the kinds of things that exist in the world and the kinds of relationships that hold among them.

The mechanistic world view again provides a useful illustration, here in its association with the positivistic paradigm of scientific research (Greene 1981, 133–135). The *positivistic paradigm* refers to a conception and practice of science in which[26]

1. The fundamental *objective* is to explain observable phenomena by formulating law-like generalizations that describe systematic relationships among variables which are unified in comprehensive, logically structured theoretical frameworks.
2. The *method* is to verify (or falsify) such generalizations by demonstrating—preferably under strictly controlled conditions—their ability (or inability) to afford prediction and control of intersubjectively observable events.
3. The *meanings* of the terms used to represent the variables and relationships of conceptual frameworks must be precisely and unequivocally—preferably quantitatively—expressed, and defined with reference to intersubjectively observable events.[27]
4. *Explanation* of the relationships between variables is in terms of cause and effect.
5. *Objectivity*, or truth, is sought through strict observance of a method which eliminates "subjectivity."[28]

While there is no relation of logical or causal necessity between mechanistic assumptions and positivistic scientific enquiry, they do form a coherent and mutually supportive whole.[29] For given the objective of developing theoretical knowledge to fulfil human intentions, it makes sense to verify (or falsify) scientific theories through their ability (or inability) to afford prediction and control of events. Once this method of verification is adopted, it makes sense that the terms denoting variables and relationships should be precisely formulated, and should refer to intersubjectively observable events, in order to be testable. The preference for quantitative or mathematical expression of relationships follows from this quest for precision, and from the view that quality has no "objective" existence. Furthermore, quantitative expression of relationships among variables promotes the objectives of prediction and control, because the kind of knowledge that can be most widely applied is that which is most generalizable or context-free, and mathematics represents the ultimate in abstraction from particular contexts or concrete relationships.

The attempt to guarantee objectivity by eliminating subjectivity is consistent with the view that generalizations are verified (or falsified) with reference to intersubjectively observable events. For when knowledge is a matter of accurately seeing what is there and not seeing what is not there, objectivity becomes a matter of putting aside all prior beliefs, expectations, and preferences in order to observe things as they really are (Lonergan 1958, 251–253, 412–416). Similarly, if the world has no inherent meaning or purpose, it makes sense that science should be objective (in the sense of being value-free) in order to avoid imposing personal preferences on data collection and analysis (Carr and Kemmis 1986, 62; Fay 1975, 20). In the positivistic view, then, science is the paradigmatic source of knowledge precisely because only the scientific method can guarantee objectivity by eliminating subjectivity:

> Because only it employs concepts which are rooted in intersubjectively evident observations, because it employs techniques of experimentation which are reproducible, because it utilizes reasoning processes which are rigorous and uniformly applicable, and because it accepts explanations only when they predict outcomes which are publicly verifiable. (Fay 1975, 21)

Once this view of science is accepted as paradigmatic, all other sources of knowledge are evaluated on the basis of how closely they approximate the positivistic ideal (*MP*, 2–3; Roszak 1972, 33–34). For given mechanistic assumptions, it makes sense to require that all claims to knowledge be accompanied by guarantees of objectivity in the form of demonstrated strict adherence to "method," and by verification in the form of the ability to predict and control. Indeed, the mechanistic world view has often been associated with the belief that science, positivistically conceived, is the *only* valid form of knowledge (Bernstein 1983, 46–47; Greene 1981, 143–144; *MP*, 2–3), and with the tendency to create a hierarchical distinction between "hard" and "soft" sciences according to how closely they resemble the positivistic ideal (Shweder 1989, 121). In this way, the attitudes, interests, norms, priorities, and practices of the positivistic paradigm of scientific enquiry are interrelated in an internally coherent and mutually supportive way with mechanistic ontological assumptions.

What are the implications of this discussion for the understanding of non-foundational justification?

THE SEARCH FOR WIDE REFLECTIVE EQUILIBRIUM

On my view, the fundamental agreements that constitute a community of enquiry's paradigm or point of view develop through an on going search for *wide reflective equilibrium*. As I define it, the search for wide reflective equilibrium proceeds through dialectical interactions within and among all levels and forms of sense-making activity. Its goal is to achieve the most overall satisfactory set of agreements in a given context of enquiry and practice, where *satisfactory* means *coherent, mutually supporting, successful,* and *defensible.* That is to say, wide reflective equilibrium is achieved among a community of enquiry's explicit beliefs, implicit assumptions, attitudes, interests, norms, priorities, and practices when they meet the following four conditions.

1. They are internally consistent and mutually supporting.
2. They are consistent with and contribute to the world view and way of life of the larger socio-historical context in which they are embedded.

3. They assist in the accomplishment of the aims and objectives of the members of that community of enquiry.
4. They are defensible in dialectical encounters with competing paradigms of enquiry.

Conversely, equilibrium can be disturbed within a community of enquiry on *any* of the following four occasions.

1. There is a perception of internal incoherence among the assumptions and commitments directing their particular form of enquiry.
2. There is a perception of incoherence between those shared agreements and the other beliefs, assumptions, attitudes, interests, norms, priorities, or practices of their broader world view and way of life.
3. Their point of view proves inadequate to fulfilling intentions to which they assign a high priority.
4. There is a perception that the set of assumptions and commitments shared within a competing community of enquiry provides a better means of accomplishing their own fundamental intentions, and a better explanation of their own limitations and failures, than their own framework can provide.[30]

On this account of rational justification, a set of assumptions and commitments guiding enquiry is vindicated to the extent it achieves wide reflective equilibrium. The relative merits of competing perspectives are properly assessed by determining which approaches the state of wide reflective equilibrium more closely than its rivals. Thus the choice of one point of view over others is justified, not by appeal to any single measure of its rational superiority, but by appeal to its overall combination of internal and external coherence, success in furthering its fundamental interests, and ability to account for the limitations of other points of view. Catherine Elgin provides a similar account of non-foundational justification in her analysis of the development and evaluation of particular scientific conclusions and their corresponding conceptual schemes:

> Justification is holistic. Support for a conclusion comes, not from a single line of argument, but from a host of considerations of varying degrees of strength and relevance. What justifies the categories

we construct is the *cognitive* and *practical utility* of the truths they enable us to formulate, the *elegance* and *informativeness* of the accounts they engender, the *value* of the ends they promote. We engage in system-building when we find resources at hand inadequate. We have projects they do not serve, questions they do not answer, values they do not realize. Something new is required. But a measure of the adequacy of a novelty is its fit with what we think we already know. If the finding is at all surprising, the background of accepted beliefs is apt to require modification to make room for it, and the finding may require revision to be fitted into place. A process of delicate adjustments occurs, its goal being a system in wide reflective equilibrium. (Elgin 1989, 91; italics added)

The process of seeking wide reflective equilibrium is non-circular as well as non-foundational because, although it begins with the interests, assumptions, and commitments of a particular group of people in a particular context, any of the starting points are open to revision or rejection as the process unfolds.

Clarification by Contrast

Those attempting to furnish foundational forms of justification have generally fallen into one of two broad groups. For those Rationalists[31] who took geometry as their ideal, a conclusion was justified if it was correctly deduced from self-evident or otherwise indubitable first principles. For those *Empiricists* who looked to natural science for their model, a generalization was justified if it was formulated by careful induction from direct sense impressions. Both Rationalists and Empiricists were sceptical about sources of knowledge or forms of argument other than their own. However, they had a strong faith in the ability of their respective methods to guarantee certain truth, largely because they granted epistemic privilege to one or another form of cognitive activity.

In contrast, the search for wide reflective equilibrium privileges neither self-evident first principles nor immediate perceptions. As Rawls (1974/75, 8) observes, in this process "there are no judgments on any level of generality that are immune to revision." Similarly, justification and evaluation through reference to the achievement of wide reflective equilibrium involves not one but many forms of argument, and many different kinds of "good reasons." For the various agreements shared within a community of enquiry can be assessed with regard to a wide variety of criteria, including the following:

Logical compatibility: Have all of the logical implications of that community's explicit beliefs been worked through, and are they compatible?

Internal coherence: Is there at least a loose fit among that community's implicit and explicit beliefs, attitudes, interests, norms, and priorities?

External coherence: Are those agreements and commitments consistent with the broader sets of implicit and explicit beliefs, attitudes, interests, norms, and priorities in which they are embedded?

Congruity with "accepted wisdom": Are those agreements and commitments consistent with what has been accepted as true because it is part of a time-tested tradition?

Economy: Do they presuppose or postulate a minimum of unsupported premises?

Performative consistency: Are the espoused commitments of that community of enquiry consistent with its actual practices?

Feasibility: Can those commitments be put into practice without taxing limited resources in an unsupportable way?

Comprehensiveness: Does the community's theoretical or conceptual framework account for a wider range of human experience than its competitors?

Empirical support: Are the empirical claims of that community of enquiry's theories compatible with evidence which those theories were not specifically developed to explain?

Generic merits: Do those theories represent a balance of simplicity, generalizability, and accuracy that is appropriate to the scope of that community's particular form or forms of enquiry?

Intuitive appeal: Do the assumptions and commitments, singly and/or together, "feel right" and "ring true"?

Aesthetic values: Are they (for example) elegant, beautiful, bold, symmetrical?

Fruitfulness or fertility: Do they spark innovative ideas, solutions, and/or ways of thinking?

Success: When put into practice, do the assumptions and commitments further the interests or purposes for which they were developed?

Ability to be self-referential: Do they provide or are they consistent with a context in which their development and success is intelligible?

Ability to accommodate new perspectives: Does that community's conceptual scheme prove elastic enough, and its members creative enough, to translate into their own language the beliefs of radically different points of view?

Ability to account for and integrate rival claims: Does that community's set of agreements explain the plausibility of competing theories or perspectives in a way that is consistent with those theories or perspectives being mistaken and that accounts for those errors arising in the first place? Do they incorporate everything that is sound within their rivals?

Freedom from distortion or bias: Is it possible to know the motivations behind having those assumptions and commitments and still hold to them? Or, would they be rejected if the reasons or motivations for holding them were known?

Unlike foundationalist forms of justification, the process of seeking wide reflective equilibrium makes no claims to attain certainty. This is in part because the search for wide reflective equilibrium—like the practice of dialectical argument in MacIntyre's account of the rationality of traditions—is an ongoing process, its conclusions open to revision in the light of new developments or discoveries. Furthermore, evaluating the degree to which a community of enquiry's agreements achieve wide reflective equilibrium involves reference to an assortment of distinct and irreducible criteria, and *these may conflict* (Nielsen 1987, 149). For example, as I have already suggested, of two possible responses to an epistemological crisis, one reformulation of a tradition's beliefs may be more internally coherent and the other more productive in practical terms. Consequently, assessments of the relative strengths and limitations of a community of enquiry's overall point of view will vary according to how much weight is assigned to the various distinct criteria. And the relative importance of those criteria in particular contexts of enquiry is itself open to debate. Indeed, traditions of enquiry that exhibit evaluative incommensurability will assign greater weight to different criteria according to the kinds of problems they hold of central importance (Kuhn 1977, 335; Doppelt 1983, 129–130; *TRV*, 10–12). As MacIntyre points out, then, that meaningful arguments can occur between rival and incommensurable communities of enquiry does not guarantee that they will always lead to consensus, particularly in the short term.

Dialectic Revisited

My characterization of wide reflective equilibrium makes explicit a number of points that are implicit in MacIntyre's account of dialectical argument, but also expands upon that account in at least three useful ways. First, my characterization of wide reflective equilibrium provides for an answer to the question of how tacit commitments, attitudes, and interests could be vindicated. I think it reasonable to propose that, because of their interrelationships, *all* of the agreements shared within a community of enquiry—and not just its explicit conceptual scheme— are justified to the extent they achieve wide reflective equilibrium. Accordingly, the implicit as well as explicit beliefs shared within traditions of enquiry are justified to the extent they form part of a coherent, mutually supporting, defensible, and successful point of view. Consider, for example, the question of how it is possible to vindicate the choice of one paradigm's "ways of seeing" over others. My discussion of the mechanistic world view indicated how assumptions carried in images can form part of a coherent whole with more explicit beliefs. Leatherdale (1974, 13–14, 19) illustrates both how members of a community of scientific enquiry typically draw upon the images associated with their world view and how those images can precipitate scientific discoveries by suggesting analogies between domains of human experience previously considered unrelated. In this manner, a particular "way of seeing" is justified by what that perspective enables people to accomplish.[32] Similarly, even though they are not part of explicit schemes of beliefs, the "ways of seeing" associated with rival paradigms can be compared on the basis of the achievements with which they are associated and the new possibilities they reveal (Brown 1983). The general point here is that a community of enquiry's implicit agreements are vindicated to the extent they contribute to successful *practice* even when they cannot be objectified and defended in propositional form.

One implication of this point is that appreciating the relative advantages of an incommensurable point of view requires the ability to adopt that new perspective, even if only temporarily. This is because the new perspective will afford an understanding of reasons and arguments that previously were unintelligible or unpersuasive.[33] Consequently, as MacIntyre has suggested, the justification for adopting a new perspective will only be apparent to those who are capable of appreciating both old and new points of view. Whether the attempt to see things from a new perspective will be worth the effort in particular cases can only be conclusively determined in retrospect, *after* the shift in perspective has been accomplished.

The second way in which my characterization of wide reflective equilibrium expands upon MacIntyre's account is by using the mechanistic world view to illustrate how particular paradigms of enquiry are related to the larger sets of shared agreements in which they are embedded. This provides for a distinction between the internal and external coherence of a scheme of beliefs, and explains why the assumptions and commitments of a community of enquiry cannot be fully understood in abstraction from its larger social, cultural, and historical context.[34]

The third and most important way in which my characterization of wide reflective equilibrium expands upon MacIntyre's account is by providing the resources to explain how the convergence of two rival traditions can occur, even when their incommensurable conceptual schemes engender conflicting standards of rational adequacy. This explanation involves four claims. The first concerns *how* a tradition of enquiry can be required to assess, revise, or even replace its current interests and priorities. I have proposed that, through the search for wide reflective equilibrium, a tradition of enquiry's beliefs, attitudes, interests, norms, priorities, and practices are all subject to critical review if perceived as incoherent, indefensible, or unsuccessful. It follows that, while evaluation and justification is always relative to some set of interests, *a tradition of enquiry's current understanding of its fundamental intentions is subject to being revised or replaced if it fails to maintain wide reflective equilibrium.* For epistemological crises may arise within a community of enquiry precisely because its members have a limited or inaccurate understanding of their actual interests.

In one such case, Laudan describes a crisis of faith in scientific progress due to a persistent failure of attempts to characterize scientific rationality. On Laudan's analysis, this crisis originated in the mistaken assumption that the primary aim of science is to discover truth, for this assumption cannot be reconciled with the actual practice of science. Against this assumption, Laudan (1977, 66, 82) argues that the fundamental aim of science has been to construct theories which provide adequate solutions to an increasing range of empirical problems. Accordingly, the theoretical frameworks of rival scientific research traditions can be evaluated with respect to their comparative problem-solving ability, as well as their capacity to generate creative responses to epistemological crises.[35] According to Laudan, once it is appreciated that rival scientific frameworks are assessed on their relative problem-solving abilities, the contradictions between theory and practice—and the crisis—are resolved and equilibrium restored. This illustrates how affirming that evaluation and justification is relative to intentions does not entail the conclusion that a tradition of enquiry's current understanding of its objectives and corresponding priorities is excepted from critical review.

My second claim is similar to the first: Because of the search for wide reflective equilibrium, *the identification of any common ground among rival communities of enquiry can provide a basis for reaching agreement on an assessment of their respective strengths and limitations.* Laudan again provides a corroborating view, this time in his rejection of Kuhn's belief that rival paradigms of scientific enquiry must be accepted or rejected on an all-or-nothing basis.[36] Laudan argues not so much that rational debate between the kind of mutually exclusive paradigms that Kuhn describes is possible, but that scientific research traditions are rarely so completely exclusive.[37] Laudan shows how the discovery of commonalities between the ontological assumptions, methodological commitments, *or* the objectives of rival research traditions can provide opportunities for productive rational debate across paradigms (Laudan 1984, 75, 84–86). For instance, where two scientific research communities share the same methodological commitments, the members of the first community may be convinced to adopt the ontological assumptions and/or the objectives of the second because the second community's scheme of beliefs is more consistent with the first community's actual practice than their own beliefs. It is in this way that one tradition's point of view may win acceptance over rival perspectives because it is understood to include a more accurate and productive understanding of a particular form of enquiry's ultimate goal. Laudan's (1984, 81–84) example of this kind of revision is twentieth-century scientific enquiry's rejection of the search for certain truth in favour of a fallibalistic conception of its goal.

My third claim concerns the conditions under which two communities of enquiry are properly understood as rivals. Various authors have remarked that, if they are to be considered rivals, paradigms of enquiry must share "*some* observational data, problems, and language" (Doppelt 1982, 125; see also Laudan 1990, 140; *WJ*, 351). Accordingly, I have proposed that competing traditions of enquiry are concerned with the same domain of human experience. I have also proposed that rival traditions share similar fundamental interests. Indeed, if two incommensurable traditions of enquiry addressed the same domain of human experience with different interests, they would be related obliquely, not antagonistically or complementarily.[38] Incommensurability of meaning results when rivals apply their respective conceptual frameworks to the same domain of human experience—frameworks which use different terms or give different meanings to the same terms. Similarly, evaluative incommensurability occurs when rivals give priority to different problems according to their respective conceptions of their common intentionality. My third claim is that, in at least some cases, *rival communities of enquiry use non-equivalent terms, and have incompatible priorities or values, because they interpret and pursue their similar fundamental interests within different world views.* For example, modern Western and Traditional eastern medicines are rival traditions of enquiry and practice because, while they are both concerned with health, they pursue different priorities according to how the sources and deficiencies of health are understood within each corresponding world view.[39] That adherents of rival communities of enquiry have incompatible world views helps explain *why* they have different conceptions of their particular form of enquiry and its fundamental intentions, *why* they have different priorities, and *why* they "see different things when they look from the same point in the same direction" (*EC*, 465; Bernstein 1983, 81–82).

My fourth claim follows from the first three. If two or more traditions of enquiry cannot agree on an evaluation of their respective strengths and limitations because they have different priorities, if those different priorities result from incompatible interpretations of simi-

lar fundamental interests, and if those incompatible interpretations reflect competing ontological assumptions, then *one way of resolving evaluative incommensurability—and of promoting the convergence of traditions—is
to evaluate the strengths and limitations of competing world views.*

How would this be possible? World views are also constrained by the
ideal of wide reflective equilibrium. As MacIntyre (*WJ,* 359) observes,
"The identification of incoherence within established belief will always
provide a reason for enquiring further." Kearney shows how world
views strive towards internal consistency or "logical-structural integration" and provides examples of how world views can be radically revised
or even abandoned when they have lost their adaptive value in physical and social environments.[40] Consequently, the relative strengths and
limitations of alternative world views can be critically assessed by asking such questions as: Which is most internally coherent? Which is most
consistent with and best contributes to the paradigms of successful
communities of enquiry? Which world view best accounts both for its
own limitations and failures and those of its alternatives? Which is most
consistent with and best contributes to a satisfactory way of life? For
although ontological assumptions shape the beliefs, attitudes, interests,
norms, priorities, and practices of particular communities of inquiry,
the success of innovative forms of enquiry can also require revisions
in the corresponding community's world view:

> In the short run, science itself is shaped by existing knowledge
> and ideas. General conceptions of nature, God, knowledge, man,
> society and history dictate what kind of science, if any, will be at-
> tempted, what methods will be employed, what topics will be in-
> vestigated, what kinds of results will be expected; social norms
> define the value and purpose of these inquiries. In the long run,
> however, if the scientist has insight and intellectual integrity, his
> findings may alter the general conceptions that shaped his inquiry
> despite his own reluctance to give up received ideas. Or he may
> adopt a radical stance and use his findings as ideological weapons,
> extrapolating science into world view.[41]

The critical assessment of competing world views against the ideal of
wide reflective equilibrium is a complex and multifaceted process. To
claim that it could promote the convergence of traditions is not to

suggest that such agreement would be easily or quickly accomplished, or that it provides a tradition-independent basis for evaluation. In later chapters, I will say more about the comparison of competing world views when I describe how the search for wide reflective equilibrium applies specifically to the project of appreciating and assessing rival *moral* traditions. By way of preparation for that description, I will conclude this chapter by summarizing the notions of truth, reality, and objectivity that correspond to my understanding of non-foundational justification.

Truth Revisited

Let us suppose that the search for wide reflective equilibrium results in agreement within a tradition of enquiry—or even across what were formerly rival traditions—on the truth conditions for a particular kind of claim. Let us further suppose that there is agreement that the truth conditions for a specific claim of that particular kind have been fulfilled. Would this mean that the claim is true? Not necessarily. Even if a claim received unanimous assent, and conviction as to its truth was supported by all current standards of rational justification, it could still be false. A claim made within a community of enquiry on the grounds that the truth conditions for that particular kind of claim have been fulfilled is only as sound as their agreements on what counts as truth conditions for that particular kind of claim. I am proposing that such agreements on truth conditions are justified to the extent that they achieve wide reflective equilibrium with the rest of a community of enquiry's explicit beliefs, implicit assumptions, attitudes, interests, norms, priorities, and practices. However, whether or not convergence within or between traditions justifies confidence in their beliefs—including their beliefs about the appropriate truth conditions for particular kinds of claims—is itself a judgment that is open to debate. My position, then, is not that the achievement of wide reflective equilibrium necessarily guarantees that truth has been attained. Rather, it is that any agreement within a particular form of enquiry that convergence does vindicate truth claims can itself only be justified as being part of the most coherent, successful, and defensible set of assumptions on the issue. In other words, I am claiming that the achievement of wide reflective equilibrium is the best grounds there are for adopting one or another set of agreements about what counts as "good reasons" for assenting to empirical or normative truth claims. Commitment to a set of agreements about the truth conditions for particular kinds of claims can be justified with reference to the achievement of wide reflective equilibrium, but justified only as the best all-around view to emerge so far, relative to alternative views.

How can my claims about wide reflective equilibrium themselves be justified? To be self-referring, my characterization of wide reflective equilibrium must be defensible by virtue of its ability to provide (a) an accurate characterization of a process discernible in what are generally taken to be good examples of justifying the sets of assumptions and commitments shared within traditions of enquiry (see, for example, Strike 1989), and (b) a framework within which the success of that process is intelligible. Because I can justify my account of non-foundational justification only in terms of its internal and external coherence, success relative to my intentions, and ability to incorporate the strengths of alternative views while explaining their limitations, I cannot claim that it is necessarily or indubitably true.

The notion of truth involves an implicit or explicit distinction between what is believed to be the case and what is actually so. One way in which beliefs are thought to be constrained is by what exists in an mind-independent way.[42] Accordingly, one way of arguing that convergence of beliefs justifies claims to truth in a particular form of enquiry is by contending that what exists in a mind-independent way is precisely what is intended in that particular form of enquiry. We have seen that, unlike foundational forms of justification, arguments that appeal to the achievement of wide reflective equilibrium do not require either that particular observations or general principles represent an unmediated description of "reality." It is assumed that any perception, judgment, or generalization expressed in language will necessarily share the limitations of one or another socially and historically conditioned perspective. At the same time, it is also assumed that a community of enquiry's assumptions and commitments will be constrained by what is prior to and independent of language, where success in their intentions depends upon an accurate representation of what exists prior to and independently of human belief. In other words, success in practice can provide grounds for confidence that a community's assumptions about the physical or social environment are true in a correspondence sense, when it seems reasonable to believe that success presupposes some degree of fidelity between representations and represented, between signs and signified.[43]

The belief that something exists in a mind-independent way requires a distinction between our experience of an event and the event itself, although we have no knowledge of events except through experience. It is worth noting that the only way we can make this distinction is to *imagine* something "outside" of our experience. For example, we can imagine that the event which gave rise to (our hearing of) the sound of thunder actually occurred seconds before the experience. We can even imagine events that would affect us directly without our being able to experience them in any usual way. An example here would be thinking about falling asleep in a vehicle that is subsequently crushed in a head-on collision. In this way, we can imagine that, when a scheme of beliefs functions to direct purposeful interaction with the physical or social environment, success is constrained by the ability of those beliefs to represent that environment in a way adequate to the task. Conversely, failures or unexpected experiences can precipitate "epistemological crises" in which the adequacy of our representational systems, linguistic and otherwise, come under doubt. As MacIntyre (*WJ*, 356) suggests, it may be that "the original and most elementary version of the correspondence theory of truth is one in which it is applied retrospectively in the form of a correspondence theory of falsity."

This account of truth and justification does not presuppose that we can step "outside" of our experience to see how well our beliefs correspond to what exists prior to and independently of those beliefs. The account does presuppose that we can distinguish between human experience and how aspects of that experience are conceptualized in the terms of various languages and theoretical frameworks. As far as evaluating the adequacy of schemes of beliefs is concerned, it makes little difference whether their truth is conceived as correspondence between belief and human experience, or between belief and something that human experience is experience *of.*

Objectivity

In my understanding, the notion of objectivity is intimately related to the notion of truth, that is, to the distinction between something being believed to be the case and it actually being so.[44] Objectivity can be attributed to the existence of objects and events, to knowledge claims, and/or to knowing subjects. For example, to describe horses as existing objectively is to claim that they exist in a way that unicorns supposedly do not, that is, independently of human imagination. To describe a knowledge claim as objective is to assert that what is claimed is not only imagined or believed or assumed to be the case, but is actually so.[45] On this view, *to describe people as objective is to assert that they manifest whatever qualities, attitudes, and/or cognitive processes are required for their claims to be objective—that is, to represent true beliefs.*

It follows from this that different theories of knowledge and truth will result in different notions of objectivity, that is, different notions of when people and/or their judgments are properly described as objective. When knowing is conceived on the analogy of taking a good look—of seeing only what is already "out there" and of not seeing what is not already "out there"—objectivity is *opposed* to subjectivity, because the subject is understood to play no active role in the production of knowledge. Hence, in the positivistic paradigm, being objective is typically equated with being dispassionate or neutral, in the sense of being free from all value commitments. Taken to its limit, this notion of objectivity can lead to the search for "the view from nowhere," a vantage point from which all of the particularities of socially and historically conditioned perspectives have been eliminated.[46] In contrast, when knowledge is understood to be the outcome of our ongoing intentional activities, mediated by language, objectivity is (to borrow Lonergan's felicitous phrase) "a function of authentic subjectivity" (1973, 265). Or, better, it is a function of authentic subjectivities because the production of knowledge (and of persons, for that matter) is always a social endeavour.

If my characterization of non-foundational justification is accepted, then members of a community of enquiry are objective to the extent that they manifest all of the qualities, attitudes, and abilities involved in the search for wide reflective equilibrium. Depending upon the form of enquiry in question, being objective could include having a sensitive appreciation of the particularities of concrete contexts, making insightful connections among events, weighing evidence fairly, testing tentative beliefs in practice, being passionately committed to the search for truth and for justice, supporting companions in enquiry, and being open to the possible merits of opposing views. Objectivity is thus properly contrasted not with subjectivity but with *bias*, where bias is defined as any human quality, attitude, or action that inappropriately obstructs, restricts, or distorts the ongoing activities through which the limitations of existing views are revealed against the ideal of wide reflective equilibrium.[47] Being biased could involve ignoring or forgetting relevant evidence, denying connections, overlooking counterexamples, rejecting potential alternatives out of hand, or accepting assumptions uncritically.

This opposition between being objective and being biased presupposes that some interests are appropriate and some inappropriate to different forms of enquiry. On this view, being objective involves elements of detachment as well as engagement: specifically, detachment from those interests or intentions inimical to the form of enquiry in question. To determine what being objective requires for a particular form of enquiry thus requires understanding which interests are appropriate and which inappropriate to its fundamental intentions, as well as which interests—the pursuit of domination, perhaps—distort *all* forms of enquiry. Lonergan (1958, 191–193, 219–227), for example, distinguishes four kinds of bias. *Dramatic bias* refers to an unconscious suppression of images or ideas that would precipitate unwanted insights—unwanted, perhaps, because they would threaten a cherished self-concept. *Individual bias* refers to an unwillingness to pursue intellectual or moral enquiry that is unrelated to egoistic self-interest. Similarly, *group bias* is an unwillingness to take enquiry beyond where it serves the status quo. "Just as the individual egoist puts further questions up to a point, but desists before reaching conclusions incompatible with his egoism, so also the group is prone to have a blind spot for insights that reveal its well-being to be excessive or its usefulness at an end" (Lonergan, 1958, 223). Finally, *general bias* refers to a preference for short-term thinking, in which immediate concerns exclude consideration of larger issues and long-term consequences.

It might be thought that the process of seeking wide reflective equilibrium would inevitably be biased because it starts from the particular interests, assumptions, and convictions of one or another socially and historically situated tradition. But this objection only underlines the importance of a community of enquiry's commitment to becoming progressively more and more unbiased, that is, to remaining open to questions that challenge their preconceptions. The assumption here is that, to the extent we remain open to further questions, our efforts in search of wide reflective equilibrium will sooner or later uncover the limitations in our initial point of view.

Converging views

Critiques of positivistic notions of objectivity are legion, as are attempts to articulate alternatives. Many authors argue that being objective is compatible with having a point of view shaped by specific interests in concrete social and historical contexts.[48] Objectivity—like rationality—so far from being opposed to it, *requires* participation in an ongoing tradition of enquiry and debate. Feminist authors in particular have argued that objectivity should be understood as situated and engaged. Haraway (1988, 589–590), for example, asserts that "situated knowledges are about communities, not about isolated individuals."

> The science question in feminism is about objectivity as positioned rationality. Its images are not the products of escape and transcendence of limits (the view from above) but the joining of partial views and halting voices into a collective subject position that promises a vision of the means of ongoing finite embodiment, of living within limits and contradictions—of views from somewhere. (Haraway 1988, 590)

Keller (1985, 115–117) develops a notion of *dynamic objectivity* in scientific enquiry which is contrasted to *static objectivity*. Both are defined as the "pursuit of a maximally authentic, and hence maximally reliable, understanding of the world around oneself." However, while static objectivity "begins with the severance of subject from object rather than aiming at the disentanglement of one from the other," dynamic objectivity starts with acknowledging the "connectivity" between subject and world. With regard to ethical enquiry, Nussbaum and Sen (1989, 308) similarly insist that being objective in evaluating a culture requires "experienced immersion" in that culture's way of life.

Looking Back, Looking Ahead

I began with the question "How can we assess the respective strengths and limitations of competing moral traditions in the search for a satisfactory moral point of view?" In chapter one, I examined the arguments for and against radical framework relativism, the position which denies that incommensurable perspectives can be evaluated in a rational way. The rationalist-relativist debate over the implications of incommensurability became focused on the question "How, if at all, can the beliefs, attitudes, interests, norms, priorities, and practices shared within communities of enquiry be justified—and their advantages and disadvantages relative to other perspectives assessed—if there is no standpoint for justification outside of traditions?" In chapter two, I presented MacIntyre's understanding of the rationality of traditions as a sound basis for responding to that question. I have used chapter three to present my own understanding of non-foundational justification by amending, systematizing, and enlarging MacIntyre's account of dialectical argument. I have claimed that the incommensurable sets of assumptions and commitments that comprise the rival points of view of competing traditions of enquiry can be assessed on their internal and external coherence, success in accomplishing their fundamental intentions, and ability to accommodate and explain competing viewpoints.

To this point, my characterization of the search for wide reflective equilibrium has been very general and abstract. This is because it is intended, like MacIntyre's account of the rationality of traditions, to apply to all forms of enquiry. In the next four chapters, I take a closer look at MacIntyre's account and then my own characterization of non-foundational justification in relation to moral enquiry. Along the way, I have more to say about how dialectical argument compares to the search for wide reflective equilibrium. Differences between the two become clearer in the light of my position on what makes moral traditions *moral*.

CHAPTER FOUR

Moral Traditions
and Dialectical Debate

Philosophy always buries its undertakers.
—Etienne Gilson

In this chapter I present MacIntyre's understanding of the rationality of traditions of moral enquiry. The chapter has four sections. In section one, I review MacIntyre's description of his own moral tradition, *the ethics of virtue*. I begin with an overview of the ethics of virtue because it illustrates the kind of interrelated beliefs that are internal to a moral point of view *and* because some of those beliefs are the necessary presuppositions of MacIntyre's account of dialectical debate among rival moral traditions. In section two, I reconstruct his understanding of the sense in which rivals to the ethics of virtue can be considered competing traditions of *moral* enquiry even while having radically incommensurable conceptions both of morality and of enquiry. In section three, I summarize MacIntyre's description of the processes through which, the criteria with respect to which, and the conditions under which the rational superiority of a moral tradition might be established in dialectical debate. In section four, I provide examples of MacIntyre's arguments for the rational superiority of his Thomistic scheme of beliefs, to illustrate how the pattern of his arguments not only conforms to his characterization of dialectical debate, but also fits my more detailed description of the process of seeking wide reflective equilibrium.

As before, I begin with MacIntyre's views not because I believe that they should be accepted without qualification, but because they are an excellent basis for further discussion. In this case, they provide a good start to describing how the "generic" understanding of non-circular and non-foundational justification presented in earlier chapters applies to the project of assessing the relative strengths and limitations of alternative moral points of view.

THE ETHICS OF VIRTUE

Practices and Their Internal Goods

MacIntyre locates himself within a Thomistic tradition of moral enquiry and practice that, following Aristotle, centres upon the virtues (*AV*, 146; *WJ*, 401–403). His account of the ethics of virtue is elaborated through several stages, beginning with a discussion of the goods internal to practices.[1] A *practice* is defined as "any coherent and complex form of socially established cooperative human activity through which goods internal to that form of activity are realized in the course of trying to achieve those standards of excellence which are appropriate to, and partially definitive of, that form of activity, with the result that human powers to achieve excellence, and human conceptions of the ends and goods involved, are systematically extended" (*AV*, 187). MacIntyre offers two clarifications-by-contrast of what he means by a practice. First, he distinguishes a practice from a set of technical skills on the understanding that the "goods and ends" which skills serve within a practice are "transformed and enriched" over time (*AV*, 193; cf. *WJ*, 31). In other words, a practice has a history in a way that the simple exercising of a set of skills does not.

> Tic-tac-toe is not an example of a practice in this sense, nor is throwing a football with skill; but the game of football is, and so is chess. Bricklaying is not a practice; architecture is. Planting turnips is not a practice; farming is. So are the enquiries of physics, chemistry, and biology, and so is the work of the historian and so are painting and music. In the ancient and medieval worlds the creation and sustaining of human communities—of households,

cities, nations—is generally taken to be a practice in the sense in which I have defined it. Thus the range of practices is wide: arts, sciences, games, politics in the Aristotelian sense, the making and sustaining of family life, all fall under the concept. (*AV*, 187–188)

Second, MacIntyre distinguishes practices from the institutions that sustain them: "Chess, physics and medicine are practices; chess clubs, laboratories, universities are institutions" (*AV*, 194).

MacIntyre's contrast between a practice and its institutional framework roughly corresponds to a distinction between the goods *internal* to and those *external* to a practice. Goods are internal to a practice when they can only be specified with reference to that practice and can only be recognized and appreciated through the experience of participating wholeheartedly in that practice's activities. Those who have no personal experience with a practice are therefore unable to recognize or make judgments about its internal goods (*AV*, 188–189). MacIntyre argues, for example, that it is not possible to appreciate the goods internal to chess without playing the game in a dedicated way (*AV*, 274). In contrast, external goods—including such institutional rewards as money, power, and prestige—are only contingently attached to particular practices.[2] External goods also differ from internal goods in their relation to individual competition within and between institutions:

> It is characteristic of what I have called external goods that when achieved they are always some individual's property and possession. Moreover characteristically they are such that the more someone has of them, the less there is for other people. . . . External goods are therefore characteristically objects of competition in which there must be losers as well as winners. Internal goods are indeed the outcome of competition to excel, but it is characteristic of them that their achievement is a good for the whole community who participate in the practice. (*AV*, 190–191)

For example, only one person will take home top prize in a chess tournament, but the whole community of chess players will benefit if the competition inspires new levels of brilliance in play.

In the light of these distinctions, MacIntyre provisionally defines a virtue as "an acquired human quality the possession and exercise of which tends to enable us to achieve those goods which are internal to practices and the lack of which effectively prevents us from achieving any such goals" (*AV*, 191). He argues that certain virtues such as "justice, courage, and honesty" are required to achieve the goods internal to any and all practices. These virtues are required because of the need for certain kinds of relationships among those who pursue the same practice, such as an absence of the kind of competition for external goods that is detrimental to practices (*AV*, 191–194). For MacIntyre, then, because institutional rewards such as positional power and prestige have the potential to corrupt practices, and yet practices cannot be sustained without institutions, the making and sustaining of forms of social life in which practices can flourish within institutional frameworks is itself a practice with its own internal goods and requisite virtues.

> For the ability of a practice to retain its integrity will depend on the way in which the virtues can be and are exercised in sustaining the institutional forms which are the social bearers of the practice. The integrity of a practice causally requires the exercise of the virtues by at least some of the individuals who embody it in their activities; and conversely the corruption of institutions is always in part at least an effect of the vices. (*AV*, 195; cf. *WJ*, 32–35)

Because practices have histories, the virtues required to sustain them will include those qualities and dispositions required to sustain relationships (although not necessarily uncritical ones) with the past. A relationship with the past must be maintained because, in practices as in traditions of enquiry, participants cannot learn to adapt the corresponding standards of judgment to new circumstances without participating in an ongoing history of internal and external debates—debates that include disputes over how the current standards of excellence internal to a practice are best formulated and pursued.

MacIntyre claims that a human life lived according to this initial characterization of the virtues would, from an Aristotelian point of view, be defective in at least three ways. First, the diversity of distinct practices allows that realization or even pursuit of their internal goods can be mutually exclusive. Consequently, without some grounds or guidelines for setting priorities among the range of possible internal and external goods, a human life would be characterized by "*too many* conflicts and *two much* arbitrariness" (*AV*, 201). Second, there are certain virtues that cannot adequately be characterized unless human life has some overall potential or purpose, the realization of which is its overriding good. MacIntyre's example of a virtue that needs such a conception of an overriding good is justice, for if justice is defined as giving to each according to their deserts, acting justly requires a standard or set of standards according to which goods and rewards can be rank-ordered. Thus, "any substantive application of an Aristotelian concept of justice requires an understanding of goods and of the good that goes beyond the multiplicity of goods which inform practices" (*AV*, 202; cf. *WJ*, 33–34, 106–107). Third, MacIntyre believes that his initial characterization of practices, because it lacks a conception of a human life as a whole or unity, leaves no application for the virtue of integrity. In light of these deficiencies, MacIntyre concludes that his scheme of moral beliefs is not complete without "an overriding conception of the *telos* of a whole human life, conceived as a unity" (*AV*, 202). Accordingly, the second stage of his account of the ethics of virtue is a set of interrelated claims outlining both how human lives are properly understood as wholes and how the overriding good of those lives can be heuristically defined.

The Narrative Unity of Human Life

MacIntyre's first claim with regard to the narrative unity of human life is that human actions cannot be characterized without reference to human intentions, for it is intentions that distinguish actions from behaviours. Behaviours and actions cannot be considered the same, because we can identify different behaviours as the same action, "as the movements involved in shaking a hand and those involved in putting out a flag may both be examples of welcoming somebody"; and, conversely, the same behaviour can be identified as different actions, "as a movement of the legs may be part of running a race or of fleeing a battle."[3] On MacIntyre's view, then, actions are identified by describing a behaviour or sequence of behaviours in terms of an individual's specific intentions.

MacIntyre's second claim is that specific intentions cannot be characterized without a narrative of the context or setting—including the individual's background beliefs, desires, and larger purposes—which make particular intentions intelligible (*AV*, 83–84, 206–215). In other words, explaining an individual's actions requires a narrative reconstruction of the personal history in light of which her or his intentions make sense.

> For all intentions presuppose more or less complex, more or less coherent, more or less explicit bodies of belief, sometimes of moral belief. So such small-scale actions as the mailing of a letter or the handing of a leaflet to a passer-by can embody intentions whose import derives from some large-scale project of the individual, a project itself intelligible only against the background of some equally large or even larger scheme of beliefs. In mailing a letter someone may be embarking on a type of entrepreneurial career whose specification requires belief in both the viability and the legitimacy of multinational corporations: in handing out a leaflet someone may be expressing his belief in Lenin's philosophy of history. But the chain of reasoning whose conclusions are expressed in such actions as the mailing of a letter or the distribution of a leaflet is in this type of case of course the individual's own; and the locus of that chain of reasoning, the context which makes the taking of each step part of an intelligible sequence, is that particular individual's history of action, belief, experience, and interaction. (*AV*, 28–29; cf. 207–208)

As MacIntyre observes, the personal histories which make an individual's actions intelligible take place within a cultural context of shared assumptions that, to the extent they could be objectified, would also be expressed in narrative form. Furthermore, those background contexts or settings have developed over time: as personal histories are embedded in broader social histories, so personal narratives are part of larger cultural narratives.[4]

MacIntyre's third claim is that constructing narratives is not an imposition of order upon human experience, for it is not the case that human actions can be independently identified and then subsequently arranged in one or another narrative framework. Rather, as we have just seen, actions *presuppose* narratives because intentions cannot be characterized outside of a narrative framework.[5] As particular human actions are moments in larger stories, so singular past events are abstractions from historical narratives (*AV*, 212–214). Furthermore, personal histories are *lived* before they are told: for MacIntyre, human lives are *enacted* narratives (*AV*, 211). On this view, it is meaningful to ask which of conflicting stories is most faithful to the actual personal or cultural history in question.[6]

The following scenario illustrates the relations among behaviours, actions, intentions, and narratives: *A man walks into a bar and asks for a glass of water. The barmaid reaches down under the bar, pulls out a large handgun, and points it at him. The man says "Thank you," and walks out satisfied.* In order to understand how the behaviours of the two characters are intelligible actions, it is necessary to expand the narrative to include their intentions: he wanted a glass of water because he had the hiccups and she wanted to help him. It is also necessary to know their shared background of assumptions, particularly that drinking a glass of water and being scared are two ways of curing the hiccups.

MacIntyre's fourth claim is that human living has a teleological or "forward-looking" character. In other words, we make choices based upon our desires to bring some possible futures to pass and to forestall others:

> We live out our lives, both individually and in our relationships with each other, in the light of certain conceptions of a possible shared future, a future in which certain possibilities beckon us forward and others repel us, some seem already foreclosed and others perhaps inevitable. There is no present which is not informed by some image of some future and an image of the future which always presents itself in the form of a *telos*—or a variety of ends or goals—towards which we are either moving or failing to move in the present. (*AV*, 215– 216)

This is equivalent to saying that our choices, individually and collectively, are shaped by the stories we tell ourselves of the past events and possible futures of our lives. Hence the narratives that other people might construct of the personal histories which make an individual's specific intentions and actions intelligible would likely include reconstructions of the stories told by that individual to himself or herself—stories of remembered events and imagined possibilities. The same would hold for narrative reconstructions of the histories of social groups. This forward-looking aspect of human living is a feature of its narrative form: just because it is characteristic of a narrative that the full significance of its events are not known until the end of the story, we often deliberate over choices among alternative courses of action by imagining the different futures each course of action could bring to pass. Thus, part of what it means for MacIntyre to claim that human lives are enacted narratives is that the significance of present actions and events is a matter as much of their possible futures as of their actual past.[7]

MacIntyre's fifth claim concerns human identity: how an individual is conceived to be (and might come to conceive herself or himself to be) the same person from birth to death. He first observes that "There is no way of *founding* my identity—or lack of it—on the psychological continuity or discontinuity of the self" (*AV*, 217). MacIntyre agrees with Hume that "identity cannot be warranted from a solely first person perspective" (*WJ*, 291). On this view, we come to conceive of ourselves as persons *not* through introspection but through learning to apply social definitions of personhood.[8] MacIntyre goes on to argue that the concept of a person, like that of an intelligible action, *presupposes* narrative. "Just as a history is not a sequence of actions, but the concept of an action is that of a moment in an actual or possible history abstracted for some purpose from that history, so the characters in a history are not a collection of persons, but the concept of a person is that of a character abstracted from a history" (*AV*, 217). Furthermore, MacIntyre understands each individual life to have a narrative unity even before the story of that life is told, whether by the individual herself or himself or by someone else. For MacIntyre, in other words, it is not just because the *concept* of a person presupposes narrative forms of explanation, and not just because our identities are part of the stories we tell ourselves about our lives, it is also because our lives have the unity of an enacted narrative that we are properly conceived as the same person from birth to death. The unity of the self, as he puts it, "is the unity of a narrative embodied in a single life."[9]

MacIntyre's sixth claim is that the concept of a person is inextricably tied to notions of agency, responsibility, and accountability. He observes that our options are limited by the actions of other people and by our concrete socio-historical context: "We enter upon a stage which we did not design and we find ourselves part of an action that was not of our making" (*AV*, 213). At the same time, because we individually and collectively can decide to work towards imagined futures, we can become co-authors of our enacted narratives to a greater or lesser degree. With agency comes responsibility and accountability: part of what it means to be a person is, in MacIntyre's eyes, to be willing and able when required (except under extraordinary conditions) to justify our actions to others; and, in turn, sometimes to require others to give account of themselves.

> Identity is socially ascribed. To be one and the same person is to satisfy the criteria by which others impute identity, and their criteria of identity govern and are embodied in their ascriptions of responsibility and accountability. The responsibility of each person is what can be imputed to that person as an originating cause, extending through the time during which there is a true first person account of his or her doings and sufferings to be given, and he or she can be held answerable in respect of such an account. Since the moral and practical life of societies always requires such responsibility and such accountability, and since the moral and practical concepts of a society are always articulated as members of a more or less coherent set in which the use of a variety of evaluative and practical judgments presupposes the applicability of the concepts of responsibility, there is no society in which the possession of a publicly usable, third-person, more or less complex conception of personal identity is not presupposed in everyday discourse. (*WJ*, 291)

This linking of personhood and accountability makes sense given MacIntyre's claims that behaviours are actions by virtue of human intentions: it is because actions presuppose intentions that we can provide a rationale for our activities with reference to our society's norms of rational action (*AV*, 209, 218). Hence MacIntyre argues that one of the strengths of the ethics of virtue is that, unlike at least some other traditions of moral enquiry, its understanding of agency, responsibility, and accountability forms a coherent whole with its understanding of narrative, intelligibility, and identity.

It is important to notice that I am not arguing that the concepts
of narrative or of intelligibility or of accountability are *more* fundamental than that of personal identity. The concepts of narrative, intelligibility and accountability presuppose the applicability
of the concept of personal identity, just as it presupposes their applicability and just as indeed each of these three presupposes the
applicability of the two others. The relationship is one of mutual
presupposition. It does follow of course that all attempts to elucidate
the notion of personal identity independently of and in isolation
from the notions of narrative, intelligibility and accountability are
bound to fail. As all such attempts have.[10]

MacIntyre's seventh claim is that the particular form of narrative that
gives human life its unity is the quest (*AV*, 219). The goal of that quest
is "to discover that truth about my life as a whole which is an indispensable part of the good of that life" (*TRV*, 197; cf. *AV*, 174–176). To
discover the "truth about my life as a whole" is in part to discover its
"overriding good." The human quest is thus a search for precisely that
knowledge of the overriding good of human life that MacIntyre needs
to complete his ethics of virtue:

It is in looking for a conception of *the* good which will enable us
to order other goods, for a conception of *the* good which will enable us to extend our understanding of the purpose and content
of the virtues, for a conception of *the* good which will enable us to
understand the place of integrity and constancy in life, that we initially define the kind of life which is a quest for the good. (*AV*, 219;
MacIntyre's italics)

MacIntyre heuristically defines the overriding good of human life as its
telos, meaning the end or activity that is the full actualization of human
potential. As MacIntyre himself observes (*WJ*, 134; *TRV*, 200), the belief that human life has such a *telos* and thereby an overriding good is
not so much the *conclusion* as the *presupposition* of ethical enquiry in the
Aristotelian-Thomistic tradition.

MacIntyre allows that, even though human imperfection might render perfect knowledge of the nature of *the* good unattainable, some
better understanding of the human *telos* is achievable. Any such progress

made in understanding the nature of the overriding human good is progress in human self-knowledge. This is because, on the assumption that every human life has the same ultimate goal, there will be some commonality as well as variation among all true answers to the question "What is the best life for *me* to live?" (*AV*, 218–219). On this view, the best human life consists of contributing to a community or social order in which pursuit of the goods internal to the various practices is organized on the basis of perfect knowledge of the overriding good of human life, to the effect that all of us eventually realize our full potential. In the absence of such perfect knowledge, the best human life consists of contributing to a community or social order in which pursuit of the goods internal to the various practices is organized on the basis of the best existing conception of that overriding good, to the effect that we both realize our potential as much possible and make progress towards a perfect conception of the human *telos* (*WJ*, 107–108, 122, 133, 298; cf. *AV*, 219).

It is worth emphasizing that it is the belief in an overriding human good existing prior to its discovery that allows MacIntyre to claim that the narrative unity of human life is lived before it is told (*RVG*, 8). Indeed, it is only from the point of view of the future realization of the human *telos* that the true significance of past and present events will be understood (*TRV*, 94, 197, 200). Progressing towards that realization will therefore involve a retelling of personal and social histories in a new light. This is a specific case of the more general claims that (a) achieving later or "higher" stages in any developmental process allows the history of progress through earlier stages to be written in a more insightful way, and (b) it is only by assuming some more or less determinate-but-unrealized potential that is it possible to speak of *stages* and *progress* at all. From the Kohlbergian point of view, as I have remarked, it is only from the perspective afforded by its final stage that the nature of moral development can be properly characterized. Similarly, for MacIntyre, is it only from the perspective afforded by knowledge of the teleological order of the cosmos that the true stories of individuals and of communities can be told, because that perspective reveals the nature of the potential that, when actualized, is the overriding human good.

Affirming that human life has the unity of a quest for realization of its overriding good allows MacIntyre to expand upon his initial characterization of the virtues.

> The virtues . . . are to be understood as those dispositions which will not only sustain practices and enable us to achieve the goods internal to practices, but which will also sustain us in the relevant kind of quest for the good, by enabling us to overcome the harms, dangers, temptations and distractions which we encounter, and which furnish us with increasing self-knowledge and increasing knowledge of the good. The catalogue of the virtues will therefore include the virtues required to sustain the kinds of households and the kind of political communities in which men and women can seek for the good together and the virtues necessary for philosophical enquiry about the character of the good. (*AV*, 219; cf. *WJ*, 44)

From this larger perspective, it is not enough to count as a virtue that a human disposition or quality contribute to the realization of the goods internal to a practice. To qualify as a virtue, a disposition or quality must also contribute to the success of a form of social life within which the various practices are integrated according to an overall view of their respective contributions to the realization of the human *telos* (*AV*, 275).

To this point, the virtues as well as the human *telos* have been defined only heuristically, that is, in terms of the places they occupy in MacIntyre's conceptual scheme. Perhaps this is in part because, to the extent that *realization* of the overriding human good is imperfect, existing *conceptions* of it are limited, and so there is room for uncertainty and disagreement over how the best human life and the virtues should be characterized. MacIntyre himself observes that different views of what success in the quest for the good might mean and of what dangers attend its pursuit have resulted—even within the Aristotelian tradition—in widely divergent descriptions of the virtues and vices (*AV*, 144, 176, 198, 243; *WJ*, 163). Because of this, formulating an adequate conception of the overriding good of human life *and* of what contributes to its realization, along with eliminating false conceptions, is of paramount importance for the ethics of virtue. How can such an adequate conception be achieved?

In MacIntyre's Thomistic scheme, knowledge of the teleological order of the cosmos is sought in metaphysics, conceived as a theoretical science. Ethics draws upon conclusions reached in metaphysical en-

quiry concerning the particular end or *telos* which is the full actualization of human potential in order to identify the kinds of educational
activities that will result in human fulfilment. It is ethics, then, conceived as a form of philosophical enquiry, that identifies those qualities and dispositions that are necessary to achieving the overriding
good of human life.

> Ethics therefore in this view presupposes some account of poten-
> tiality and act, some account of the essence of man as a rational ani-
> mal and above all some account of the human *telos.* The precepts
> which enjoin the various virtues and prohibit the vices which are
> their counterparts instruct us how to move from potentiality to act,
> how to realize our true nature and to reach our true end. To defy
> them will be to be frustrated and incomplete, to fail to achieve that
> good of rational happiness which it is peculiarly ours as a species
> to pursue. The desires and emotions which we possess are to be put
> in order and educated by the use of such precepts and by the cul-
> tivation of those habits of action which the study of ethics pre-
> scribes; reason instructs us both as to what our true end is and as
> to how to reach it. (*AV,* 52–53)

By furnishing ethics with an account of the human *telos,* metaphysics
provides knowledge of the overriding good that provides human life
with a narrative unity.

The Virtues and Tradition

The third stage in MacIntyre's account of the ethics of virtue is a discussion of the necessary role of tradition in the human quest for the
good. His key claim here is that we are "never able to seek for the good
or exercise the virtues only *qua* individual" (*AV,* 220). MacIntyre has
maintained that being rational presupposes the context of a tradition
of enquiry just because there is no place outside of one or another particular community of enquiry from which to offer or evaluate arguments. Becoming a member of a tradition of enquiry therefore involves
learning how to take up its arguments as our own, including its debates
over the standards appropriate to argument. In the same way, he asserts
that moral enquiry and practice presuppose the context of one or

another tradition's current "shared beliefs about goods" and corresponding norms and priorities for human life (*MA*, 222; *WJ*, 122–123, 133–134; *TRV*, 60–66). Becoming a member of a moral tradition thus involves learning how to live faithfully to its current conception of the best human life. Consequently, in the same way as the virtues required to sustain practices and communities of enquiry include those which preserve relationships with the past, the virtues required to sustain the quest for the good include those qualities and dispositions necessary to preserve moral traditions.

> The virtues find their point and purpose not only in sustaining those relationships necessary if the variety of goods internal to practices are to be achieved and not only in sustaining the form of an individual life in which that individual may seek out his or her good as the good of his or her whole life, but also in sustaining those traditions which provide both practices and individual lives with their necessary historical context. Lack of justice, lack of truthfulness, lack of courage, lack of the relevant intellectual virtues— these corrupt traditions, just as they do those institutions and practices which derive their life from the traditions of which they are the contemporary embodiments. (*AV*, 223)

Asserting that traditions play a necessary role in an individual's quest for the good forms part of a coherent whole with MacIntyre's claims that individual identity is that of a character in a narrative, and narratives always have a social and historical context. In his view, there is no personal identity that is not also social and historical (*AV*, 221). Cultural traditions are the carriers of a social group's norms and priorities, including their assumptions about what it means to be a person and their corresponding expectations concerning "normal" behaviour. To share such a tradition is, for MacIntyre, in part "to share schemata which are at one and the same time constitutive of and normative for intelligible action by myself and are also means for my interpretation of the actions of others. My ability to understand what you are doing and my ability to act intelligibly (both to myself and others) are one and the same ability" (*EC*, 453–454). Different traditions have different views of what it means to be a person, and so have different expectations of what is normal—that is, intelligible and acceptable— behaviour. Accordingly, MacIntyre asserts that how we interpret our own and other people's behaviours varies according to the concepts available within our shared schemes of beliefs (*WJ*, 24–25, 183). For example, while all cultures have norms regulating human desires and emotions, different traditions have varied views on the nature of the emotions, on which emotions are appropriate, and on how individuals are related to their desires (*WJ*, 21, 76–77). MacIntyre further suggests that a tradition's shared expectations concerning what is and is not normal human behaviour are rarely explicitly defended, but more often form part of its shared background assumptions or world view. In light of this, he argues that appreciating any such tradition's point of view (including one's own) requires a familiarity with the normative expectations carried in the "stock of stories which constitute its initial dramatic resources."[11]

In this context, MacIntyre contends that the quest for the good must begin in, although it need not always be limited to, the resources of the communities through which we achieve moral self-consciousness.

> The fact that the self has to find its moral identity in and through its membership in communities such as those of the family, the neighbourhood, the city and the tribe does not entail that the self has to accept the moral *limitations* of the particularity of those forms of community. Without those moral particularities to begin from there would never be anywhere to begin; but it is in moving forward from such particularity that the search for the good, for the universal, consists. (*AV*, 221)

While MacIntyre believes that we can progress beyond the limitations of the tradition(s), we inherit through our communities, he also asserts that the particularities of our pasts "can never be simply left behind or obliterated" (*AV*, 221). Where, when, and to whom we were born is always part of the enacted narratives that constitute the unities of our lives and identities (*AV*, 172–173). Because of this, what living virtuously requires of us will vary according to the particularities of our personal, social, and historical contexts. This holds even for members of a moral community sharing the same conception of the overall *telos* of human life and corresponding list of virtues and vices.

From this affirmation of the significance of differences among particular personal, social, and historical contexts, MacIntyre draws an important conclusion: we need more than just an accurate conception of the human *telos* in order to know what is best for us to do. To live the best possible human life, we also need to know how to determine the implications of a conception of the overriding human good for our own particular circumstances (*RVG*, 8). Because of this, MacIntyre's list of the virtues necessary to success in the human quest is not complete without the qualities and dispositions we need to be practically rational, that is, to identify, choose, and accomplish what is best for us to do in specific contexts. Hence the fourth stage of his account of the ethics of virtue is an elaboration of a Thomistic understanding of practical rationality.[12]

The Virtues, Practical Rationality, and Moral Education

To be practically rational is to have acquired and to exercise a capacity to make sound practical judgments. As I have argued in chapter one, the rationality of practical judgments is not a simple matter of applying general rules or principles to specific cases. What, then, from the point of view of the ethics of virtue, makes practical judgments rational?

Aristotle
In MacIntyre's interpretation of Aristotelian practical rationality, actions must be in our best interests in order to be rational. On this view, we are rational when our actions are based upon our own judgments about what is in our best interests *and* those judgments are sound (*WJ*, 125). A sound practical judgment correctly determines the implications of a "more or less adequate" conception of the overriding human good for immediate action (*WJ*, 125). It calculates the immediate implications for action of a general conception of the good by constructing a practical syllogism:

> What immediately precedes and generates action is that form of deductive reasoning which commentators have called "the practical syllogism," although Aristotle himself never uses that expression. Such a syllogism consists of two premises or sets of premises, a first initiating premise (often misleadingly referred to as the major premise) in asserting which the agent declares what good is at stake in his acting or not acting as he should, and a secondary premise (correspondingly referred to as the minor prem-

ise) in asserting which the agent declares what the situation is in which, given this good is at stake, action is required. The conclusion drawn from these premises is the required action (*DA* 434a16–21, *De Motu Animalium* 701a7–25, *NE* 1146b35–1147a7 and 1147a25–31). (*WJ*, 129)

Practical syllogisms are constructed in two stages. Deliberation provides major premises by deriving from the overriding good of human life general principles or ends of action for certain kinds of contexts. Perception supplies the minor premise or premises by grasping how the current situation provides an opportunity to realize the good named in the major premise (*WJ*, 20, 44–45, 125–126, 130–132, 137–138, 188–189). In other words, on this deductive model of practical judgment, deliberation and perception combine to identify an action as "good" in the sense that it contributes to achieving the final goal of human life.

The rational agent then is set the task of constructing a major premise which states truly what good it is which is his particular good here and now . . . the good specified in it will only be his genuine good if it not merely is consistent with but is derivable from *the archē*, the set of ultimate first principles and concepts, which specifies the good and the best for human beings as such. The completion of this derivation is the central task of deliberation. (*WJ*, 130)

In Aristotle's terms, as noted earlier, the ability to make a sound practical judgment by combining an accurate conception of *the* good with a discerning grasp of particulars is *phronēsis* (*AV*, 154; *WJ*, 115–116, 125–126; *TRV*, 139).

In MacIntyre's account, sound practical judgment requires *prohairesis*, "desire guided by reason." *Prohairesis* is necessary first because untutored desires or passions represent a potential distraction to the calculations of practical deliberation. Hence MacIntyre's admonition, noted earlier, that "the desires and emotions . . . are to be put in order and educated by the use of such precepts and by the cultivation of those habits of action which the study of ethics prescribes" (*AV*, 53, cf. 154; *WJ*, 301; *TRV*, 139). Educated desire is also necessary because, to be practically rational in the full sense, we must be disposed to complete our practical syllogisms by performing the requisite action (*WJ*, 126, 136, 189; *TRV*, 62). As MacIntyre observes, one implication of this is that an action can be rational without being immediately preceded by a process of deliberation culminating in a practical judgment: an action could be rational because it is motivated by *prohairesis*, which results from the *previous* exercise of sound practical reasoning (*WJ*, 131, 135). On this view, then, an action can be rational *either* because it is immediately preceded by the exercise of practical rationality *or* because it could retrospectively be justified in that way. Accordingly, MacIntyre claims that we can sometimes know and do what is in our best interests simply because of our "natural traits and talents." To act rationally *consistently*, however, we must develop both the intellectual virtues, which are the capabilities that we exercise in sound practical judgment, *and* the virtues of character, which are the dispositions that motivate us to act on the conclusions of theoretical enquiry and practical judgment (*AV*, 149, 154).

MacIntyre elaborates his interpretation of Aristotelian practical rationality with two further points. One, acting rationally is not simply a matter of following rules or laws, not only because discretion is needed to apply rules and laws correctly in specific contexts (*AV*, 150–154; *WJ*, 116–120), but also because acting rationally is doing what is right *knowing* it to be right: "The genuinely virtuous agent . . . acts on the basis of a true and rational judgment" (*AV*, 150; cf. *WJ*, 113). Two, acting rationally is not necessarily a matter of acting *contrary* to the passions, as if passions were inherently irrational. Rather, the fully virtuous person acts on the basis of passions educated—that is, *transformed*—in light of true knowledge of the good.

> Virtues are dispositions not only to act in particular ways, but also to feel in particular ways. To act virtuously is not, as Kant was later to think, to act against inclination; it is to act from inclination formed by the cultivation of the virtues.[13]

For Aristotle, a number of distinct human qualities and dispositions— such as honesty, courage, justice, temperance, and generosity—are necessary to achieve the human *telos* and so are integral to the best human life. Moreover, it is an important part of Aristotle's understanding of the virtues that each requires the others in order to be complete. The relationship between justice and *phronēsis* is a good example (*WJ*, 106–107, 119; cf. *VSD*, 5). For Aristotle, justice is a matter of distributing resources and rewards among citizens according to their relative contributions to the *polis*, the political order in which the activities of the various practices are organized according to a shared conception of the overriding human good. Consequently, in order to act justly, members of the *polis* need both to know the relative contribution of each particular virtue to the best human life and to be disposed to act according to that knowledge. Because people must themselves embody each virtue in order to appreciate its relative contribution to the *polis*, they must possess all of the virtues in order to distribute rewards and administer punishments according to desert. In particular, because what acting justly demands in particular cases can be difficult to establish, individual members of the *polis* must possess the virtue of *phronēsis* in order to be just (*WJ*, 115–116). And, because individuals cannot achieve the goods internal to practices without the virtues, they must possess the virtue of justice in order to judge and act in a practically rational way.

It is clear from this account that, on MacIntyre's Aristotelian view, individuals must develop both the intellectual virtues and the virtues of character in order to know and do what will further their quest for the overriding good. These two different kinds of virtue are acquired through two distinct but inseparable forms of education:

> Aristotle's distinction between these two kinds of virtue is initially made in terms of a contrast between the ways in which they are acquired; intellectual virtues are acquired through teaching, the virtues of character from habitual exercise. We become just or courageous by performing just or courageous acts; we become theoretically or practically wise as a result of systematic instruction. Nonetheless these two kinds of moral education are intimately related. . . . According to Aristotle . . . the excellence of character and intelligence cannot be separated. (*AV*, 154)

The two kinds of virtue and corresponding forms of moral education cannot be separated because building character through the performance of virtuous acts needs sound judgment in order to know *which* inclinations and desires to cultivate, *which* acts to perform. Conversely, developing judgment through learning from systematic instruction requires a well-formed character in order not to be distracted from self-development by more immediate gratifications (*WJ*, 110, 128–129; *VSD*, 5; cf. *NE* 1095a1–11).

As MacIntyre (*WJ*, 118) remarks, Aristotle's affirmation of the interdependence of these two forms of education seems to result in a vicious circle. For the deliberation that precedes sound practical judgment combines accurate perception of the relevant features of particular situations with an adequate conception of the overriding human good. MacIntyre claims that, according to Aristotle, accurate perception of particulars comes with experience, while an adequate conception of the human *telos* develops through the combination of *epagōgē* and dialectical debate. *Epagōgē* refers to the formulation of a general concept or principle by abstracting what is common to a group of particulars. In other words, *epagōgē* is a process in which human intelligence selects a number of particular objects or events and discerns something with respect to which they all can be considered examples of the same kind of thing. *Dialectical debate* compares, among other things, the relative strengths and weaknesses of the general concepts and principles developed through *epagōgē*.[14] The formulation of an adequate theoretical conception of the overriding human good thus *presupposes* a number of sound practical judgments, in which some implicit conception of the *telos* of human life can be discerned (*WJ*, 91–93, 118). At the same time, however, on MacIntyre's interpretation of Aristotelian practical rationality, sound practical judgments *presuppose* the prior formulation of an adequate conception of the overriding good of human life. How can either develop if each depends upon the other?

This vicious circle can also be expressed in the following way: we become just through the performance of just acts, courageous through the performance of brave acts. However, it is only *retrospectively* that we can appreciate how being just or courageous is in our best interests.

> The virtues are, on Aristotle's view, dispositions to act in specific ways for specific reasons. Education into the virtues involves the mastery, the disciplining, and the transformation of desires and feelings. This education enables one to exercise the virtues so that one not only values each of the virtues for its own sake, but un-

derstands the exercise of the virtues as also being for the sake of being *eudaimon*, of enjoying the good and the best life for human beings. And the knowledge which enables one to understand why this kind of life is in fact the best is only to be had as a result of having been a virtuous person. (*WJ,* 109)

In the same way that we have to be dedicated to a practice over a period of time in order to appreciate fully its internal goods, so we have to gain experience in living a life informed by an accurate conception of the human *telos* in order to appreciate the point of the virtues. "It follows that for those who have not yet been educated into the virtues the life of the virtues will necessarily seem to lack rational justification; the rational justification of the life of virtue within the community of the *polis* is available only to those who already participate more or less fully in that life" (*WJ,* 110; cf. *FP,* 15; *PPI,* 74–75). If we can only fully appreciate the virtues *after* we have become virtuous, then how is it that we can be motivated to perform virtuous acts, or even recognize what the genuinely virtuous person would do? In brief, then, the vicious circle is this: "We cannot judge and act rightly unless we aim at what is in fact good; we cannot aim at what is good except on the basis of experience of right judgment and action" (*WJ,* 118; cf. *TRV,* 63).

MacIntyre claims that this appearance of circularity is deceptive: it disappears with a closer look at how *phronēsis* actually develops. To illustrate his point, he describes the educational process through which an individual gains the capacity to make sound practical judgments about what the virtue of justice requires in particular circumstances. The process begins with the individual following specific injunctions or precepts that define just conduct in relatively straightforward situations. A respected teacher, representing the accumulated wisdom of one or another tradition, provides the individual both with rules to follow and with inspiration to follow them (*WJ,* 114, cf. 194; *TRV,* 63, 130). This early training in obeying rules of just behaviour—supplemented, perhaps, with stories or poems of other situations in which justice was or was not served (*WJ,* 382–383; *RVG,* 8–9)—provides opportunities for two complementary kinds of learning, for it provides the practical experience (a) through which individuals can develop accurate perception of the relevant features of particular contexts and (b) in reflection upon which they can grasp through *epagōgē* general concepts and principles of just behaviour. Learning to formulate principles of justice not only enables them to appreciate the reasoning behind the rules they have followed, but also helps them to discern what justice requires in situations too complex for the simple application of rules. "So the order of learning is such that we first have to learn in certain initial situations what is *always* enjoined or always prohibited, in order that later we may become able to extrapolate in a non-rule-governed way to other types of situations in which what courage or justice or truthfulness, together with prudence, demand is more than conformity to the universal rule" (*RVG*, 10; *WJ*, 115, 121). MacIntyre thus suggests that the interdependence of the systematic development of intellectual virtues on the one hand and the cultivation of virtues of character on the other is not a vicious circle. On the contrary, it is a back and forth interaction through which both can improve: "In developing both our conception of the good and the habit of right judgment and action—and neither can be adequately developed without the other—*we gradually learn to correct each in the light of the other, moving dialectically between them*" (*WJ*, 118, my italics; *TRV*, 128–130).

In this and related discussions of moral education, MacIntyre notes that if the educational process he describes is to be understood as resulting in accurate knowledge of what is virtuous and hence practically rational, then at least three things must be presupposed: one, that teachers who possess accurate knowledge of virtuous behaviour are available; two, that individuals have the innate potential to be able to learn from their experiences, including the potential ability to construct general principles from particular cases (*TRV*, 136); and three, that individuals have some way of confirming whether or not their particular practical judgments are correct and their general principles of virtuous behaviour justified. With regard to the third prerequisite, MacIntyre describes confirmation of correct judgment as coming in two ways, using learning about justice as his example. First, the principles of justice used in particular judgments receive support to the extent that they are defensible in dialectical debate with competing positions. Second, on MacIntyre's Aristotelian view, any sound practical judgment by definition correctly grasps the implications for a particular situation of an accurate conception of the overriding human good. Accordingly, principles of justice formulated through reflection on particular cases receive confirmation to the extent they are compatible with the conception of the overriding human good formulated in theoretical enquiry (*WJ*, 118; *ITC*, 106). Thus, on MacIntyre's view, "the *phronimos* can then always look forward to the vindication of his present judgments by their according with that conception of the good and the best which dialectical enquiry establishes" (*WJ*, 119; cf. 117).

Aquinas

MacIntyre presents Aquinas' account of the virtues, practical rationality, and moral education as generally following and elaborating Aristotle's account (*WJ*, 188–189, cf. 192; *VSD*, 9–10). For both, it is not possible for individuals to be practically rational—that is, to know and do what is truly in their best interests—without first acquiring the intellectual virtues and the virtues of character (*WJ*, 176–177). For both, individuals develop virtuous dispositions by performing virtuous actions, and so initially require guidelines as to what should and should not be done (*WJ*, 181). For both, what is truly good, truly in an individual's best interests, is good because it has some relation to the overriding good of human life. Whatever is rightly desired is therefore rightly desired as an integral part of the best human life (*WJ*, 165). For both, the nature of the cosmos determines what kind of human life will lead to fulfilment of its highest potential: each derives his conception of the virtues and of the *telos* of human life from a "metaphysical theology" (*WJ*, 166, 171, 198; *TRV*, 137–138). Finally, both affirm the necessity of acquiring the ability—Aquinas' term for *phronēsis* is *prudentia*—to adapt or adjust general principles to the needs of particular situations. In Aquinas' terms, to have a good conscience is to be able to derive general moral principles from a conception of the overriding good, and then to combine those principles with an accurate perception of immediate circumstances (*WJ*, 185; cf. 196–197).

MacIntyre also observes that, their substantial agreements notwithstanding, Aquinas judges Aristotle's overall position to be defective in two major respects. First, Aquinas rejects Aristotle's conception of the human *telos*. For Aristotle, the most divine human activity is *theōria*, a form of contemplation, and, while the best human life includes many other activities that are properly desired as ends in themselves, they are all secondary to *theōria* (*WJ*, 107–108). Furthermore, while not all of us will necessarily be able to experience the satisfaction that accompanies contemplation, its attainment in this life is humanly achievable. Against this view, Aquinas uses Aristotle's own criteria of the human *telos* to argue that no finite state attainable in this present life can properly be considered the supreme human good, because every such finite state falls short of perfection (*TRV*, 137). Aquinas concludes that the human *telos* must therefore be "outside and beyond this present life":

> Nothing, so Thomas argues, can be the ultimate end of human beings except that state of perfect happiness which is the contemplation of God in the beatific vision, in which contemplation all of human nature finds its completion (*S.T.* I–IIae, 3,7). (*WJ*, 192)

For Aquinas, not only is the ultimate end of human life beyond attainment in this present life, it transcends theoretical understanding. Yet, even so, Aquinas, like Aristotle, understands theoretical enquiry in ethics as properly progressing towards a more adequate understanding of the human *telos* through dialectical enquiry, because the deliberations of practical rationality require the best possible conception of the overriding human good (*WJ*, 193).

The second way in which Aquinas finds Aristotle's position unsatisfactory is in its lack of recognition of the inability of the will to obey the dictates of reason. MacIntyre proposes that Aquinas' psychology is more Augustinian than Aristotelian in holding both that the will is required to initiate action and that it has been corrupted by original sin. Accordingly, although Aquinas agrees with Aristotle that any one virtue needs the others to be complete, Aquinas adopts Augustine's list of the four cardinal virtues: prudence, justice, temperateness, and courage (*WJ*, 197–198; *TRV*, 154). Furthermore, in a way that is completely foreign to Aristotle, Aquinas holds that these "natural" virtues are only brought to completion by the "supernatural" virtues of faith, hope, and charity (*TRV*, 140). From this Thomistic point of view, Aristotle's list of the virtues is seen as defective in omitting the humility required to accept divine grace, which purifies the will of pride (*WJ*, 181, 205). MacIntyre summarizes a Thomistic critique of Aristotle as follows:

> The virtues understood only in Aristotelian terms are incapable of perfecting human beings in such a way that they can attain their *telos*, partly because of Aristotle's inadequate understanding of what that *telos* is and partly because the natural virtues themselves can only perfect when informed by that *caritas* which is a gift of grace. (*WJ*, 182)

With regard to moral education, MacIntyre understands Aquinas to follow Aristotle in three important respects. First, Aquinas believes that bringing the passions in line with reason is both possible and necessary, because being genuinely virtuous involves having the right intentions as well as performing the right actions. Second, Aquinas holds that it is through obedience to precepts of virtuous behaviour that individuals not only cultivate virtuous dispositions, but also eventually learn to judge what actions are appropriate in situations too complex for the straight-forward application of rules (*WJ*, 195–196). Third, like Aristotle, Aquinas refers to a kind of learning through personal experience that complements the intellectual process of formulating general principles from particular examples (*TRV*, 139; *ITC*, 106). Aquinas refers to such practical knowledge of the virtues as "knowledge by way of connaturality" (*WJ*, 194; *TRV*, 128).

Summary

As reconstructed by MacIntyre, the ethics of virtue is a tradition of moral enquiry and practice concerned to cultivate those human qualities and dispositions required for success in the quest for the overriding human good. The virtues vital to realization of the human *telos* are those that sustain (a) practices, (b) the institutions within which practices are maintained, (c) the larger social and political frameworks within which the various practices are coordinated, and (d) the traditions that provide practices, institutions, and larger forms of social life with historical continuity. The qualities and dispositions necessary to living the best human life include the intellectual virtues required for sound practical judgment and the virtues of character required for acting on those judgments. The virtues are acquired through a tradition-informed process of moral education that combines theoretical enquiry into the nature of the overriding human good with practical learning through judgment and action in specific contexts. Both Aquinas' and Aristotle's conceptions of the virtues, and of the proper role of the virtues in human life, form part of a coherent and mutually supporting whole with their fundamental ontological and epistemological beliefs. Hence, in his adaptation of Aristotelian concepts to an Augustinian theological framework, Aquinas' beliefs about God, the cosmos, and human nature result in a distinctively Christian account both of the human *telos* and of the virtues necessary to its realization.

The ethics of virtue and framework relativism

MacIntyre agrees with framework relativists that empirical claims are only as reliable as the assumptions and commitments shared within the corresponding community of enquiry—in particular, its shared agreements on truth conditions for specific kinds of claims. According to the ethics of virtue, practical judgments make a kind of truth claim in holding that the actions which conclude practical syllogisms accurately embody the immediate implications of a correct understanding of the overriding human good. MacIntyre therefore acknowledges—indeed, insists—that particular practical judgments are only as sound as the agreements shared within the corresponding community of moral enquiry, most particularly the "shared beliefs about goods and shared dispositions educated in accordance with those beliefs, both rooted in shared practices" (*MA*, 222; cf. *WJ*, 122–123, 321).

We have seen how MacIntyre, in his account of the rationality of traditions, opposes framework relativism by arguing that a community of enquiry's standards for rational judgment can themselves be vindicated in a non-circular and non-foundational way. It follows that, if MacIntyre's arguments against framework relativism are to apply to the moral domain, he must show how the perspective of one particular moral community can be supported against competing moral points of view. How, then, according to MacIntyre, is it possible to justify confidence in the assumptions, commitments, and practices of one or another particular moral community, and to assess its strengths and limitations relative to its rivals, without presupposing a particular moral perspective? How is it possible to justify confidence in one among competing conceptions of the best human life?

MORAL TRADITIONS

To understand his account of the rationality of moral traditions it is necessary first to understand what, for MacIntyre, makes a moral tradition *moral*. In Aristotle's distinction between intellectual and moral virtues, *moral* means something like *pertaining to character* (*AV*, 38; cf. Barnes 1976, 27). However, MacIntyre's understanding of *moral* is not always the same as Aristotle's, because *moral education* in MacIntyre's terms includes intellectual as well as character education (*AV*, 154,

WJ, 115). MacIntyre uses *moral* in such contexts as more or less syn-onymous with *ethical* to mean *concerned with identifying and living the best human life*. In some cases, then, MacIntyre understands *moral* in a way that is specific to the Aristotelian-Thomistic teleological tradition (*AET*, 507–508; *RVG*, 3). Yet MacIntyre also refers to non-Aristotelian and even anti-Aristotelian communities of enquiry and practice as repre-senting rival moral traditions. In such contexts, MacIntyre is using a third and much broader understanding of *moral* that, even while in-ternal to the ethics of virtue, enables him to recognize its competitors (*TRV*, 3). How, then, does MacIntyre recognize rivals to his Thomistic scheme of moral beliefs?

MacIntyre states that "if two moral traditions are able to recognize each other as advancing rival contentions on issues of importance, then necessarily they must share some common features" (*AV*, 276). Un-fortunately, however, he provides no succinct account of what "com-mon features" are possessed by rivals to the ethics of virtue in light of which they are properly also considered to be traditions of *moral* enquiry—even when they give neither the virtues nor the overriding human good a place in their schemes of beliefs. To redress this omis-sion, in what follows I attempt to identify the common features that, for MacIntyre, make moral traditions *moral* (in the broadest sense of the term). This examination of how he describes moral traditions will serve not only to reconstruct MacIntyre's understanding of their com-mon features, but also to introduce his account of how moral points of view are properly assessed.

Overall Conceptual Schemes and Forms of Social Life

In *Whose Justice? Which Rationality?*, MacIntyre compares the concep-tions of justice and of practical rationality that are internal to the ethics of virtue with those that are internal to its rivals. His comparison involves a narrative reconstruction of the history of each tradition's origins and subsequent development through internal and external de-bates. MacIntyre is concerned in that book to show how each tradition's conception of justice is closely linked to its conception of practical ratio-nality *and* how each tradition's understanding of justice-and-practical-rationality is both incommensurable to and irreconcilable with the understandings of its rivals (*WJ*, 39–43, 328–329, 389).

Through the course of his narrative, MacIntyre illustrates how each rival understanding of justice-and-practical-rationality, like the understanding of justice-and-practical-rationality that is internal to the ethics of virtue, is part of a (more or less) coherent and mutually supporting overall scheme of beliefs. He shows, for example, how each rival tradition's understanding of justice-and-practical-rationality is closely tied to its conceptions of the other virtues, to its theory of the self, and to its view of the cosmos (*WJ*, 349). MacIntyre also illustrates how each of these overall conceptual schemes (of which particular conceptions of justice-and-practical-rationality are an integral part) arises out of and informs specific "forms" or "modes" of social life, which are institutionalized to a greater or lesser degree (*WJ*, 349, 391–392; *SH*, 1). He claims, for instance, that moral beliefs typically inform economic, judicial, and political systems that define acceptable procedures for allocating resources, settling conflicts, and justifying legal authority. Schemes of moral belief are also embodied in such aspects of social life as "rituals and ritual dramas, masks and modes of dress, the ways in which houses are structured and villages and towns laid out, and of course by actions in general" (*WJ*, 355). In addition, moral beliefs are embodied in and legitimated through individuals who occupy the special social role of *characters*: "Characters . . . are the moral representatives of their culture and they are so because of the way in which moral and metaphysical ideas and theories assume through them an embodied existence in the social world" (*AV*, 28).

Towards the end of his narrative, MacIntyre summarizes the conclusions of his comparison of moral traditions in this way:

> It has become evident that conceptions of justice and of practical rationality generally and characteristically confront us as closely related aspects of some larger, more or less well-articulated, overall view of human life and of its place in nature. Such overall views, insofar as they make claims upon our rational allegiance, give expression to traditions of rational enquiry which are at one and the same time traditions embodied in particular types of social relationship. (*WJ*, 389)

Throughout the narrative, MacIntyre uses *overall conceptual scheme* (*WJ*, 23, 29), *overall view* (*WJ*, 389), and *scheme of overall belief* (*WJ*, 394) as equivalent to his earlier terms *moral theory, scheme of moral belief,* and *moral scheme* (e.g., *AV,* 51–54; cf. *RVG,* 11). MacIntyre thus characterizes rival moral traditions as irreconcilable and incommensurable socially embodied moral theories, where the term *moral theories* refers very broadly to the overall conceptual frameworks that are embodied in distinctive ways of life. MacIntyre's very broad definition of *moral theory* is consistent with his view that any community's understanding of what *moral* means is integral to their most basic metaphysical and epistemological beliefs.

By describing moral traditions as *socially embodied* moral theories, MacIntyre is underlining that they are properly concerned with practice as well as enquiry. In his terms, a scheme of moral beliefs cannot exist solely in minds or texts and count as a moral tradition (*WJ,* 391).

> When I speak of an overall moral scheme . . . I do not merely mean a theory, but rather a theory that is actually embodied in the practices and relationships of a specific society, a theory which if and when it is articulated at the level of explicit theorizing will have to be able to give an account of its own embodiment, if it is to sustain its claims. (*AET,* 507; *AV,* 118)

By characterizing moral traditions as socially embodied moral *theories,* MacIntyre is maintaining not only that particular forms of social life implicitly affirm a set of moral norms and priorities, but also that ongoing moral enquiry is generally an integral part of social life that, like other forms of social interaction, can be institutionalized to a greater or lesser degree (*WJ,* 349).

To characterize moral traditions as socially embodied moral theories is to beg the question "What makes a theory moral?" This question can be reformulated as "What interest or fundamental intention can be discerned as common among those traditions MacIntyre considers moral, that they interpret and pursue in different terms according to their basic ontological and epistemological assumptions?" The reformulation works like this: In chapter three, I defined a world view as a set of fundamental ontological beliefs, including assumptions about the origin, history, and structure of the cosmos and the nature of humans and their place in the world order. I subsequently used the mechanistic world view and positivistic paradigm of science to illustrate a general claim that the assumptions and commitments shared within a community of enquiry can be understood, at least to some degree, as the application of a world view to a particular domain of human experience. It would follow from my general claim that the assumptions and commitments shared within a community of moral enquiry and practice could be explained, at least to some degree, with reference to their basic beliefs about the world and human nature. MacIntyre supports this conclusion (and so, indirectly, my general claim) by providing examples of how basic ontological and epistemological assumptions interrelate to form a conceptual framework for particular moral judgments. For one example, in *Whose Justice? Which Rationality?* MacIntyre illustrates how conceptions of justice-and-practical-rationality are "closely related aspects of some larger, more or less well-articulated, overall view of human life and of its place in nature." Similarly, in another context, he shows how "there is no sphere of morality independent of the agent's metaphysical or theological (or antitheological) view of the world and, more particularly, of God and the self" (*MP*, 14). More specifically, MacIntyre explains Hobbes's morality with reference to Hobbes's assumptions concerning determinism, human nature, and language (*SH*, 138–139); he indicates how the existentialist Sartre "locates the basis of his moral view in a metaphysics of human nature, just as much as the Catholic or the Marxist does" (*SH*, 269); and he shows how moral philosophies implicitly or explicitly contain views of human agency—of "the relationship of an agent to his or her reasons, motives, intentions, and actions" (*AV*, 23, cf. *WJ*, 74–77)—and of the proper relationship between the virtues and social institutions (*AV*, 225). Other examples include his remarks on the Stoics (*WJ*, 148–149), on Augustine (*WJ*, 154–158), and on Aquinas (*WJ*, 164–166).

Also in chapter three, I proposed that rival communities of enquiry use non-equivalent terms, and have incompatible priorities or values, because they interpret and pursue *similar fundamental interests* regarding the same domain of human experience *within different world views.* It is clear that MacIntyre understands rival moral traditions to be rooted in competing views of the world and human nature. This justifies reformulating the question "What, for MacIntyre, makes a moral tradition moral?" as "What interest(s) or fundamental intention(s) can be discerned as common among those traditions MacIntyre considers moral, that they interpret and pursue in different terms according to their basic ontological and epistemological assumptions?"

At least one such common interest can be discerned in MacIntyre's narrative of competing traditions in *Whose Justice? Which Rationality?* That is an interest in establishing shared norms and priorities for human living. MacIntyre proposes that in early heroic societies, conceptions of the virtues formed part of an unquestioned world view in which persons were defined by their social roles, and social roles were presumed to mirror the order of the cosmos (*WJ*, 12–29; cf. *SH*, 5–13; *AV*, 121–126). Consensus on those world views eventually broke down, creating a need to justify norms and priorities with reference to which individual behaviours could be judged and collective objectives established. Aristotelian traditions justified their norms and priorities— represented by their conceptions of the virtues and their rank-ordering of the various ends of human activity—with reference to shared visions of the best human life, which in turn were based upon shared conceptions of humanity's highest potential. Even Aquinas, who equated principles of justice with God's law, understood obedience to divine commandments as rational because it furthered realization of the human *telos* (*WJ*, 203; *TRV*, 154). Within such traditions, individuals were enjoined to achieve their highest potential by transforming their desires to accord with what theoretical enquiry established as the overriding human good.

According to MacIntyre, teleological world views fell out of favour with the rise of formal or "technical" conceptions of rationality. From the time it was first denied that social norms and priorities could or should be justified with reference to a shared conception of the good life, efforts to ground moral principles have generally followed one of two basic alternatives.[15] One is to justify norms and priorities with reference to moral principles self-evident to any rational person. MacIntyre presents the scheme of moral beliefs and corresponding forms of social life of the seventeenth- and eighteenth-century Scottish intellectual tradition as the exemplar of this alternative (*WJ*, 223, 253–255). In this and similar conceptual schemes, moral principles are justified *without* reference either to human desires or the human good— although it may be a matter of divine providence that people individually and collectively benefit from fulfilling their moral obligations. Human desires are not transformed but mastered or disciplined by reason, which is understood to be capable of motivating action independently of desire or self-interest. Indeed, as MacIntyre observes, once moral principles are founded upon reason as *opposed* to interests or desires, it is often held that "it is just insofar as actions are explicable by interests or advantages that they cease to have moral worth" (*WJ*, 265).

In MacIntyre's narrative, the Scottish intellectual tradition was subverted from within by Hume, whose conceptual scheme reflected eighteenth-century English mercantile society. Hume's scheme represents the second possible way of justifying social norms and priorities, once it is no longer possible to appeal to shared conceptions of the human *telos* and best human life. This second alternative is to justify norms and priorities with reference to one or another conception of the passions or human desires.[16] In Hume's terms, *the passions* are prelinguistic and preconceptual responses which, because they contain no judgments concerning the objects to which they respond, can be neither true nor false. For Hume, all human action is motivated by one or another of these passions. In contrast, "reason . . . cannot motivate us. And the passions, which do motivate us, are themselves neither reasonable nor unreasonable" (*WJ*, 301). Therefore, although reason can suggest which passions if acted upon will promote long-term interests and so calculate the most expeditious means to the fulfilment of human desires, its conclusions affect human action only to the extent its exercise is itself motivated by a passion (*WJ*, 300–313). Consequently, any social norms regulating people in their pursuit of satisfaction of their desires are only justified so long as and to the extent those norms promote long-term interests.

> We and everyone else want on the one hand to be able to prosecute our ends, whatever they are, within a framework which provides peace, order, and stability in the transactions and exchanges of social reciprocity; we and everyone else are, however, also on occasion moved by the immediacies of particularity and self-interest to disrupt that peace, order, and stability. We suffer, that is, from contrary passions. Nevertheless, reason assures us that it is by giving the primacy to the former set of passions and by controlling and, if necessary, frustrating the latter that our and everyone else's most extensive and enduring satisfaction will be achieved. So Hume

concludes that "however single acts of justice may be contrary, either to public or private interest, 'tis certain, that the whole plan or scheme is highly conducive, or indeed absolutely requisite, both to the support of society, and the well-being of every individual" (*Treatise* III, ii, 2). (*WJ*, 309)

Through such examples, MacIntyre illustrates how incommensurable conceptions of justice-and-practical-rationality, along with their corresponding overall schemes of beliefs and forms of social life, are rooted in conflicting views of the proper respective contributions of deliberative reason and pre-reflective desire to directing human action (*WJ*, 21, 43–46, 76–77, 213–214; cf. *AV*, 228–229, 235–236). It makes sense that this issue should be central to moral traditions, because every social group has to contend with the conflicting interests of its members, and all individuals are potentially faced with having to decide which of their various inclinations to pursue at the expense of some others (*AV*, 48; *WJ*, 174; *RVG*, 3–8). MacIntyre's narrative in *Whose Justice? Which Rationality?* thus suggests that the fundamental interest common to rival traditions of *moral* enquiry (in the broadest sense of the term) is a concern *to establish norms and priorities for human life consistent with an accurate view of human nature and the world, and particularly with a correct understanding of the respective roles that deliberative reason on the one hand and pre-reflective interests, passions, and desires on the other should play in directing human action.*

Versions of Moral Enquiry and Narrative Structures

MacIntyre's characterization of moral traditions in *Whose Justice? Which Rationality?* is further developed in *Three Rival Versions of Moral Enquiry.* The three incommensurable versions or modes of moral enquiry he compares are *encyclopaedia, genealogy,* and *tradition. Encyclopaedia* is represented by the authors of the Ninth Edition of the *Encyclopaedia Britannica* and particularly by its editors, Thomas Spencer Baynes and William Robertson Smith. Genealogy is represented primarily by the Nietzsche of *Zur Genealogie der Moral,* and secondarily by Foucault and Deleuze. *Tradition,* unsurprisingly, is represented by Aquinas, understood by MacIntyre as perfecting the dialectical mode of enquiry originating with Socrates, Plato, and Aristotle.[17]

The title notwithstanding, rival versions of enquiry are not the only focus of comparison in *Three Rival Versions*. We have already seen how MacIntyre claims both that human life has the unity of an enacted narrative and that, according to the ethics of virtue, human life has the unity of a quest for the good. In addition, MacIntyre claims that rival moral traditions have competing views about *which form* of enacted narrative gives human life its unity (*AV*, 128–129, 144, 173; *TRV*, 77–78). He illustrates and supports this latter claim by presenting the encyclopaedic, genealogical, and dialectical versions of moral enquiry as closely tied to incommensurable views of the narrative structure of human life.

In what follows, I reproduce MacIntyre's characterization of the three rivals by summarizing (in much condensed form) his description of each tradition's version of moral enquiry and corresponding narrative framework. This serves two important purposes. First, it rounds out MacIntyre's characterization of moral traditions presented in *Whose Justice? Which Rationality?* Second, it further illustrates how competing conceptions of enquiry—moral enquiry in particular—form an integral part of the epistemological and ontological assumptions of competing world views.

Encyclopaedia
For the encyclopaedists, all forms of enquiry are one or another kind of science, and therefore most usually are differentiated by their subject matter rather than their methods. All encyclopaedic sciences have the same four "constitutive elements." First, there are "the facts," which are to be gathered. Second, there are "the unifying synthetic conceptions supplied by methodical reflection upon the facts" which "order the facts by making them intelligible as exemplifying laws." Third, there are two kinds of methods, those by which the unifying conceptions and laws are derived from the facts and those by which they are confirmed. Fourth, there is continuous progress represented by "ever more adequate unifying conceptions which specify ever more fundamental laws" (*TRV*, 19–20). The human sciences are differentiated from the sciences of nature only by explaining, as well as making, human progress:

> The human sciences, like all natural sciences, exhibit progress in enquiry, but progress of all kinds, moral, scientific, technological,

theological, is their central subject matter and conceptions of progress and of its inevitability are among their most important unifying conceptions. So the sciences concerned with the distinctively human were taken to reveal to us a law-governed history whose climax so far is their own emergence. (*TRV*, 21)

The editors of the Ninth Edition believe that further human development is advanced by identifying the laws that have governed human progress to its current pinnacle, as represented by the encyclopaedic sciences. Accordingly, the overall objective of encyclopaedic enquiry is to furnish, either in philosophy or natural theology, a unified description and explanation of human progress from savage to civilized (*TRV*, 21–24). By charting the process of past development, the encyclopaedia itself sets the course for future rational progress.

The encyclopaedists understand moral enquiry, like their other sciences, as differentiated by its subject matter rather than its methods. MacIntyre asserts that Enlightenment moral philosophers were united in a conviction that "plain persons do not need the moral theorist to tell them what the requirements of morality are, except insofar as religious or political interests have obfuscated and distorted true morality, sometimes with the aid of false moral theory." For those who hold such a view, "the only role left open for theory is the vindication and clarification of the philosophically uninfected plain person's judgments, so as to protect them against false theory" (*TRV*, 175). By the nineteenth century, however, it had become clear that both plain persons and their interpreters continued to disagree on moral matters. These differences were attributed to greater and lesser degrees of progress in moving from primitive to civilized belief. This progress was understood as a process whereby rational moral rules were gradually detached from superstitious customs and rites. Accordingly, the writers and editors of the Ninth Edition conceive their task as "organizing and harmonizing" the pretheoretical moral judgments of civilized peoples into a system of moral rules that would elicit agreement from the largest number of rational persons (*TRV*, 176–177).

The moral philosopher's aim then is or ought to be that of articulating a rational consensus out of the pretheoretical beliefs and judgments of plain persons. But not all such beliefs and judgments are equally to be taken into account. It depends in part on where they are to be placed in the developmental scheme. (*TRV*, 177)

By systematizing the beliefs of those who have achieved the highest degree of moral development, and thereby promoting rational agreement on moral rules, the encyclopaedists hope to advance the cause of civilization.[18] In this way, the history of progress in moral philosophy is thought to coincide with the history of progress in morality itself, which is a history of more or less continual movement toward rational consensus (*TRV*, 178). This reveals that "the narrative structure of the encyclopaedia is one dictated by belief in the progress of reason" (*TRV*, 78). When constructed according to this narrative form, the story of a person's life is the story of his or her relationship, positive or negative, to the history of reason's progress:

> Many of the articles in an encyclopaedia such as the Ninth Edition were designed to identify what some particular individual did either by way of a contribution to that progress or by way of obstructing such progress. Articles of a certain length and tone were the encyclopaedist's equivalent of canonization. Such canonized individuals were taken to have advanced our realization that nothing falls outside the bounds imposed by and prescribed by reason; reason does and can know nothing of anything external to itself. So what reason discovers, when it is successful, is always in some sense itself, some instantiation of the coherence of reason. (*TRV*, 78)

It is of the essence of reason and the laws of rational progress, as understood by *encyclopaedia*, that they are everywhere and always the same. Accordingly, the encyclopaedic narrative of progress in moral enquiry toward rational consensus is, like the narrative of moral progress itself, a story of emancipation from the strictures and superstitions of past traditions.

Genealogy

MacIntyre presents Nietzsche's *Zur Genealogie der Moral* as providing "not only an argument in favour of, but a paradigm for, the construction of a type of subversive narrative designed to undermine the central assumptions of the Encyclopaedia, both in content and in genre"

(*TRV*, 25). On one interpretation of Nietzsche, such genealogical narratives are committed to an interrelated set of psychological, epistemological, historical, and literary claims that are in direct opposition to the encyclopaedic scheme of beliefs (*TRV*, 35–42). For example, the psychological claim would be something to the effect that all motivation is directly or indirectly an expression of a will to power, and that aspirations to rationality or objective truth are variations on the same repressive, "life-denying ascetic ideal" represented by the "priestly" virtues of faith and humility. The epistemological claim would be something to the effect that the encyclopaedist's search for *the* truth is a deluded pursuit of an imaginary goal.

> The encyclopaedist's conception is of a single framework within which knowledge is discriminated from mere belief, progress towards knowledge is mapped, and truth is understood as the relationship of *our* knowledge to *the* world, through the application of those methods whose rules are the rules of rationality as such. Nietzsche, as a genealogist, takes there to be a multiplicity of perspectives within each of which truth-from-a-point-of-view may be asserted, but no truth-as-such, an empty notion, about *the* world, an equally empty notion. (*TRV*, 42)

On this interpretation, genealogy is a form of historical enquiry whose narrative task is to disclose what conventional histories conceal (*TRV*, 39–40, 78). The corresponding story of an individual's life would be a narrative of success or failure in achieving and maintaining freedom from false consciousness (*TRV*, 79; cf. 209).

As MacIntyre remarks, if genealogy is understood in this way, then it risks contradicting itself by making the claim "There is no absolute, non-perspectival truth" in the form of a claim to absolute, non-perspectival truth (*TRV*, 36). However, in his description of the discourse of truth as a mask for the will to power, Nietzsche declares that argument is better understood not as an offering of reasons but as a "play of forces," and "it is not by reasoning that at a fundamental level anyone moves from one point of view to another" (*TRV*, 39, 42). In light of such statements, genealogical assertions are perhaps best understood not as truth claims, but as strategic moves in the verbal equivalent of guerilla warfare in which there are no fixed positions to defend.

On this interpretation, genealogy is rival to *encyclopaedia* and to *tradition*, not because it offers an incommensurable scheme of moral beliefs or an alternate form of moral enquiry, but because it rejects all discursive claims to rationality or objective truth:

> Nietzsche's final standpoint, that towards rather than from which he speaks, cannot be expressed as a set of statements. Statements are made only to be discarded—and sometimes taken up again— in that movement from utterance to utterance in which what is communicated is the movement. Nietzsche did not advance a new theory against older theories; he proposed an abandonment of theory. (*TRV*, 48–49)

Understood in this way, genealogy could be seen as being profoundly anti-narrative in rejecting *any* attempt to discover *the* final true story, whether of individual lives or of human history (*TRV*, 145; cf. *AV*, 21–22). The genealogist would at best accept one version of events as a temporary resting place in an ongoing journey to a destination as yet unknown.

> Every piece of writing, like every spoken word . . . is utterance on the move, in which the utterer is actively responding to what has gone before and actively expecting both others and him or herself either to react or to act in further response, so that he or she may move beyond it to something else. So the genealogical genre is one in which present theses about what has been are presented in a genre open to what is not yet. (*TRV*, 44–45)

Tradition

MacIntyre argues that neither the faith in rational progress nor the unified view of the sciences espoused by the editors of the Ninth Edition are currently tenable (*TRV*, 23–24). He is quick to add, however, that genealogy is not the only alternative when *encyclopaedia* is rejected. For MacIntyre believes that Aquinas' dialectical mode of enquiry represents the epistemological middle ground between *encyclopaedia*'s naive objectivism and genealogy's radical relativism. Accordingly, in *Three Rival Versions*, MacIntyre elaborates his understanding of the dialectical rationality of traditions that is internal to the Thomistic ethics of virtue, principally by explaining how both Aristotle and Aquinas understood enquiry as a kind of craft. Crafts are themselves a kind of practice, in MacIntyre's use of the terms, although not all practices are crafts. He asserts that learning how to participate in and contribute to a community of enquiry is like learning how to participate in and contribute to a craft in that it requires the development of both the intellectual virtues and the virtues of character. In other words, there is no progress in learning any craft unless individuals correct the shortcomings in their beliefs, intellectual capacities, dispositions, and habits that are revealed when they measure themselves against the standards of excellence internal to that practice (*TRV*, 61–63). MacIntyre further remarks that although progress and success in a craft are measured against its current standards of excellence, those standards are open to reformulation when experience reveals them inadequate in relation to the materials with which they are concerned (*TRV*, 68). Therefore, to master a craft—including the craft of enquiry—is to learn when and how to revise and extend its standards of excellence, thereby adding another line to its history of development or decline (*TRV*, 127–128). MacIntyre thus reiterates that, in contrast to both encyclopaedic and genealogical versions of enquiry, the rationality of traditions requires a reappropriation, even if a critical one, of the past.

> Just because at any particular moment the rationality of a craft is justified by its history so far, which has made it what it is in that specific time, place, and set of historical circumstances, such rationality is inseparable from the tradition through which it was achieved. To share in the rationality of a craft requires sharing in the contingencies of its history, understanding its story as one's own, and finding a place for oneself as a character in the enacted dramatic narrative which is that story so far. (*TRV*, 65)

Moral enquiry
MacIntyre proposes that, within this Thomistic scheme of beliefs, moral enquiry is conceived to be a kind of virtue-guided craft (*TRV*, 63). Its goal is "excellence in the achievement not only of adequate theoretical understanding of the specifically human good, but also of the practical embodiment of that understanding in the life of the particular enquirer" (*TRV*, 63). Hence, within the ethics of virtue, an individual's

critical reappropriation of the past in moral enquiry is understood to proceed through the combination of theoretical study and practical experience. We have already seen that the goal of Thomistic theoretical enquiry is to formulate an adequate conception of the overriding human good through the combination of *epagōgē* and dialectical debate. And we have seen that, in such enquiry, people evaluate competing conceptions of the good in terms of the coherence of those conceptions within an overall theoretical framework, which is evaluated in turn with reference to its own criteria of progress. MacIntyre describes in *Three Rival Versions* how Aquinas developed Aristotelian theoretical enquiry into a systematic and orderly construction of a comprehensive conceptual scheme through dialectical arguments with previous positions on topics arranged in order of their logical priority. Thus, in the Thomistic tradition of theoretical moral enquiry, "at every stage what emerges is the outcome of some particular learner's debate with all those distinct pasts" (*TRV*, 79, cf. 88–89). Moral practice in the Thomistic tradition embodies in forms of social life the schemes of moral beliefs formulated through such critical appropriations of past moral enquiry:

> What such enquiry has disclosed is, on the Thomistic view, a set of answers to such questions as: What is the *telos* of human beings? What is right action directed towards the *telos*? What are the virtues which issue in right action? What are the laws which order human relationships so that men and women may possess those virtues? *To live a practically well-ordered life is to embody the universal concepts which we comprehend and justify in those enquiries in the particularities of our moral lives.* (*TRV*, 79–80, my italics; cf. 127–129)

As I have already shown, narrative plays two important roles in all forms of enquiry considered within MacIntyre's account of the rationality of traditions. First, the reappropriation and justification of a tradition of enquiry requires familiarity with the history of its internal and external debates, and that history is reconstructed in narrative form. Second, resolving epistemological crises requires the construction of narratives linking later to earlier formulations of a tradition's fundamental agreements. In addition, because of the need to translate theory's "universal concepts" into practice, narrative plays a third role in moral enquiry. For MacIntyre, it is through learning how to tell the story of her or his life from a tradition's point of view that an individual comes to understand what kind of life she or he would have to lead in order to learn more about what is in her or his best interests (*TRV*, 129–130). The same holds true for social groups. For MacIntyre, then, *rival moral traditions interpret human lives through competing narrative structures because narratives illustrate in a concrete way the implications of overall schemes of beliefs for particular forms of individual and social life.*

> In moral enquiry we are always concerned with the question: what *type* of enacted narrative would be the embodiment, in the actions and transactions of actual social life, of this particular theory? For until we have answered this question about a moral theory we do not know what that theory in fact amounts to; we do not as yet understand it adequately. And in our moral lives we are engaged in enacting our own narrative, so revealing implicitly, and sometimes also explicitly, the not always coherent theoretical stance presupposed by that enactment. Hence differences between rival moral theories are always in key part differences in the corresponding narrative. (*TRV*, 80; cf. *AV*, 23; *RVG*, 8)

MacIntyre argues that, from the point of view of *tradition*, not only does each rival version of moral enquiry hold a different narrative structure to be "appropriate and necessary in recounting and enacting narratives of the moral life," but also "it is through contrasting and comparing the different and rival ways in which each understands the structure of such narratives that the issues which divide them can most easily be defined and perhaps even resolved" (*TRV*, 77–78). MacIntyre's claim here is that contrasting and comparing the narrative structures of rival moral traditions will resolve their conflicts *if that process identifies which tradition and corresponding moral point of view best enables its adherents to integrate all rival stories within one intelligible and plausible narrative framework.*

> So the encyclopaedic, the genealogical, and the Thomistic tradition-constituted standpoints confront one another not only as rival moral theories but also as projects for constructing rival forms of moral narrative. . . . that narrative prevails over its rivals which is

able to include its rivals within it, not only to retell their stories as episodes within its story, but to tell the story of the telling of their stories as such episodes. (*TRV*, 80–81, see also 144–145; *RVG*, 12–13)

Summary

I have been engaged in reconstructing MacIntyre's understanding of moral traditions. On the basis of how rivals to the ethics of virtue are characterized in his texts, I conclude that MacIntyre understands a moral tradition to be a historical succession of communities of moral enquiry and practice in which participants individually and collectively reappropriate that tradition's overall scheme of beliefs—its "moral theory"—and enact its corresponding narrative of human life. In other words, by learning to tell and to live the story of our lives from the point of view of a moral tradition, we come to understand what, given that tradition's view of human nature and the world, are the proper norms and priorities (if any) for human life. How, then, can those committed to one narrative of human life demonstrate that their tradition is rationally superior to competing moral points of view?

As champion of the Thomistic version of moral enquiry, MacIntyre asserts that the relative superiority of one moral tradition over a competitor is properly established by showing how it can more plausibly integrate the rival's point of view within its narrative framework than the reverse. To elaborate his claim, I will summarize in the next section MacIntyre's description of the processes through which, the criteria with respect to which, and the conditions under which the rational superiority of a moral tradition can be demonstrated in dialectical debate.

THE RATIONALITY OF MORAL TRADITIONS

MacIntyre argues that the evaluation of moral traditions, like that of other traditions of enquiry, is historical as well as dialectical. It is historical first in the sense that it is undertaken from the point of view of one or another tradition at some particular stage of its development: no evaluation is context-free. It is historical also in the sense that the relative strengths and weaknesses of competing moral traditions are evaluated only by way of narrative reconstructions of their histories,

and particularly their histories of internal and external debates. Mac-
Intyre holds that, although traditions of enquiry properly aim at historical truth, there is no tradition-independent access to the past against
which their rival narratives could be compared. How a tradition is presented as having fared in its debates therefore depends upon the point
of view from which the history of that tradition is told (*TRV*, 117–118,
151, 191–192). Accordingly, MacIntyre maintains that the first step in
the dialectical assessment of rival and incommensurable schemes of
moral beliefs is to appreciate them in their own terms.

The Process of Appreciating Incommensurable Moral Perspectives

Coming to appreciate an incommensurable moral tradition's point of
view in its own terms involves, as with any tradition of enquiry, a process of learning its "language-in-use" as "a new and second first language." By a language-in-use, MacIntyre is referring not only to a
natural language such as German or Japanese but also to the set of specialized or technical terms in which a particular tradition's scheme of
beliefs is expressed (*ITC*, 111).

> Every tradition is embodied in some particular set of utterances
> and actions and thereby in all the particularities of some specific
> language and culture. The invention, elaboration, and modifica-
> tion of the concepts through which both those who found and
> those who inherit a tradition understand it are inescapably con-
> cepts which have been framed in one language rather than an-
> other. (*WJ*, 371–372)

As the meaning of a scheme of moral beliefs is not fully understood
without a grasp of its implications for practice, so its concepts are not
fully understood without a familiarity with how they are embodied in
particular forms of social life. For MacIntyre, then, the process of
learning to understand an incommensurable moral tradition in its own
terms is analogous to the process whereby an anthropologist learns the
language-in-use of a foreign people by living among them and im-
mersing himself or herself in their culture. Such immersion is necessary because a culture is embodied in what people do, and in what they
don't say as much as in what they say. MacIntyre thus submits that a

member of one moral community wishing to appreciate the perspective of another in its own terms must participate in that second community (to whatever degree possible) until he or she can "pass as a native" (*WJ*, 375). Because of this, learning to perceive the world from the point of view of a rival moral tradition might well require initiation into the "form of life" defined by its institutions and practices (*TRV*, 98). At the very least, it will involve learning to inhabit imaginatively the rival tradition's conceptual scheme through familiarity with its texts (*WJ*, 394–395).

When speakers of one language-in-use learn to speak that of an incommensurable point of view as a second first language, they come to understand what terms from each language lack equivalents in the other and so cannot be translated without conceptual and linguistic innovation on the part of one or both languages (*WJ*, 375; *TRV*, 114; *ITC*, 111). They also come to understand which terms from each conceptual scheme cannot easily be translated into the other language because they represent beliefs which are necessarily false from the point of view of the other conceptual scheme (*WJ*, 376–381). For MacIntyre, because rival schemes of moral beliefs exhibit evaluative incommensurability as well as incommensurability of meaning, those who speak the language of a rival tradition as a second first language do so only as actors speak parts which "in their own person" they do not believe (*WJ*, 395; cf. *AV*, 245–246). MacIntyre cites himself as an example. Prior to his characterization of *encyclopaedia* and genealogy, MacIntyre describes himself as having attempted to learn "the idiom of each from within as a new first language, much in the way that an anthropologist constitutes him or herself a linguistic and cultural beginner in some alien culture" (*TRV*, 43). At the same time, he acknowledges that any translation of a rival tradition's conceptual scheme, including his rendering of *encyclopaedia* and of genealogy, is shaped by interests and assumptions internal to the interpreter's own perspective.

> In characterizing the variety of standpoints with which I have been and will be concerned, I too must have been and will be speaking as a partisan. . . . It is not that the adherent of one particular standpoint cannot on occasion understand some rival point of view both intellectually and imaginatively, in such a way and to such a degree that he or she is able to provide a presentation of it of just the kind

that one of its own adherents would give. It is even in so doing the mode of presentation will inescapably be framed within and directed by the beliefs and purposes of one's own point of view. (*TRV*, 117)

Thus, while MacIntyre attempts in each case to present *encyclopaedia* and genealogy as someone committed to those points of view, his intent in doing so derives from his on-going commitment to the Thomistic tradition of dialectical theoretical moral enquiry.

MacIntyre argues that no real engagement with a rival moral tradition is possible if its positions on particular issues are considered apart from their place within that tradition's overall scheme of beliefs (*WJ*, 172, 182; *TRV*, 77, 99, 135). Therefore, part of what it means to appreciate an incommensurable moral scheme in its own terms is to understand how each of its individual theses gains support from its contribution to the overall theory. In addition, to appreciate an incommensurable scheme in its own terms is in part to understand how it is a response to the interests, issues, and problems of its larger social and historical context (*AV*, 268– 269; *WJ*, 9, 12–13, 143–144, 205, 258, 389–390; *FP*, 64; *PPI*, 74, 81).

The second step in the dialectical assessment of rival and incommensurable moral traditions, once they have both been appreciated from within, is to formulate explicitly whatever parts of their schemes of beliefs have remained implicit in their practices or other commitments. For MacIntyre, this task of objectifying implicit beliefs falls to philosophy.

Philosophical theories give organized expression to concepts and theories already embodied in forms of practice and types of community. As such they make available for rational criticism and for further rational development those socially embodied theories and concepts of which they provide an understanding. Forms of social institution, organization, and practice are always to a greater or lesser degree socially embodied theories and, as such, more or less rational according to the standards of that type of rationality which is presupposed by tradition-constituted enquiry. (*WJ*, 390; cf. *AV*, 268; *MA*, 222)

MacIntyre contends that forms of social life embody implicit philosophical commitments because all societies must provide answers to
basic philosophical questions. On this view, the job of the academic philosopher "is to make explicit and to pursue with some persistence questions that are posed to and answered by everyone" (*PPI*, 66).

Criteria for Assessing Incommensurable Schemes of Moral Beliefs

Once the socially embodied moral theories of rival traditions have been
both appreciated and objectified, the third step in their dialectical assessment is to evaluate their successes and failures, their strong points
and their limitations. MacIntyre argues that such evaluation is necessarily undertaken from the perspective of one or another historical
tradition of moral enquiry because there are no tradition-independent
or tradition-neutral standards that are sufficient to resolve the substantive conflicts between rival schemes of moral beliefs. Indeed, it is
in large part precisely because of their different criteria of success and
failure that rival moral traditions are characterized by evaluative incommensurability as well as incommensurability of meaning.

In his argument against the idea of tradition-independent justification or evaluation, MacIntyre considers two candidates for the role of
tradition-neutral standards: "the facts" and self-evident moral principles. With regard to the first candidate, he maintains that conflicts between rival moral traditions cannot be resolved simply by referring to
"the facts" of the matter, because each tradition will construct "the
facts" according to the categories of its scheme of beliefs. One of Mac-
Intyre's examples is the conflict between Aristotle's and Hume's accounts of the relation of reason to action. He submits that this conflict
cannot be resolved by appealing to "the facts" because there is no
theory-independent way of describing instances of human action:

> When individuals articulate to and for themselves the processes
> through which they proceed to action or when observers describe
> those processes in others, they cannot do so except by employing
> some particular theory-informed or theory-presupposing scheme
> of concepts, by conceptualizing that which they do or undergo or
> observe in a way which accords with one theory rather than an-
> other. There are no preconceptual or even pretheoretical data,
> and this entails that no set of examples of action, no matter how

comprehensive, can provide a neutral court of appeal for decision between rival theories. I do not of course mean to say, and it would be absurd to say, that the empirical facts about action and its generation are not such as to impose constraints upon what can constitute a plausible or workable conceptualization. But those constraints are, unsurprisingly, consistent with a range of theories at least as wide as, and possibly a good deal wider than, the set of rival, mutually incompatible theories which emerged from the histories of previous chapters. (*WJ,* 332–333, cf. 77; *TRV,* 111–112)

Similarly, while MacIntyre recommends that rival metaethical positions be compared on the basis of the "theory of human nature and of the physical universe" that each presupposes, he warns that such comparison is necessarily always from the perspective of one or another tradition's own world view.[19]

With regard to the second candidate for neutral standards, MacIntyre submits that all efforts to date to identify moral principles that are self-evident to all rational and reflective persons have failed. He concludes that while such failures do not prove that such principles could never be formulated, they do provide "strong grounds" for conceiving standards of rational adequacy as internal to traditions (*WJ,* 346, cf. 329–332, 334–335; *AV,* 21, 66–68). By whose criteria, then, are the strengths and limitations of competing moral traditions to be evaluated in dialectical debate?

In MacIntyre's characterization of the rationality of traditions, the dialectical assessment of competing points of view requires no reference to standards neutral between them: the successes and failures of rival traditions are evaluated with reference to their own intentions. One tradition of enquiry emerges from dialectical debate as rationally superior to its rivals when it has the resources both (a) to succeed where rival traditions fail by their own standards of success, and (b) to provide a better explanation of those failures than the rival traditions can themselves provide out of their own resources. MacIntyre characterizes the rational superiority of a *moral* tradition over its rivals in essentially the same way:

It is in the ability of one particular moral-philosophy-articulating-the-claims-of-a-particular-morality to identify and to transcend the limitations of its rival or rivals, limitations which can be—although

they may not in fact have been—identified by the rational standards to which the protagonists of the rival morality are committed by their allegiance to it, that the rational superiority of that
particular moral philosophy and that particular morality emerges.
(*AV*, 268–269; see also *MA*, 222–223; *WJ*, 143–144; *TRV*, 145–146,
173; *PPI*, 78–79)

A moral tradition is assessed, not only on its ability to identify, explain,
and transcend the limitations of its rivals, but also on its own ability to
avoid or resolve epistemological crises. Accordingly, like any other
scheme of beliefs, a moral theory should be comprehensive (leave
nothing out which can be shown to be relevant), coherent (suffer from
no logical or performative self-contradictions), and resourceful (address successfully its own recognized problems, either by providing solutions or by showing them to be misconceived, and make progress
relative to its own objectives). Hence, the aspiration of theoretical
moral enquiry as exemplified in the work of Aquinas is to formulate a
conceptual framework that, in its ability to integrate the strengths as
well as identify the limitations of rival traditions, demonstrates itself
to be more comprehensive, coherent, and resourceful than any rival
moral framework.

> *His* counterposing of authority to authority was designed to exhibit
> what in each case could withstand dialectical testing from every
> standpoint so far developed, with the aim of identifying both the
> limitations of each point of view and what in each point of view
> could not be impugned by even the most rigorous of such tests.
> Hence the claim implicitly made by Aquinas against any rival out
> of the past is that the partiality, one-sidedness, and incoherences
> of that rival's standpoint will have already been overcome in the
> unfinished system portrayed in the *Summa*, while its strengths and
> successes will have been incorporated and perhaps reinforced.
> Against any similar claim from the future the corresponding claims
> would be that it too could be brought into the dialectical conver-
> sation at every point and that the test of Aquinas' standpoint would
> lie in its ability to identify the limitations and to integrate the
> strengths and successes of each rival into its overall structure.
> (*WJ*, 207; cf. *TRV*, 146)

From this we see that when MacIntyre characterizes dialectical debate between rival moral traditions in general terms, he describes it in much the same way as he describes debate between any two competing and incommensurable schemes of beliefs. At the same time, MacIntyre presents moral traditions as having two distinctive features that result in correspondingly distinctive characteristics of the arguments between them. The first distinctive characteristic of debate among moral traditions is its scope. Because the strength of the individual beliefs of an overall moral scheme is, in part, a function of their contribution to a coherent whole, and the strength of the overall scheme is, in part, a function of the plausibility of its individual beliefs, *and* because moral theories integrate positions on a wide range of historical, normative, empirical, and logical issues, the scope of dialectical argument between moral traditions is very broad. For example, given the expectation that any conception of the proper norms and priorities for human life should form a coherent whole with an associated set of ontological and epistemological beliefs, the questions debated between rival moral traditions will include how human nature should be conceived and which forms of knowledge should be considered valid (*AV*, 259; *TRV*, 230).

The second distinctive characteristic of debate among rival moral traditions is related to their common interest. The foundational assumption of Thomistic dialectic is that "the world is what it is independently of human thinking and judging and desiring and willing. There is a single true view of the world and of its ordering, and for human judgments to be true and *for human desiring and willing to be aimed at what is genuinely good they must be in conformity with that divinely created order*" (*TRV*, 66–67; my italics). In line with this assumption, Thomism holds that the scheme of moral beliefs that best represents the true nature of the world and the human condition is able (a) to articulate norms and priorities for a form of social life that will eventually be recognized as most satisfying or fulfilling, and (b) to explain the practical failings and disappointments of those committed to the norms and priorities of rival traditions (*AV*, 195–196, 199, 261–262; *WJ*, 89, 111–112). In MacIntyre's Thomistic version of moral enquiry, then, the rationally superior moral tradition will integrate the points of view of rival traditions within its own narrative framework by incorporating strengths and identifying limitations of a particular kind. Its scheme of beliefs and corresponding narrative will prove more able than the equivalent resources of rival traditions (a) to incorporate what its competitors have correctly identified, explicitly or implicitly, to be essential and integral aspects of the best human life; (b) to name those aspects of the best human life that they have failed to appreciate explicitly but are unable to do without; and (c) to uncover what in their practices or point of view accounts for that failure.[20] It is in this way that members of one moral tradition could demonstrate that their point of view is rationally superior to the perspective of its competitors.

Conditions for Productive Debate among Incommensurable Moral Traditions

MacIntyre cautions that because there are no tradition-independent standards of rational assessment—in particular, no agreement on the proper narrative structure of human life—there is no guarantee that those committed to rival moral traditions will emerge from dialectical debate with their conflicts resolved. It may happen that, for some indefinite period of time, neither of two conflicting moral traditions will provide its members with the resources required to demonstrate its superiority according to its own standards of rational adequacy, much less those of its rival (*WJ*, 328). This may happen in part because the adherents of one or both traditions are unwilling or unable to acknowledge their own limitations and the strengths of their competitors.[21] And it may happen because the relative degree of satisfaction that attends different sets of priorities for human living only becomes evident over a long period of time.

In his more general account of the rationality of traditions, MacIntyre acknowledges that although participating in an encounter with a genuinely different perspective can lead to greater self-knowledge, it can be a difficult and demanding process, in part because self-knowledge can require self-transformation. The same holds true *a fortiori* in encounters between rival and incommensurable moral points of view (*TRV*, 120). For example, MacIntyre states that to have reached understanding across linguistic and cultural differences, a moral tradition may have had "to enrich itself significantly in order to be able to provide a representation of some of the characteristic positions of the other, and this enrichment will have involved both conceptual and linguistic innovation, and quite possible social innovation too" (*WJ*, 370). Such difficulties are doubled when the members of *both* of two incommensurable traditions are actively trying to appreciate the other perspective in its own terms. Because of the effort required to succeed in understanding across differences—or even to make the attempt—MacIntyre holds that productive debate between adherents of two rival and incommensurable moral traditions is likely to occur only under certain psychological, socio-cultural, economic, and political conditions.

To begin with, already we have seen how MacIntyre believes that productive dialectical debate is more likely to occur if at least one of the traditions involved has previously passed through an epistemological crisis. The assumption is that a tradition which has had to revise and/or replace some of its fundamental agreements will be more likely to allow both that its current self-understanding is also open to improvement, and that a rival scheme of beliefs might be more adequate to their problems than their own (*WJ*, 388). Like many other philosophers, MacIntyre understands a willingness to explore unfamiliar perspectives, even at the price of discomfort, to be a basic psychological condition for understanding across frameworks.

In addition, if it is to be possible to appreciate rival points of view in their own terms, there must be material resources sufficient to support ongoing theoretical enquiry, in which, for example, texts must be collected, preserved, translated, and interpreted; and the commitments implicit in social practices must be objectified in a systematic way.[22] There must also be people both willing and able to undertake systematic scholarly activity, *and* people able and (ideally) willing to support such activity. Similarly, with regard to the political conditions of dialectic, MacIntyre contends that there must exist hospitable or at least tolerant institutional contexts in which ongoing theoretical enquiry can take place without undue interference, and in which rival perspectives can be admitted without distortion (*TRV*, 6–7, 151–152). Finally, dialectical assessment requires that at least one tradition has the resources, and at least one of its members the insight and creativity, to construct a framework within which the strengths and limitations of the rival traditions can be compared in a meaningful way (*WJ*, 143; *TRV*, 119–120, 181; *PPI*, 79–80). Because of these conditions, MacIntyre believes that instances of productive dialectical debate in which moral traditions are substantively transformed through encounters with their rivals are comparatively rare.

Summary

MacIntyre argues that moral traditions are evaluated, like other traditions of enquiry, from the point of view of one or another historical tradition and with respect to their degree of success in internal and external debates. To be successful in internal debates, a scheme of beliefs must be coherent, comprehensive, and resourceful with respect to that tradition's problematic. In addition, to be successful in external debates, it must be able to render competing schemes of beliefs "intelligible in a way that cannot be achieved by their own adherents from their own point of view and to distinguish their defects and limitations from their insights and merits in such a way as to explain the occurrence of what they themselves would have to take to be their defects and limitations at points at which their own explanatory capacities are resourceless" (*TRV*, 125). Thus, in MacIntyre's Thomistic view of dialectical debate among rival *moral* traditions, the rationally superior scheme of beliefs will be that which is able to show itself to be more comprehensive, coherent, and resourceful than its rivals, but especially resourceful in one particular way: Because it represents the most accurate view of the world and the human condition—including, in particular, the most adequate conception of the overriding human good—*the rationally superior moral tradition will prove to be a more reliable guide than its rivals to living the most fulfilling human life.* It will be able to integrate the stories told by those committed to rival traditions within its own narrative framework precisely because it will be able to show both how and why their norms and priorities for human life are distorted by a false conception of human potential.

Can the Thomistic ethics of virtue demonstrate its rational superiority in these terms?

THE CASE FOR THE ETHICS OF VIRTUE

To be consistent with his account of the rationality of moral traditions, MacIntyre must do two things to justify his confidence in his Thomistic scheme of beliefs. First, he must show through internal debates how the Thomistic scheme is not only comprehensive and coherent, but also resourceful enough to address successfully the problems internal both to the Aristotelian and Augustinian traditions while maintaining continuity with their core assumptions. Second, MacIntyre must show through external debates how the Thomistic ethics of virtue has the conceptual resources both to succeed where rival moral traditions fail and to provide explanations for their failures.[23] With regard to his first task: MacIntyre provides a narrative reconstruction of the ethics of virtue in which he argues that Aristotle solved many of Plato's problems (*WJ*, 85; *FG*, 243, 246); and that Aquinas integrated the strengths of the Aristotelian and Augustinian schemes in a comprehensive, coherent framework that corrected each tradition's previous limitations (*TRV*, 123–124). In the first section of this chapter, I have summarized some of the key claims and arguments of MacIntyre's reconstruction of Thomism. Whether or not the result is faithful to Aquinas' point of view, and whether or not Aquinas did succeed in integrating Aristotle into Augustine's Christian neo-Platonism, are both important questions. However, they are outside my present concern, which is with what can be learned from MacIntyre's account of the rationality of traditions about the external debates through which rival and incommensurable moral points of view might be assessed. Consequently, I will limit myself to illustrating MacIntyre's external debates, presenting his arguments for the rational superiority of the Thomistic point of view relative to its foremost current contenders, Nietzschean genealogy and Kantian liberalism.[24]

The Case against Genealogy

MacIntyre portrays genealogy as attempting to undermine claims to objectivity both by discrediting discourses of truth as products of power-relationships and by discounting notions of a perspective-independent world as metaphysical fictions (*TRV*, 42, 205; cf. *AV*, 258). MacIntyre's case against the genealogical project is based largely on an argument that, in the act of engaging in "polemical conversations"—whether by writing texts, giving lectures, or participating in verbal exchanges—genealogy is involved in a performative self-contradiction. On the one hand, he argues, the practice of engaging in even polemical conversations is only intelligible if continuity of identity is ascribed to the participants (*TRV*, 45–46, 196); on the other hand, genealogy is necessarily committed to denying continuity of identity as just another "metaphysical fiction." MacIntyre thus seeks to reveal an internal incoherence in the genealogical project by asking "Who is undertaking it, for whom is it intended, and for what reasons?"

Having raised these questions, MacIntyre considers a possible Nietzschean response to the effect that personal identities are fictions which, like masks, can be adopted for the purpose of a momentary encounter and then later discarded. But, argues MacIntyre, if genealogy adopts such a view of identity, then it faces the problem of explaining "how to combine the fixity of particular stances, exhibited in the use of standard genres of speech and writing, with the mobility of transition from stance to stance; how to assume the contours of a given mask . . . without ever assenting to the metaphysical fiction of a face which has its own finally true and undiscardable representation" (*TRV*, 47). Through such arguments, MacIntyre registers strong doubts that anyone would be able to construct an intelligible narrative of the genealogical project, or even use language in a meaningful way, without implicitly affirming metaphysical commitments of the kind that genealogy explicitly rejects.

> For in making his or her sequence of strategies of masking and unmasking intelligible to him or herself, the genealogist has to ascribe to the genealogical self a continuity of deliberate purpose and a commitment to that purpose which can only be ascribed to a self not to be dissolved into masks and moments, a self which cannot but be conceived as more and other that its disguises and concealments and negotiations, a self which just insofar as it can adopt alternative perspectives is itself not perspectival, but persistent and substantial. Make of the genealogical self nothing but what genealogy makes of it, and that self is dissolved to the point at which there is no longer a continuous genealogical project. Or so I am suggesting. (*TRV*, 54; cf. 213–214)

MacIntyre has included within the conceptual scheme of the ethics of virtue a belief that continuity of personal identity is provided by an enacted narrative. Unsurprisingly, then, MacIntyre not only discerns substantive selves behind genealogical masks, but also "shadow narratives" behind genealogical histories (*TRV*, 209). He suggests that both selves and narratives remain unacknowledged within genealogy precisely because it lacks a conceptual scheme within which they could find a fitting place.

MacIntyre believes that genealogical utterances have succeeded in undermining confidence in encyclopaedic rationality (*TRV*, 55–56, 229). He also allows that genealogy might find the resources within itself to resolve its internal problematic. Nevertheless, from his Thomistic point of view, all attempts to date to carry through the genealogical project have lapsed into performative self-contradiction in their dependence upon traditional genres of argument and of narrative (*TRV*, 53–55, 209, 215, 218). In other words, genealogy has been unable to avoid internal incoherence because, in rejecting objectivity, truth, and the continuity of personal identity, it has removed the necessary presuppositions of its practices of argument and social criticism.

Through such arguments, MacIntyre maintains that the Thomistic scheme of beliefs provides resources for identifying what genealogy has lacked in order to make progress. He further maintains that, in contrast, genealogical critiques of encyclopaedic conceptions of and pretensions to universal rationality have no force against a Thomistic account of the rationality of traditions (*AV*, 257). Indeed, he contends that the ethics of virtue succeeds where genealogy fails precisely because its conception of dialectical enquiry provides a coherent standpoint for rejecting objectivistic claims without lapsing into incoherent forms of relativism. And, finally, he argues that Thomism provides an explanation of how Nietzsche came to conceive genealogy in a way that is fundamentally flawed. For in rejecting the morality of his European contemporaries, Nietzsche cut himself off from the kind of participation in a community which is, from the Thomistic point of view, the precondition of successful moral enquiry (*AV*, 258). And, in his self-proclaimed isolation from his contemporaries, Nietzsche displayed precisely the kind of pride that the Thomist understands to be the root of intellectual and moral error.

Where Nietzsche saw the individual will as a fiction, as part of a mistaken psychology which conceals from view the impersonal will to power, the Thomist can elaborate out of materials provided in the *Summa* an account of the will to power as an intellectual fiction

> disguising the corruption of the will. The activity of unmasking is
> itself to be understood from the Thomistic standpoint as a mask
> for pride. (*TRV*, 147)

Of course, in showing that the ethics of virtue provides an explanation
for genealogy's difficulties, MacIntyre is not thereby demonstrating
that this explanation is true. That explanation would be plausible to
the extent that the Thomistic scheme as a whole achieves wide reflective equilibrium, which, as he himself observes, MacIntyre has yet to
show. Thus, MacIntyre proposes that the case for and against genealogy is still open (*TRV*, 115). At the same time, he believes that the evidence to date gives good grounds for confidence that the Thomistic
scheme of beliefs is and will continue to be the more rationally defensible point of view.

The Case against Liberalism

MacIntyre portrays liberalism as attempting to formulate universal
moral principles that could not consistently be denied by any rational
person. Some versions of Kantian liberalism, for example, try to derive
moral principles from a conception of rational agency. On MacIntyre's
analysis, liberalism seeks to provide some such universal, rational basis
or ground for morality because it rejects any proposal to justify moral
principles with reference to a particular conception of *the* good, or of
the best human life.

> On the dominant view it is held that either because rational agree-
> ment on the nature of the good life for human beings cannot be
> reached or just because as a matter of fact it has not been reached
> or because it is a key part of the freedom of each individual to
> choose whatever he or she takes to be the best life for him or her-
> self, the rules that constitute morality must be neutral between al-
> ternative and conflicting views of the good for human beings.
> Pluralism about the good is to coexist with rational agreement on
> the rules of morality. (*AET*, 499)

MacIntyre's case that liberalism has failed according to its own criteria
of success is based upon three related claims. The first is that liberal-

ism is unable to account adequately for the existence of widespread disagreement on moral principles. He argues that if the fundamental
principles of morality were truly undeniable by any rational person,
then liberalism should be able to explain disagreement on moral principles as a symptom of irrationality. However, moral philosophers (who
one might expect to be paragons of rationality) have only multiplied
their conflicts since the Enlightenment (*TRV*, 189; cf *WJ*, 234–235).
And, more significantly, even those who are committed to the liberal
project and so share a basic philosophical purpose and method have
been unable to reach agreement on which moral principles rational
agency entails (*AV*, 21; 45–47, 259, 271; *WJ*, 334–335).

MacIntyre's second claim is that liberalism fails, not only because its
advocates are unable either to resolve or to explain their disputes, but
also because they are unable to justify the moral principles they profess
in a way that is neutral with respect to competing accounts of the good.
As a test case for this claim, MacIntyre examines the arguments of Alan
Gewirth, which he cites as an exemplary attempt to derive principles
of justice from an analysis of rational agency. Gewirth's attempt fails,
on MacIntyre's reading, because it covertly introduces normative assumptions in the form of a notion of "natural" human rights—rights,
that is, that are conceived without reference to the beliefs of any particular religious, political, social, or contractual context (*AV*, 66–68).

MacIntyre argues that human rights cannot be derived from a conception of rational agency that is neutral to competing moral traditions
because rights claims are unintelligible when abstracted from the conceptual scheme and social practices of particular historical traditions.
To drive home this point, he remarks that trying to claim a right in a
social context that has no concept of rights is like trying to cash a
cheque in a society which has no money and no banks. MacIntyre asserts that "natural" rights of the kind invoked by Gewirth are a fiction,
they "plainly" do not exist, and "belief in them is one with belief in
witches and in unicorns." In this way, MacIntyre argues that conceptions of rational agency are either too "thin" to ground useful principles of justice or too "thick" to be neutral among competing moral
traditions. Consequently, liberals must appeal to notions such as natural rights, moral intuitions, and utility to provide the semblance of justification for the supposedly universal principles of justice they profess.
Upon closer inspection, however, these notions prove either to be empty

or to incorporate substantive normative beliefs particular to one or another liberal point of view (*AV*, 69–70; cf. *WJ*, 176).

MacIntyre's third claim is that, because it relies upon normative commitments specific to its particular point of view, liberalism, like genealogy, becomes involved in a performative self-contradiction. For in denying any influence upon public policy to the beliefs of those committed to particular accounts of the human good, liberalism privileges its own scheme of moral beliefs, including its view of the best human life. MacIntyre argues, in other words, that its political ideals entail "not only that liberal individualism does indeed have its own broad conception of the good, which it is engaged in imposing politically, legally, socially, and culturally wherever it has the power to do so, but also that in so doing its toleration of rival conceptions of the good in the public arena is severely limited" (*WJ*, 336; cf. 345; Moon 1993, 7–8). Liberalism compounds its failure to provide a tradition-independent rational justification for its moral principles by imposing those principles upon people who subscribe to other traditions, because this imposition contravenes liberalism's own principles of justice, tolerance, and respect for persons. Kohlberg's theory again serves as a case in point; here, in its attempt to provide a secular, universal basis for moral education in a pluralistic democracy. As Fernhout (1989) argues, the liberal individualism of Kohlberg's theory is *not* neutral with respect to rival traditions, and cannot form the basis of a society that would be neutral to competing accounts of the good.

As in his analysis of genealogy, MacIntyre proposes that the Thomistic scheme of beliefs has the resources to explain why its rival has failed in its own terms. The reason that modern liberalism, whether Kantian or otherwise, is unable to make progress is that it has inherited the limitations of its Enlightenment predecessors. MacIntyre contends that Kant's attempt to base moral principles upon practical rationality, Hume's attempt to base moral principles upon the passions, and Kierkegaard's attempt to ground morality in choice all failed and indeed *had* to fail because their conceptual schemes all lacked certain key features of a teleological world view. What were they missing?

On MacIntyre's definition, a teleological moral scheme has three basic components: (a) an analysis of how people are now, (b) a conception of how people could be if they realized their full potential, and (c) a description of how people could make the transition from the former to the latter state (*AV*, 52–53). Because it is assumed within such teleological frameworks that we all have the same basic human nature and potential, it is believed that we will all experience frustration and disappointment to the degree that we fail to realize the human *telos*.[25] Accordingly, within teleological schemes, ethical virtues and precepts are justified to the extent they help people achieve the highest form of human satisfaction or fulfilment. This means that teleological ethics can be rational in two senses: (a) because it is arguably in everyone's best interests to cultivate moral virtues and to observe moral precepts and (b) because reason is capable of identifying both the highest human potential and the way of life required to fulfil it (*WJ*, 44–45).

In MacIntyre's narrative, as I have already mentioned, belief in teleological frameworks broke down with the rise of a formal or "technical" view of reason. On this view, "reason is calculative; it can assess truths of fact and mathematical relations but nothing more. In the realm of practice therefore it can speak only of means. About ends it must be silent" (*AV*, 54). MacIntyre submits that Enlightenment thinkers as diverse as Hume, Kant, and Kierkegaard all accept that reason apprehends no innate potentiality in either human nature or the world, and so all reject "any view of man as having an essence which defines his true end" (*AV*, 54). In thus eliminating from ethics the teleological notion of human nature in a perfected state, the Enlightenment conception of rationality left its philosophers without a clear basis for the justification of ethical virtues or laws.[26] Thus the liberal project is doomed to failure, in MacIntyre's narrative, for two related reasons: (a) the moral principles, rules, and practices they are trying to justify were originally part of one or another teleological world view, and require belief in an overriding human good in order to be fully intelligible;[27] and (b) liberalism's technical or formal conception of rationality provides no basis for new substantive moral principles. In other words, because it remains preoccupied with the Enlightenment ideal of context-free justification, liberalism is blind to the way in which a tradition's commitments can receive historical vindication (*WJ*, 7).

To support his explanation of liberalism's lack of success, MacIntyre identifies a number of problems with its scheme of beliefs that are directly related to its rejection of teleology. One problem concerns the meaning and force of the word *ought* in moral prescriptions. Within a teleological framework, the meaning and force of saying that we ought to obey ethical precepts and/or ought to cultivate intellectual and moral virtues is clear: we *ought* to do so *if* we wish to live the kind of life that will lead to realization of our highest good (*WJ*, 203). The force of saying we *ought* to desire our highest good more than we desire anything else is also clear: we *ought* to do so *if* we wish to avoid the frustration that inevitably arises when desires run contrary to human nature. In contrast, once the notion of innate human potential no longer plays a central role in ethics, it is no longer clear what the *ought* of moral prescriptions could mean or why they should be heeded (*AV*, 60; *TRV*, 193–194).

Earlier we have seen how MacIntyre maintains that once norms and priorities can no longer be justified with reference to the overriding human good, then they are generally justified with reference *either* to reason independently of desire *or* to pre-reflective passions. In the first case, the force of *ought* is not hypothetical but simply categorical: we are expected to do our moral duty simply because it is our moral duty. The problem MacIntyre sees in this approach is that it leaves it unexplained how or why anyone would or should be motivated to be moral (*TRV*, 178, 187; *RVG*, 12–13). In the second case, the force of ought derives simply from our existing scales of preferences: we ought to do what will maximize the accomplishment or fulfilment of what we now happen to desire. The problem MacIntyre finds with this approach is that it eliminates any distinction between what we desire and what we ought to desire, and so it fails to provide an adequate basis for critical social and political practice. Furthermore, when our desires are not educated in light of the human *telos*, what we now happen to desire might well not be what is in our true best interests (*RVG*, 13).

MacIntyre identifies two further, closely related problems internal to liberalism that arise from its rejection of teleology: "that of the liberal self and that of the common good in a liberal social order" (*WJ*, 346). When we share a teleological world view, then the diverse ends of our various activities and practices can be coordinated with reference to our shared vision of the best human life. Within such a social context, the aspects of our identities corresponding to the various spheres of activity in which we participate—as family member, student, worker, citizen, artist, friend—can be integrated in a harmonious way. Furthermore, we can learn through membership in forms of activity such as practices that are directed towards common goals, goals that in turn contribute to a way of life directed towards *the* good, how everyone's best interests are interconnected: "goods are so ordered and understood that the self cannot achieve its own good except in and through achieving the good of others and vice versa" (*TRV*, 192). Conversely, when the possibility of an overriding human good is rejected, and there is a "growing disagreement as to what the goods of human beings are and how or whether they are to be hierarchically ordered," then we have no clear basis either for prioritizing our individual desires or for social cooperation (*WJ*, 337–338; *TRV*, 190–193).

MacIntyre further supports his analysis of liberalism's limitations by arguing that its failures explain certain features of contemporary North American societies in which the language of liberal individualism is predominant. First, that liberalism invokes notions of rights or of utility that are either empty or ungrounded explains why current moral debates are interminable. Second, that there is no shared agreement within a liberal social framework on what should count as a good reason for a moral commitment, combined with the fact that moral language is still used in arguments for and against particular social policies, explains why (a) moral principles are often left vague and imprecise, (b) people tend not to defend their moral claims so much as to declare them, and (c) people can unmask the pretensions of other people's claims to moral objectivity (*AV*, 70–72; cf. *AET*, 510; *WJ*, 2–3).

If liberalism truly exhibits these philosophical shortcomings, why then has it become the dominant language of moral discourse in the West? MacIntyre attributes the domination of liberalism in part to its easy conformity with capitalist market economies (*WJ*, 336). In other words, MacIntyre endeavours to show that liberal views of persons, of justice-and-practical-rationality, and of the market economy form a coherent and mutually supporting whole (*WJ*, 335–339). He also suggests that those educated in accordance with a liberal conception of rationality will likely not recognize the limitations of its point of view. This is because the individual so educated will lack training in the moral virtues and therefore will likely not experience the way of life in which the human *telos* is apprehended and appreciated (*WJ*, 176– 179). Finally, MacIntyre offers an explanation of why liberalism continues to seek rational justification for moral concepts and practices that have no coherent place in its basic ontological and epistemological framework. It is part of the Thomistic scheme of beliefs that every person has an innate grasp of fundamental moral precepts, a "natural knowledge of divine law." Although it can be left undeveloped in some cultural contexts or distorted in others, this initial apprehension of moral precepts is ineradicable. MacIntyre proposes that it is because they have such an innate moral sense that liberals are reluctant to abandon traditional moral values. He concludes that, because he is able to construct a narrative framework that both incorporates liberalism's strengths and identifies the source of its limitations, Thomism is a more rationally defensible moral tradition than liberalism (*TRV*, 194, cf. 76; *WJ*, 179–180).

Looking Back, Looking Ahead

Through his various publications, MacIntyre presents a narrative reconstruction of the history of moral enquiry in which the ethics of virtue is portrayed as a more coherent, comprehensive, resourceful, and dialectically defensible scheme of moral beliefs than its rivals. In MacIntyre's narrative, Thomism emerges superior from its encounter with genealogy and liberalism because it can match their accomplishments while avoiding their failures *and* integrate them into its narrative framework. It does so by showing how their failures are intelligible within its account of moral enquiry as a quest for the overriding human good that depends for its success upon the natural and supernatural virtues (*RVG*, 12–14). In contrast, according to MacIntyre's analysis, genealogy and liberalism are unable to succeed either in their own objectives or in dialectical debate with the ethics of virtue because they both lack two essential aspects of the Thomistic scheme of beliefs. One, because they lack an understanding of the rationality of traditions, they are faced with the sterile alternatives of radical relativism or empty universalism. Two, because they have rejected teleological world views, they are unable to recognize explicitly the narrative unity of human life, or to justify the normative commitments implicit in their political practices. In addition, or so MacIntyre maintains, both genealogy and liberalism cannot avoid implicitly affirming normative commitments that have no place in their schemes of belief—and so cannot avoid engendering performative self-contradictions—because they cannot escape either their innate apprehension of basic moral precepts or their desire for human fulfilment.

In making the case for his Thomistic ethics of virtue against *encyclopaedia* and genealogy, MacIntyre illustrates the practice of dialectical debate among rival and incommensurable moral traditions. As I have characterized the process of seeking wide reflective equilibrium, the set of fundamental agreements shared by members of a community of enquiry—their beliefs, attitudes, interests, norms, priorities, and practices—are justified to the extent that (a) they together form a coherent and mutually supporting whole; (b) they also form a coherent and mutually supporting whole with the world view and way of life in which that community of enquiry is embedded; (c) they result in satisfactory progress in fulfilling that community of enquiry's fundamental intentions (which includes resolving epistemological crises); and (d) they are defensible in dialectical encounters with rival paradigms of enquiry. This chapter has shown how MacIntyre's arguments for the rational superiority of his Thomistic scheme of moral beliefs conform both to his general account of dialectical debate and to my more detailed characterization of non-foundational justification.

In chapter three, I proposed that the process of vindicating agreements shared within a community of enquiry involves more than internal and external debates among explicitly formulated schemes of beliefs. In the next three chapters, I develop that proposal by showing how the search for wide reflective equilibrium within and among rival moral points of view incorporates an experiential dimension that is largely absent from MacIntyre's account of the rationality of moral traditions. Precisely because it neglects this crucial dimension of moral development and moral discourse, the ethics of virtue will be seen to fall short of its own criteria of success.

CHAPTER FIVE

The Intellectualist Bias

"Finding I could speak the language of ants, I approached one
and inquired, 'What is God like? Does he resemble the ant?'
He answered, 'God! No, indeed—we have only a single sting,
but God, He has *two*!'"

—Indries Shah, *Thinkers of the East*

In this chapter, I present a critical review of MacIntyre's ethics of
virtue. My purpose in this book is not to defend a comprehensive moral
theory, but to argue for the possibility of productive moral discourse in
a pluralistic world. Consequently, although I have questions about
many of his claims, I limit my review of MacIntyre's scheme of beliefs
to those aspects that substantially affect his characterization of the rationality of moral traditions, and so directly concern the issue of how incommensurable moral perspectives can be assessed in a non-circular
and non-foundational way.

My review is focused on indications of an intellectualist bias in
MacIntyre's work. By *an intellectualist bias*, I refer to a set of related
tendencies

1. to equate the highest, most uniquely human faculty with reason
   (where *reason* is identified with the intellect; and *the intellect* is the capacity for having, formulating, and deductively developing *ideas* into
   an abstract, logically consistent conceptual framework), and to overlook, deny, or disparage other cognitive faculties;
2. to equate cognition primarily or even exclusively with the exercise
   of the intellect, and to overlook, deny, or disparage other forms of

cognitive activity—in particular, to equate learning with theoretical enquiry, conceived as the construction of abstract conceptual schemes through the objectification and justification of beliefs, and to privilege theoretical over practical enquiry;[1]

3. to equate knowledge primarily or even exclusively with some subset of the beliefs that are capable of being formulated as propositions (e.g., the set of true and justified beliefs), and to overlook, deny, or disparage other forms of knowledge;

4. to equate the justification of points of view primarily or even exclusively with dialectical comparisons of the relative coherence of explicit schemes of beliefs, and to neglect other forms or criteria of justification; and

5. to equate what exists, or what exists in the highest, truest, fullest sense, with what is intellectually intelligible.

I refer to this set of tendencies as a bias because, as I will argue later, it operates to restrict enquiry in ways that are both unwarranted and unnecessary. Although theoretical enquiry is an important and powerful form of learning, it is not the only or even the most important form, particularly in the moral context. Nor is reasoning the only or even the most important human cognitive activity.

Although my critical questions are addressed specifically to MacIntyre, I do not wish to suggest that the set of tendencies listed above is peculiar to his work. On the contrary, I understand the intellectualist bias to be firmly rooted in Hellenistic dualism and so—particularly since its reinforcement by positivism—a persistent feature of mainstream Western culture.[2] I focus on indications of an intellectualist bias in my review of MacIntyre because I believe that it contributes to a widespread uncertainty about the nature of intrinsic moral value and so presents a serious obstacle to the project of assessing rival moral points of view.[3] Conversely, I hope that my challenge to the intellectualist bias will contribute to productive moral discourse in a pluralistic world.

PRACTICAL RATIONALITY AND MORAL EDUCATION

One significant difficulty with MacIntyre's ethics of virtue indicative of an intellectualist bias is that he examines the contributions of theoretical enquiry to ethics in great detail, but he pays scant attention to other components of practical judgment and moral education that *on his own account* are equally important. As a consequence, he leaves the following crucial questions unanswered.

What Is *Perception?*

MacIntyre refers to perception of particulars as a critical component of practical judgment (*WJ*, 116, 125). This is consistent with his claim that incommensurable theoretical perspectives produce conflicting characterizations of "the facts" (*WJ*, 332; *TRV*, 111–113; *PPI*, 68). For if concrete contexts of practice cannot be characterized in a way that is neutral to competing moral traditions, then deliberation, decision, and action will be shaped by what perception selects as the salient moral features of a situation (*ITC*, 110). On this view, it would follow that we can only arrive at sound practical judgments if we have already developed a capacity for accurate perception.

In a discussion of the work of Simone Weil and Iris Murdoch, MacIntyre underlines the necessity of accurate perception to sound practical judgment by remarking that "one *sine qua non* of human goodness is the ability to see things as they are; and to see things as they are is a morally difficult task." He concludes that "A part of moral philosophy and moral psychology must therefore be concerned with how we do come to see things as they are, the varieties of ways in which we may fail, the variety of causes of failure, and the kind of discipline that can overcome these obstacles" (*MP*, 12–13; *WJ*, 92). How, then, according to MacIntyre, can we come "to see things as they are"?

MacIntyre insists that moral education is a prerequisite to sound practical judgment, and he provides a brief account of how abstract principles of justice can be formulated through reflection upon the experience of following precepts of just behaviour. However, he provides no analysis of *how* people's explicit beliefs—much less their tacit assumptions—affect their ability to perceive accurately the morally relevant features of a given situation. Furthermore, although he maintains that accurate perception of particulars develops only through the process of making and acting upon practical judgments, MacIntyre does not explain in what sense, under what conditions, or through what processes we could learn from our experience to perceive things "as they are." Indeed, it is not clear how or even whether it would be possible to reconcile this notion of perceiving things "as they are" with his claim that "the facts" are always characterized in the terms of one or another conceptual scheme. How can the ideal of accurate perception be articulated without returning to discredited notions of "the view from nowhere"? This important question remains unanswered because MacIntyre does not explain (a) in what the capacity for accurate perception of particulars consists, (b) how it interacts with other aspects of practical judgment such as the formulation, application, and revision of general moral principles, or (c) how it can be improved through the experience of following precepts of virtuous behaviour.

How Does Habit Educate the Passions?

Like accurate perception, educated desire is critical to MacIntyre's account of practical rationality. He characterizes the fully virtuous person as someone whose passions have been *transformed* (as opposed to merely having been disciplined) through following precepts of virtuous behaviour. Furthermore, he states that it is through the same day-to-day lived experiences by which the passions are transformed that people learn *why* the virtues are correctly desired for their own sake, as well as for their part in living the best human life. He insists that, for these reasons, the transformation of the passions effected by moral education and the corresponding practical, experiential knowledge of the goodness of the virtues is a prerequisite to sound practical judgment: "To be uneducated in the virtues is precisely to be unable as yet to judge rightly what is good or best for oneself" (*WJ*, 109). But *how* does the following of precepts of just behaviour lead to (for example) the love of justice for justice's own sake, as well as for justice's role in the best human life? That the passions, like perception, are transformed only through sincere efforts to do what the genuinely virtuous person would do suggests that the love of justice arises from some aspect of the actual experience of practising just actions (*WJ*, 114–115). Again, however, MacIntyre does not explain how or under what conditions emulating virtuous action is educational. Nor does he explain what the love of justice for justice's own sake contributes to Aristotelian practical rationality such that, in its absence, even the person who does exactly what the just person would do falls short of fully possessing the virtue of justice (*WJ*, 112–113). That is to say, MacIntyre does not explain *why* it is so important that, in Aristotle's understanding, virtues of character are dispositions to *feel* as well as to act in certain ways.[4]

How Can We Know *Which* Actions to Perform in Order to Educate the Passions?

The question of how habit transforms the passions raises the related question of how *reason* can serve to identify, in specific situations, the actions that should be performed in order to build virtues of character. We have already encountered this question in the form of what appears to be a vicious circle: Virtuous dispositions are formed and cultivated through virtuous actions. *Truly* virtuous actions—defined heuristically as what the genuinely virtuous person would do—are identified in sound practical judgments. Sound practical judgment requires reliable conceptions of the overriding good of human life provided by the successful outcome of theoretical moral enquiry. However, both successful theoretical enquiry and sound practical reasoning *presuppose* the prior acquisition of virtuous dispositions (*WJ*, 176–177). How, then, can someone cultivate good character without already possessing the virtues?

I have noted that, in response to this question, MacIntyre proposes that young people can receive sufficient guidance from teachers to acquire enough of the moral virtues to engage productively in theoretical and practical moral enquiry (*TRV*, 82–83, 91–92, 130). The difficulty with this answer is that it does not explain either how young people can be expected to recognize trustworthy teachers or how the teachers themselves learned to be virtuous. Perhaps because he anticipates these concerns, MacIntyre further proposes that we can benefit from instruction because we have an inborn capacity to learn from our experience: "Aquinas held that all education is in an important way self-education: 'a teacher leads someone else to the knowledge of what was unknown in the same way that someone leads him or herself to the knowledge of what was unknown in the course of discovery' (*Quaestiones Disputate De Veritate* XI, 1)" (*TRV*, 129; cf. *WJ*, 177). However, as I have also noted, if individuals are to learn from their experience of making and acting upon practical judgments, then they must have some way of recognizing when their actions do and do not conform to what the genuinely virtuous person would do. MacIntyre's suggestion here is that the soundness of practical judgments will receive retrospective confirmation from the conclusions of theoretical moral enquiry (*WJ*, 119; *FP*, 13). Again, however, because such enquiry relies upon *epagōgē* from sound practical judgments in addition to dialectical debate, then either individuals have the capacity to make or recognize sound practical judgments *prior to* and *independently of* theoretical moral enquiry, or they remain caught within the vicious circle.

MacIntyre's final proposal in regard to this problem of circularity is that there can be a back and forth interaction between moral theory and practice in which "we gradually learn to correct each in the light of the other, moving dialectically between them" (*WJ*, 118). This proposal suggests that it is not enough that the conceptions of the overriding human good formulated through *epagōgē* be tested in dialectical debate, in which only the outcomes of *previous* practical judgments and actions are included (*WJ*, 206–207). It suggests that, in addition, the provisional conclusions of theoretical enquiry must be tested with reference to the success or failure of *subsequent* judgments and actions that adopt those provisional conclusions as guides to achieving the human *telos* (*WJ*, 331). In other words, given the interdependence of the intellectual virtues and the virtues of character within the Thomistic scheme of beliefs, the very possibility of sound practical judgment and effective moral education would seem to presuppose that members of a moral tradition are able to learn, individually and collectively, through a combination of theoretical reflection and practical action. The central importance of this dialectical form of *learning* to MacIntyre's ethics of virtue (an educational process that includes but goes beyond dialectical *argument*) warrants a closer look at practical rationality and moral education in light of how he characterizes the theory-practice relationship.

MORAL THEORY AND MORAL PRACTICE

Roughly speaking, there are three ways of characterizing the relation between theoretical reflection and practical action. Deductive accounts locate learning in theory, seeing practice as the straightforward implementation of general principles developed and justified independently—in metaphysics, perhaps, conceived as first science or first philosophy. Inductive accounts locate learning in practice, seeing theoretical frameworks as mere summaries of convictions developed and justified through particular moments of active engagement with the concrete world. Dialectical accounts locate learning in the back and forth interaction between reflection and action, seeing both theory and practice as incomplete without the other. It is this third way of conceiving the theory-practice relationship that MacIntyre appeals to in order to avoid a vicious circularity within the ethics of virtue. Therefore, it is another significant difficulty indicating an intellectualist bias that, in some cases, MacIntyre appears to locate moral learning *exclusively* in philosophical reflection and to understand moral practice as the implementation of conclusions established through dialectical debate. The result is an unresolved tension within MacIntyre's texts between deductive and dialectical ways of characterizing the theory-practice relationship. In what follows, I show how this unresolved tension manifests in both his characterization of moral traditions as socially embodied moral theories and his deductive model of rational judgment.

Moral Traditions as Socially Embodied Moral Theories

I have noted that MacIntyre often speaks as if a moral point of view is equivalent to a scheme of moral beliefs that either is or could be formulated in propositional form. Indeed, he sometimes gives the impression that moral communities are simply the social embodiment of pre-existing moral philosophies (*MA*, 222–223; *WJ*, 159, 301, 393; *TRV*, 79–80). Perhaps because of this, MacIntyre often speaks as if the rational justification of a moral tradition is equivalent to the vindication of an explicitly formulated conceptual scheme through dialectical debate. Even when he describes moral theories as abstracted from the practices of pre-existing forms of social life, MacIntyre suggests that the further development of a tradition whose scheme has been objectified occurs through the dialectical arguments of those of its members who are engaged in systematic ethical enquiry (*WJ*, 144, 390; *TRV*, 62, 79–80). For example, he implies that the kind of knowledge developed through and implicit in successful moral practice is incapable of response when changing forms of social life demand new kinds of virtuous acts, when "old virtues have to be embodied in new ways and rules extended to cover new contingencies." Only theoretical reflection seems able to generate innovative responses: "In such situations we are forced back to a reconsideration of first principles and how they apply to particulars" (*TRV*, 128–129).[5] On the one hand, then, MacIntyre sometimes speaks as if the kind of collective learning required for a moral tradition's historical development is located purely in the theoretical reflection of its members, whose innovative solutions to epistemological crises are then subsequently embodied in new forms of social life.[6]

On the other hand, MacIntyre also sometimes speaks as if a moral tradition's point of view incorporates more than what is objectified in its moral theory. One example is his suggestion that those wishing to appreciate the incommensurable perspective of a rival tradition must participate as much as possible in its forms of social life, because meaning is embodied in how people act and in what they do not say as much as in what they say.[7] This recognition of the unspoken, tacit dimension of a tradition's point of view supports the earlier conclusion that its development necessarily takes place through embodied practical action *as well as* abstract dialectical debate.

Even after a close reading of MacIntyre's texts, I find it difficult to resolve the tension between the two ways in which he characterizes the theory-practice relationship in his references to the historical development of moral traditions. My problem is that MacIntyre cites no actual cases that would illuminate *how* the day-to-day experiences of people committed to a teleological moral tradition can force them to revise their conceptions of the virtues and/or the proper goal of human living. That he provides no concrete illustrations of the role of experiential knowledge reinforces my overall impression that MacIntyre privileges theory over practice in ethics, even though such a hierarchy cannot be reconciled with other elements of his position. For example, with respect to the historical development of the communities of enquiry committed to Aristotle's teleological ethics, MacIntyre says little about the kinds of considerations to which Aquinas appeals in his arguments for rejecting Aristotle's conception of the overriding good of human life (*WJ*, 192; *TRV*, 137; *RVG*, 15). More generally, in his account of how practices evolve, MacIntyre refers to a kind of "knowing how" that enables the masters of a craft both to reshape what previously were the standards of excellence definitive of that practice *and* to help others to gain the same level of mastery (*TRV*, 65–66, 127–128; cf. *WJ*, 31; *AV*, 222–223). Although he proposes that this kind of proficiency is very relevant to the development of moral enquiry as a kind of virtue-guided craft, he does not examine the nature of this "knowing how to act," which is also a "knowing how to learn how to act," or the way in which it is gained through experience. Instead, he quickly moves on to de-scribe the kind of systematic construction of theoretical frameworks exemplified by Aquinas' *Summa Theologica*, the "metaphysical and theo-logical studies which complete all enquiry" (*TRV*, 130–131). Again, then, even when he suggests that practical experience plays an indis-pensable role in a tradition's development, MacIntyre implies that the kind of learning that comes from attempting to embody moral theo-ries in concrete forms of social life is subordinate to (and perhaps even replaceable by) the conclusions of dialectical debate.

Ethics as Science, Deliberation as Deduction

An unresolved tension between two different ways of understanding the theory-practice relationship is also present in MacIntyre's charac-terization of the role of ethical science in practical deliberation. To ex-plain: In a way that is consistent with his Thomistic view of a perfected science, MacIntyre maintains that theoretical enquiry should aspire to construct and justify through dialectics a set of first principles that would enable the philosopher to derive *deductively* all of the truths rele-vant to that science (*WJ*, 174; *FP*, 26–27; 43–44). Accordingly, Mac-Intyre understands the goal of theoretical enquiry in ethics to be a dialectically defensible conceptual scheme in which first principles for human action are derived from a conception of the overriding good of human life, which forms the "ultimate and basic" first principle of the scheme (*WJ*, 117; cf. 100, 175). And he further maintains that not only is it from one or another conception of the human *telos* that ethical sci-ence should derive general norms and priorities for human action, but it is with reference to the resulting set of first principles that practical judgment should select one from alternative courses of action in par-ticular situations (*WJ*, 125; *FP*, 6–7). On this syllogistic model of prac-tical judgment, in other words, deliberation provides major premises by *deducing* immediate priorities for human action from the general principles and "additional premises" supplied by reflection.[8] The minor premise or premises are supplied by perception, which serves only to establish that a particular situation affords an opportunity to re-alize one of the "goods" deductively derived (*AV*, 162; *WJ*, 44–45, 129, 139, 188–189, 275). Apparently, in this interpretation of Thomistic practical rationality, the emotions or passions also contribute nothing to identifying the goods they have been trained by reason to desire: the virtues of character supply only the motivation to act on what practical rationality commands (*AV*, 154, 162; *WJ*, 114, 130, 189, 197, 301; *TRV*, 139). On the one hand, then, MacIntyre frequently appears to locate knowledge of the goodness of a virtuous action *exclusively* in theoretical enquiry. For (a) actions are known to be genuinely virtuous only if they can be justified by a sound practical syllogism; (b) the major premise of a sound practical syllogism establishes the goodness of an action with reference to conceptions of the *telos* or overriding good of human life; (c) conceptions of the overriding good are formulated in philosophical reflection; and (d) dialectical debate identifies one conception of the overriding good as the most adequate of current competing conceptions by demonstrating that it is internal to a conceptual scheme that is more able to withstand objections than rival moral theories (*WJ*, 100–101, 117–119, 130, 144, 172, 206–207; *RVG*, 9).

The impression that MacIntyre privileges theoretical over practical knowledge in ethics is reinforced when he speaks as if confidence in the soundness of practical judgments is only achieved when the human intellect goes beyond mere experience with particulars to grasp "unchanging and primary definitions." Furthermore, in a way that is consistent with locating learning in dialectical debate, MacIntyre regularly speaks as if the kind of qualities that constitute good character *and* the particular actions through which the virtues of character should be cultivated can be deductively derived from theoretical conclusions about the nature of the overriding human good (*AV*, 162; *WJ*, 269, 275; *TRV*, 62, 111). In such references to the role of ethical science, the problem of the circularity arising from the interdependence of the intellectual virtues and the virtues of character has vanished. That MacIntyre understands the conclusions of theoretical reflection to be competent to dictate to practice is further implied when he recommends dialectical enquiry to those who are looking for a rational way to evaluate competing moral traditions (*WJ*, 398–399). For this suggests that the methods of dialectical enquiry can be successfully employed even by those who as yet have no practical, experiential knowledge of the virtues—the kind of knowledge that MacIntyre himself describes as resulting only from efforts to embody the teachings of a moral tradition (*WJ*, 122–123).

On the other hand, in a way that limits the role of ethical science in deliberation, MacIntyre also states that any set of first principles only achieves perfection when dialectical enquiry is complete *and* that the conclusions of dialectic are never final: they are always open to revision (*WJ*, 164, 175, 224, 252; *FP*, 46). Furthermore, he himself sometimes allows that first principles are open to revision in the light of inadequacies revealed, not just through further reflection, but also through the experiences of living out their practical implications (*WJ*, 185; *TRV*, 95–96, 129). And, perhaps most importantly, MacIntyre often insists that it is not possible even to understand the dialectical arguments employed in theoretical moral enquiry without the lived experience of virtuous action that comes from practising the teachings of one or another moral tradition (*WJ*, 176–179, 396–397; *FP*, 15; *TRV*, 62–63, 133, 204; *RVG*, 16). Again, on this version of MacIntyre's position, it would seem that philosophical and theological conclusions about the "specifically human good" must be vindicated by practical success, which in turn requires that there is some way of *recognizing* the rightness and wrongness of particular practical judgments independently of the conclusions of theoretical enquiry. In other words, if we are to learn by evaluating theoretical conclusions about the overriding human good on the basis of our practical experience, then we must have some way of learning to recognize in particular circumstances what the genuinely virtuous person would do: what actions truly conform and conduce to the best human life.

There are three additional features of MacIntyre's ethics of virtue that suggest it is incomplete without an explanation of the nature and conditions of experiential knowledge of the goodness of virtuous actions. First, MacIntyre allows in general that those with practical experience can make sound judgments prior to and independently of philosophical reflection (*FP*, 13). Indeed, he cites with apparent approval Aristotle's observation that practical judgments based only upon experience with particulars are often more accurate than those informed only by philosophical theories.[9] Second, the possibility of such experiential knowledge would seem to be a necessary implication of MacIntyre's (*FP*, 39–40; cf. *TRV*, 134) statement that the practical judgments of a teleological ethics are a kind of empirical truth claim with testable consequences, for to invoke an analogy with modern science is to suggest that experimentation plays an indispensable role in learning along with theory-construction (*AV*, 81). Third, and most significantly, when distancing himself from Aquinas' "tidy" classification of the virtues, MacIntyre explicitly refers to an "empirical" knowledge of

the qualities of good character that is distinct from theoretical conclusions. And he does so in a way that casts doubt on reason's compe-
tence to guide practice simply by deducing priorities for action from
Thomistic metaphysical first principles:

> A Linnaeus or a Mendeleev may indeed have grasped by a brilliant
> intuition an ordering of the empirical materials which is vindicated
> by a later theory; but where our knowledge is genuinely empirical
> we have to be careful not to confuse what we have learnt empiri-
> cally with what is inferred from theory, even from true theory. And
> a good deal of our knowledge of the virtues is in this way empiri-
> cal: we learn what kind of quality truthfulness or courage is, what
> its practice amounts to, what obstacles it creates and what it avoids
> and so on only in key part by observing its practice in others and
> in ourselves. And since we have to be educated into the virtues and
> most of us are incompletely and unevenly educated in them for a
> good part of our lives, there is necessarily a kind of empirical un-
> tidiness in the way that our knowledge of the virtues is ordered,
> more particularly in respect of how the practice of the each relates
> to the practice of all the others. In the face of these considerations
> Aquinas' treatment of the classification of the virtues and his con-
> sequent treatment of their unity raises questions to which we find
> in his text no answer.
>
> For on the one hand the theoretical backing for his classificatory
> scheme has two parts: one is a reiteration of the Aristotelian cos-
> mology and the other is specifically Christian and theological. Yet
> we have every reason to reject Aristotle's physical and biological sci-
> ence, and the part of Christian theology which concerns man's true
> end and which is not Aristotelian metaphysics is on Aquinas' own
> account a matter of faith, not of reason. (*AV*, 178–179)

As with his other references to learning from practical experience, it is
hard to determine the implications of this allusion to an empirical
knowledge of the virtues because MacIntyre never describes how it
could be acquired. In this case, for example, he does not explain *how*
people could learn from observing virtuous practices without *already*
having some ability to recognize *which* actions are genuinely virtuous.

Not only does MacIntyre himself refer to an empirical knowledge of the virtues, he also, as I noted earlier, presents Aquinas as attesting to "a kind of knowledge . . . which is not at all that produced by intellectual enquiry. We can learn what a virtue is through the experience of having our will directed by that virtue" (*WJ*, 194). Aquinas refers to people learning in this way as learning "*per inclinationem*, through the directedness of their lives in living out the virtues" and to the result as "knowledge by way of connaturality" (*WJ*, 194; *TRV*, 128–129). As before, however, it is difficult to ascertain MacIntyre's interpretation of the theory-practice relationship within Thomism because he focuses his attention almost exclusively upon dialectical theoretical enquiry. Indeed, while MacIntyre frequently explains how theoretical reflection can serve to remedy the deficiencies of practical knowledge— "limitations rooted in the relative inarticulacy of the merely practical" (*RVG*, 19; also *WJ*, 117; *ITC*, 106)—nowhere does he illustrate *how* experienced practitioners are able to correct the limitations of general moral principles. For example, MacIntyre reports that intellectual and practical enquiry were "closely intertwined" in the Augustinian understanding of progress toward human perfection, but he describes only the contribution of dialectic to that progress, and not how the "life of faith" informs theoretical reflection (*TRV*, 94–96). Similarly, even though his scheme of beliefs depends so heavily upon the possibility of practical knowledge of the good, and even though he is usually careful to avoid using Thomistic terms without explanation (*TRV*, 197), MacIntyre offers no interpretation of Aquinas' references to "knowledge by way of connaturality," to "the relatively inarticulate apprehensions of those who learn *per inclinationem*," to "the kind of knowledge that faith provides," or to the "plain person's unclouded moral apprehension" (*TRV* 128, 137, 140, 141). Consequently, even if I assume that he accepts Aquinas' position with minor qualifications, MacIntyre's failure to elaborate upon the specifically Christian aspects of that position leaves me unclear about his view of the role of experiential learning in practical judgment and moral education.

Looking Back, Looking Ahead

I have been engaged in examining MacIntyre's references to learning with respect both to the historical development of moral traditions and to the education of character. The examination reveals an unresolved tension in MacIntyre's work between two conflicting ways of characterizing the theory-practice relationship. The tension between his references that locate learning in *epagōgē* and dialectical argument and those that present the conclusions of theoretical enquiry as provisional upon further practical vindication is difficult to resolve because MacIntyre only alludes to the kind of "empirical" knowledge of the virtues that would complement theoretical reflection. It is ironic that, although the necessity of *phronēsis* or *prudentia* to sound practical judgment is a key feature of MacIntyre's ethics of virtue, *how* people can learn from experience to go beyond rules—to co-determine a universal ethical concept or principle by grasping that it is properly instantiated in *this* particular—is left an unexplored mystery (*WJ*, 93, 175, 195–196; *RVG*, 10; *TRV*, 139). MacIntyre thus fails to supply an account of the experiential component of the back and forth interaction between theoretical reflection and practical action within moral traditions, an account that the ethics of virtue requires *in addition to its characterization of dialectical debate* in order to explain how people can learn to be virtuous.

The question of how people could learn to recognize when an action should be performed for its own sake because it is what the genuinely virtuous person would do is closely related to a second, broader question: "What could it mean to say that an end or action *should* be desired for its own sake?" MacIntyre does recognize that if he is to explain why virtues such as justice should be valued as ends and not only as means, then he requires an answer to this second question (*FG*, 250). However, in what follows, a closer look at how MacIntyre characterizes the goodness of the virtues and of the *telos* of human life will again reveal an unresolved tension in his work that manifests an intellectualist bias.

INTRINSIC GOODNESS AND THE VIRTUES

What Is Meant by *Good*?

On MacIntyre's Thomistic view, all actions aim at one or another good (*AV*, 148). Thus, when the term is used without qualification, a *good* is an end at which an action or actions aim.[10] Distinctions among different kinds of goods correspond to distinctions among different kinds of ends. Three such distinctions are important to the ethics of virtue. The first distinction is among (a) *external goods*, those ends that are desired for the sake of (as means to) something else; (b) *internal goods*, those ends that are desired for their own sake as well as being desired for the sake of (as means to) something else; and (c) *the overriding good*, the only end of human action that is desired purely for its own sake—the only end of action that is not also a means. The second distinction is between (a) those goods where the end or purpose of the action is the action itself, as can be the case in playing music or competing at chess; and (b) those goods where the end or purpose of the action is an outcome distinct from the action itself, as can be the case in building houses or studying for exams.[11] The third distinction is between (a) the goods that are mistakenly desired, either as a wrong means to a right end, a wrong means to a wrong end, a right means to a wrong end, or a wrong end; and (b) the goods that are correctly desired, either as a right means to a right end, or a right end. Building upon these distinctions, I will refer to any end that is *correctly* desired for its own sake (regardless of whether or not it is *also* desired for the sake of something else) as *intrinsically* good; and to any end that is *correctly* desired as a means—that is, *only* for the sake of an intrinsic good—as *instrumentally* good.[12] The questions facing the ethics of virtue can now be put more precisely. The broader question is "What could it mean to say that an end (whether an activity or an outcome distinct from the activity that produced it) is correctly desired for its own sake?" The related, more specific question is "In what sense is virtuous activity intrinsically as well as instrumentally good?"

Competing Narratives of the Best Human Life

To begin with the latter question: MacIntyre emphasizes that "every particular view of the virtues is linked to some particular notion of the narrative structure or structures of human life" (*AV*, 174). Therefore, it is significant that there are two important structural differences between Aristotle's and Aquinas' respective narratives of the best human life. The first way in which the Thomistic medieval Christian narrative of human life is not Aristotelian is that its conception of the final end of human striving allows for the redemption of an entire life at its last hour. In contrast, "Aristotle takes the *telos* of human life to be *a certain kind of life;* the *telos* is not something to be achieved at some future point, but in the way our whole life is constructed" (*AV*, 175; MacIntyre's italics). The second way in which the Thomistic narrative is not Aristotelian is that "the notion of a human life as a quest or a journey in which a variety of forms of evil are encountered and overcome requires a conception of evil of which there are at most only intimations in Aristotle's writings" (*AV*, 175). The Thomistic narrative of life as a quest incorporates Augustine's view of evil along with his conception of the will: "Evil is somehow or other such and the human will is somehow or other such that the will can delight in evil. This evil is expressed in defiance of divine law and of human law insofar as it is the mirror of divine law; for to consent to evil is precisely to will to offend against the law" (*AV*, 175). Hence, in MacIntyre's account, Aristotle's scheme of moral beliefs has no equivalent conception of evil at least in part because it has no equivalent conception either of the will or of divine law.

Why the change in narrative form?

MacIntyre suggests that Aquinas adopted Augustine's conceptions of evil and of the will to explain what is unintelligible within Aristotle's scheme: that people can have their desires under rational control and still do what they plainly know to be against their best interests. Aquinas' recourse to the doctrine of redemption can be understood as a response to Aristotle's view that possession of the intellectual and moral virtues is only a *necessary* condition for living the kind of life that is the overriding good of the human species. Possession of the virtues is not a *sufficient* condition, from the Aristotelian point of view, because the best intentions can be frustrated by a lack of material resources or other external conditions. It is not difficult to appreciate why a narrative of human life in which reaching its highest goal is contingent upon good fortune would be rejected by those committed to belief in the all-powerful, just, and beneficent God of Christian theism (*AV*, 158, 176). Accordingly, Aquinas' conception of the virtues as the natural and supernatural qualities required to overcome evil in the quest for final redemption can be understood as a response to these two perceived shortcomings in Aristotle's ethics.

What MacIntyre does not explicitly acknowledge is that, in departing from the Aristotelian form of narratives of the best human life, the structure of Thomistic narratives creates a significant problem for the ethics of virtue. In Aristotle's scheme of beliefs, each intellectual virtue and virtue of character represents the perfection of a particular capacity of the human species. Hence, Aristotle can be read as defining the human *telos* as an entire life in which these capacities are actualized in various kinds of activities, in which the end or good is the activity itself and not some outcome distinct from the exercise of the virtues.[13] In this Aristotelian view, virtuous feeling and conduct is correctly desired for its own sake *because* the overriding good *is* the life of virtuous activity (Ackrill 1980, 19–22). In other words, because the various kinds of virtuous acts are understood within Aristotle's teleological scheme as the perfections of the various potentials of a biologically given human nature, they can all be considered components of the best human life by definition. For Aquinas, in contrast, because the overriding good is seen as something that is achieved only "outside and beyond this present life," the virtues are the *means* to attaining the human *telos*. The problem, then, is that, given the form of Aquinas' narrative, it is no longer clear in what sense—if any—virtuous acts can be affirmed as intrinsically good.

It is this problem that results in a tension between the ways in which MacIntyre characterizes the goodness of the virtues. On the one hand, he seems to wish to retain the Aristotelian view that virtuous feeling and conduct are intrinsically good. I have noted, for example, how he maintains that part of what makes genuinely virtuous people virtuous is that they perform just and brave and generous acts for the love of justice and courage and generosity for their own sakes and *not* for the sake of their consequences (*AV*, 150, 198; *WJ*, 112–113; cf. Williams 1985, 10). On the other hand, having adopted the Thomistic narrative, MacIntyre almost invariably describes the goodness of the virtues in *instrumental* terms, as qualities that are desirable because they are necessary to success in the quest for the overriding good (*AV*, 144, 219, 223, 233; *WJ*, 122, 194; *TRV*, 62, 130, 140).

Although MacIntyre does not explicitly acknowledge this tension between intrinsic and instrumental conceptions of the virtues, I believe some recognition of the problem is implicit in his presentation of Aristotle's ethics. For although MacIntyre does describe significant differences between Aristotle and Aquinas, his interpretation of Aristotle tends to highlight those elements of Aristotle's position that can be assimilated to the Thomistic narrative structure and, conversely, to leave in the shadows those elements that contradict the Thomistic point of view. In what follows, I show how this tendency to assimilation *and* its inherent instability results in four sets of difficulties within MacIntyre's attempt to combine Aristotle's and Aquinas' ethics of virtue.

Intrinsic goods and the overriding good

The first set of difficulties concerns whether or not, or to what extent, the variety of intrinsic goods pursued within human life should be considered subordinate to one particular kind of activity identified as the overriding human good. This question is important because, if the construction of a single practical syllogism is to furnish a clear priority for action in a particular situation, then it must refer to a conception of the overriding good that presents one unitary end as the ultimate goal of human action. That conception of the overriding good must also make perfectly clear how pursuit of other intrinsic goods is subordinate to the final end, which becomes the only good desired purely for its own sake. Otherwise, the conclusion that some particular course of action represents an opportunity to realize a genuine good will be insufficient to justify that action *unless* further deliberation *also* establishes that the situation offers no opportunities to realize *other* genuine goods that might take priority over the first (*WJ*, 139–141; *RVG*, 18). MacIntyre uses an example from the game of hockey to illustrate this point:

> A hockey player in the closing seconds of a crucial game has an opportunity to pass to another member of his or her team better placed to score a needed goal. Necessarily, we may say, if he or she has perceived and judged the situation accurately he or she must immediately pass. What is the force of this "necessarily" and this "must"? It exhibits the connection between the good of that person *qua* hockey player and member of that particular team and the action of passing, a connection such that were such a player not to pass, he or she must *either* have falsely denied that passing was for their own good *qua* hockey player *or* have been guilty of an inconsistency *or* have acted as one not caring for his or her good *qua* hockey player and member of that particular team. That is to say, we recognize the necessity and the immediacy of rational action by

someone inhabiting a structured role in a context in which the
goods of some systematic form of practice are unambiguously ordered. (*WJ,* 141)

If the objective of playing hockey is understood *not only* as winning by
scoring more goals than the opposing team, *but also* (suppose) as sixty
minutes of enjoyment for all members of *both* teams, or as winning
fairly, then the player's judgment whether or not to pass is more complicated.[14] Conversely, his or her judgment can be justified with reference to a single practical syllogism *only* if the overriding good of a
person *qua* hockey player is understood simply as playing on the team
that has the higher score at the end of the game.

For Aquinas, the overriding good of human life is such a unitary
final end: "the state of perfect happiness which is the contemplation
of God in the beatific vision" (*WJ,* 192). In *Whose Justice? Which Rationality?,* Aristotle is assimilated to this scheme when MacIntyre presents
contemplation or *theoria* as Aristotle's conception of the overriding
good. Note that when he interprets Aristotle in this way in the following reference, MacIntyre describes the virtues in instrumental terms,
as desirable for their contribution to the achievement of the human
telos conceived as a single kind of activity.

So the life of moral and political virtue exists for the sake of and
must be subordinated to the life of contemplative inquiry. But the
latter is impossible for the individual, let alone for any group of individuals, without the former. Hence the two modes of life must be
combined in the overall life of the *polis,* which itself has to be understood, in this light, as existing for the sake of that in human beings which links them to the divine. All rational practical activity
has as its ultimate final cause the vision, so far as it is open to
human beings, of what God sees. (*WJ,* 143)

It is uncontroversial to observe that Aristotle ranked the virtues according to his hierarchical view of the parts of the human soul. It is also
relatively clear that he considered the capacity for *theoria* to be the highest and "most divine" aspect of the rational part of the human soul, and
held contemplation to be the most self-sufficient of those ends properly desired for their own sake. Nevertheless, as MacIntyre himself ob-

serves (*AV*, 158; cf. *WJ*, 142–143), the tensions within Aristotle's own references to the virtues and the good life leave his position open to conflicting interpretations: while some of Aristotle's remarks do, others do not support the conclusion that practical judgment should always subordinate pursuit of other human excellences to the activity of contemplation. Similarly, it is clear that Aristotle equated the overriding human good—the end of human activity that is desired purely for its own sake—with *eudaimonia:* "being well and doing well" (*AV*, 148). However, that *eudaimonia* cannot simply be equated with the activity of contemplation, and that there are other activities that are correctly desired for their own sake as ends-in-themselves, receives support from MacIntyre's own assessment of Aristotelian scholarship.[15] Therefore, when he presents Aristotle as holding that *theoria* is the ultimate *telos* for the sake of which all other actions should be performed, MacIntyre is selecting a reading of Aristotle that is particularly amenable to the Thomistic point of view.[16] Furthermore, its relation to Aristotle aside, if Thomism understands contemplation to be the only activity that is desired *purely* for its own sake, then how contemplative and political activity should be combined within the best human life remains an unresolved issue within MacIntyre's ethics of virtue (*TRV*, 142–143).

A final point regarding this first set of difficulties: If it is granted that the deductive model of practical deliberation requires a conception of an ultimate goal of human action to which all other ends are clearly subordinate, then Aristotle's affirmation of different kinds of virtuous feeling and conduct as intrinsic goods in their own right (*NE* 1144a1) suggests that conceptions of the overriding good supplied by metaphysics play a different role in his account of *phronēsis* than they do in Aquinas' account of *prudentia.* In other words, it seems reasonable to expect that, as MacIntyre himself sometimes allows (*AV*, 162; cf. *WJ*, 188–189, 192–197, 205), there would be radical differences between Aristotle's and Aquinas' conceptions of practical rationality corresponding to the differences between the structures of their narratives of human life. In this context, it is significant that MacIntyre (*WJ*, 131–132) provides only one example of an "Aristotelian" practical judgment in which immediate priorities are deduced from a conception of the overriding good of human life, and it remains very much open to question how well this illustration of *phronēsis* is faithful to Aristotle's own discussion of practical rationality. In particular, when

MacIntyre interprets Aristotle (*WJ*, 92–93, cf. *NE* 1144a31–33) as stating that deliberation always reasons with a mind to *the* end, *the* good, Aristotle could be read as stating that deliberation always reasons with a mind to *an* end, a *particular* good such as health. My point here is that if conceptions of the human *telos* provided by metaphysics can play only a limited role in practical judgment, then it is all the more important to determine how people can learn from experience to recognize what is genuinely virtuous.

Virtues: primary or secondary concept?

The second set of difficulties within MacIntyre's efforts to combine Aristotle and Aquinas concerns whether the virtues should be defined with reference to a conception of the good life or the reverse. MacIntyre initially acknowledges that because of the differences in structure between Aristotle's and Aquinas' narratives of human life, their corresponding conceptions of the virtues are significantly different (*AV*, 175–176; cf. *WJ*, 182). It is puzzling, therefore, that he later presents their conceptions of the virtues as essentially the same (*AV*, 185; cf. *WJ*, 165–166). More specifically: MacIntyre initially argues that because Aristotle defines *eudaimonia* as a life of activity according to the human excellences, his conception of the good life *presupposes* his account of the virtues.

> For what constitutes the good for man is a complete human life lived at its best, and the exercise of the virtues is a necessary and central part of such a life, not a mere preparatory exercise to secure such a life. *We thus cannot characterize the good for man adequately without already having made reference to the virtues.* (*AV*, 149; my italics)

Later, however, MacIntyre seems to contradict himself in the context of his construction of a "core concept" of the virtues. For there he proposes that as "in the Homeric account the concept of a virtue is secondary to that of *a social role*," so "in Aristotle's account it is secondary to that of *the good life for man* conceived as the *telos* of human action" (*AV*, 186; MacIntyre's italics). Thus, in some of MacIntyre's references, the Aristotelian and Christian conceptions of the virtues are described as structurally different; in others they are described as structurally the same. In the latter references, MacIntyre again presents the virtues as means—albeit the *internal* means—to reaching the human *telos:*

The New Testament account of the virtues, even if it differs as much as it does in content from Aristotle's . . . does have the same logical and conceptual structure as Aristotle's account. A virtue is, as with Aristotle, a quality the exercise of which leads to the achievement of the human *telos. The* good for man is of course a supernatural and not only a natural good, but supernature redeems and completes nature. Moreover the relationship of virtues as a means to the end which is human incorporation in the divine kingdom of the age to come is internal and not external, just as it is in Aristotle. It is of course this parallelism which allows Aquinas to synthesize Aristotle and the New Testament. A key feature of this parallelism is the way in which the concept of *the good life for man* is prior to the concept of a virtue in just the way in which on the Homeric account the concept of a social role was prior. Once again it is the way in which the former concept is applied which determines how the latter is to be applied. In both cases the concept of a virtue is a secondary concept. (*AV*, 184–185; MacIntyre's italics)

In such passages, the disparity that MacIntyre originally identified between Aristotle's and Aquinas' conceptions of the virtues has mysteriously disappeared from view.

Consequentialism

The third set of difficulties arising from the structure of Aquinas' narrative concerns the relation between teleological and consequentialist ethics. On the one hand, MacIntyre is concerned to point out that teleology is not necessarily wedded to a consequentialist view of the goodness either of virtues or of rules. He cites with approval Aristotle's conviction that not only should virtuous actions be done for their own sake, but also some vicious actions should be absolutely prohibited (*AV*, 150; *WJ*, 113, 121). On the other hand, however, MacIntyre seems to lack the resources within the scope of his Thomistic teleological framework to explain the sense in which actions can be categorically right or categorically wrong. It is striking how the virtues and vices are approved and prohibited in MacIntyre's account in terms of their *consequences* for advancing or obstructing realization of the human *telos*. For example, in his reconstruction of an Aristotelian view of natural justice, MacIntyre describes absolutely prohibited actions as those that undermine solidarity and so preclude the achievement of goods internal to practices. Deeds such as "the taking of innocent life, theft and perjury and betrayal" are prohibited because they produce harm "of such an order that they destroy the bonds of community in such a way as to render the doing or achieving of good impossible in some respect at least for some time" (*AV*, 151; cf. *WJ*, 111). Similarly, MacIntyre presents Aquinas as unconditionally forbidding lying because "Insofar as I lie I make myself into the sort of unjust person incapable of achieving my ultimate end. And to this immediate considerations must be subordinated" (*WJ*, 203). It would appear that, because the Thomistic narrative framework reconceives the virtues as means to an overriding good that is located outside and beyond human life, it results in precisely the kind of consequentialist ethics that MacIntyre wishes to avoid.[17]

The distinction between internal and external means

MacIntyre attempts to reconcile intrinsic and instrumental conceptions of the virtues by finding in Aristotle's work an implicit distinction between means that are *external* and those that are *internal* to their end. MacIntyre proposes two criteria to distinguish them. Means are external to their end when (a) they are contingent to the achievement of that end, and (b) the end can be adequately characterized without reference to those particular means. Conversely, means are internal to their end when (a) they are necessary to the achievement of that end, *and* (b) that end cannot be adequately characterized without reference to those particular means (*AV*, 149, 184; cf. *WJ*, 132). Perhaps in an effort to avoid consequentialism, MacIntyre argues that it makes no sense to consider whether or not vicious or unlawful actions could ever be justified with reference to some higher good because the virtuous life is an internal means to the realization of the human *telos*: "The exercise of the virtues is itself a crucial component of the good life for man" (*AV*, 184).

So far from resolving the tension between intrinsic and instrumental conceptions of the virtues, the distinction MacIntyre draws between internal and external means-ends relationships only results in a fourth set of difficulties and contradictions within his texts. With regard to the first criterion of the distinction: MacIntyre's example of a means that is necessary to the achievement of an end is the rule that "one should be scrupulous in laying out one's theses and putative proofs so that they are maximally vulnerable to objection and refutation." He argues that, on the assumptions that there is an internal relation between truth and the ability to withstand refutation *and* that truth is the goal of enquiry, it would make no sense to argue that it could be justified, in the name of some other good, to set aside this rule in the practice of enquiry (*RVG*, 11). However, even if the virtues are internal to living the best human life in a way that is analogous to how this rule is internal to the pursuit of truth, the first criterion of the internal-external distinction does not supply a sense in which the virtues can be affirmed as ends-in-themselves. For in MacIntyre's own example, the importance of the rule regarding refutation is argued on instrumental grounds. Arguing that following such rules is necessary to achieving truth provides no grounds for affirming the virtues of precision, care, and honesty in enquiry for their own sakes *as well as* for their necessary role in producing knowledge. In the same way, arguing that lying should never be permitted because it is invariably detrimental to achieving the final goal of human life provides no grounds for judging the telling of falsehoods to be categorically wrong.

With regard to the second criterion: MacIntyre suggests that the goodness of the virtues is not purely instrumental because they are a necessary feature of the good life. However, it is hard to reconcile MacIntyre's emphatic claim in this context that the good life cannot be characterized independently of the virtues with his other statements that the virtues are secondary and derivative concepts in Aristotle's ethics. Even if we accept MacIntyre's claim that the virtues should be conceived as "a crucial component of the good life for man," this provides no explanation *why* we should consider the virtues to be intrinsically good or *in what sense* an account of the virtues is a necessary part of any characterization of the best human life. Therefore, even aside from the question of whether or not it is faithful to Aristotle's conception of the human excellences and their relation to the best human life, MacIntyre's description of the virtues as internal means for attaining the human *telos* does not establish that they are correctly desired for their own sake. It merely establishes that the virtues are necessarily, as opposed to contingently, instrumentally good.

The structure of Aquinas' narrative of the best human life creates problems for MacIntyre even if the virtues are reconceived as instrumental goods. For if it is only by reference to their consequences for achieving a goal outside and beyond human life that the goodness of

actions can be justified, then it is uncertain how the virtues could ever
be recognized or appreciated this side of death. In other words, it is
difficult to imagine how we could learn either to recognize what the
genuinely virtuous person would do or to love virtue for its own sake
if the point of virtuous actions is only fully appreciated by those who attain the final human good in contemplation of God.[18]

Having posed the question "In what sense can the virtues be affirmed as intrinsically as well as instrumentally good?", I have presented
four sets of difficulties arising within MacIntyre's texts, each set related
to the shift from an Aristotelian to a medieval Christian way of struc-
turing narratives of human life and the resulting tension between intrinsic and instrumental conceptions of the goodness of the virtues. In
what follows, I will illustrate how the contradictions within MacIntyre's
references to the goodness of the virtues are symptomatic of a more
basic problem internal to his metaethics. This basic problem will be revealed by considering MacIntyre's response to the broader question
posed above: "What could it mean to say that an end is correctly desired
for its own sake?"

The Human *Telos* and the Supreme Good

In MacIntyre's Thomistic scheme of beliefs, the human *telos* is a paradigm of intrinsic goodness because it is by definition the only end of
human action that is not also desired for the sake of some other good.
This suggests that MacIntyre's general understanding of the nature of
intrinsic goodness can be sought in his answer to the question "In what
sense is the overriding good of human life *correctly* desired *for its own
sake?*"

For MacIntyre, there are three senses in which the human *telos* is *correctly* desired. To begin with, he follows both Aristotle and Aquinas in
linking achievement of the overriding good to performance of the specific function(s) for which the human species is designed—in other
words, with perfection of the potential that is unique to humans. For
example, MacIntyre shows how Aristotle and Aquinas arrive at their
respective characterizations of the proper goal of human life by em-
ploying metaphysical reasoning to identify the potential by which the
human species is distinguished from those lower and higher on the ontological hierarchy (*TRV*, 134). For MacIntyre, then, the first sense in

which realizing the human *telos* is correctly desired is that the specific nature of human potential is not accidental or contingent, but forms part of the intelligible order of the cosmos. Accordingly, I conclude that one criterion of an adequate conception of the overriding good—adequate, that is, to the interests of the Thomistic ethical scheme—is that it is consistent with knowledge of the true natures of things.[19]

Even if a potential unique to the human species is identified, there is no reason to affirm that the human *telos* is correctly desired *for its own sake* unless it is *good* in a sense that means more than simply being *consistent with the cosmic order*. Perhaps because of this, MacIntyre again follows both Aristotle and Aquinas in describing the overriding human good as the activity or activities that not only actualize human potential, but also afford complete satisfaction of human desire. For example, part of Aristotle's argument that *eudaimonia* is the human *telos* is that *eudaimonia* meets the expectation that the final human good will be self-sufficient.

> The self-sufficient we now define as that which when isolated makes life desirable and lacking in nothing; and such we think *eudaimonia* to be; and further we think it is the most desirable of all things, without being counted as one good thing among others— if it were so counted it would clearly be made more desirable by the addition of even the least of goods; for that which is added becomes an excess of goods, and of goods the greater is always more desirable. *Eudaimonia*, then, is something final and self-sufficient, and is the end of action.[20]

Aristotle and Aquinas assume that all things naturally desire to fulfil the *telos* for which they are suited by nature, and that we will therefore experience frustration or dissatisfaction if we act upon false beliefs about the proper priorities for human life (*AV*, 52, 60). Accordingly, as MacIntyre observes, Aristotle and Aquinas support their respective conceptions of the human *telos* with empirical claims that we do achieve greater or lesser degrees of fulfilment according to how closely the ends that we pursue conform to what metaphysical reflection has identified as the overriding good. On this view, although we can choose whether or not to pursue the kind of life that would culminate in the perfection of our nature, we cannot choose to have any other overriding good; or, indeed, to change what we most fundamentally desire (*RVG*, 6). Thus, the second sense in which MacIntyre understands realization of the human *telos* to be correctly desired is that it and only it will afford total contentment: only those who fully actualize their human potential will experience the complete satisfaction that they seek (*WJ*, 192; *TRV*, 152; cf. *SH*, 52, 118–119; Gilson 1971, 339, 344). Accordingly, I conclude that a second criterion of an adequate conception of the overriding good is that a life lived faithfully to its implications affords at least some promise or taste of future fulfilment.

In many of his references to the goal of moral education and of sound practical judgment, MacIntyre speaks as if these first two senses of *correctly desired* are all that is meant by *good*.[21] However, if that were the case, then it would still be unclear why the human *telos* is correctly desired for its own sake, as opposed to being correctly desired for the sake of the satisfaction of human desire. Perhaps because of this, in a few other references MacIntyre again follows both Aristotle and Aquinas in adverting to a notion of goodness in which *intrinsically good* means more even than the combination of *actualizing the highest human potential* and *affording complete satisfaction of desire*. The term Aristotle uses to refer to goodness in this third sense is *kalon* (χαλόν: noble, fine).[22] Aristotle characterizes *eudaimonia* as the good life at least in part because it consists of activities that *should* be desired—that is, by nature *merit* being desired for their own sake—*because* they are noble and fine. For Aristotle, in other words, not only is the virtuous life good because it completely satisfies desire, it completely satisfies desire because it actualizes what is *intrinsically good* (*NE* 1176b4–9). For example, it is because just and brave actions are *kalon* that Aristotle maintains they are properly done for their own sake, and only incidentally for their consequences (Owens 1981, 263, 272). Similarly, Aristotle claims that genuinely virtuous people can be recognized according to whether or not they take pleasure in what is "pleasant by nature" *because* it is noble and fine.

> Now for most men their pleasures are in conflict with one another because these are not by nature pleasant, but the lovers of what is noble find pleasant the things that are by nature pleasant, and virtuous actions are such, so that these are pleasant for such men as well as in their own nature. Their life, therefore, has no further

need of pleasure as a sort of adventitious charm, but has its pleasure in itself. For, besides what we have said, the man who does not rejoice in noble actions is not even good; since no one would call a man just who did not enjoy acting justly, nor any man liberal who did not enjoy liberal actions; and similarly in all other cases. If this is so, virtuous actions must be in themselves pleasant. But they are also *good* and *noble*, and have each of these attributes in the highest degree, since the good man judges well about these attributes. . . . *Eudaimonia* then is the best, noblest, and most pleasant thing in the world, and these attributes are not severed as in the inscription at Delos.[23]

Although MacIntyre (*WJ*, 108, 113) mentions Aristotle's contrast between feeling and conduct which is noble or fine and that which is base, he does not explore what *kalon* might mean in modern terms. Rather, in explaining why realization of the human *telos* is correctly desired for its own sake—and not just for the sake of its part in a cosmic scheme or for the enjoyment it affords—MacIntyre, like Aquinas, follows Augustine. The Augustinian-Thomistic view is similar to Aristotle's in holding that realization of the human *telos* affords complete satisfaction of desire *because* it is a realization of what is intrinsically good. It adds the important point that realization of what is intrinsically good satisfies human desire completely because *the* good—that which in itself *merits* being desired—is what humans long for most deeply.[24] And, finally, the Augustinian-Thomistic view is similar to Aristotle's in holding that there is a supreme good, the experience of which fully illuminates the intrinsic goodness of particular virtuous actions.[25] In Augustine's Christianized neo-Platonism, the perfect good that all humans desire—the Being, Truth, and Goodness that is the ground of all particular objects, truths, and goods—is God.[26] MacIntyre is thus committed to the belief that we will only fully appreciate why the human *telos* is correctly desired *for its own sake* when we achieve knowledge of the goodness of God: "that divine goodness by reference to which alone, in Augustine's Platonic terms, the unity underlying and ordering the range of uses and applications of the concept of good can be discovered" (*TRV*, 137–138, 154; cf. *WJ*, 178; *RVG*, 10–11). On this view, it is in contemplation of the divine nature that our quest for *the* good attains its final end.

Everyone desires perfect happiness, and everyone has as the true end of their nature, that for the sake of which they move towards all other goods in the way that they do, the goodness of God (*S.T.* Ia, 6,1). This latter movement toward their final cause human beings share with all other created beings, but nonrational beings cannot of course know or acknowledge this about themselves. Human beings can and before Adam's fall did. In their present state they often do not recognize, what nonetheless they possess all the means for recognizing, if only they would attend to them, that in being moved by a love for their own good, they are being moved by a love of and desire for God (*S.T.* Ia–IIae, 109,3). (*WJ*, 192)

I have been seeking MacIntyre's general understanding of intrinsic goodness by reconstructing his answer to the question "In what sense is the human *telos* correctly desired for its own sake?" I have indicated how MacIntyre follows Augustine and Aquinas in asserting that the meaning of *intrinsically good* is fully appreciated only in knowledge of the goodness of God. Therefore, if MacIntyre wishes to affirm that the human *telos* is intrinsically good, then he must provide some account of the sense of *good* in which God is believed to be perfect goodness, and of how the actualization of human potential is correctly desired for its own sake because it is good in the same or an analogous way. That is to say, a third criterion of a conception of the overriding good that would be adequate to the interests of MacIntyre's Thomistic ethics of virtue is that it is sufficiently clear about the senses in which the final human end is *good* that other instances of intrinsic goodness could also be recognized.

In what, then, does divine goodness consist and how is it known? How does that knowledge help us know and do what is genuinely virtuous from a love of virtue for its own sake?

In seeking MacIntyre's answers to these questions, I am again confounded by the unresolved tension in his texts between two conflicting views of the theory-practice relationship. For, on the one hand, MacIntyre sometimes speaks as if the kind of knowledge of divine goodness attained through dialectical enquiry in the Thomistic mode is sufficient for directing practical judgment and moral education. For example, MacIntyre equates the knowledge that God exists and that "his attributes make him worthy of honour, reverence, and worship" with the "rational knowledge of God" attained through metaphysical reflection (*WJ*, 188). And, he states that although the knowledge of divine goodness afforded by theoretical enquiry is limited, it is enough "to guide us further" (*WJ*, 193). This view is consistent with MacIntyre's account of deliberation on the first model of the theory-practice relationship, in which the goodness of an activity is established with reference to the conception of the human *telos* provided by metaphysics.

On the other hand, as we have seen, if the conception of the overriding good provided by theoretical dialectical enquiry is to be enriched "in the course of our education and self-education into the virtues" (*WJ*, 194), then it must be complemented with a practical, experiential knowledge of intrinsic goodness, and this means that dialectical enquiry is *not* sufficient in itself. MacIntyre strongly supports this conclusion when he states that we are not capable of self-education "into the virtues" until our pride has been transformed into charity (*caritas*) by God's gift of grace.

> For just as and because justice is continually the victim of the vice and sin of pride, so justice cannot flourish, cannot indeed, so it turns out, even exist as a natural virtue, unless and insofar as it is informed by the supernatural virtue of *caritas*. Charity is the form of all virtue; without charity the virtues would lack the specific kind of directedness which they require. And charity is not to be acquired by moral education; it is the gift of grace, flowing from the work of Christ through the office of the Holy Spirit (*S.T.* Ia–IIae, 23 to 44). (*WJ*, 205, cf. 182; *TRV*, 84, 91–92)

It is important to note that divine grace, in transforming the will, remedies radical defects in our *ability to know* as well as in our *motivation to do* what is intrinsically good (*TRV*, 140). This belief that the apprehension of intrinsic goodness is internal to the life of faith is consistent with MacIntyre's claim that in the same way we must be dedicated to the internal goods of practices in order to know their worth, so we must *experience* genuinely virtuous activity in order to appreciate why virtuous acts should be done for their own sake (*WJ*, 106, 109–110, 177–180). Unfortunately, however, MacIntyre does not describe the transformation that enables us to be charitable and so genuinely virtuous, or the apprehension of divine goodness that comes from learning to love God "more and more" (*WJ*, 154), or the knowledge of the virtues that is made possible by God's gift of grace. Again, then, because he says very little about the specifically Christian component of Thomistic ethics, MacIntyre's account of how we can learn to recognize what is genuinely virtuous is radically incomplete: I can only guess at what it could mean within his moral theory to speak of God as supremely good, and at how contemplating the divine nature would fully illuminate the intrinsic goodness of the virtues.

A final point on this topic: MacIntyre states that "even the best theoretical enquiry yields an inadequate knowledge of our ultimate end, and even the revealed truth that that end is the enjoyment of the beatific vision involves a reference to aspects of the divine nature of which we can only have the most inadequate apprehension." Yet, he also quickly adds that the knowledge afforded by theoretical enquiry is only inadequate in comparison to "that which we shall enjoy if we achieve our ultimate end" (*WJ*, 193). MacIntyre does not explain how he is able to be confident in these claims about the relation of present to future knowledge of the ultimate end of human development without having already achieved that end. In this connection, it would be strange if MacIntyre accepted Aquinas' appeals to Scripture (on which, see *S.T.* I) to establish the existence of things unknowable by reason *unless* MacIntyre had grounds *other than* Scriptural authority for accepting the authority of Scripture. In any event, because "the part of Christian theology which concerns man's true end . . . is on Aquinas' own account a matter of faith, not of reason," even theoretical knowledge of the supreme good in MacIntyre's scheme presupposes whatever it is that he means by *faith*.

Looking Back, Looking Ahead

Having raised the general question "In what sense can an end be affirmed as *correctly* desired for *its own sake*?", I have indicated how MacIntyre's inability to characterize the intrinsic goodness of virtuous actions is symptomatic of his inability to characterize the third and full sense of what *good* can mean. Similarly, his explanation of why the human *telos* should be desired for its own sake is incomplete because he does not delineate the supreme goodness of God that is apprehended through faith. I wish to propose that it is precisely because Mac-

Intyre lacks an adequate account of intrinsic goodness that he is unable to explain how we can learn to recognize in particular situations what the genuinely virtuous person would do. In other words, I suspect that it is because he is unclear on the full sense in which something is correctly desired for its own sake that MacIntyre is unable to characterize the experiential knowledge of intrinsic goodness that is required for sound practical judgment and effective moral education.

If I am correct in this assessment, then one possible explanation for the limitations of MacIntyre's metaethics is that the Thomistic tradition lacks the resources to characterize intrinsic goodness. Indeed, this line of thought is suggested by some of MacIntyre's own remarks. Specifically, in his narrative of the development of the ethics of virtue, he interprets Aristotle as intending to remedy defects in Plato's notion of the form of the good (*WJ*, 85). Later, however, MacIntyre remarks that, even at the end of Aristotle's last work, "the goodness of the final object of contemplation, whether understood as the form of the good or as the unmoved mover, remains both in itself and in its effects too obscure" (*FG*, 255). And, with regard to the problem of "the relationship of the human good to the goodness of that in the contemplation of which the final human *telos* is to be found," MacIntyre says only that "it is scarcely surprising that in Aquinas' account of the supreme good Platonic elements re-appear alongside Aristotelian, in a way that would scarcely be possible if Aristotle and Plato were fundamentally at odds on these matters," and "To what extent Aquinas solves the problem and to what extent it remains unsolved is another question that must be deferred" (*FG*, 261). Finally, to add to MacIntyre's inconclusive remarks on this issue, one could observe that Plato is unwilling to speak directly in the *Republic* about either the form of the Good or the "dialectical" process whereby the human soul could ascend to its grasp, and that Aristotle promises an account of the kind of education that would produce people of good character, but on this issue his surviving works are, like MacIntyre's, radically incomplete.[27]

These observations notwithstanding, I wish to propose another explanation for the limitations of MacIntyre's ethics of virtue. I suspect that he overlooks the resources within the Thomistic tradition for characterizing intrinsic goodness at least in part because he continues that tradition's subordination of practical to theoretical knowledge. Consider the case of an apprentice to the healing arts who learns from experience to recognize that such and such specific treatments will cure such and such particular people. In Thomistic terms, that apprentice has practical knowledge of particulars but as yet lacks the understanding of causes that theoretical knowledge would supply: *why* and not just *that* those kinds of treatments will restore people to health. Within the Thomistic tradition, it is only such an understanding of causes that is considered knowledge (*epistēmē, scientia*) in the full sense of the term (*NE* 1139b30–35; *FP*, 13–14). Accordingly, with regard to the question of *why* the virtues should be valued as ends and not only as means, MacIntyre seems to be looking for a *moral theory* to supply the answer.[28] It is conceivable that dialectical enquiry could supply a theoretical answer to this question of why the virtues are intrinsically good if knowledge of the good was understood to consist simply in a representation of the intelligible order of the cosmos. On this understanding, as medical science would provide an explanation of why certain treatments are effective and others are not, so moral theory would provide an explanation, in the form of a classification of the human species and its final cause, of why certain kinds of activity satisfy human desire and others lead to frustration. However, as I have indicated above, the ethics of virtue needs more than this kind of theoretical knowledge of the good. A representation of the cosmic plan would *not* describe why actualization of human potential is desirable for its own sake except in the sense of affording complete satisfaction of desire. And MacIntyre himself insists, following Aquinas, that even the supreme enjoyment attendant upon achieving the human *telos* does not *constitute* actualization of the overriding good, but only *supervenes upon* it.[29] In addition, given that MacIntyre presents sound practical judgment as resulting only from a life of faith infused with *caritas*, it would seem that becoming able to recognize what is genuinely virtuous is more like coming to appreciate why health is desired for its own sake than like coming to understand the causes and remedies of disease. What I want to suggest by this analogy is that MacIntyre, to the extent he is concerned exclusively with moral theory, is looking for knowledge of the good in all the wrong places.

As I described in the previous chapter, MacIntyre's case for the rational superiority of the ethics of virtue appeals to the success of its dialectical mode of argument and its theistic, teleological world view. He argues that Thomistic theoretical enquiry can justify a conception of the final end of human life that is necessary to, but absent from, rival moral traditions. Consequently, the ethics of virtue has the resources both to succeed where its rivals fail according to their own criteria of success *and* to explain the precise source of their lack of progress. In the next chapter, I sketch a similar argument. I indicate how my interpretation of intrinsic moral value and its apprehension can, by paying proper attention to our reasons of the heart, both progress beyond the limitations of MacIntyre's moral point of view *and* locate their origin in its intellectualist bias.

CHAPTER SIX

Reasons of the Heart

"The men where you live," said the little prince, "raise five
thousand roses in the same garden—and they do not find in
it what they are looking for."

"They do not find it," I replied.

"And yet what they are looking for could be found in one
single rose, or in a little water."

"Yes, that is true," I said.

And the little prince added:

"But the eyes are blind. One must look with the heart. . . ."

—Marie-Antoine-Roger de Saint-Exupéry, *The Little Prince*

This chapter has two sections. In the first, I present my understanding of intrinsic moral value and its apprehension, drawing from
the conceptual resources of Mahāyāna Buddhism to forestall anticipated objections to my account. In the second section, I argue that
my characterization of intrinsic moral value provides for answers to
the questions that I have identified as important to, but unaddressed
within, MacIntyre's ethics of virtue. My arguments are intended, not
just to build support for my notion of reasons of the heart, but also to
indicate how the limitations of MacIntyre's moral point of view reflect
an intellectualist bias. I thereby hope to show, as MacIntyre illustrated
in his critiques of genealogy and liberalism, how someone committed
to one moral standpoint can assess the moral theory of another in that
second perspective's own terms.

APPREHENSIONS OF INTRINSIC MORAL VALUE

Intrinsic Moral Value

Intrinsic goodness
There are two distinct senses in which something is judged to be intrinsically (as opposed to instrumentally) good. In the first sense, the object, event, state of affairs, attitude, action, principle, policy, or person is judged intrinsically good because it affords satisfaction of a human interest or desire. In the second sense, it is judged intrinsically good because it embodies or actualizes what *merits* being valued because it is *good*. The key difference between the two senses is that, in the first, intrinsic goodness is dependent upon or relative to human interests or desires; and, in the second, it is not. When I refer without qualification to *intrinsic value* in the following discussion, I will mean intrinsic goodness or intrinsic badness in the second, unconditional, not-relative-to-human-interests sense of the term. It is an account of intrinsic goodness in this second sense that MacIntyre's teleological ethics of virtue requires—but does not provide—in holding God to be the perfect Good to which all things are drawn.

My first point with regard to intrinsic value in general is that, precisely because goodness is generally judged with reference to human interests, it is not at all clear what, if anything, *intrinsically good* could mean.[1] That is to say, it is not at all clear how or why something could merit being desired if considered independently of human interests. Yet some such notion seems to be necessary to capture what is affirmed in at least some people's value judgments: MacIntyre is not alone in relying upon a notion of intrinsic goodness that remains unexplained. To cite a few examples, there is Moore's reference to "good" as a simple, unanalysable property; Williams' (1985, 182–183) discussion of "simply important"; Rawls's (1971, 9, 44; cf. 1974/75, 8) appeal to moral intuitions or "considered moral judgments"; and Moon's (1993, 33) reference to what is "truly valuable."

My second point is that our judgments of intrinsic value—in both the relative and non-relative senses of the term—commonly appeal, explicitly or implicitly, to the quality of human experience. In speaking of *the quality of human experience* I am referring very broadly to all kinds of feelings, agreeable and disagreeable, including sensations, moods, sentiments, and emotions. The connection between the quality of human experience and judgments of intrinsic value is relatively straightforward when *intrinsically good* is defined with reference to human interests and passions. For example, when intrinsic goodness is defined in this relative sense, chocolate might be said to be correctly desired for its own sake simply because of how it tastes. Thus, in some contexts at least, enjoying its flavour and texture is all the reason someone needs to answer "yes" to the question "Is chocolate good?" To understand fully what that person means in saying that it is good, we must appreciate something of the quality of her or his experience when eating chocolate.[2]

When *intrinsically good* is defined as what *should* be valued for its own sake independently of human interests and desires, the connection between the quality of human experience and judgments of intrinsic value is less clear. Nevertheless, I have often observed that part of what people mean when they say something is intrinsically good in the non-relative sense is that it *merits* a certain degree and kind of qualitative response. An example would be the aesthetic judgment of a person who, in exclaiming that a field of yellow daffodils is very beautiful, both expresses the degree and quality of her response to what she sees *and* implicitly affirms that her experience is appropriate or "fitting" to that to which it is a response. The implication is that those who are unmoved by daffodils dancing in the sunlight are either not paying sufficient attention or lack poetry in their souls. In such judgments, then, *meriting that degree and quality of response* is at least part of what people mean in ascribing intrinsic value.

Of course, judgments of intrinsic value can be negative as well as positive. Objecting that an act is cruel (think of flogging a horse for no fault of its own) cannot only describe the degree and quality of the objector's response to the act, but also express a judgment that the cruelty of the act *should* be met with responses such as horror and outrage. Indeed, I think that someone whose feelings are not affected by witnessing an act of cruelty does not fully understand what is meant in calling cruelty *reprehensible* and *deplorable* and just plain *wrong*.

My third point is that if it is granted that we commonly appeal directly or indirectly to the agreeable and disagreeable qualities of human experience in making judgments of intrinsic value, then it is reasonable to consider the possibility that the degree and quality of human response can exercise a cognitive function; that is, that it can help us identify what is truly intrinsically good or intrinsically bad. In any event, that is the view I wish to propose: that certain degrees and qualities of human experience can, under certain conditions at least, accurately apprehend aspects of that to which they are a response.

Two possible versions of my proposal can be distinguished, taking the field of daffodils again as an example. In the first version, it is possible that what is responded *to* in the experience of beauty could be apprehended in some other way. In other words, it is a purely *contingent* fact that the beauty of the daffodils is apprehended in *that* particular degree and kind of qualitative response, and that meriting some such degree and quality of response is part of what being beautiful *means*. Similarly, it could be said that seeing things as yellow can accurately reflect features of what is being seen, but it is a purely contingent fact that there is a consistent correlation between particular features of the environment and that particular visual quality. In contrast, in the second version of my proposal, it is not possible that what makes the field of daffodils beautiful could be appreciated through a degree or quality of human experience very different from the typical "Oh! How beautiful!" response. The assumption here is that there is (in at least some cases) a *necessary* connection between the particular quality and degree of response and what is apprehended through/in that response.[3] I favour the second version, but my fourth point is that, so far as judgments of value are concerned, not much hangs on which of these two versions is preferred, in the same way that there is little pragmatic difference between realist and instrumentalist conceptions of scientific laws.

My fifth point is that various kinds or categories of intrinsic values— in both the relative and the non-relative senses of *intrinsic*—can be differentiated according to distinctions among the degrees and qualities of the responses involved in the corresponding judgments. So, for example, one could distinguish *aesthetic* (harmonious vs. discordant, elegant vs. crude), *sensual* (delicious vs. unsavory), *artistic* (uplifting vs. degrading), *moral* (admirable vs. contemptible), and *religious* (sacred vs. profane) kinds of qualitative responses. One implication of this point is that we should not equate what is good with what is pleasant (or what is bad with what is painful) unless we follow Aristotle (*NE* 1175a23– 1176a) in both differentiating distinct and irreducible kinds of pleasure (and differentiating equally distinct and irreducible kinds of pain or suffering) and understanding enjoyment as supervening upon what is good.

My sixth and last point concerning judgments of intrinsic value in general is that, the distinctions among them notwithstanding, there is something common among all of the different kinds of qualitative responses appealed to in ascriptions of intrinsic goodness (a subset of *positive* judgments of value, which include ascriptions of both intrinsic and instrumental goodness), and something common among all of the different kinds of qualitative responses incorporated in ascriptions of intrinsic badness (a subset of *negative* judgments of value). It is for this reason that the same word can be used to describe similar or analogous qualitative responses in different-but-comparable kinds of judgments. So, metaphorically speaking, our characters can be colourful, grating, odious, sweet, rough, warm, and so forth.

Intrinsic moral values

The distinction between what is *moral* and what is *nonmoral* has been drawn in a variety of ways within different philosophical, religious, cultural, and political traditions.[4] For instance, we have seen how MacIntyre uses *moral* in one sense to differentiate virtues cultivated by habit from those learned through systematic instruction; in a second sense, to refer to a concern with character and the overriding good; and, in a third sense, to designate those traditions of enquiry that are concerned with establishing proper norms and priorities for human life (*proper* being variously interpreted). Since Kant, *moral* is often used in a fourth sense to refer to what is either categorically good (obligatory) or bad (forbidden) without reference to human desires (Williams 1985, 174–175).

As I understand it, the distinction between moral and other kinds of intrinsic values—and, even more so, the distinction between moral and egotistical concerns—is important because we commonly feel that some kinds of considerations should have more weight than others in establishing norms and priorities for human living. I believe that *moral* is appropriately as well as commonly used to designate those values that *ought* to take priority over other considerations in guiding action (however *ought* is interpreted).[5] This way of differentiating *moral* from other kinds of intrinsic values is consistent with the understanding that moral values provide good and perhaps even sufficient reasons to choose one course of action over others and so cannot be reduced to purely egotistical, non-generalizable interests.[6] It is also consistent with the view that moral judgments are inherently prescriptive.[7]

In this context, I can articulate one of the key claims of my meta-ethics, which is that however *moral* is defined within distinct traditions, what it means for something to be intrinsically morally good or intrinsically morally bad is always appreciated, as with intrinsic values in general, in part with reference to the degrees and qualities of cognitive-affective human responses. In particular, I propose that it is at least in part because people are *profoundly moved* in positive ways by experiencing or witnessing (for example) freedom, solidarity, and compassion, and *profoundly moved* in negative ways by experiencing or witnessing oppression, alienation, and indifference, that the corresponding moral values are given priority (if in different ways) in practical judgments. I further propose that if intrinsic moral values are apprehended in part through the quality of human experience, then it is in part with reference to these kinds of profound human responses that moral judgments and commitments should be justified.

In making these proposals I take Aristotle as my exemplar, for it seems that it is with reference to the quality of human experience that Aristotle differentiates what is intrinsically noble and fine (χαλόν, *kalon*) from what is only pleasant or useful. According to Owens, *kalon* is the neuter form of *kalos*, meaning *beautiful*, precisely because people in Aristotle's day named as noble or fine what they experienced as inherently and profoundly *appealing*.[8] Furthermore, and most significantly in this context, Owens argues that *kalon* means for Aristotle what we would mean by "moral goodness" precisely because part of perceiving something to be noble or fine is experiencing it as intrinsically *compelling:* "In its own way it prescribes fulfilment. It presents itself as something that *ought* to be done." Indeed, it is precisely because what is *kalon* is experienced or perceived as intrinsically obligatory—as something that by its nature *ought* to be done—that only those who do what is noble or fine for its own sake are deemed to be genuinely virtuous in Aristotle's ethics.

A morally good action is one that is performed for the sake of the χαλόν. No motive for it other than its own self is recognized. For example, to remain at one's post in the face of death, because to do so under the circumstances is χαλόν, constitutes a morally good action. To perform the same external action through fear of the military penalty or to escape the troubles of life or for any other such motive would not be genuine courage. . . . The sole acceptable motive for bringing about the χαλόν is the χαλόν itself. (Owens 1981, 263)

Furthermore, it is also precisely because what is genuinely virtuous is recognized by the quality of human response that, for Aristotle, the person of good *character* is the measure of what is truly intrinsically good (*NE* 1113a30). And, finally, as Aristotle points out, it is precisely because what is *kalon* is apprehended through the quality of human response that moral arguments will have no effect upon those unfortunate souls who, through lack of proper education, "have not even a conception of what is noble and truly pleasant, since they have never tasted it" (*NE* 1179b15). It is for this reason that the cultivation of dispositions to *feel* as well as act correctly is so important within Aristotle's ethics.[9]

An important implication of the claim that moral values are apprehended through the degree and quality of human response is that if we are to understand why people are committed to the particular moral values that they enact, then we must have some appreciation of what they personally have experienced as most profoundly intrinsically good and/or most profoundly intrinsically bad. My original inspiration to investigate the connection between intrinsic moral values and the quality of human experience came from reflection upon the roots of my own commitments, moral and otherwise. An informal part of that investigation has been to ask people how they arrived at their most deeply held convictions about what is categorically right or good and what is categorically wrong. The answers they gave most often took the form of narratives of significant events in their personal histories—events in which the quality of experience played a central role. Because of this, I am not at all surprised to read that, according to Bernstein (1983, xv), "the *experience* of solidarity and friendship is fundamental in the thought of Gadamer, Habermas, Rorty, and Arendt." Nor do I think it a coincidence that, in the biblical prophetic tradition, to be compassionate is to be moved in one's heart (or in one's very bowels) by the sight of injustice.[10] In any event, as far as I can tell, my ability to make real sense out of the moral commitments of the people I talk to depends upon how well I can use my own personal experiences of things worth caring about as a bridge to appreciating theirs.[11]

The notion that moral goodness is analogous to beauty in its apprehension has been advanced by many philosophers and poets other than Aristotle. And, in contemporary discourse, one can still encounter exhortations to do "the right thing" with their implicit appeals to an intuitive, qualitative, quasi-aesthetic sense of what is *right*. At the same time, the views of those who have thought of the good as analogous to the beautiful have been severely criticized (Murdoch 1970, 3–4). In proposing that we are potentially able to apprehend intrinsic moral value in part through the degree and quality of our experience, I must anticipate two objections. The first objection points to the radical disagreements that exist between people's deep convictions on the appropriate norms and priorities for human living. It also points to the difficulty of explaining what it is that apprehensions of intrinsic moral value are responses *to*—what it is about something that would make it categorically right or wrong independently of human interests. It concludes that, contrary to what I have proposed, the degree and quality of human experience is simply a product of our psychological makeup and it justifies no inferences about the nature of that to which it is supposedly a response. The second objection argues that particular responses on specific occasions do not provide sufficient grounds to affirm universal moral principles, and concludes that moral intuitions cannot justify generalizable norms and priorities for human living.[12]

To provide the conceptual resources to address these objections, in what follows I introduce a non-dualistic metaethics by way of Mahāyāna Buddhist teachings on egolessness of self (*anatman*), emptiness (*śūnyatā*), Buddha-nature (*tathāgata-garbha*), the distinction between absolute truth (ultimate truth, *paramārtha-satya*) and relative truth (conventional truth, *samvriti-satya*), and the skilful means (*upaya*) of a *bodhisattva*.

Mahāyāna Buddhism

Buddhism originated in the life and words of Siddhārtha Gautama (Shākyamuni Buddha), who is generally considered to have lived and taught from approximately 566 to 486 B.C.E. in what is now Nepal.[13] Since that time, Buddhism has crossed many geographical, political, linguistic, and cultural boundaries. In the process, it has developed a great variety of teachings, practices, institutions, and traditions. In speaking of *Mahāyāna* (lit. "Great Vehicle") Buddhism, I am referring to a collection of teachings and associated practices that presuppose while adding to the earlier *Hīnayāna* (lit. "Small Vehicle") or *Theravāda* (Way/Speech of the Elders) viewpoint commonly summarized in the Four Noble Truths and the Eightfold Path.[14] The understanding of the Mahāyāna point of view that I will present is based principally upon the oral and written instructions of the Vidjadhara the Venerable Chö-gyam Trungpa Rinpoché, a meditation master and scholar within the Tibetan Buddhist tradition.[15] Although I will often refer to other works, I cite Trungpa's teachings as my principle source because what little insight I have achieved into the "definitive meaning" (*nitartha*) of Ma-hāyāna texts has been through the practice of Buddhism according to his instructions. That said, the more I practice and study Mahāyāna Buddhism the more I realize how much I have yet to learn. Accordingly, I do not presume to claim that I present here an adequate account of even a Tibetan version of that overall point of view.[16] My intent is more modest: to summarize certain fundamental Mahāyāna concepts that have come to form an important part of my interpretation of intrinsic moral value and of my overall moral framework.

The egolessness of self

According to Buddhism, we all (with a few exceptions) cling tightly to the assumption that we exist as separate, autonomous selves. We are all heavily invested in protecting and fostering the "me" that we presume somehow remains the same from our birth to our death (and perhaps even beyond). Our self-attachment is prior to and somewhat independent of any particular ideas that we might have about who we are. That is to say, even if we are intellectually convinced that our identities are socially constructed (for example), we still tend to feel and act *as if* we were each a single, permanent self. As one contemporary Buddhist teacher has observed, "we all act as if we had lasting, separate, independent selves that it is our constant pre-occupation to protect and foster. It is an unthinking habit that most of us would normally be most unlikely to question or explain. . . . We are so enormously involved with and attached to this 'self' that we take it for granted" (Gyamtso 1988, 20). This *self* with which we are so preoccupied is a conspicuous feature of the languages (and corresponding thoughts) that have a subject-object structure: it is the *I* of "*I* think," "this is *mine*," and so forth.[17]

Buddhism further observes that, however closely we examine our experience, we will *not* find separate, independent, continuously existing selves. Although we implicitly believe that we are the thinkers of our thoughts, no such independent entities have ever actually been observed. According to Buddhism, our sense of continued existence as subjects is an illusion, analogous to that produced by watching a film. Even though the film is composed of distinct frames, they follow each other so quickly that we generally do not notice the gaps between them, and so perceive the movie as continuous. Buddhism teaches that, similarly, our sense of self-continuity is based on missing—indeed, ignoring—the "gaps" in our experience of self. On this view, the distinction between a subject and its activities or experiences—the distinction between perceiv*er* and perceiv*ing*—exists only by virtue of the conceptual frameworks through which immediate experiences are interpreted and articulated.[18] Buddhism thus rejects as unwarranted Descartes' belief that the occurrence of thinking proves the existence of a thinker; proposing instead that the affirmation of a thinker is simply another thought. Conventionally speaking, then, we exist as separate selves; but only, according to Buddhism, because separate selves exist by convention. Strictly speaking, our belief that we are continuously existing subjects can neither be validly deduced nor empirically confirmed, whether through introspection or otherwise.[19]

The claim that there are no grounds for believing that we exist in the way that we usually assume we do is referred to within Buddhism as the doctrine of the egolessness of self (*anātman*). To avoid confusion, however, we should note that the term *ego* can be used—even just within Buddhism—in at least three distinct senses. In the first sense, *ego* refers to the *deep conviction* that we exist as continuous, independent subjects; this is the assumption that Buddhism argues is unwarranted. In the second sense, *ego* refers to that *separate, continuously existing part of ourselves* that we believe makes us the same persons today as we were yesterday. It is in this second sense of the term that the self is said to be without ego. In the third sense, *ego* refers to the *collection of habitual patterns of perceiving, feeling, thinking, and acting* that culminates in and continually reproduces conviction in the separate existence of subjects and objects. Ego in this third sense refers to the processes whereby experience comes to be *interpreted* dualistically, as arising from a self that is separate from the world.[20]

Emptiness

Virtually all Buddhist traditions point to the egolessness of self. In the *prajñāpāramitā* literature, Mahāyāna Buddhism goes further in proclaiming the egolessness of other.[21] It asserts that, however closely we examine our experience, we will find no solid, separate, independent, continuously existing objects: the perceiv*ed* as well as the perceiv*er* is not found separately from perceiv*ing*, which is transitory. The Mahāyāna term that is usually translated as *emptiness* (*śūnyatā*) refers to the existential realization that all objects (including subjects) do not exist separately or independently and so are "empty" (*śūnya*) of inherent existence. The realization of *śūnyatā*, contrary to what the translation *emptiness* might suggest, is not the experience of a featureless void. The phenomenal world does not vanish in emptiness; what disappears is the naive belief in underlying, independent, permanently existing objects. Loy's translation is revealing: "*Śūnyatā* . . . comes from the root *shu*, which means 'to swell' in two senses: hollow or empty, and also full, like the womb of a pregnant woman. Both are implied in the Mahāyāna usage: the first denies any fixed self-nature to anything, the second implies that this is also a fullness and limitless possibility, for lack of any fixed characteristics allows the infinite diversity of impermanent phenomena."[22] Because the claim is that all things are empty of self- or inherent-existence, *śūnyatā* is closely related to the doctrine of dependent origination (*pratītya-samutpāda*), which asserts that all things arise interdependently.[23] In Mahāyāna non-dualism, then, objects as well as subjects are understood to exist independently only by convention (Gyamtso 1988, 39).

The egolessness of self and other can be suggested by a variety of analogies. Consider a computer that has had almost every original part of its hardware replaced over five years of upgrading. Its operating system has been changed, and most of the original data stored on its hard drive is gone, a portion remaining only in altered form. In what sense, if any, can it be said to be the same computer now that it was five years ago? The point of this analogy is that there is no continuously existing single "thing" that corresponds to the word *computer*. Rather, *computer* is simply a convenient label for a set of components, programs, and their functional interrelationships, all of which change over time and are subject to eventual, inevitable decay. It is only because we tend to think that labels correspond to things that we might speak as if the "same" machine existed over five years. The suggestion here is that the kind of continuity that can be attributed to personal identities is essentially no different.[24] Buddhism would thus agree with MacIntyre that "persons" are characters abstracted from narratives. Buddhism would also allow that such narratives capture a certain kind of continuity, similar to the limited kind of functional continuity that could be attributed to the computer in my example.[25] It would not accept that there is the kind of continuity provided by an eternal soul, notions of which Christianity adopted, with adaptation, from the Greeks.[26]

Another illustration of how things are empty of inherent existence describes an organism's relation to its environment. Conventionally speaking, we refer to particular plants and animals as if they had a separate existence. On closer examination, however, the boundaries between organisms and environment dissolve into a web of interrelationships, an ever-changing exchange or "dance" of energy and elements. I might for the sake of convenience speak of the tree at the bottom of my garden as if it were a separate, continuously-existing object or "thing," but it is actually only a relatively stable, continuously changing composite of earth, air, water, and sunlight. Modern physics has confirmed that even energy and matter transform each into the other, ultimately separable only in thought. No permanent boundaries or solid building blocks have been discovered anywhere in the universe, not even at atomic or subatomic levels.[27]

When people hear Mahāyāna teachings on emptiness they typically ask, "If *I* exist only by convention, then who is it that is having *my* experience? If people are not eternal souls or autonomous subjects, then what are we? Who is it that is speaking and listening here?"

Buddha-nature

Such questions bring us to the teachings on Buddha-nature (*tathāgata-garbha*). Mahāyāna Buddhism reports that if we learn to relax our clinging to a sense of self, then in the gaps between our thoughts we can

discover an awareness that is completely unconditioned. It is unconditioned in the sense that it is not created or manufactured, but is always already there, primordial. It is unconditioned also in the sense
that it is prior to and so free from all reference points, including the
basic duality of *self* and *other*. Buddhism reports that, contrary to what
we might believe, it is not the "self" that is aware. Rather, all self-centred
emotions and all thoughts of self arise within the "space" of unconditioned awareness. One traditional analogy for glimpsing this is the experience of being on an elephant and discovering that, rather than you
riding the elephant, it is the elephant that is carrying you!

Mahāyāna Buddhism teaches that unconditioned awareness or
wakefulness is our basic nature. (It is called Buddha-nature because
buddha is Sanskrit for *awake*.[28]) It is what we most fundamentally are.
Indeed, as is realized in *śūnyatā*, all "beings" are nothing other than
Buddha-nature.[29] Mahāyāna Buddhism reports that this unconditioned
awareness naturally manifests as inseparable insight and compassion,
and it is only our habit of imposing the reference points of *self* and *other*
that obscures the boundless clarity and warmth of "our" basic nature.
In one traditional analogy, Buddha-nature is compared to the sun and
the sky; self-centred thoughts and emotions are likened to clouds. In
the same way that the light and warmth of the sun can be blocked by
clouds without being altered in any way, so the transcendent insight
and limitless compassion of Buddha-nature is not affected when obscured by our confusion. Unconditioned awareness itself is like the sky:
vast, fathomless, without measure.[30]

To attain our full human potential is, according to this point of view,
simply to realize our true nature. To do so, we do not need to fabricate anything or import anything from an external source: *unconditioned awareness, insight, and compassion are always already there*.[31] The
Mahāyāna path to the realization of Buddha-nature is essentially a process of allowing it to manifest, which happens naturally when the habit
of self-attachment is unlearned.

Absolute and relative truth

The fourth topic of Buddhist teaching I wish to introduce is a distinction between absolute (conceptually unmediated) and relative (conceptually mediated or conventional) truth.[32] Mahāyāna Buddhism states
that Buddha-nature cannot be conceptualized—or even imagined—
precisely because it is unconditioned. In that sense, it is ineffable. Simi-

larly, the transcendent insight or clear perception (*prajñā*) that is inseparable from unconditioned awareness and compassion is described as unmediated, as arising prior to the habitual attempt to fix points of reference, including the superimposition of conceptual schemes (Kongtrül 1992, 26, 52). Because Mahāyāna Buddhism holds that dualistic conceptualization superimposes upon what is inherently without reference points, it maintains that only transcendent insight is really accurate: only those experiencing non-dualistically perceive things as they actually are. In Mahāyāna Buddhist terms, the content of such clear perception or "discerning awareness wisdom" is *absolute truth*. Absolute truth is non-propositional or non-discursive because, as non-dualistic, it cannot be expressed in the terms of languages based upon the polarities of either/or, A or not-A, subject or object (Loy 1988, 4). It follows that, for Buddhism, claims expressed in language can be considered to be true in a limited, conventional sense, but not absolutely. What is affirmed in justifiable propositions is considered *relative truth*.[33]

If absolute truth cannot be grasped by thought, then is logic and relative truth to be discarded by those seeking enlightenment?

Mahāyāna Buddhism does understand direct, non-conceptual insight to transcend the limitations of propositional knowledge and associated conceptual schemes. At the same time, however—not least because Buddhism understands that most of us still mistake subject-object mediated perception for reality—it holds relative truth to be indispensable. The reference points for thinking and acting provided by conceptual schemes are limited to a greater or lesser degree, but can be very useful nonetheless. It is difficult when communicating through language to avoid speaking and writing as if subjects and objects exist in an independent way (this book being a case in point). From the absolute point of view, this is inaccurate. Yet, there is no harm in drawing imaginary boundaries around relatively stable processes and speaking as if they were objects to which qualities can be attributed—so long as we remember that such boundaries no more exist "out there" in an absolute sense than the ones that we draw to create nation-states and historical traditions.[34]

In fact it is crucial for the Madhaymaka to accept the everyday conventional world, as it forms the basis for religious practice and without it enlightenment cannot be attained. Nevertheless, the everyday conventional world must be accepted not as an ultimate world but precisely as what it really is—the everyday, conventional world. (Williams 1989, 70)

One traditional use of relative truth within Mahāyāna Buddhism is philosophical argument against dualistic assumptions, particularly the conventional belief that subjects and objects have inherent existence. The arguments are not intended to prove that non-duality is true. This is because non-duality cannot be proved: to realize the truth of emptiness is to experience what goes beyond words, not to grasp the conclusion to an argument.[35]

From the absolute point of view, it is as equally unwarranted to assert that subjects and objects do not exist as it is to claim that they have self-nature. Similarly, it is as incorrect to say that subjects and objects are different (two) as it is to say that they are the same (one). The best approximation to expressing *śūnyatā* in language is to say that things are "not two" (hence "nonduality"). Ultimately, the intent of Mahāyāna philosophy is *not* to replace dualistic assumptions with a non-dualistic conceptual scheme. Its arguments against dualism are primarily intended not so much to change how we think—for thinking is understood to be inherently dualistic—as to *interrupt* our habitual thought patterns, and thereby open us to a glimpse of things "as they are." Teachings in the form of substantive, propositional truth claims—for example, declarations that neither we nor even the spiritual path really exist—are not meant to capture absolute truth, but to shatter conventional assumptions (Gyamtso 1988, 56–57, 66). On one Buddhist analogy, those who grasp the emptiness of *self* and *other* are like those roused from a dream in which they were desperately trying to escape from a burning house. Upon awakening, they realize that both the danger and the one trying to escape it never existed outside of their imagination.[36] Hence, for the benefit of those still caught in the belief that there is a permanent self or soul that will one day experience realization, it is necessary to proclaim that "In emptiness, there is . . . no path, no wisdom, no attainment and no nonattainment" (*The Sūtra of the Heart of Transcendent Knowledge,* Nālandā Translation Committee; cf. Conze 1958, 89–90).

In this context, it seems fair to say that Mahayana Buddhism shares the "pragmatic" approach to relative truth presented in this thesis, in which particular conceptual frameworks and corresponding ways of thinking are justified if they assist the people using them to accomplish (and, if necessary, reformulate) their fundamental objectives.[37] For example, many Mahāyāna Buddhist traditions make the apparently substantive claim that "something"—variously called Buddha-nature, non-conceptual Wisdom Mind (*jñāna*), the Clear Light (*prabhasvara*) Nature of Mind, Thusness (*dharmatā*), and so forth—is the true "ground" of dualistic experience. Such assertions arise from meditative experience as opposed to metaphysical speculation, and what they affirm cannot be grasped conceptually or even imagined (Gyamtso 1988, 38–39, 77–78, 84; Williams 1989, 100). As already suggested, the main purpose of such assertions is to focus attention on immediate experience and so to reinforce the occasional glimpses of the egolessness of *self* and *other* that might otherwise be dismissed, ignored, or misinterpreted. Positive assertions, taken metaphorically, also serve to counteract any tendency to draw nihilistic conclusions from too literal an interpretation of emptiness. Within the Mahāyāna, then, it is taught that it is a grave mistake to cling to any concept or teaching, Buddhist or otherwise, most particularly that of emptiness.[38] For it is expected that all conceptual schemes will sooner or later have to be abandoned in the movement towards what "cannot be expressed as a set of statements."[39]

> Thus most, if not all, of the Buddha's teachings have a relative value and only a relative truth. They are to be used like ladders, or, to use an age-old Buddhist image, like a raft employed to cross a river. There is no point in carrying the raft once the journey has been completed and its function fulfilled. When used, such a teaching transcends itself. (Williams 1989, 143).

As one contemporary Buddhist instructor remarked during a talk on meditation: "All these teachings are designed to self-destruct at the appropriate moment"—including the distinction between relative and absolute truth![40]

I would like to make three final points related to the Mahāyāna distinction between absolute and relative truth. First, the Mahāyāna view of relative truth is incompatible with the understanding that propositional truth claims recover pre-given features of a world that exists independently of the subject (Bai and Vokey 1995). Relative truth concerns the relation between propositions (whether uttered, written, or just thought) and more immediate conditioned experience (mind), *both* of which arise within the space of unconditioned awareness (Mind).

Thus, it would be more consistent with the Buddhist understanding of relative truth to say that it is concerned with representing what exists prior to concepts than to say it is concerned with representing what exists in a "Mind"-independent way.[41]

Second, I hope it is clear by now that Buddha-nature is not some Ultimate Reality that is separable from and ontologically superior to what is experienced by those who remain caught in conventional views. There is nothing other than Buddha-nature, the inseparable non-duality of *form* (phenomena) and *emptiness* (unconditioned awareness), perceived either with or without the overlay of relative reference points. From the absolute point of view, then, there is no ontological distinction between *samsara* and *nirvana*.[42] Consequently, in Buddhism there is no basis for depreciation of the sensible or the material in favour of the intellectual or spiritual. The root cause of suffering and wrong action is held to be not sense-experience or even desire *per se*, but ignorance and subsequent dualistic superimposition in the forms of *grasping* and *fixation*.[43]

Third, although non-duality cannot be proved, neither can it be disproved simply by accepting only dualistic experience as normal or veridical, for to do so would beg the question. Further, as Loy (1988, 6–9; cf. Williams 1989, 102) contends, *only someone who has experienced both is capable of understanding the relationship between absolute and relative truth*, a relation that in principle cannot be conceived in dualistic terms. This suggests that, as there is no general rule for making exceptions to general rules, so there is no formula for identifying when the expectation of logical consistency should and should not be put aside. From the Buddhist point of view, knowing when rational argument does and does not enhance understanding is a matter of practical judgment which, when fully manifest, is *prajñā:* immediate, intuitive insight.

I initiated my discussion of Buddha-nature and the two truths by raising the question "Who is it that is having *my* experience?" That question can now be answered. From the relative point of view the answer is: whoever I think I am. The answer from the absolute point of view is: *no one knows*.[44]

The skilful means of a bodhisattva

Because *śūnyatā* is usually translated as *emptiness*, Western students of Buddhism sometimes worry that enlightenment will be experienced as nothingness. Similarly, because the fruition of the Buddhist spiritual path is often described as detachment, they can become concerned that meditation practice will result in quietism, a passive acceptance of suffering and injustice. It is thus important to note that the single most distinguishing characteristic of Mahāyāna Buddhism is the ideal of the *bodhisattva*. A bodhisattva is someone with a high degree of spiritual realization who works tirelessly for the benefit of others.[45] Indeed, within Tibetan Buddhism at least, the very first step on the Mahāyāna path is to make a commitment to attain enlightenment in order to lead all sentient beings to the state of liberation that is free from suffering. Mahāyāna Buddhism proclaims that because all beings are nothing other than Buddha-nature, all are worthy of our concern. Furthermore, since we ourselves are nothing other than Buddha-nature, we can awaken to a boundless wisdom and energy that would accomplish whatever any particular situation required to effect the liberation of beings. All we have to do to awaken to innate insight and compassion is to unlearn the habit of self-attachment. But how?

In the Buddhist analysis of the human situation, realization of our true nature is obstructed by confusion or ignorance, which gives rise to (and subsequently is reinforced by) habitual patterns of dualistic perceiving, feeling, thinking, and acting. Happily, those habitual patterns can be unlearned because the inertia or momentum created by previous experiences conditions—but does *not* determine—subsequent events. In other words, although the law-like patterns in which phenomena arise have enough stability to make relative truth useful, they are not immutable; and so there are often "gaps" in our dualistic fixations.[46] Furthermore, although the unconditioned clarity and warmth of *tathāgata-garbha* is clouded by confusion, it is still sufficient to create within us a haunting sense that there is a better way of being in the world than grasping and that there could and should be less dissatisfaction, less suffering in the world (Trungpa 1976, 149–150). Buddha-nature thus provides for the possibility, if not the necessity, that confusion will be dispelled.[47]

None of the journeys of those who do embark upon a spiritual path—even within the same tradition—are exactly the same. At the same time, there are enough similarities that those who come later can often learn—even across traditions—from those who went before.[48] The Karma Kagyū Buddhist tradition strongly recommends a combination of study and practice as path: intellectual comprehension is a useful precursor to the personal realization of *śūnyatā* that dispels confusion.[49] Buddhist study, as I have noted, is primarily concerned with learning how to correct the false views that reinforce our dualistic preoccupations. Buddhist practice is divided into two broad categories: formal periods of meditation on the one hand and post-meditation disciplines on the other. In meditation practice, use of one or another of a variety of techniques within a favourable environment serves to interrupt habitual patterns, thereby encouraging non-dualistic insight and compassion to emerge. The understanding is that, because these practices are "in tune" with our fundamental nature, eventually unconditioned awareness will be self-liberated: the "knot" of confusion will untie itself.

Mahāyāna post-meditation disciplines, like the techniques used in meditation practice, work holistically with *body*, *speech*, and *mind*. Essentially, they are means of cultivating compassion by putting others before oneself.[50] In Buddhism, to have compassion (Tib. *nyingje*, lit. "noble heart") is to feel that there is no difference between the suffering of others and one's own suffering, no difference between the happiness of others and one's own happiness. This pure motivation is referred to as *bodhicitta*, "the heart of the Enlightenment Mind."[51] Teachers of the Mahāyāna path emphasize again and again and again that, because our confusion is so strongly tied to our self-attachment, rousing *bodhicitta* is the key to realization: "His Holiness the Dalai Lama has said somewhere, speaking from the Mādhyamaka perspective, that in Mahāyāna there are no absolutes, but if there were one it would be compassion" (Williams 1989, 198).

One final aspect of the Buddhist path is worth noting. According to Catholicism, salvation from the state of sin occurs only through the unmerited gift of God's grace; yet, at the same time, it requires our freely willed cooperation (Tarnas 1991, 237). Similarly, from the Buddhist perspective, "we" (meaning the autonomous subjects that we believe ourselves to be) cannot remove the obscurations represented by our self-centred thoughts and emotions because "we" *are* those self-centred thoughts and emotions.[52] Hence, in enlightenment, it is said that confusion is "self-liberated." Even so, from the relative point of view, recognizing Buddha-nature is understood to require individual effort to establish the appropriate circumstances. Mahāyāna practitioners are therefore trained to acquire good habits as a means of developing beyond them. Thus, the entire Buddhist path, including the various formal practices of meditation and the post-meditation disciplines, involves both the "conditioned" and the "unconditioned" aspects of experience.[53]

The fruition of the Buddhist path can be described as the elimination of the confusion that obscures Buddha-nature, resulting in a state of being in which the distinction between meditation and post-meditation no longer applies.[54] Such complete realization of Buddha-nature gives rise to *skilful means* (*upaya*), which can be defined as "any behaviour . . . which is done through the motivation of compassion, animated by wisdom, for the benefit of others" (Williams 1989, 144; cf. Kongtrül 1992, 75; Trungpa 1976, 120). I have three points related to the Mahāyāna ideal of skilful means that are particularly relevant to my interests in this thesis. My first point is that in the same way that the distinction between experienc*er*, experienc*ing*, and experienc*ed* is understood within Buddhism to exist only by convention, so the conviction that actions result from the decisions or volitions of subjects is considered only relatively true. In the nondualistic skilful means of the *bodhisattva*, agent, intention, and act are inseparable.

Parallel to the superimposition of thought on percept, the mental "overlay" of intention also superimposes thought on action and thereby sustains the illusion of a separate agent; but without such thought-superimposition no distinction is experienced between agent and act, or between mind and body. Nondual action is spontaneous (because free from objectified intention), effortless (because free from a reified "I" that must exert itself), and "empty" (because one wholly *is* the action, there is not the dualistic awareness *of* an action).[55]

From the perspective of non-duality, the schema of subject, decision, and action is only a convenient way of describing at the level of relative truth how one egoless event can "condition" the arising of another when unconditioned awareness is "clouded" by ignorance of the true nature of mind.[56]

My second point is that, within the Thomistic tradition, virtuous action depends upon sound practical judgment to adapt general ethical principles to the particularities of actual situations. Because genuinely virtuous activity is situation specific, it can only be described generically as what would be done by someone possessing both the intellectual virtues and the virtues of good character. Similarly, Mahāyāna Buddhism holds that only those who have realized the truth of non-duality have the clear perception and pure motivation to do what any given situation requires. In the most common example, it is claimed that our giving will always be coloured by some more or less subtle agenda to the extent that we continue to interpret our experience in terms of *self* and *other*. In contrast, the generosity of the *bodhisattva* is described as perfect precisely because the distinctions between giver, giving, and gift have been transcended.[57] It is for this reason that, although moral codes play an extremely important role in the Buddhist path, the Mahāyāna practitioner is also eventually encouraged to go beyond conventional concepts of good and evil, right and wrong, that are based upon the reference points of *self* and *other* (Williams 1989, 144–145). To do what one *thinks* one should do in order to live up to one's self-concept as a "good" person (regardless of whether "good" means rational, liberal, charitable, caring, honourable, egalitarian, sensitive, or something else) is only an intermediary step, even if a very important one, in the Buddhist schema of moral development.

My third point, which concerns the relation between intrinsic value and the quality of human experience, is that people typically begin Buddhist study and practice to alleviate their own suffering or dissatisfaction. The clear perception that emerges through meditation practice reveals that the suffering of others is fundamentally no different and no less important than our own: this is the root of *bodhicitta* and the *bodhisattva* ideal. As practice matures, glimpses of Buddha-nature are accompanied by moments of profound joy, which eventually ripen into an unconditioned and so unshakeable contentment. Thus, the entire Buddhist path could be described as inspired by the negative and positive qualities of human experience: there is no question that those qualities play a motivational role. Does Mahāyāna Buddhism also hold that the qualitative dimension of human experience plays a cognitional role? The answer to this is not as clear, but the Mahāyāna definition of skilful means as accomplishing whatever a situation requires does presuppose that some actions are right and others wrong independently of ego's concerns. Furthermore, there are at least some suggestions that the "fitting" thing to do is apprehended directly or "intuitively," and that this apprehension has a qualitative dimension:

Whenever Dogen-zenji dipped water from the river, he used only half a dipperful, returning the rest to the river again. . . . At Eiheiji when we wash our face, we fill the basin to just seventy percent of its capacity. And after we wash, we empty the water towards, rather than away from, our body. This expresses respect for the water. This kind of practice is not based on any idea of being economical. It may be difficult to understand why Dogen returned half the water he dipped to the river. This kind of practice is beyond our thinking. *When we feel the beauty of the river, when we are one with the water, we intuitively do it in Dogen's way.* It is our nature to do so. But if your true nature is covered by ideas of economy or efficiency, Dogen's way makes no sense. (Suzuki 1970, 92–93; my italics)

Mahāyāna Buddhism *is* clear that those who have realized Buddha-nature do not deduce what is right and wrong, arouse the appropriate motivation, and then act. Rather, what is truly beneficial is accomplished spontaneously by the inseparable insight (*prajñā*) and compassion (*karuna*) of Wisdom Mind (*jñāna*).[58]

In sum
To provide conceptual resources for responding to two anticipated objections to my understanding of intrinsic moral value, I have introduced a number of teachings that are central to the Mahāyāna Buddhist tradition as interpreted and practised within the Tibetan Karma Kagyü and Nyingma lineages. According to those teachings, human potential is actualized and human longing fulfilled in the realization of our true nature, which is unconditioned awareness, non-discursive insight, and limitless compassion.

A "Mahāyāna" Metaethics

Reasons of the heart
In the context of these Mahāyāna teachings I can articulate another key claim of my moral point of view: It is in the state of unconditioned awareness prior to the imposition of relative reference points—particularly and most fundamentally the reference points of *self* and *other*—that non-relative intrinsic value, moral and non-moral, is apprehended. That non-relative intrinsic value is apprehended non-dualistically is suggested by the very idea of something being unconditionally good

or unconditionally bad. Dualistic judgments of value by definition presuppose the distinction between *self* and *other*. Therefore, they necessarily presuppose human interests, however altruistic those interests might be. Conversely, then, apprehensions of what is categorically good or bad presuppose a perspective that is completely free of subject-object duality and its attendant self-preoccupation.

To refer to non-dualistic apprehensions of intrinsic value I will adopt Pascal's (1910, 99) phrase "reasons of the heart."[59] The reference to *heart* captures something of a Mahāyāna view of wisdom—recall the definition of *bodhicitta*—and (I hope) makes what I am trying to describe more familiar to readers unused to the notion of non-dualistic insight. I worry that the unconditioned experiencing to which I refer might seem very mysterious, something achieved only through years of esoteric exercises. It is my understanding that, on the contrary, non-dualistic experiencing is perfectly ordinary. According to Buddhism, independent subjects and objects do not exist and never have; those who "wake up" realize that perceiving, feeling, thinking, and acting are and always have been non-dualistic. In other words, experiencing does not result from the interaction of an independent subject and independent world, even when that dualistic interpretive framework is subsequently imposed. Therefore, what takes training is not experiencing phenomena prior to conceptualization, but relaxing our habitual preoccupations long enough to notice. For example, we all have many moments of "pure" perception in any given day, such as when a flash of colour arrests our eyes, or a sudden noise cuts through our internal dialogues.[60] If such moments are unfamiliar, it is only because of how quickly we generally pass from percept to concept, from "Thusness" to "whatness" (Bai and Vokey 1995, 5). And we all have experiences of non-dualistic activity of the kind described by musicians, dancers, athletes, and other performers, wherein there is no separation between action and agent. It is my understanding that, similarly, we commonly experience what I am calling reasons of the heart: immediate cognitive-affective responses, both "positive" and "negative," that arise in the unself-conscious space of Nowness. Indeed, I think it is precisely because non-dualistic apprehensions of intrinsic value happen constantly "in the gaps" between our thoughts that the notion of non-conceptual moral intuitions is a perennial feature of ethical theories.[61] One of the strengths of Mahāyāna Buddhist traditions, and one of the reasons that I draw from their teachings, is that they include well-developed ontological, epistemological, and psychological frameworks within which the notion of moral intuition becomes philosophically and educationally workable.

An example of what I am referring to as an "immediate apprehension" might be the moment in which we encounter someone on the street and respond with compassion for his or her evident suffering. The dualistic imposition that might follow (in a fraction of a second) could include a perception that the person is very dirty and reeks of alcohol; followed by a feeling of aversion; and subsequent internal dialogue over what one "should" do in this kind of situation, however we have come to label it. I offer this example not to moralize, but to draw attention to the tension we might feel in such situations between an unconditioned and a conditioned response—between "opening up" and "closing down." I think that how we are feeling when we walk away from such situations tells us something important.

If non-dualistic experiencing is as common as I have claimed, then one would expect that references to it would not be limited to Buddhist teachings—or even to "Eastern" philosophy altogether. It is true that, for whatever reason, mainstream "Western" traditions of enquiry have tended to take dualistic interpretations of experience for granted.[62] Even so, expressions of and arguments for non-duality can be found throughout the history of Western religion, literature, and philosophy. For example, the accounts of their experiences left by Western contemplatives exhibit a striking set of similarities to those left by their Eastern counterparts—differences in world view notwithstanding—including wide agreement that the highest form of knowledge is non-conceptual and so ineffable, transcending our usual *self* and *other* frames of reference (Huxley 1994, 147–170; Smith 1989, 47–76). Similarly, throughout the ages there have been those who describe aesthetic experience in a non-dualistic way, contrasting such experience to our more familiar, conceptually mediated perception.[63] Iris Murdoch makes the link to ethics, referring to a kind of "unselfing" that is important to moral virtue as well as to art. Murdoch's description captures well the "ordinariness" of immediate experience that is prior to subject-object differentiation:

> Beauty is the convenient and traditional name of something which art and nature share, and which gives a fairly clear sense to the idea of quality of experience and change of consciousness. I am looking

out of my window in an anxious and resentful state of mind, obliv-
ious of my surroundings, brooding perhaps on some damage done
to my prestige. Then suddenly I observe a hovering kestrel. In a
moment everything is altered. The brooding self with its hurt
vanity has disappeared. There is nothing now but kestrel. And
when I return to thinking of the other matter it seems less important. (Murdoch 1970, 84)

Erazim Kohák restores the link between beauty and goodness in his
characterization of a quasi-aesthetic form of perception through which
we apprehend the moral value of nature.

The sense of nature includes also a dimension of value, not merely
as utility but as intrinsic, absolute value ingressing in the order of
time. The chipmunk peering out of the stone fence is not reducible
simply to the role he fulfils in the economy of nature. There is not
only utility but also an integrity, a rightness to his presence. When
humans encounter that integrity in a trillium of a lady's slipper,
they tend to acknowledge it by speaking of beauty, and it is not inappropriate. It is, though, also more—the presence of absolute
value, the truth, the goodness, the beauty of being, the miracle that
something is though nothing might be. (Kohák 1984, 70–71)

Even in the natural sciences there are references to forms of perception in which the self is displaced. Keller, for example, describes *dynamic
objectivity* as "a form of attention to the natural world that is like one's
ideal attention to the human world: it is a form of love."[64] It would be
premature to say that all references to forms of unself-conscious apprehension report equivalent experiences; more work would need to
be done to chart their similarities and differences before any such conclusion would be warranted. At the same time, testimonies to the power
of perception that is prior to conceptions of *self* and *other*—Buber's
I and Thou comes to mind here—are numerous and similar enough
to lend credence to my notion of *reasons of the heart*.

Replies to objections
A non-dualistic interpretation of intrinsic value and its apprehension
provides for responses to the two objections to moral intuition men-

tioned above. The first objection argues from the fact of moral disagreement and from "queerness"—the difficulty of explaining what
moral claims are claims *about*—to the conclusion that moral values are
"subjective" in the sense of *not* being part of the "fabric of the world."
Those sympathetic to one or another notion of moral objectivity have
already assembled counterarguments to the case for subjectivism based
on moral disagreement. They have argued that, in morality as in science, the persistence of even fundamental disputes does not in itself
rule out that some views are more justifiable than others (Frankena
1973a, 110). They have also maintained that there are more satisfactory
explanations for the persistence of opposing viewpoints in morality and
science than the "subjectivity" hypothesis, which has trouble accounting for the substantial agreements that do occur.[65] Some such alternative explanations for persistent disagreement refer to the difficulty of
the questions or problems under consideration; others to the differences among the contexts in which opposing views are maintained.
And, particularly in the moral domain, persistent disagreement is often
attributed to the different degrees of cognitive and/or affective maturity achieved by those representing opposing views—Kohlberg's stage
theory of justice-reasoning again serving as a case in point (cf. *WJ*, 278).

My reply to the "disagreement" argument is that a Mahāyāna metaethics reinforces developmental explanations for the persistence of opposing moral points of view, because fully awakening to unconditioned
awareness is a rare achievement. In our usual experiencing, clear perception is "clouded" by the superimposition of dualistic thoughts and
emotions. And when we conceptualize non-dualistic experiencing in
judgments and principles, we necessarily articulate it in the terms of
our socially and historically conditioned perspectives. In this way, the
conceptual resources and forms of social life available within moral traditions affect how we interpret our moral intuitions.[66] Whether non-
dualistic apprehensions of intrinsic value are even recognized at all
thus depends upon such factors as what are and are not accepted as
"good reasons" for moral commitments. If the intellectualist bias is as
deeply rooted in Western ways of thinking as I have suggested, then it
is only to be expected that neglect of our reasons of the heart will
contribute to disagreement on moral matters.

A Mahāyāna metaethics also provides for a reply to the argument
from "queerness." That apprehensions of intrinsic value are non-dualistic explains why it is so difficult to characterize what true judgments

of intrinsic value, moral and otherwise, are knowledge *of;* why it is so hard to explain what it could mean to say that something is *good* (or bad) independently of human interests; why, as Murdoch (1970, 74) puts it, "Good is non-representable and indefinable." Intrinsic goodness eludes conceptualization because, in non-dualistic apprehension, there *is no* knowledge of something separate from the knower. At the level of relative truth it is necessary to attribute intrinsic value to events, objects, people, or actions in order to communicate something of what is immediately experienced in our reasons of the heart. However, from the perspective of absolute truth, the contrast between what is good relative to human interests and what is good "in itself" vanishes because it presumes an "either-or" perspective that does not arise in *śūnyatā.* Thus, from the absolute point of view of "not two," the *Euthyphro* question, "whether the gods love piety because it is pious, or whether they merely call pious whatever they love" (de Sousa 1987, 9), is seen to admit of no satisfactory answer just because it presents false alternatives.

The second objection mentioned above submits that as particular empirical observations do not suffice to prove a scientific law, so moral intuitions cannot in themselves justify universal moral principles. My short reply to this objection is that it does not pertain to my non-dualistic metaethics, for I have no wish to establish universal moral principles; that is, principles that could be applied to all practical contexts without substantive adaptation. My longer reply is that our reasons of the heart can and do contribute to the justification of generalizable norms of conduct. Our non-dualistic apprehensions of intrinsic value can be expressed as particular judgments of value, whether aesthetic, moral, or otherwise; and, in turn, the convergence of a number of widely accepted particular judgments of value can result in the formulation of general guidelines for practical judgment, including aphorisms and moral principles.

That we interpret nondualistic apprehensions of intrinsic value in different ways corresponding to the conceptual and other resources of different traditions has two important implications. One is that reasons of the heart cannot play the same foundational epistemological role in ethics as observations were understood to do in classical empiricism.[67] Rather, as experiences can only be used to justify choice among competing scientific theories when articulated in the terms of one or another theoretical framework, so immediate apprehensions of intrinsic value can only be invoked to defend moral judgments and commitments when objectified in the language of one or another moral tradition. The other implication is that persistent disagreement among what people judge to be intrinsically worthwhile can be explained by positing different levels of maturity among traditions as well as individuals. For all of their emphasis upon personal experience, Mahāyāna Buddhist traditions hold that our chances of realizing our true nature are substantially affected by whether or not we hear the right teachings.

THE ETHICS OF VIRTUE REVISITED

I have proposed that it is in part with reference to the quality of human experience that judgments of intrinsic moral value should be justified. I have also proposed that it is in the state of non-dualistic awareness that intrinsic values, moral and non-moral, are apprehended. In what follows, I shall reconsider MacIntyre's ethics of virtue in the light of these two claims. My intent is first to show how a non-dualistic moral point of view that grants a cognitive function to the quality of human experience affords answers to questions that MacIntyre has left unaddressed. My intent is also to indicate how the intellectualist bias has obstructed progress within the ethics of virtue by inclining MacIntyre to overlook or reject those elements of his own tradition that concern our reasons of the heart.

Answers to Unaddressed Questions

Perception, the passions, and practical judgment
Mahāyāna Buddhism reports that accurate perception arises naturally once the filters and distortions of ego's preoccupations are self-liberated. The Mahāyāna characterization of *prajñā* as transcendent, non-conceptual insight, combined with the distinction between absolute and relative truth, provides an interpretation of the ideal of "seeing things as they are" that respects the situated, conditioned nature of propositional claims.[68] Further, its traditional teachings on unlearning dualistic fixations at least begin to describe the conditions under which experience does and does not cultivate accurate perception, thereby filling one of the gaps in MacIntyre's account of moral education.

The Mahāyāna characterization of *prajñā* also provides a conceptual framework for the claim that practical reasoning includes a form of direct insight that *codetermines* universals and particulars and so undergirds deliberation. Affirming the possibility and importance of non-discursive insight is consistent with how Aristotle links *phronēsis* with *nous*, describing the exercise of *nous* as immediate, intuitive "perception" in contrast to the discursive reasoning of the intellect (*dianoia*).[69]

Mahāyāna Buddhism's conceptual framework also provides for an account of how good character can be cultivated by habit. In that scheme, the responses that we would call emotions are *not* understood as immediate, but as conditioned by the residual effects of previous experiences, which are retained in the form of dispositions and beliefs. That is to say, an emotion results from the pre-reflective superimposition of a dualistic interpretive framework upon an immediate cognitive-affective response. Buddhist theories about how habitual patterns of perceiving, feeling, thinking, and acting are formed and reinforced are too complicated to attempt to reproduce here. However, the educational application of those theories is not unfamiliar: because our emotional responses are conditioned by previous experiences, dispositions can be deliberately cultivated. That is why habit and discipline have important roles to play in moral education. The link between cultivated dispositions and sound practical judgment is that *emotions establish saliency*. In other words, because deliberation, decision, and action will be shaped by what perception selects as the salient moral features of a situation, emotions play a cognitive role in that "they indicate to us where importance is to be found" (Nussbaum and Sen 1989, 316).

Without minimizing their importance, I would like to emphasize that emotions are not the apprehensions of intrinsic value to which I have referred as *reasons of the heart*. Emotions and the deliberative judgments they inform are in the realm of mediated and hence relative truth because they involve the superimposition of a dualistic framework upon experience. While they are indispensable to moral development and do admit of a degree of objectivity, emotional responses are susceptible to bias and so cannot be exempted from critical scrutiny.[70]

Experiential knowledge of intrinsic goodness
We have seen that, because of the interdependence of the intellectual virtues and the virtues of character, learning *which* actions to perform to cultivate good habits requires an ability to recognize instances of

intrinsic goodness, a "knowing how" that can be prior to and independent of theoretical enquiry. We have also seen how, concerning this ability, MacIntyre says little beyond observing that it comes from the experience of attempting to embody the values of one or another tradition. In contrast, the view that what is intrinsically good or intrinsically bad is apprehended in the quality of immediate, cognitive-affective responses explains why the internal goods of practices, the excellences of the *polis* and its citizens (*WJ*, 110), and the contemplative virtues and practices of the monk—"celibacy, fasting, penance, mortification, self-denial, humility, silence, solitude" (*VSD*, 10; cf. *TRV*, 95–96)—are only appreciated through wholehearted participation in the associated forms of social life. That view also explains why the experiences that transform the passions are the same as those that afford knowledge of what is genuinely good. The key point here is that the capacity of the intellect to transform our behaviour is limited, whereas the profoundly positive and negative qualities of our immediate apprehensions of intrinsic value are inherently motivating. MacIntyre himself describes the intellect and even the will as relatively ineffectual in the face of temptation (*WJ*, 154, 181). A similar view of the limitations of the intellect is implicit in the Mahāyāna scheme of the transcendent virtues (*paramitas*), where, for example, patience is characterized *not* as the ability to restrain impatient impulses on rational grounds but as the complete absence of aggression, of which impatience is one manifestation.[71] Theoretical enquiry into the good might lead me to the conclusion that I *ought* to be patient in that way, but it will *not* enable me to do so, because it will not in itself remove my aggression. Theoretical enquiry is further limited because, on the view that only non-dualistic perception is truly accurate, deductive reasoning can issue helpful generalizations but cannot determine what the genuinely patient person would do in particular situations. It is thus our reasons of the heart, in which cognition and affect are inseparable, that affords the pre-theoretical ability to recognize what is genuinely virtuous—*and* desire it for its own sake—that is required by, but absent from, MacIntyre's account of practical judgment and moral education.

Why be moral? Reason, the passions, and rival moral traditions

A closely related issue concerns whether or not the ethics of virtue provides a more satisfactory account of moral motivation than its rivals. MacIntyre argues that those who base moral principles upon pre-reflective desires can provide no reasons to honour such principles when they conflict with personal interest. Conversely, those who base moral principles upon the formal elements of rational judgment divorce morality from desire and so can provide no "reasons" to be rational. MacIntyre thus argues that the Thomistic tradition is rationally superior to utilitarian and deontological moral theories because the desires are transformed, not merely overruled, by reason. Again, however, "morally good" must mean more than simply "directly or indirectly affording human fulfilment" if reason is not to become the "servant of the passions"—the alternative that MacIntyre vehemently rejects. That is to say, if moral motivation is not to be reduced to desire, however enlightened, then the ethics of virtue requires a *rational* knowledge of intrinsic goodness that is motivating independently of self-oriented desires. This is why, perhaps, MacIntyre claims that reason is independently motivating for both Plato and Aristotle: "it has its own ends and it inclines those who possess it toward them, even if it is also necessary that the higher desires be educated into rationality and that the bodily appetites be subordinated to it" (*WJ*, 156; cf. 285, 301; *TRV*, 111, 140).

On my reading of Aristotle—a reading earlier confirmed by MacIntyre himself—it seems clear that neither the demonstrative and dialectical arguments of theoretical enquiry nor the deliberative reasoning of practical judgment are motivating independently of the appetite.[72] In what other sense of *reason*, then, is there rational knowledge of the good that is motivating independently of desire?

This question is directly related to MacIntyre's complaint that basic disagreement is "recurrent and ineliminable" in modern philosophy because its participants come to the table with "commitments to some extra-philosophical standpoint" and such "ideological *weltanschauungen* cannot be provided support by contemporary philosophy" (*TRV*, 159). On this analysis, what contemporary philosophy lacks is a *substantive* (as opposed to a formalistic) view of reason. Therefore, if the ethics of virtue is to provide for productive debate among those representing rival moral traditions, then MacIntyre must explain in what sense of *reason* we could be motivated on purely rational grounds to select one among competing conceptions of *the* good, with its corresponding narrative of the best human life, to inform the education of our desires. However, no such explanation is forthcoming in the ethics of virtue, no account of a form of *reason* other than the capacities for dialectic, deduction, and deliberation.

From the point of view of a Mahāyāna metaethics, knowledge of the good is motivating independently of self-oriented desires because wisdom is inseparable from compasson in nondualistic apprehensions of intrinsic value. My suggestion here is that "for Aristotle and Plato, as for other ancient writers, reason is an active goal-setting, goal-achieving power" (*TRV*, 154) because *reason* in such contexts refers to a capacity for an apprehension of Goodness that is analogous to the appreciation of Beauty. Even on the basis of my limited knowledge of their thought, it seems clear to me that what Plato and Aristotle mean by *nous* goes far beyond what MacIntyre means by reason. This claim is supported by Voegelin's characterization of *nous* as the presence of the "divine ground" within human experience.

> In the Platonic-Aristotelian experience, the questioning unrest carries assuaging answer within itself inasmuch as man is moved to his search of the ground by the divine ground of which he is in search. The ground is not a spatially distant thing but a divine presence that becomes manifest in the experience of unrest and the desire to know. The wondering and questioning is sensed as the beginning to a theophantic event that can become fully luminous to itself if it finds the proper response in the *psyche* of concrete human beings—as it does in the classic philosophers. Hence, philosophy in the classic sense is not a body of "ideas" or "opinions" about the divine ground dispensed by a person who calls himself a "philosopher," but a man's responsive pursuit of his questioning unrest to the divine source that has aroused it.[73]

Similarly, according to Barnes (1976, 42), Aristotle's claim that *theoria* is the most self-sufficient and intrinsically desirable form of human activity reflects his conviction that "*nous*, which is the faculty of contemplation, is the most complete and perfect faculty of the soul and is, in a sense, identical with the real self of man."

Questions of what *nous* means for Plato and Aristotle aside, even if MacIntyre were successful in finding a plausible substitute for Aristotle's metaphysical biology (in itself no small problem), his resurrection of Thomistic teleology cannot save reason from becoming a servant of the passions so long as reason means no more than dialectic, deduction, and deliberation. In contrast, there is no difficulty in conceiving a rational knowledge of intrinsic goodness that is inherently motivating if *reason* can refer to an immanent "divinity," the "ground" of our reasons of the heart. Here again, then, a non-dualistic Mahāyāna metaethics provides the conceptual resources to address issues important to but unresolved within MacIntyre's account of the ethics of virtue.

The preconditions of education in virtue

Appreciating the cognitive role of the quality of human experience can also illuminate MacIntyre's references to an innate potential for moral education, a "natural aptitude for virtue" (*WJ*, 179). Again, MacIntyre says little to clarify these references beyond proposing that our innate potential for moral development is actualized through our participation in practices, which provide a social context and direction for our *inclinationes* (*RVG*, 7; cf. *WJ*, 173–174; *TRV*, 137). In contrast, Mahāyāna teachings on Buddha-nature can explain how it is that we can appreciate particular instances of intrinsic goodness through the degree and quality of our immediate cognitive-affective responses: it is because unconditioned awareness is never completely obscured that we can recognize, however dimly, when particular actions are genuinely virtuous.

A closely related point concerns the question of why, in the Thomistic moral scheme, we are unable to know or do what is genuinely virtuous until our will has been transformed by the supernatural virtue of *caritas*, and how that gift of grace relates to the kind of knowledge that only faith provides. My answer is that charity is nothing other than unconditional love, unconditional precisely because it is *unconditioned* by the reference points of *self* and *other* (Lewis 1960, 117). On this interpretation, the kind of knowledge of intrinsic goodness afforded by God's gift of grace is equivalent to that afforded by non-dualistic awareness, which is a "gift" from ego's point of view. My answer is inspired by the Christian teachings that those who transcend self-preoccupation eliminate the source of pride, impatience, anger, envy, and greed, and thereby remove the obstacles to being filled with the love of God; and "In the measure that one's love of God is complete, then values are whatever one loves, and evils are whatever one hates so that, in Augustine's phrase, if one loves God, one may do as one pleases, *Ama Deum et fac quod vis*" (Lonergan 1973, 39; cf. *WJ*, 204–205; Murdoch 1970, 66–67). In this context, acquiring faith might be understood not as learning to accept on authority nine impossible things before break-fast, but as developing the confidence required in order to *surrender* the self-attachment that obscures insight and compassion.[74] In Chris-tianity, *devotion* plays an important role in the process of self-surren-der, hence the importance of learning to love God "more and more." Devotion is also an integral component of the Mahāyāna Buddhist path, so it is not necessarily inconsistent with the teachings on non-duality that inform the interpretation of *caritas* I propose. On my un-derstanding of the Mahāyāna point of view, devotion to what is represented as "other" is a way of guarding against ego's tendency to self-aggrandizement; ultimately, subject and object of devotion are "not two."

I have been engaged in showing how my Mahāyāna metaethics pro-vides for responses to questions that are important to, but unanswered within, MacIntyre's moral theory. In particular, I have argued that my notion of reasons of the heart describes the experiential knowledge of intrinsic goodness that is indispensable to practical judgment and moral education within the ethics of virtue. I have also indicated that counterparts to the notions of non-conceptual insight (*prajñā*) and un-conditional compassion (*karuna*) can be found within the Thomistic tradition. This invites the question "If *caritas* is the precondition to all genuine virtue, and unconditioned love the "heart" of the Thomistic point of view, then why does MacIntyre say so little about charity, and so much about theoretical enquiry into the overriding good?"

The Ethics of Virtue and the Intellectualist Bias

I have proposed that MacIntyre's account of the ethics of virtue lacks an adequate conception of intrinsic moral value at least in part because he privileges theoretical enquiry over other forms of learning. I have also suggested the intellectualist bias in MacIntyre's ethics can be at-tributed in part to the dualisms that Thomistic Christianity absorbed from Hellenist philosophy and Manichean religion.[75] However, it is dif-ficult to say that MacIntyre's intellectualist bias is simply inherited, for a predilection for theory seems to influence what he does and does not adopt from the Thomistic tradition itself. In what follows, I want to provide further support for my interpretation of the limitations in Mac-Intyre's ethics by showing how his failure to characterize an experiential knowledge of intrinsic goodness forms part of a coherent and mutually supporting whole with his subordination of the emotions to reason, his anti-nominalistic metaphysics, and his mistrust of non-conceptual insight.

Reason and the emotions

That MacIntyre overlooks the cognitive function of the quality of human experience is evident in his presentation of Aristotle, in which the virtues of character are relegated to a motivating role and the importance of appreciating what is *kalon* is almost entirely neglected. This is consistent with a Thomistic view of human nature in which "the interiority that is constitutive of the human act, which is identical with the moral act, is a matter of mind and will (*ratio et voluntas*)"; hence, "the human act is one that originates in a man's own deliberate willing (*voluntas deliberata*)" (Rigali 1974, 88–89). On this view of what it is to be human, the emotions originate in our "lower" nature and must be sternly disciplined by the intellect lest they upset its deliberations:

> Now, human passions do influence the *perfection* of the voluntariness of the agent. When a passion *precedes* the act of rational deliberation, it tends to becloud and impede the use of reason. Hence, an antecedent passion can diminish the voluntariness of any given act of the moral agent. An act performed, even partly, as a result of passion, is less than perfectly human; it is a partly animal act. If such an act is morally good, it is less meritorious, when it springs from passion, than it would be if resulting from pure reason and will. (Bourke 1966, 73)

In this we can see why the emotions seem to contribute nothing to knowledge of the good in MacIntyre's ethics: given the Thomistic metaphysics of human nature, "an otherwise good act is less good, if it springs from uncontrolled passion, than it would be if dictated by reason."[76] Indeed, because of the elevated status of rational deliberation within Thomistic ethics, even the contribution of *caritas* to practical judgment is at best obscure (Rigali 1974, 90).

That *caritas* takes second place to deliberative and theoretical reason in MacIntyre's ethics is also consistent with the Thomistic characterization of our ultimate end, in which love is equated with enjoyment—the "highest of all pleasures"—that *supervenes* upon attainment of the Supreme Good that is grasped *only* by the intellect (*WJ*, 191; cf. Gilson 1979, 340; *S.T.* I–II, 3,5,c). It is worth noting that Rigali argues against a Thomistic view that the essentially human and hence moral act is one "of reason and rational appetite or will." Rigali submits that a very different interpretation of the human act is more faithful to Christ's commandments to love: "The human or moral act and the act of charity must be one reality." Rigali's discussion of moral meaning underlines the indispensability of qualitative, experiential knowledge of moral goodness.

> If the human act and the act of charity are one and if the primary locus of moral meaning is therefore the interiority of charity itself, then love is meaning—the meaning par excellence. To know love is the only way in which love can be known as a reality, that is, to experience love, is to know human or personal reality, to know the moral order as a reality and not merely as a notion. To experience love is to know moral meaning in its primordial and fullest form, from which are derived mediately, through a discursive process and the natural affectivity of habits respectively, the moral meanings known in intellectual judgments and in judgments of connaturality. (Rigali 1974, 104)

My conclusion is that MacIntyre's ethics of virtue contains so few references to *caritas* in part because he has adopted a metaphysics in which our humanity is equated with our rational will and intellect, and in which the quality of experience—even unconditional love—is granted only a motivating role.

Regarding anti-nominalist metaphysics
MacIntyre's tendency to equate learning with theoretical enquiry and corresponding neglect of experiential learning also forms part of a coherent and mutually supporting whole with his position on the nature of being and its relation to language. To explain: MacIntyre equates truth with the re-presentation in propositional form of the pre-existing

characteristics of objects. This is because he believes that being is inherently intelligible in the sense of conforming to the logical "laws" of thought, particularly the law of the excluded middle.[77] Similarly, it is because he adopts the neo-Platonic, Augustinian-Thomistic view that the cosmos is ordered according to "ideas" in the mind of God that MacIntyre can hold both that created things have their own predetermined ends and that theoretical enquiry should aspire to grasp immutable first principles (*FP*, 43–44; *TRV*, 90, 166). Because being is intelligible, everything that truly exists is potentially knowable, and everything that is knowable can—at least in principle—be grasped by the intellect, formulated in logically consistent propositions, and justified in dialectical argument.

MacIntyre's commitment to the complete intelligibility of being appears to be based upon a dichotomy reminiscent of that underlying the Cartesian anxiety. In this case, the dichotomy is that *either* conceptual schemes "mirror" the world *or* they are arbitrary. MacIntyre refers to this dichotomy to explain Nietzsche's rejection of propositional truth. MacIntyre reasons that if the possibility of propositions being true or false requires that linguistic structures reproduce a cosmic order preordained by God, then "without God there is no genuine objectivity of interpretation or conceptualization" (*TRV*, 98). MacIntyre enlists the same either/or assumption to explain why Foucault's mockery of classical epistemology and his movement towards "the preconceptual, the presystematic, and the prediscursive" results from his rejection of all forms of structuralism (*TRV*, 52). From the Buddhist point of view, this dichotomy is false. According to the Mahāyāna understanding of absolute and relative truth, the adequacy of conceptual schemes to a given purpose can be constrained by "what is," but "being" does *not* necessarily conform to the laws of logic, and so ultimately eludes conceptualization.[78] From the Mahāyāna standpoint, the Thomistic belief in immutable first principles and the genealogical rejection of "truth" are respectively examples of eternalism and nihilism, both confused "extreme views." The upshot is that if the possibility of propositional truth does *not* require that conceptual schemes "mirror" the order of being, then nominalist epistemologies are *not* necessarily open doors to radical relativism, and MacIntyre need *not* defend a neo-Platonic ontological and epistemological scheme or equate *the* truth with propositional knowledge in order to "ground" his moral commitments.

Regarding non-conceptual insight

Is being intelligible? If what exists always respects the law of the ex-cluded middle, then there is no apparent need for non-discursive in-sight. Conversely, if the law of the excluded middle does not hold invariably in experience, then knowledge of being is not complete with-out something beyond theoretical enquiry. In this context, it is signifi-cant that any claim within the Thomistic tradition for the complete intelligibility of being faces an apparently insurmountable problem. The problem is to define the intelligibility of God, who, as transcend-ing all dichotomies, is the ultimate Mystery that lies far beyond the power of the human intellect. MacIntyre recognizes, with Aquinas, "that there is indeed that which lies beyond concepts, beyond saying" (*TRV*, 166). Furthermore, MacIntyre acknowledges that Aquinas was a contemplative as well as a theologian. MacIntyre refers briefly to the mystical experience Aquinas enjoyed shortly before his death: "such things have been revealed to me that all that I have written seems to me as so much straw."[79] And, on MacIntyre's own interpretation, Aristotle subordinated all other human activities to *theoria*. Why, then, does con-templation, like *caritas*, merit so little attention within the ethics of virtue?

There are indications that MacIntyre mistrusts non-conceptual forms of knowing. He proposes, for example, that "the introduction of the word 'intuition' by a moral philosopher is always a signal that some-thing has gone badly wrong with an argument" (*AV*, 69). He dismisses experience that is not conceptually mediated: "A world of textures, shapes, smells, sensations, sounds and nothing more invites no ques-tions and gives no grounds for furnishing any answers" (*AV*, 79–80). He seems far less comfortable than either Aristotle or Aquinas with the idea that first principles are apprehended by direct insight, for Mac-Intyre subordinates the apprehensions of *nous* to the conclusions of dialectical enquiry (*WJ*, 224; cf. *S.T.* Ia, 1,2 and 1,5). And, while he is unstinting in his criticism of the liberal and genealogical traditions, MacIntyre reserves his unqualified condemnation for the mysticism of Meister Eckhart. He denounces Eckhart for originating a rhetorical form of preaching (in the pejorative sense of *rhetorical*), suggesting that the "irrationalism" of such preaching is the converse of the "hyper-rationalism" of the academic nominalist philosopher. (The either/or dichotomy rears its head once again.) MacIntyre accuses preaching in

Eckhart's tradition of "fetishistic appeals to a particular kind of experience," comparing such appeals to the rationalizations of Scripture
employed by "modern" evangelical fundamentalists (*TRV*, 168–169).
The least we could say is that MacIntyre regards any claims for non-
discursive religious knowledge with suspicion.

To propose that MacIntyre's disregard of contemplation is rooted
in a mistrust of non-conceptual insight invites the further question
"What is threatening about nonconceptual insight?" Some possible answers are to be found in MacIntyre's discussion of Eckhart, which draws
on John D. Caputo's *The Mystical Element in Heidegger's Thought* (1986).
MacIntyre indicates how Eckhart's appeal to a direct experience of God
in "a mode of speech unconstrained by logic, by the structures of
rational theory and practice" rejects the priority of theological and
philosophical reason over religious experience. MacIntyre's apparent
concern is that "a mode of discourse which claims allegiance independently of and, if necessary, in defiance of reason" inevitably serves
to protect self-serving manipulators of public opinion from rational
accountability. In other words, he suggests that placing religious experience outside ecclesiastical authority opens the doors to rampant
irrationality. The irony here is twofold. First, that MacIntyre here presents accountability to "some public standard" of rationality as the
proper defence against demagoguery *in contrast to* the virtues internal
to a practice, in this case, the practice of preaching. The ideal of an
educated public sharing standards of rationality is a noble one, but
MacIntyre himself insists that such standards are internal to a community of enquiry and corresponding form of social life. And it is not
clear that the standards of rationality internal to a tradition are less susceptible to corruption and rationalization than the norms internal to
a practice such as preaching, simply because that tradition unifies a
number of practices under a conception of the overriding human
good. Nor is it clear how MacIntyre's appeal to shared standards of
rationality could cohere with his suggestion that unaided reason should
defer to institutionally mediated revelation.

The second irony in MacIntyre's condemnation of "late medieval
mysticism and pietism" is that his denunciation itself evidences the irrationality he deplores. MacIntyre offers no historical evidence to support his insinuation that those following Eckhart affirmed the priority
of direct religious experience over theological argument as a strategic

move to avoid "public" accountability. Instead, MacIntyre employs rhetorical devices and inflammatory language to damn Eckhart's mysticism by association with "those who place effectiveness in persuasion above rationality of argument" (*TRV*, 168). MacIntyre does not appear to entertain the possibility that Eckhart prized "effectiveness as a preacher" over "rationality of discourse" because he wanted to communicate or evoke something of an experience of God that is inaccessible to argument.

I share MacIntyre's unqualified opposition to those who manipulate public opinion for personal gain. I heartily endorse his ideal of a public educated into the shared standards that make rational discourse productive. And I would strongly disagree with those who see contemplative practice as necessarily antithetical to philosophical argument. At the same time, I believe that the claims of contemplatives within and without the Catholic tradition regarding the limitations of the discursive intellect deserve careful treatment in the light of a balanced presentation of the historical record. Indeed, on MacIntyre's own characterization of the process of appreciating an incommensurable point of view, it is indefensible to interpret a text such as the *Summa Theologica* without considering the practices such as prayer and contemplation that form its context.[80] I can only conclude that MacIntyre's failure to engage seriously either with the nature and implications of contemplative experience or with the associated critiques of Thomist views of language further evidences an intellectualist bias.

The roots of the intellectualist bias: A hypothesis
MacIntyre's characterization of the rationality of traditions recommends that those representing one point of view not only detail the limitations of rival perspectives but also explain their origin. This invites the question "Why does MacIntyre evidence an intellectualist bias?" In suggesting an answer, I could appeal to the Christian emphasis upon ortho *doxis* as opposed to ortho *praxis*. Or, similarly, I could refer to the concern within the Catholic Church that admitting the historicity of all propositional knowledge would undermine the authority of Catholic dogma.[81] Alternatively, I might speculate on the occupational hazards faced by academic philosophers who earn their bread by arguing—hazards with which I have some acquaintance. However, such answers would not explain why the intellectualist bias has recurred

in various forms within both Eastern and Western traditions of enquiry. Consequently, I seek an answer to a question that looks beyond the Thomistic and even the Aristotelian traditions: What is at the root of all the ontological, epistemological, and ethical hierarchies that reinforce the intellectualist bias, hierarchies such as those of spirit over matter, the immutable over the changeable, the intelligible over the sensible, the intellect over the emotions, the "masculine" over the "feminine"?[82]

My hypothesis draws first upon the relation between efforts to identify permanent, absolute, and indubitable frames of reference—including universal standards of rational judgment—and the priority of establishing and maintaining control. This relation is illustrated clearly within the mechanistic world view and associated positivistic paradigm of knowledge, wherein reason is valued over the emotions, what is "objective" is rated higher than what is "subjective," what is quantifiable is preferred over what is unquantifiable, and the universal is favoured over the particular because they all conduce to control.[83] My hypothesis draws also upon the psychological truism that the need for control varies directly with lack of confidence: the more insecure we feel, the more we attempt to master our environment. It draws heavily upon the Buddhist observation that we all experience insecurity to a greater or lesser degree, an insecurity that is most fundamentally a fear of self-extinction. And, finally, it adopts the not uncommon insight that our fear of death arises with our capacity to conceive a future in which we do not exist: "Aquinas says that because of the way intellect thinks, humans conceive and then desire immortality" (Coleman 1994, 75; cf. Copleston 1955, 169).

Buddhist and other non-dualistic traditions teach that our fear of non-existence is based upon a fundamental misunderstanding: we do not realize that there is no permanent self to die. On this view, we fear death and seek control precisely because we identify with our thoughts (which are impermanent) rather than with "our true nature": the unconditioned awareness in which thoughts arise (which is primordial, prior to concepts of existence and nonexistence). Conversely, we will only move beyond fear and the desire to control when we learn to dis-identify with our thoughts and other dualistic frames of reference. The contemplative path can thus pose a threat to those who hope to maintain their self-identity for eternity, because the price of "salvation" is unconditional self-surrender—or, more graphically, "crucifixion."[84] MacIntyre recognizes (*TRV*, 166–169) that Eckhart's conception of obedience to God as "not conformity of the human will to the divine will, but loss of human will altogether" threatens "the destruction of the integral self." My hypothesis, then, is that the intellectualist bias—and the corresponding hierarchies of spirit over matter, mind over body, reason over emotion, what is "hard" over what is "soft," and so forth—originates in the insecurity that follows from ignorance of our true nature.

In advancing this hypothesis, my intent is not to single out any particular person or tradition as driven more than others to seek control by a fear of death. Rather, my intent is to draw attention to an elemental "dynamic" of human psychology that (I suspect) is relevant to the persistence of many forms of alienation including, but not limited to, the intellectualist bias.

Looking Back, Looking Ahead

I have presented and subsequently reviewed MacIntyre's account of the rationality of moral traditions to consider how the general understanding of non-foundational justification developed in earlier chapters applies to assessing moral points of view. I have argued that MacIntyre's ethics of virtue leaves important questions unanswered because he fails to provide an adequate account of intrinsic moral value. Specifically, because he is unclear on the full sense in which something is correctly desired for its own sake, MacIntyre is unable to characterize the experiential knowledge of intrinsic goodness that is essential to sound practical judgment and effective moral education. I have proposed that intrinsic moral value is apprehended in immediate, cognitive-affective responses that are prior to the imposition of dualistic frames of reference, and that moral commitments are therefore appropriately justified in part with reference to the quality of human experience. I have demonstrated that this Mahāyāna metaethics can both progress beyond the limitations of MacIntyre's moral point of view *and* locate the origin of those limitations in its intellectualist bias. I have thereby indicated how, in dialectical argument, the conceptual resources of one moral tradition can apply to the unanswered questions of another, even when they conduct their enquiries in incommensurable terms.

In moral as in other forms of enquiry, more than dialectical argument is involved in the search for wide reflective equilibrium. In my final chapter, I consider the implications of my characterization of nonfoundational justification, combined with a Mahāyāna metaethics, both for the search for a satisfactory moral point of view and for the practice of moral discourse in a pluralistic world.

CHAPTER SEVEN

Moral Discourse

Simab said:
"I shall sell the Book of Wisdom for a hundred gold pieces,
and some people will say that it is cheap."
Yunus Marmar said to him:
"And I shall give away the key to understanding it, and almost
none shall take it, even free of charge."
—Indries Shah, *Thinkers of the East*

In the first section of this chapter, I revisit my account of moral points of view and the common intentionality that makes rival moral traditions *moral*. This serves to identify criteria of satisfactory moral standpoints; criteria that distinguish the search for wide reflective equilibrium within moral enquiry. In the second section, I consider how different forms of narrative contribute to moral development through the dialectical interaction of theory and practice. This serves to show that much more is involved in moral enquiry than comparing explicit schemes of beliefs. In the third section, I remark upon a few of the conditions under which moral discourse might be productive in a pluralistic world. This serves to summarize what my characterization of non-foundational justification, when combined with a Mahāyāna metaethics, might contribute to the convergence of moral points of view. In the fourth section, I take stock of what has and has not been accomplished in this book, which serves to bring its arguments to conclusion.

THE SEARCH FOR A SATISFACTORY MORAL POINT OF VIEW

Moral Traditions and Points of View Revisited

I have heuristically defined moral points of view as the sets of implicit assumptions, explicit beliefs, attitudes, interests, norms, and priorities that can help explain why we choose and act in the way that we do. We construct our moral points of view from the resources of moral traditions, which include schemes of beliefs, stories, images, rituals, paradigms of enquiry, formal institutions, and living exemplars of moral virtue. Defining our moral points of view in this way underlines that we enact them in a way of life.[1] It also allows that, although there will be substantive overlap among the points of view of the members of a particular tradition, no two perspectives will be exactly the same because each person has a unique history. A related point is that our personal histories and corresponding moral perspectives condition but do not determine our decisions, and so cannot explain our actions completely, even retrospectively: Standpoints and corresponding horizons are shaped by our personal decisions as well as the reverse. Even when relatively stable, individual and collective moral points of view are subject to change without notice.

Following MacIntyre, I have used *moral theory* to refer to our most comprehensive scheme of beliefs. Moral theories have been distinguished from other elements of our moral points of view that cannot be objectified in propositional form. In this way, the distinction between a moral theory and the corresponding moral point of view is analogous to the distinction between a conceptual scheme and the corresponding paradigm of enquiry. The difference between a moral point of view and the paradigm of a particular community of enquiry is that the former is broader, comprising the assumptions and commitments that inform an overall way of life.

Typically, the norms and priorities that differentiate a particular way of life are derived from, justified with reference to, and/or generate preference for beliefs about "the true natures of things"—the loose fit among ontological and ethical beliefs notwithstanding. That is to say, the norms and priorities of a particular way of life tend to form a coherent and mutually supporting whole with an overall view of the world and human nature, as we saw in the example of the mechanistic world view. Different world views in turn tend to correspond to different definitions of *moral* in a narrower sense: definitions that derive from different theories of what it is about certain kinds of norms and priorities that they *ought* to take precedence in practical judgment. This distinction between broad and narrower senses of *moral* is consistent with my earlier claim that teleological, deontological, utilitarian, and other types of moral traditions can be rivals because they share a fundamental intentionality that they articulate in different—and sometimes incommensurable—terms.

In my general account of non-circular and non-foundational justification, I argued that it is by virtue of their shared intentionality that rival paradigms of enquiry—scientific, historical, literary, moral, or otherwise—are rivals, even when they characterize their interests in incommensurable terms. It is this shared intentionality that allows for the possibility that rival paradigms of enquiry will converge *and* that provides for continuity between earlier and later formulations of a tradition's scheme of beliefs. Indeed, it is only by positing some such underlying intention that changes in a tradition of enquiry's self-understanding can be deemed a development or a decline. Therefore, to identify criteria of satisfactory moral points of view we must ask what, from the perspective of a Mahāyāna metaethics, is the common interest that makes rival moral traditions *moral.*

Moral Intentionality

In my reconstruction of MacIntyre's most general sense of *moral,* I articulated the fundamental interest shared among rival moral traditions as establishing norms and priorities for human life that are consistent with an accurate view of human nature and the world—and most particularly with a correct understanding of the respective roles deliberative reason and pre-reflective desire should play in directing human action. I believe it is more to the point to define moral traditions as those that are centred on moral values, and to define moral values as what we care about most deeply. This is consistent with understanding moral values as the core values of traditions that prescribe norms and priorities for overall ways of life. For example (to oversimplify), hedonists prize sensual pleasure; utilitarians maximize happiness; Kantian deontologists value autonomy and rational agency; critical social theorists and feminists uphold the cause of justice; deep-ecologists defend the integrity of nature; Machiavellians seek power; existentialists commend authenticity; Buddhists pursue enlightenment; and Christians seek to embody the redeeming power of God's unconditional love. Of course, even members of such traditions will make their practical judgments with reference to a variety of norms and priorities that are more or less integrated within more or less coherent ways of life. Other values than core values can be given priority in practical judgment at different times according to how point of view interacts with context.

I see many advantages in defining our moral values as what we care about most deeply. One is its recognition that of the things we believe are genuinely worth caring about, some are held to be more important than others. Lonergan (1973, 31–32), for example, lists vital, social, cultural, personal, and religious values in an ascending order of importance. Similarly, MacIntyre ranks the ends internal to practices (and so the practices themselves) in a hierarchical scheme. Even those who do not single out one end or principle of practical judgment as always taking precedence over the rest generally consider some kinds of considerations to be more important than others. Typically, whether explicit in a moral theory or implicit in a way of life, such orderings of values are not considered to be arbitrary. They are held to represent what truly makes greater and what truly makes lesser contributions either to the satisfaction of human desire or to actualization of what *merits* being desired because it is intrinsically good. However, what I see as common to rival moral traditions is more *that* they assign highest importance to a *particular* value or set of values than the kinds of justifications they provide for those commitments. In any event, if I am correct, then naming as their moral values what each believes should be cared about most deeply identifies an important dimension of what makes liberalism, utilitarianism, Marxism, Christianity, Buddhism, and other such rival traditions *rivals*.

Naming what we care about most deeply as our moral values also provides a useful perspective on the question of whether morality can be independent of religion. The answer is yes, morality can be independent of religion if by *religion* we mean a cosmology, theistic or otherwise: What we apprehend as most important is not determined by our ontological beliefs, even when we interpret the significance of such experiences in the terms of our world view. The answer is no, morality cannot be independent of religion if by *religion* we mean commitment to a way of life that is rooted in a particular historical tradition: Moral values do not enjoy an independent basis in tradition-free rationality.[2] To the extent that a particular set of norms and priorities is justifiable, it is justifiable as part of a socially and historically situated moral point of view that comes closer to achieving wide reflective equilibrium than its competitors; and this holds equally true for religious, philosophical, and political traditions. (On how I distinguish religious moral traditions and values from philosophical and political ones I say more below.)

A related advantage of defining moral values as what we care about most deeply is that it challenges the curious belief that liberal traditions enjoy some special status simply because they affirm the right over the good. As MacIntyre and others have argued, liberalism has no *a priori* claim to set the terms of argument between rival moral points of view because liberalism also presupposes substantive moral commitments that are internal to a historical tradition.[3] Those who wish to defend liberal moral values must address such questions as "What is it about rational autonomy (or a stable democratic society) that you care about it so much?", "What does it mean to say that all people are intrinsically worthy of respect, that people *ought* to be respected?"[4] I should add that I have yet to hear people answer such questions without directly or indirectly appealing to the quality of experience: what they and others have personally *felt* is worth caring about. For one example, Habermas states that "we learn what moral and in particular immoral action involves *prior* to all philosophizing; it impresses itself upon us no less insistently in feelings of sympathy with the violated integrity of others than in the experience of violation or fear of violation of our own integrity" (cited in Gaon 1996, 20). For another, Richard Rorty appeals to the quality of human life when he says that "the pragmatists' justification of toleration, free inquiry, and the quest for undistorted communication can only take the form of a comparison between societies which exemplify these habits and those which do not, leading up to the suggestion that nobody who has *experienced* both would prefer the latter" (1989, 43; my italics).

Defining moral values with reference to what we care about most deeply also avoids the difficulties of limiting morality to a particular issue. For example, the problem with equating morality and justice is that the selection of justice as definitive of morality presupposes, and so privileges, the substantive assumptions of one particular moral point of view. Similarly, the problem with equating morality with the issue of how people should treat other people is that moral values are concerned more with what *kind* of relationships we have (for example, just or caring relationships) than with *whom* those relationships are with. Concern for *all* sentient beings and not just people is important to advocates of many moral traditions. Again, what is common among the communities embodying rival moral traditions is more the depth than the content of their concerns.

As a final advantage, equating moral values with what we care about most deeply spares us the vain attempt to find a universal, context-free, convincing-to-any-rational-person basis for our moral commitments. I say this because some theorists apparently are seeking such a "rational" basis for the values implicit in their emancipatory projects without reflecting upon *why* they have come to be committed to those values in the first place. Indeed, I arrived at my notion of the intellectualist bias in part through my attempts to understand why, in such cases, human suffering and joy are not sufficient to "ground" moral norms and corresponding obligations.[5] I should reiterate that, in defending the importance of our reasons of the heart, I do *not* wish to suggest that the moral judgments and commitments arising from immediate cognitive-affective responses should be immune from critical scrutiny. Although we can apprehend what is genuinely worth caring about in such responses, we formulate our judgments in the terms of one or another socially and historically conditioned moral point of view. Consequently, our moral values must be examined for the ideological and other biases that distort our reasons of the heart in the processes whereby they are interpreted and articulated in dualistic terms.

Defining our moral values as what we care about most deeply has its limitations. One is that it does not rule out such things as the pursuit of domination that some people might prize more than anything else but would be considered immoral in most other people's terms. I accept this limitation because I prefer to err on the side of inclusiveness: I do not wish to rule out unilaterally any set of values that someone might wish to defend in moral discourse. The problem of how to relate to people who are either unable or unwilling to resolve conflict peacefully is a difficult issue that is not to be resolved by simply labelling their conduct immoral.

The trap I am hoping to avoid is of prejudging substantive issues by assuming a particular definition of the subject at hand. So, for example, the issue of whether or not computers are intelligent can be foreclosed by assuming that if a computer can do something, then, whatever that something may be, it is not a sign of "true" intelligence.[6] Similarly, the issue of what should count as knowledge can be foreclosed by assuming that only *knowing that* represents "true" knowledge, as opposed to *knowing how*. I mention this latter case because of how it can evidence and reinforce an intellectualist bias in ethics: once meaningful experience becomes limited to that which is conceptually mediated, morality can be reduced to a matter of engaging in the right kind of reasoning (cf. Murdoch 1970, 6–9). These examples illustrate that, if it is not to prejudge what is at stake in moral discourse among competing and incommensurable religious, philosophical, political, and other traditions, a definition of *moral* needs to be as broad as possible while still capturing something of what is at the "heart" of the rivalry.

In light of the above, I propose that what makes rival moral traditions *moral* is a common concern to establish norms and priorities for human life based upon a true scale of moral and other values, that is, upon a correct understanding of what is genuinely worth caring about in the right relative order. I further propose that it is because of this concern that questions about the true natures of things—and, particularly, questions about the proper respective contributions of deliberative reason and pre-reflective desire to human action—have become important within and among rival moral traditions.

Criteria of Satisfactory Moral Points of View

In my generic account of nonfoundational justification, I proposed that the agreements shared within a community of enquiry are considered *satisfactory* when they are internally and externally coherent, inform successful practice, and are defensible in dialectical debate. I also proposed that what counts as successful practice is constrained by the fundamental interest of a particular form of enquiry. It would thus follow from my definition of *moral* that the explicit beliefs, implicit assumptions, attitudes, interests, norms, and priorities of our moral perspectives are satisfactory to the extent they meet these four conditions.

1. They are internally consistent and mutually supporting.
2. They are consistent with the assumptions and commitments of the other, more specific traditions of enquiry and practice in which we are engaged (physics, sociology, literary criticism, medicine, education, and so forth).
3. They yield a way of life that is consonant with our apprehensions of what is more and what is less genuinely worth caring about.
4. They are defensible in dialectical encounters with the points of view of competing moral traditions.

Conversely, we might become dissatisfied with our moral point of view for *any* of the following reasons:

1. There are contradictions among the assumptions and commitments directing our overall way of life.
2. There are contradictions between those overall assumptions and commitments on the one hand and, on the other, the beliefs, attitudes, interests, norms, and priorities that direct the more specific forms of enquiry and/or practice in which we are engaged.
3. There are conflicts between our way of life and our apprehensions of what is more or less genuinely worth caring about.
4. Our moral point of view proves less adequate to our deepest concerns than an alternative and incommensurable moral perspective, which also reveals the source of the limitations of our own assumptions and commitments.

On this view, two things distinguish the search for wide reflective equilibrium in moral enquiry. One is its scope, for it is concerned with world views and overall ways of life. The other is its appeal to moral values that we apprehend in the depth and quality of human experience.[7] It is this concern with our reasons of the heart that differentiates moral from other forms of enquiry with a broad scope, such as science. At the same time, because satisfactory moral points of view are those that achieve *wide* reflective equilibrium, the outcomes of all forms of enquiry and practice are relevant to assessing their strengths and limitations.

I argued in chapter five that MacIntyre tends to equate a moral tradition's point of view with its explicitly formulated scheme of beliefs, and that he often speaks as if moral enquiry should be first and foremost theoretical. MacIntyre is not alone in focusing his attention almost exclusively upon the role of argument and theory in moral enquiry. Although I have no quarrel with the importance of dialectical argument or the project of constructing a coherent scheme of moral beliefs, I have argued that they alone do not suffice to justify a moral standpoint. If I am correct, then we need to look more closely at how moral theory is informed by practical experience to understand the processes involved in developing satisfactory moral points of view.

MacIntyre looks to narrative to illustrate how a comprehensive scheme of beliefs should be embodied in a particular form of social life. But *how* do narratives help us enact a moral theory *and* learn from the attempt?

NARRATIVE AND MORAL ENQUIRY

Narrative and Theory in the Ethics of Virtue

MacIntyre is clear that narratives can play three important roles in moral enquiry. First, they can justify confidence in a particular scheme of moral beliefs by reconstructing the history of the internal and external debates through which it was developed, stage by stage. Second, they can contribute to the resolution of epistemological crises by linking later to earlier formulations either of a person's assumptions and commitments or of a moral tradition's fundamental agreements. Third, they can portray the practical applications of the theories formulated though dialectical moral enquiry (*TRV*, 80).

All this notwithstanding, MacIntyre is *not* clear on the relation within moral enquiry between the kind of understanding afforded by images and narratives and the kind afforded by abstract concepts. He raises the question of whether "the narrative forms of the heroic age are not mere childlike story-telling, so that moral discourse while it may use fables and parables as aids to the halting moral imagination ought in its serious adult moments to abandon the narrative mode for a more discursive style and genre" (*AV*, 130). In apparent support of the abandonment option, MacIntyre characterizes Plato's ability to resolve Athenian disputes over the Homeric legacy in the terms of a movement from the "poetic" to the "philosophical" mode, a movement in which the "imaginative universal" is replaced by the "intelligible universal." Furthermore, when he states that "images are more fundamental to the Periclean standpoint than either concepts or arguments," MacIntyre links the use of images and other non-discursive forms of argument to *rhetoric* in a pejorative sense of the term, associating narrative with forms of communication that persuade in some non-rational, manipulative way (*WJ*, 56–57, 67). Even when he allows that some uses of images and narrative are legitimate, MacIntyre often seems to believe that they require interpretation in the terms of one or another theory to become true knowledge: "The uneducated understand themselves through the images of scriptural narrative which the educated interpret to them" (*TRV*, 99). On the one hand, then, MacIntyre often speaks as if images and narratives should either be replaced by or be held subordinate to theory in moral enquiry, once the "final stages in the Viconian journey from the imaginative universal to the conceptual universal" have been accomplished.[8]

On the other hand, MacIntyre also suggests that "to raise the question of truth need not entail rejecting myth or story as the appropriate and perhaps *the only appropriate form in which certain truths can be told*" (*EC*, 457; my italics). Further, MacIntyre characterizes Plato as opposing not so much dramatic poetry *per se* as the "teachers of rhetoric and certain sophists" understood as representatives of the goods of effectiveness.[9] Finally, MacIntyre notes both how Plato cannot dispense with "the images and narratives of the poet and the storyteller" in making his case for the pursuit of excellence as a way of life (*WJ*, 88) and how Sophocles' *Oedipus* serves to challenge Periclean and Athenian *hubris* (*WJ*, 57–58). MacIntyre thus implies that there are valid forms of rational persuasion other than philosophical argument.[10] In one case, he actually suggests that discursive reasoning is *constrained by* the images conveyed in poetry and dramatic narrative.

> It is important also to notice how poetry and philosophy can co-exist within a tradition. Dante for his own time, if not for ours, was both philosopher and poet. . . . Poets, until the unfortunate notion of literature was invented, were teachers as well as makers, presenting truth through images, *images which on occasion played a key part in controlling the direction of argument.* (*TC*, 10, my italics)

On my reading, the way in which MacIntyre's texts present the relation between narrative and discursive reasoning is analogous to how they
present the relation between practical and theoretical knowledge. First,
although both narrative and practical experience are included in moral
education, they both appear to be subordinated to theory precisely because theory affords knowledge of what is universal and context-free.
For example, MacIntyre portrays philosophy as transcending and com-
pleting the kind of self-understanding afforded by stories.

> An ability to put ourselves to the question philosophically . . . in key
> part depends upon the prior possession of some measure of nar-
> rative understanding, but this ability transcends the limitations of
> such understanding. For in stories, as contrasted with theories, we
> encounter the universal *only* in and through the particular. What
> we need are stories which provoke us to move beyond stories—
> although everything then turns upon what direction it is that our
> movement takes. Narratives which point beyond themselves toward
> the theories that we in fact need are to be found in many places: in
> some folk-tales, in Sophoclean and Shakespearean drama, and
> above all in Dante's *Commedia*, which directs us beyond itself to-
> ward the kind of theoretical understanding provided by Aquinas'
> commentaries on the *Ethics* and *Politics*. (*RVG*, 8–9; cf. *WJ*, 63)

MacIntyre is not clear whether he intends "theoretical understanding"
to complement or to replace "narrative understanding" in such cases,
but it does seem that *knowledge* in the full sense of the term is again
equated with the context-free generalizations of *epistēmē* and *scientia*.

The second way in which the presentation of narrative is analogous
to that of practical knowledge is that, in both cases, it is difficult to ascertain MacIntyre's position on their respective contributions to moral
enquiry because the relevant references are not developed. The most
important example of this in the case of narrative is where MacIntyre
describes Dante's work as complementing Aquinas' *Summa* because the
former implicitly supplies a standard for the superior moral point of
view. Dante's work demonstrates, on MacIntyre's interpretation, that
the superior moral perspective is the one that is able to include its rivals
within it, "not only to retell their stories as episodes within its story,
but to tell the story of the telling of their stories as such episodes"

(*TRV*, 81). It is hard to appreciate why MacIntyre believes such narratives will contribute to reconciling conflict among incommensurable moral points of view, because members of a moral tradition *cannot* demonstrate its superiority simply by showing how their tradition provides the resources for the construction of a "master story." They must also demonstrate *why* their version of events should be accepted over competing narratives, *why* (for example) a Thomistic representation of Nietzsche's *hubris* is to be preferred over a Nietzschean characterization of Aquinas' "emasculation and impoverishment."[11] *How* is the superior among rival narratives of human life to be identified?

MacIntyre responds to the conflict among competing master stories by returning to dialectical argument (*TRV*, 142–148, 192–215). And, while he states that we do not adequately understand a moral theory until we know what type of enacted narrative would be its embodiment, *MacIntyre does not explain what, if anything, other than deductive deliberation would be involved in grasping a moral theory's implications for a way of life.* What, if anything, narratives portraying the practical applications of moral theories contain that is not already present in those theories, MacIntyre does not say. I conclude, finding no clear examples to indicate otherwise, that narratives as well as practical judgments within MacIntyre's ethics of virtue are ultimately justified through, and so subordinate to, theoretical moral enquiry.

I argued in chapter five that the ambiguities surrounding MacIntyre's references to an experiential knowledge of intrinsic goodness can be attributed in part to his ontological assumptions and corresponding intellectualist bias. I suspect his apparent lack of clarity on the relation of images and narratives to theory can also be explained in part with reference to his Thomistic world view and associated epistemological commitments. This is because if being is completely and wholly intelligible such that the material differences among particular instances of the same universal are incidental, and if the quality of human experience contributes nothing to knowledge of the good, then it is not clear that any form of knowing other than theoretical understanding is required for sound practical judgment and effective moral education.

To address MacIntyre's unresolved question of how image and narrative are related to theory, I present in what follows an analysis of different forms of narrative, each form defined by its relation to the "worlds" we construct through language.

Forms of Narrative

I have proposed that moral points of view establish the horizons within which we make practical and moral judgments. I further propose that moral points of view take their basic orientation from a myth. Building upon the structuralist analysis of John D. Crossan (1975, 48–54), I am using the term *myth* here in a restricted, technical sense to refer to a particular *form* of narrative. In this conceptual scheme, myths are narratives that point the way to the reconciliation, accommodation, resolution, or transcendence of *binary oppositions* that are understood to be fundamental to human life. Invariably, these binary oppositions are between what is considered good (or somehow desirable) and what is considered evil (or somehow undesirable). Obviously, then, myths admit of great variation in content, according to what they place in opposition. For example, some narratives interpret human experience in terms of a fundamental opposition between social groups (the opposition between property owners and workers, perhaps), while others interpret human experience in terms of an opposition within the self (perhaps the attraction to sin and death on the one hand and a longing for repentance and life on the other). Myths also vary in content in the sense that some portray a way of life through which a fundamental opposition has been overcome (Buddhist stories of the enlightenment of Siddhartha Gautama), while others offer visions of as yet unrealized future possibilities (feminist visions of the post-patriarchal world).

Whatever their specific content, *myths orient moral points of view by defining the fundamental limitations and possibilities of human life.* That is to say, whatever binary opposition we take to be fundamental to human life defines the basic structure of the interpretive framework within which we perceive and respond to some issues as *moral.* Swimme and Berry's *The Universe Story* (1994, 250) illustrates this point very well. They envision the future in terms of "the tension between the Entrepreneur and the Ecologist, between those who would continue their plundering, and those who would truly preserve the natural world, between the mechanistic and the organic, between the world as a collection of objects and the world as a communion of subjects, between the anthropocentric and the biocentric norms of reality and value." MacIntyre's work also furnishes a prime example of how the binary oppositions of myth orient standpoints and corresponding horizons. The basic structure of his narrative reconstruction of the history of moral enquiry is that of the struggle between the soldiers of light (champions of the goods of excellence) and the gathering forces of darkness (proponents of the goods of effectiveness).[12]

If this characterization of myth is correct, then (given that a scheme of moral beliefs is the partial objectification of a moral point of view) theoretical moral enquiry *presupposes* the binary oppositions of a mythical horizon, which continues to shape enquiry within the corresponding tradition (cf. Frye 1990a, 168–169). Indeed, that myths establish the horizons of theoretical enquiry and practical judgment explains why rival accounts of the virtues correspond to rival accounts of the narrative structure of human life.

Crossan defines four forms of narrative other than myth (making five in total) according to their distinct relationships to the horizon or "world" that myth creates: "Story establishes world in *myth*, defends such established world in *apologue*, discusses and describes world in *action*, attacks world in *satire*, and subverts world in *parable*." Crossan's term *apologue* refers to fictional or historical narratives that aim to demonstrate the truth of the basic structure of a myth. If I have represented it correctly, MacIntyre's work illustrates *apologue* in providing a narrative reconstruction of the history of moral philosophy that attempts to vindicate a Thomistic point of view and associated dualisms.

Crossan's term *action* refers to stories that also defend and describe the point of view established in myth, but do so more indirectly than narratives of the apologue form. Action stories work by representing or creating characters "about whose fates we are made to care, in unstable relationships which are then further complicated until the complication is finally resolved." How the resolution is achieved is consistent with, and so confirms, the moral point of view implicit in the story. In this way, action stories elaborate and validate the binary opposition that structures a particular mythic "world."[13] Jane Austen's novels—*Sense and Sensibility* comes to mind here—have been put forward as candidates for the *action* category.[14]

Satire, in Crossan's conceptual scheme, refers to narratives that counter the stories of apologue and action by ridiculing the assumptions, institutions, practices, and characters of a particular socially constructed world. Examples of satire include Swift's *Gulliver's Travels* and Trudeau's *Doonesbury* cartoons (Crossan 1975, 61–62).

Finally, Crossan (1975, 60) uses *parable* to denote narratives that are "deliberately calculated to show the limitations of myth, to shatter world so that its relativity becomes apparent." It is worth emphasizing that the term *parable* is used here in a narrow technical sense that would exclude many cautionary tales—biblical and otherwise—that are referred to as parables. A true parable, in Crossan's sense of the term, is a narrative structured to confound our expectations by *reversing* whatever binary opposition we understand to be fundamental to human experience. Crossan's examples of early parables are the biblical stories of Ruth and Jonah, which subvert legal and prophetic oppositions between the righteous and the unrighteous in order "to remind Israel about the difference between the traditions of God and the God of traditions."[15] If Crossan is correct, then parables serve not to eliminate mythic "worlds" or to question their necessity, but to relativize them—to reveal their limits as human constructions.

What contributions do these distinct forms of narrative make to moral enquiry through the dialectic of theory and practice, reflection and action? To answer this question, I return to issues pertaining to moral education and the development of sound practical judgment.

Narrative and Practical Judgment

Perception and "framing"

Which principles or values are deemed relevant to a practical judgment depends upon how the situation in question is interpreted. In other words, perception is crucial to practical judgment because problems do not come ready made, but are the result of how we "see" or "frame" equivocal situations.[16] Research on effective professional judgment reports that the expertise of those dealing with concrete situations lies not so much in finding solutions as in defining problems. That research also suggests that experienced professionals are able to select fruitful problem-definitions because they have a large repertoire of different *frames* through which equivocal situations can be interpreted. On this view, the larger our repertoire of different ways of "seeing" situations as instances of particular *kinds* of situations, the better our chances of finding one that will afford an appropriate and effective response.[17]

One way in which we can increase our repertoire of frames for interpreting situations is through creative experimentation in personal, firsthand experience. Another is through hearing stories, particularly those of the *action* category, that provide new ways of interpreting events. Swapping "war stories" is an important means by which nurses, doctors, teachers, counsellors, architects, and other practitioners learn from each other's experiences.[18] Similarly, listening to folk tales and reading novels can help people enhance the sensitivity of their pre-reflective moral perception.[19]

Education of the emotions

A related point concerns the earlier claim that virtuous dispositions contribute to practical judgment, not only by furnishing appropriate motivation for action, but also by establishing proper saliency in perception. In other words, our ability to act virtuously in a given situation is in part a matter of interpreting or "seeing" that situation in the right way, which in turn is in part a matter of responding with the right kind and degree of emotional response. Helping us learn what responses are appropriate to particular kinds of situations is another way in which stories can promote sound practical judgment. There are two aspects to this educational process: specific emotions must be evoked and associated with particular kinds of situations. Narratives both visual and textual can evoke specific emotions in a thousand ways, as marketing executives and Hollywood film directors know only too well. One way is by incorporating *affective symbols*, which are events, objects, actions, or persons associated with particular kinds of qualitative response.[20] Narratives—especially of the *action* and *satire* form—can sanction or discourage evoked emotions by illustrating their connection to decisions and actions that lead, in turn, to desirable or undesirable events. Narratives can also shape dispositions by portraying the responses of exemplary characters—human or otherwise, with whom we will tend to identify and so wish to emulate—to particular kinds of situations. In these and other ways, *stories share the power of actions to speak louder than words* (Lonergan 1973, 73).

MacIntyre himself refers to the relative impotence of having a purely theoretical knowledge of the good as compared to witnessing its enactment.

Everyone can discover within his or her own mind that timeless form or conception of justice which is the measure of right action. But not only is it the case that many individuals do not exercise their ability to become intellectually aware of that standard, something for which Plato and the Neoplatonists did offer an explanation; it is also inescapable, so Augustine took himself to have discovered both in his own life as recorded in the *Confessions* and in the life of others, that the full intellectual apprehension of the form of justice is not by itself sufficient to generate right action. And this from the standpoint of a Platonic or Neoplatonic psychology is unintelligible.

What more is needed? To direct our love . . . toward that form is something which we are only able to achieve when our love is directed toward a life which perfectly embodies that form in its actions, the life of Jesus Christ. The particularities of that life alone can evoke from us a response of love which is both love directed toward that particular person and toward the form of justice. And Jesus points us toward that immutable form of justice in God which we first directly apprehended within our own minds, but toward a clearer apprehension of which we continually move, as we come to love God more and more, as He is revealed in Jesus Christ (*De Trinitate* IX, 13). (*WJ*, 154)

Even without such theological commitments, we can agree that it is because what moral values such as *justice* and *compassion* mean is revealed most fully in their embodiment in ways of life that stories shape our moral dispositions more powerfully than theories.

A related point concerns the ability of images presented through narratives to communicate our reasons of the heart. I have argued that we apprehend intrinsic moral value in the state of awareness that is prior to the imposition of dualistic frames of reference. Ames (1991, 231) submits that "imaging permits direct access to concrete detail and nuance—the immediate noninferential intuition of a world—unmediated by abstract and intellectual discourse." As the saying goes, a picture is worth a thousand words. By embedding in descriptions of human action the images that capture apprehensions of intrinsic moral value—portraying, perhaps, a specific instance of feeling and conduct that is noble and fine—narratives can validate the kinds of concrete experiences through which people come to recognize and love what is genuinely virtuous. Narratives can also participate in the power of metaphors to "annihilate" dualistic boundaries: it can happen through the telling of a story that "the present becomes a moment in which, in Eliot's phrase, the past and future are gathered" (Frye 1990d, 7–8). Speaking directly to our hearts is another way in which various forms of narrative can make unique contributions to the search for a satisfactory moral point of view.

Deliberation and imagination

Stories and storytelling can also enlist the power of the imagination to assist the process of deliberation that combines with perception in practical judgment.[21] Through their ability both to portray temporal sequences of events and to evoke particular kinds of affective response, stories can inform decisions among alternative courses of action by describing not only *what* consequences are likely to ensue, but also how experiencing those consequences might *feel*. Similarly, imaginatively projecting into the characters of historical or fictional narratives allows us to "experience" in a safe way the consequences of decisions and actions made from different moral points of view—Twain's *Huckleberry Finn* comes to mind in this connection. In thus linking emotion and action, stories play another indispensable role in developing sound practical judgment.

Experience and generalization

Dispositions are one form in which the lessons of experience are retained and subsequently applied to future situations requiring practical judgment. Other forms of retention include rituals, pictures, proverbs, poems, aphorisms, mottos, epigrams, homilies, dramas, epics, and sagas (to name a few), as well as the explicit, formal principles of theoretical frameworks. Narrative can contribute to practical judgment by assisting us both in formulating and interpreting the genres in which generalizations are communicated. With respect to formulation, storytelling involves reflecting on experience in order to give it meaningful form. Particularly when guided by skilfully posed questions, such reflection can help us articulate the implications of events for subsequent decision and action. In other words, telling a story to others about significant events and/or telling *oneself* the story can facilitate the formulation of generalizable conclusions from particular experiences.[22] It is not surprising that we would spontaneously use storytelling to draw out the morals of our personal experiences, or the experiences of acquaintances, for we are exposed as children to the fables or similar didactic narratives that serve as paradigms of the process.[23]

With respect to interpretation, all forms in which the lessons of experience are retained are more or less ambiguous; hence the indispensability of practical judgment. Do we look before we leap, or recall that those who hesitate are lost? MacIntyre has argued both that moral principles require judicious application to specific contexts and that narratives interpret moral theories by portraying their embodiment in specific forms of social life. What he does not mention is that *action* stories serve to make abstract moral principles concrete because, by presenting the universal in the particular, they are uniquely suited to communicating the practical insights in which universal and particular are *codetermined*. Theoretical moral enquiry can thus no more adequately replace narrative than it can substitute for *phronēsis* or *prudentia*. Taylor (1984, 28) makes a similar point when discussing *phronēsis:* "If you had to explain or communicate this knowledge you would often have to have recourse to paradigm actions, or people, or tell stories."

Thus far, I have proposed that the binary oppositions of *myth* structure the moral points of view that establish the broadest horizon of moral enquiry and practice. I have discussed the potential contributions of *apologue, action,* and *satire* forms of narrative to the development of sound practical judgment. What of *parable*? To explain the importance of stories and actions that challenge the oppositions created in myth, I need to say more about the role of narrative in providing for continuity through change in moral points of view.

Continuity through Change

MacIntyre describes moral and other traditions of enquiry as developing only by maintaining continuity through radical reformulations of their fundamental agreements. This raises the question of how it is possible for a tradition to maintain its identity through the large-scale conceptual innovations precipitated by epistemological crises. MacIntyre suggests that historical narratives provide the needed continuity by showing how later schemes of beliefs are related to earlier schemes as more to less adequate characterizations of the final goal of that particular form of enquiry. However, he also recognizes that if the emergence within a moral tradition of a more accurate conceptualization of the final end of human life is not to represent a new and incommensurable moral tradition, then some "core of shared belief, constitutive of allegiance to the tradition, has to survive" (*WJ*, 356).

With regard to what this core of belief might be, or what form it might take, or how narratives provide for its continuity, MacIntyre says little. His own analysis of the process suggests that moral theories cannot remain constant in the movement from earlier to later stages of a moral tradition. This is because it is precisely through conceptual innovation that epistemological crises are resolved and, given that comprehensive schemes of beliefs must exhibit internal coherence, conceptual innovation in one aspect of the framework will necessitate corresponding revisions in the other parts of the scheme. What, then, if not its moral theory, is the "core" of a tradition that provides for continuity through changes in moral point of view?

Many stories, particularly when taken out of the context in which they were originally told, are equivocal. Like experience itself, they are rich in many possible meanings.[24] Consequently, re-telling such stories can bring new meanings to light and suggest new ways of perceiving, feeling, thinking, and acting. For example, we can give familiar stories new endings, as Alfred Lord Tennyson does in his poem *Ulysses*. Alternatively, we can place a narrative of events alongside other stories that affect its interpretation, as the authors of the gospels give very similar narratives of events different meanings according to where they are positioned within the overall story of Jesus. Similarly, we can substantially alter the "original" meaning of a story by highlighting previously unimportant elements and leaving once key figures in the background. Marion Zimmer Bradley's *Avalon* provides a good example of this in her creative re-telling of King Arthur's rise and fall from a woman's point of view.

Why is this important?

Religious narratives

It is the capacity of stories to take on successive different but related meanings that can provide for continuity through change in at least one kind of moral tradition. Or so Slater (1978) argues on the basis of the comparative study of religious traditions. He contends first that a religious tradition has a *central symbol* as its core. A central symbol is a person, text, or event that communicates a way of life through which (or in which) the fundamental oppositions plaguing human existence can be (or are) transcended. A central symbol points the way to radically new possibilities for human life and so becomes an image of hope for the realization of a very different and better world. Examples of such symbols include "Jesus the Christ, Gautama the Buddha, the Torah in Judaism, the Qur'an in Islam, the Veda in India, the Sage in China, Socrates the Lover of Wisdom, and Mao the True Comrade" (Slater 1978, 34). Slater then observes that the implications of a central symbol for norms and priorities in a particular historical context are elaborated by *secondary symbols.* In one time and place, what follows from affirming Jesus as Christ could be elaborated through narratives of Jesus as Good Shepherd. As social or personal conditions change, new possibilities could be revealed through stories of Christ as King, Judge, Rabbi, Healer, or Lord (Slater 1978, 44). Such narratives could portray very different ways of life. At the same time, each in its own way centres on the redemptive power of God represented by Jesus as Messiah. Slater thus illustrates how, through re-interpretation of its central symbol in successive narratives, adherents of a religious tradition can preserve its identity while developing new perspectives and new comprehensive schemes of beliefs. The central symbol is at least part of the "core" of a religious tradition that provides for continuity through change.

Following Slater, I will stipulate that it is their transcendent end or goal that differentiates religious from other kinds of moral traditions. What makes a way of life religious, on this analysis, is that it is understood to lead to a time or place or state that is beyond the fundamental opposition that previously plagued human life. This end is transcendent in the sense that it is radically different from life as we now know it. It need not be otherworldly: examples of a transcendent end in these terms would include at least some visions of the classless or post-patriarchal society. This characterization of religious ways of life suggests that different kinds of moral traditions could be differentiated by the structures of their corresponding myths. I am thinking here of distinctions (similar to those proposed by Northrop Frye) among *romance,* in which conflict is resolved when one side of the opposition defeats the other, as MacIntyre apparently hopes Good will triumph over Evil;

tragedy, in which conflict is inevitable and at best coped with, as in Moon's (1993, 10) political liberalism; *comedy*, in which conflict turns out to be based upon simple misunderstanding, as in more optimistic versions of liberalism; and *irony*, where the opposition itself is called into question, as in Madhyamika Buddhist dialectics, thereby opening up the possibility of resolving conflict by shifting to a radically new standpoint, from which the opposition is seen as false.

This characterization of religious ways of life also explains why religious values are sometimes understood to trump moral values: in such cases, moral values would be equated with the norms and priorities of the status quo, and as such would be relativized by the perspective of some transcendent end. So, for example, the Buddhist goal of going completely beyond the reference points of *self* and *other* relativizes (without eliminating or disparaging) ideas of good and bad that presuppose a dualistic framework. The Tao Tê Ching is particularly eloquent on the limitations of conventional morality when compared to the perspective of not-two.[25]

Given the distinctive nature of religious narratives and corresponding ways of life, it is an open question whether or to what extent Slater's research on continuity through change applies to moral traditions, such as liberalism, which are not so directly associated with a particular way of life understood as leading to a transcendent end. What I know of liberalism's history suggests that the image of the Rational Individual might function as its central symbol, elaborated through successive points of view according to changing world views, theories of the self, and conceptions of rationality.[26] However, even if Slater's model would require substantial modification to apply to non-religious moral traditions, it suggests that what remains constant through successive versions of a moral point of view is more a vision of the limitations and potentials of human life (although that also undergoes substantive change) than a particular cosmology or theory of knowledge. The history of Catholicism illustrates this well in its adaptation to new world views (*SH*, 110–120; Slater 1978, 83–95). Similarly with liberalism: my impression is that Rawls can be located within the same tradition as Kant, in spite of radical differences between their respective world views and social contexts, because of their shared commitment to the possibility and desirability of rational autonomy and to a way of life based on respect for persons.

There is a "moral" to this story. If a tradition of moral enquiry and practice must be open to change while also retaining some moral vision at its core, then there is a danger in its norms and priorities becoming tied too closely to a particular world view, or even too closely to a particular version of its mythic narrative.[27] The danger of too tight a fit among explicit beliefs, implicit assumptions, interests, norms, priorities, and practices is that "mutually supporting" can become "self-fulfilling": it can become more and more difficult for people inhabiting such "worlds" to imagine alternatives at all, much less for them to accept other perspectives as valid. In the language of systems theory, the danger is that adaptation can preclude adaptability: the more "tightly coupled" a form of social life, the less able its members might be to respond positively to changing circumstances.[28] The Catholic Church's response to heliocentric views of the cosmos and the unfortunate struggle that resulted between reason and "faith" well illustrate the costs of inhabiting a mythical horizon that is too closed and complete.[29]

MacIntyre argues, and I think correctly, that truth claims should be evaluated in part with reference to whether or not they find a place within an internally consistent conceptual scheme. At the same time, he also counts it a strength of Aristotle's and Aquinas' dialectical mode of enquiry that the corresponding tradition can accommodate new world views and evolve in unanticipated ways. Hence, to be healthy, a moral tradition must include stories that relativize its mythic framework, reminding us of the fragility of all human meaning-making in the face of the Absolute. Here is the importance of *parable* to the ongoing development of satisfactory moral points of view: Stories that confound binary oppositions can undermine ideologies and their corresponding biases, ideally opening our minds and hearts to fresh perspectives. I think it no coincidence that Jesus, who brought a new vision of the Kingdom of Heaven to challenge old narratives of the Israel-God relationship, taught his followers with parables.[30]

In the previous chapter, I interpreted MacIntyre as caught within a false dichotomy: either language can mirror the intelligible order of the cosmos or no conceptual scheme can be judged more adequate than any other—"anything goes." Against this assumption, I proposed that the adequacy of competing conceptual schemes relative to a given purpose can be constrained by "what is" even though "being" ultimately eludes conceptualization. I will here advance what I understand as a complementary view: there is no alternative to thinking in terms of oppositions at the level of relative truth, and we cannot dispense with language. Therefore, as Frye (1990a) reminds us, myth is *not* something we can leave behind in favour of theory. At the same time, the adequacy of the binary oppositions that structure our points of view is constrained by the needs of a given social and historical context. Myths can and should be (and have been) reinterpreted or even replaced if they do not serve human well-being. *Parables can help us recognize that all binaries are suspect—that all literal truth is metaphorical—and so help us to "let go" of old ways of thinking and old stories if they no longer afford the transformations we desire.*

These arguments provide a context for Cascardi's (1988) and Davis' claims that "narrative understanding" would help us avoid the sterile alternatives of objectivism and radical relativism. Davis (1986, 6) states that "a recognition that symbolism is the appropriate form of knowledge and expression for substantive questions of meaning and value in relation to human existence can preserve society from a destructive swing between metaphysics and nihilism, between oppression and empty freedom, and allow the development of a pluralist world order with the convergence and complementarity of diverse cultures." An image or idea functions well as a symbol to the extent it points beyond itself to what can only be directly experienced. To recognize the value of such symbolism is thus to acknowledge the limitations of language, particularly in expressing our immediate apprehensions of intrinsic moral value. The implication is that we will remain caught in the "destructive swing between metaphysics and nihilism" to the extent we look to one moral theory for a timeless truth that it cannot provide. Even time-tested schemes of moral beliefs must prove their emancipatory potential with every new generation.

Summary

I have been exploring the contributions of image and stories to the theory-practice dialectic. In response to MacIntyre's ambiguity on the topic, I have indicated how, for many purposes, narrative can neither be replaced by nor subordinated to theoretical enquiry in the search for a satisfactory moral point of view. There are many other analyses of the forms and functions of narrative than the one I have presented.

Even so, my discussion serves to show that the ways in which stories mediate between moral theory and practice are many and complex. The least that could be said is that the search for wide reflective equilibrium in moral enquiry is a multi-faceted process.

MORAL DISCOURSE IN A PLURALISTIC WORLD

I have used *moral discourse* to refer to attempts at reaching agreement across differences in moral points of view. By definition, discourse attempts to reach consensus in a rational way, and so is centrally concerned with assessing the respective strengths and limitations of different viewpoints. The term *discourse* implies conversations, but they need not be face-to-face. Conversations can take place through texts and many other mediums of communication. We can even speak of dialogue, if somewhat metaphorically, with people long passed away (Bernstein 1983, 162).

As an integral part of their search for satisfactory moral points of view, advocates of competing religious, philosophical, political, and other traditions have engaged in moral discourse for the last three thousand years. The plurality of moral standpoints is not exclusively a modern phenomenon; nor are efforts to assess the strengths and limitations of incommensurable moral perspectives against the expectation of wide reflective equilibrium. We do not need to invent new forms of enquiry, argument, or practice to pursue the convergence of moral points of view. Rather, we need to challenge the unnecessarily narrow conceptions of rationality and morality that have displaced moral discourse to the margins of modern society.

My account of non-foundational justification in terms of a search for wide reflective equilibrium, combined with a Mahāyāna metaethics, provides a philosophical framework within which the possibility of reaching agreement among incommensurable viewpoints can be affirmed. Unfortunately, the obstacles to a convergence of moral points of view are not simply philosophical. Although I cannot present a complete response to pessimism about the prospects for agreement across moral traditions, I consider in what follows some of the conditions under which moral discourse could be productive in a pluralistic world.

Mahāyāna Metaethics and Moral Consensus

One basic condition of productive moral discourse is the existence of mature traditions of moral enquiry and practice. Mature traditions are those whose members have realized from passing through epistemological crises that they do not possess the whole and absolute truth. We need such traditions to teach us to be open to what we might learn from other points of view. In saying this, I am agreeing with MacIntyre that we achieve moral self-consciousness only through appropriating, critically and/or uncritically, the narrative and other resources of some concrete social context. I am also agreeing that there is no place from which we can engage in moral discourse that is not historically and socially situated. I am also saying—disagreeing, perhaps, with MacIntyre—that productive moral discourse requires that no point of view be exempted by an appeal to authority from critical scrutiny in the light of present experience. The Mahāyāna distinction between absolute and relative truth is useful in this connection, for it allows us to accept the limitations of all schemes of beliefs without falling prey to moral scepticism. Happily, there are many educators contributing towards general recognition of the value of multiple perspectives through their work in areas such as open-mindedness, critical thinking, multi-culturalism, anti-racism, and post-conventional thinking.

A second condition of productive moral discourse is that people representing incommensurable moral points of view understand each perspective in its own terms.[31] I agree with MacIntyre that coming to understand the viewpoint of an incommensurable tradition of enquiry is usefully compared to learning another language as a second first language. On this analogy, learning to speak the "language" of an incommensurable moral point of view involves not only deciphering terms that have no counterpart in one's own scheme of beliefs, but also coming to appreciate assumptions, interests, norms, and priorities that are not explicitly formulated. For example, it requires appreciating the metaphors, images, concepts, models, and narrative frameworks through which people from other traditions "see" the world. As MacIntyre suggests, this might entail participation in unfamiliar forms of social life. Developing a deeper understanding of people who have a different moral perspective could involve dwelling in their homes, joining in their music-making, listening to their stories, and enlisting in their struggles—or just sitting with them in silence.[32]

Reaching understanding across differences is one thing; reaching agreement is another. To achieve a convergence of our own with other moral points of view we must be willing to undergo new kinds of experiences and to follow creative leaps of imagination. Such willingness is necessary because transformations of experience and corresponding shifts in horizon can reveal beliefs that we previously considered absurd to be both intelligible and persuasive.[33] Open-mindedness is thus a necessary but not sufficient condition for success in moral discourse. Depending upon what we have and have not experienced, we might be willing but as yet unable to appreciate the power of another moral point of view. We might have to do more than study texts and oral traditions to understand why people are committed to their projects: we might have to walk a mile in their shoes. In its attention to the quality of experience, a Mahāyāna metaethics reminds us that as developing sound practical judgment necessarily involves an experiential knowledge of intrinsic goodness, so understanding an incommensurable moral tradition requires a personal appreciation of the core values of its corresponding way of life.

It is important to recall here that objectivity in enquiry is opposed not to subjectivity, but to bias. The process of seeking wide reflective equilibrium is self-correcting only so long as we do not consciously or unconsciously ignore any feature of experience relevant to the issue at hand. A Mahāyāna understanding of non-discursive insight reaffirms the possibility of objectivity by allowing us to retain the ideal of "seeing things as they are" while honouring the conditioned nature of propositional truth. Acknowledging the role of narrative in moral enquiry— in particular, the power and pervasiveness of myth—reinforces the need for "educated imaginations" and "critical poetics" in appropriating the resources of our moral traditions.[34] In addition, if morality is as centrally concerned with the quality of human experience as I have claimed, and the intellectualist bias as deep-rooted as I have declared, then our neglect of the reasons of the heart explains the lack of current moral consensus in a way that holds out some hope for future progress.[35]

Discourse and Common Ground

For moral discourse to make progress, there must be a prior understanding that the only force involved will be the force of rational persuasion, where *rational* is defined in opposition to what is manipulative or coercive. The ideals of unconditional respect for persons and commitment to truth are shared among many moral traditions: they are the heart of any formal criteria of dialogue we might define. Our ability to reach agreement across fundamental differences would only be enhanced by feeling genuine respect for other people, however objectionable their standpoints might seem. In this connection, it is a strength of Mahāyāna Buddhism and many other religious traditions that they provide practical instruction in how to educate ourselves so that the unconditional worth of persons becomes a matter of direct experience instead of an abstract ideal.

As well as commitment to genuine consensus, productive moral discourse requires some substantive agreements among participants, because efforts to resolve conflict must have some common ground to which to appeal. Productive argument and instruction always presuppose prior assent to some minimal set of norms and beliefs.[36] My interpretation of a Mahāyāna metaethics supplies a defensible framework for an appeal to moral intuitions. More generally, my account of wide reflective equilibrium underlines that *anything*—belief, attitude, interest, norm, priority, or practice—can provide a point of departure for productive moral discourse. Kohlberg's cognitive-developmental paradigm of moral education once again affords an illustration. His moral philosophy reflects a particular set of interrelated beliefs about the nature of persons, history, knowledge, morality, and the cosmos itself.[37] Within his scheme of beliefs, the fundamental commitment to equal respect for the dignity of persons is closely tied to a conception of persons as rational, autonomous wills, or "self-determining and rule-following agents" (Boyd 1980, 200). This view of persons is reflected in Kohlberg's characterization of the highest stage of moral reasoning, and in his neglect of the affective or qualitative dimension of moral development (Wallwork 1985, 96–97). Seyla Benhabib shows how feminist dissatisfaction with this set of assumptions born of very different experiences both of the content and of the processes of moral judgment has led to an embodied and relational view of persons. Given

Kohlberg's fundamental commitment to respect for human dignity, it is reasonable to suppose that he would have been open to adopting a more relational and situated view of persons, if it could be shown that the moral significance of "difference" must be appreciated to resist systemic oppression. Adopting this view of persons would entail a corresponding paradigm shift in how the whole sphere of morality is conceived (Benhabib 1987, 77–95).

Even where common ground exists, moral discourse is unlikely to take place, much less succeed, unless we believe that efforts to achieve a convergence of moral viewpoints are worthwhile. Worsfold (1993) challenges this belief by arguing *for* Rawls's "overlapping consensus" approach to creating agreement, and *against* MacIntyre's "tournament of the traditions." Worsfold proposes that dialectical debate among rival moral traditions is undesirable, unworkable, and, above all, unnecessary. Worsfold endorses Rawls's belief that liberal democracy has been around long enough, and worked well enough, that a moral consensus sufficient for a just and stable pluralistic society could be formed out of the intuitive ideas latent in our political culture.

Against Worsfold, I have argued that MacIntyre's and Rawls's responses to pluralism can be seen as complementary, at least to some degree (Vokey 1993). On the one hand, MacIntyre says little about how we would arrive at consensus upon the "large areas of agreement without which conflict and disagreement themselves would necessarily be sterile." Obviously, Rawls's project of identifying an overlapping consensus is relevant to this task, even if short on detail regarding how it would proceed. On the other hand, Rawls provides no evidence to support his claim that enough of an overlapping consensus already exists, waiting to be identified, to form the basis of a just and stable democratic society. From where I look, Rawls's optimism appears unwarranted. Because of substantive differences in world views, the appearance of agreement on basic moral principles often dissolves in attempts to translate them into practice. For example, so long as we are working with very different assumptions about what it means to be a person, agreement on "respect for persons" will provide little guidance on issues such as euthanasia, infanticide, and abortion.[38] Rawls's efforts towards an overlapping consensus, like Habermas' analysis of the norms implicit in speech oriented to communication, would seem only to help us arrive where moral discourse should begin.

Lest the "common ground" condition for productive moral discourse appear unrealistic, I should also mention some of what we would *not* need to agree upon at the start. We do not need to agree upon which moral values are most important, how moral values are distinguished from other valid concerns, whether or not there are universal moral values, whether or not emotions play a cognitive role in practical and moral judgment, how persons are best conceived, or which of the various criteria for a satisfactory moral point of view should have greater and lesser weight in comparing rival traditions. Agreement on these and other issues is not necessary, because moral discourse can bring them all into the process of seeking wide reflective equilibrium. So, for example, liberals and communitarians can compare their respective viewpoints against the expectation of internal and external coherence, examining whether or to what extent their assumptions about human nature and the world form a coherent and mutually supporting whole with their moral values and actual practices. MacIntyre and others (Sandel 1982) model this process in their critical analyses of liberal views of the self. More generally, my review of MacIntyre illustrates how wide the search for reflective equilibrium can be. Theories of language, the emotions, personal identity, the virtues, narrative, practical judgment, objectivity, rationality, beauty, truth, goodness, and being itself can all come under question in moral discourse.

My discussion of narrative illustrates that moral discourse encompasses much more than arguments among moral philosophers and other academics. Even so, the chances of resolving conflict among rival moral standpoints would be improved if university research was enlisted in the search for satisfactory moral points of view. What kind of institution of "higher education" could sustain the practice of moral discourse?

MacIntyre and the Post-Liberal University

According to MacIntyre, public life and moral philosophy have *both* suffered as a result of being separated within modern liberal democracies. Public life has lost accessible forums for productive debate on the appropriate norms and priorities for social life:

Thinking has become the occupational responsibility of those who discharge certain social roles: the professional scientist, for example. But those topics thinking about which is of general social concern, thought about goods and the good, about the relationship of justice to effectiveness or the place of aesthetic goods in human life, about the tragic, the comic, and the farcical not only in literature, but also in politics and economics, *either* are handed over to certain disciplined, but limited because professionalized, specialists, *or* are dealt with in forums in which the constraints of disciplined exchange are almost entirely lacking.[39]

Modern moral philosophy, isolated in the academy, has lost its connections to the issues facing one or another particular community of enquiry in some particular historical, social, political, cultural, and economic context. By holding its concepts and arguments to the expectation of timeless and universal validity, it abstracts itself from the very conditions under which its conflicts could be resolved in a rational way (*EP*, 33; *TRV*, 192–194)

MacIntyre's goal is to re-establish the conditions for productive public debate on substantive moral issues. He believes that in order for public debate to be productive, participants must agree on the standards they will use to differentiate stronger from weaker claims, arguments, and positions. He further believes that public debate is only fully rational when the standards to which participants appeal can themselves be vindicated. Ideally, in MacIntyre's view, "universities are places where conceptions of and standards of rational justification are elaborated, put to work in the detailed practices of enquiry, and themselves rationally evaluated." Indeed, MacIntyre proposes that vindicating rational standards for public enquiry and debate is the "peculiar and essential function" of a university (*TRV*, 222).

MacIntyre charges that the modern liberal university cannot fulfil this "essential function." He cites three grounds. First, he claims that it has institutionalized the *encyclopaedic* position on the issue of rational justification, for it assumes that arguments must earn the assent of "any rational person whatsoever" (*EP*, 33). Second, he observes that, because it typically treats different kinds of claims separately in different disciplines, the modern liberal university renders impossible the kind of critical comparisons of competing world views through which competitors to *encyclopaedia* could demonstrate their rational superiority. MacIntyre's objection here is that the competing conceptions of rational justification internal to Thomism and other traditions rival to liberalism are neutralized by the modern liberal university's disciplinary framework and dominant forms of discourse. Third, MacIntyre complains that the modern university renders its liberal values immune to challenge from competing moral standpoints by relegating moral commitments to "the realm of privatized belief." In MacIntyre's eyes, the first and third features of the liberal university are connected: It is precisely because no substantive moral norm has been found to be justifiable in a context-free way—that is, to any rational person whatsoever—that the liberal university has pushed moral issues to the disciplinary sidelines. Ironically, by excluding meaningful debate among rival moral points of view, the modern liberal university has contributed to a social context in which it is unable to justify many of its endeavours to a public increasingly reluctant to support research that has no visible economic payoff (*EP*, 28, 33; *TRV*, 217–222, 227).

MacIntyre proposes that, to generate standards for public debate on substantive moral issues, the post-liberal university should be a place "where rival and antagonistic views of rational justification, such as those of genealogists and Thomists, are afforded the opportunity both to develop their own enquiries, in practice and in the articulation of the theory of that practice, and to conduct their intellectual and moral warfare" (*TRV*, 222). To contain such "warfare," post-liberal universities must be institutions of constrained disagreement. Enquiry would be productive because members would each play a double role. One role would be that of protagonist of the point of view of a particular religious, philosophical, political, or other tradition. As protagonists of particular viewpoints, members of post-liberal universities would "advance enquiry from within that particular point of view, preserving and transforming the initial agreements with those who share that point of view and so articulating through moral and theological enquiry a framework within which the parts of the curriculum might once again become parts of a whole." They would also engage with representatives of rival perspectives, "doing so *both* in order to exhibit what is mistaken in that rival standpoint in the light of the understanding afforded by one's own point of view *and* in order to test and retest the central theses advanced from one's own point of view against the strongest possible objections to them to be derived from one's opponents" (*TRV*, 231).

The other role that members of post-liberal universities would be expected to play is that of guardians of the agreements that make encounters among rival traditions fruitful. In this role, their task would be to sustain the university as an "arena of conflict in which the most fundamental type of moral and theological disagreement was accorded recognition." For example, all members of the institution would be expected to negotiate the "modes of encounter" among points of view and to ensure that "rival voices were not illegitimately suppressed" in debate.

MacIntyre's recommendations for university reform can serve as a beginning point for thinking about how institutions of higher education could support moral discourse. Two features of his proposals require clarification in this regard. One feature concerns the question of whether or not rational standards for debate on substantive moral issues can themselves be rationally justified. On the one hand, one of MacIntyre's own conditions for the existence of an "educated public" is general agreement on a form of rational justification for the standards with reference to which stronger and weaker positions are identified in enquiry and debate. On the other hand, MacIntyre also suggests that agreement on rational standards for enquiry and debate within a community of enquiry is properly achieved by simply excluding dissenters from that community. Taking eighteenth-century Scottish society as a "paradigmatic example" of an "educated public," MacIntyre states that its universities were able to help create public forums for enquiry and debate on substantive moral issues because of a "high degree of homogeneity in fundamental belief, especially as regarded standards of rational justification, within the wider community as well as in the universities and colleges" (*TRV*, 223). In his narrative reconstruction of the rise and fall of Scotland's "educated public," MacIntyre identifies three ways in which universities helped achieve and maintain homogeneity of belief. First, agreement on rational standards was achieved through reflection on successful practice (*EP*, 33; *TRV*, 223). Second, there were "the enforced exclusions from the universities and colleges of points of view too much at odds with the consensus underpinning both enquiry and education" (*TRV*, 223). Third, "a counterpart to these enforced exclusions was the use of preferments and promotions to ensure that upholders of the consensus, including those who extended, corrected, and otherwise improved the standards of rational justification embodied in it, occupied the relevant professorial chairs" (*TRV*, 224).

MacIntyre goes on to argue that the conditions for productive moral enquiry and debate were lost when the founders of modern liberal universities correctly judged many pre-liberal exclusionary practices to have been unjust, but mistakenly concluded that rational enquiry should be freed from such "external constraints," most particularly the use of religious affiliation as a basis for hiring and promotion. Their mistake, in MacIntyre's view, was to imagine that universities could do away with enforced consensus and instead rely upon context-free rationality or the practice of enquiry itself to furnish the agreement on rational standards. MacIntyre argues that this mistake has done comparatively little harm to enquiry and debate in the natural sciences because there had already been substantive agreement on the procedures and standards of its research methodologies when liberal universities were inaugurated, agreement that has been maintained through "quiet, informal, characteristically unstated policies of enforced exclusion" (*TRV*, 225; cf. *WJ*, 400). In contrast, there was no such agreement on appropriate procedures and standards for enquiry in the humanities and social sciences, and methods borrowed from the natural sciences could not serve as an adequate replacement.

MacIntyre leaves it unclear whether or not he believes that, in order to restore sufficient common ground for productive moral enquiry and debate within universities, it would be necessary to return to policies of enforced consensus. However, to the extent that post-liberal universities achieved consensus by policies of exclusion, they would do nothing to restore the social and cultural conditions for public debate on substantive moral issues. MacIntyre himself clearly distinguishes an educated public from a group in which participation is restricted (*EP*, 18). Therefore, if the post-liberal university is to contribute to a wider social consensus upon standards for public moral enquiry and debate, then it must be possible to arrive at such agreement in the way MacIntyre originally prescribed: through systematic assessment of competing theories of justification in the light of moral enquiry and practice.

This point leads to the second feature of MacIntyre's proposals that needs clarification. He has argued that moral philosophy within modern universities is unproductive to the extent it abstracts from the issues that in part define particular social and historical contexts. It is therefore surprising that MacIntyre says nothing about how members of the post-liberal university could compare their rival moral standpoints in terms of their consequences for life inside and outside the academy. When MacIntyre refers to *practice* in the moral context, he always seems to have the "practice" of theoretical enquiry and dialectical debate in mind. However, if the post-liberal university is to help restore the conditions for productive public debate on substantive moral issues; if one of those conditions is shared understanding of how stronger and weaker moral claims, arguments, and positions are to be identified; and if such shared understanding is fruitfully sought in the dialectic of theory and practice; then two general implications follow. The first is that we need to look at the successes and failures where university research already inform practice in courthouses, schools, hospitals, laboratories, factories, theatres, and the like. The second is that before universities can credibly claim to justify standards for productive moral debate, they must show that their *own* organizational structures, policies, and practices enact a consensus on moral values reached in a rational way.

CONCLUSION

Looking Back

Building upon Alasdair MacIntyre's account of the rationality of moral traditions, I have identified processes through which, and criteria with respect to which, advocates of incommensurable moral traditions might assess the strengths and limitations of their moral points of view. In addition, I have given some account of what makes moral judgments true or false beyond the thoughts, feelings, and desires of the person or persons making the claim; gone some way towards explaining how the possibility of true moral judgments is compatible with the facts of moral diversity and disagreement; and identified some of the conditions under which moral discourse has potential to be productive. My hope is that, by undertaking these four tasks, I have made some small contribution to the case against moral scepticism.

A defender of moral subjectivism might observe that I have not explained what knowledge of intrinsic moral goodness is knowledge *of;* what it could mean to say that something *merits* being valued independently of human needs and interests. To this I could only agree. Yet, I could also observe in reply that this inarticulacy about intrinsic goodness has not previously prevented our reasons of the heart from playing a central role in our search for satisfactory moral points of view. It need not represent an obstacle in the future. I would add that, similarly, it is not necessary to accept a non-dualistic Mahāyāna metaethics to agree that moral discourse appropriately involves appeals to the quality of human experience.

A defender of liberalism, genealogy, or other tradition might observe that it is easy to look superior in dialectical debate when arguing with one's own interpretation of opposing points of view, rather than with the opponents themselves. Again, to this I could only agree. I have no illusions that I have gone very far in comparing the respective strengths and limitations of Mahāyāna and Thomist traditions. My intent has not been to do so, nor to formulate a comprehensive scheme of moral beliefs, but to illustrate the potential of a certain form of argument. If I interpret him correctly, MacIntyre's priorities are similar. He seems most concerned to defend those aspects of his Thomistic scheme of moral beliefs that are necessary to his account of the rationality of traditions—traditions of moral enquiry in particular.[40] MacIntyre's approach is sensible, for we might wish to accept the broad outlines of his characterization of non-foundational justification without also adopting *all* of the epistemological and theological assumptions of his overall moral point of view. For example, we might agree that evaluating rival moral traditions usefully involves comparing their competing narratives of human life without embracing MacIntyre's belief that life is a quest for a pre-given human *telos.*

To argue that at least a partial convergence of moral points of view is philosophically possible is, of course, a very limited contribution to the cause of reducing conflict and oppression. I appreciate that many people are unable to participate in moral discourse because of economic inequality within and among nation states. At the same time, I believe that some degree of moral consensus would be the best long-term solution to economic disparity and other forms of injustice. I am not saying that it is advisable or even possible for us to refrain from acting unilaterally until such a consensus is achieved. On the contrary, because the strengths of a particular moral point of view are demonstrated in part through its association with effective *praxis*, confidence in a particular standpoint must be justified through present action as well as historical recollection (cf. *WJ*, 403). Precisely because it appeals to successful practice, however, working towards a convergence of moral traditions is necessarily a long-term project. I should add that the necessity of acting in the absence of shared agreement can apply to conflicts between an individual and a community where what is at issue is competing interpretations of a tradition, as much as to disputes between those representing rival moral points of view.

For the foreseeable future, there will be people unwilling to participate in moral discourse to the extent their participation conflicts with self- or group interest. I have no general solution to this problem. I suspect none is possible: what we would judge to be an appropriate and effective response to people who employ strategic means to effect their goals will vary according to how our moral points of view interact with the particulars of the given context. I can only say that moral discourse cannot be considered productive in the full sense unless and until whatever agreements are reached are translated into forms of social and political life.

My characterization of moral discourse has said little about differences rooted in the inequalities of power tied to class, gender, and other forms of systemic oppression. Perhaps the criteria I propose for assessing competing moral perspectives are distorted by my privileged point of view. For that reason, I must allow that people unwilling to participate in moral discourse might have very good reasons for their decision. In this context, I should reiterate that the convergence of moral points of view that I envisage does not involve the elimination of all differences (or even of all conflict), because I believe that diversity, like competition, is healthy when balanced by shared agreements.

Looking Ahead

I would have to do much more to show that my characterization of non-foundational justification, when combined with a Mahāyāna meta-ethics, could itself achieve a tolerable degree of wide reflective equilibrium. I have only begun to explore the implications and consequences of Mahāyāna Buddhism for my own way of life to find out if my confidence in its teachings is warranted. Also, I would have to go much further developing and defending my position in dialectical encounters with alternative points of view. To invite such further debate—and mindful of MacIntyre's exhortation to lay out "theses and putative proofs so that they are maximally vulnerable to objection and refutation"—I will list some of the more contentious beliefs to which I am committed by my moral point of view. These claims as material for, not presuppositions of, moral discourse.

With regard to moral philosophy, I predict that, because we apprehend intrinsic moral values in immediate cognitive-affective response such that the quality of human experience is at the heart of moral enquiry, all purely formalistic attempts to ground substantive moral commitments will prove unsatisfactory. Nor will rehabilitating a teleological world view succeed in rescuing us from the moral objectivism-relativism dilemma so long as it does not explain why and in what sense the human *telos* (however conceived) is intrinsically *good*. Furthermore, because immediate apprehensions of value can only be evoked through symbolic language, we will find that philosophers, critical pedagogues, deconstructionists, and other theorists wax increasingly metaphorical and lyrical (not to mention emotional) to the extent they attempt to communicate the "reasons" behind their moral commitments.

With regard to world view, I predict that, because separate subjects and objects do not and never have existed except in our frames of reference, empirical research will support non-dualistic over dualistic ontologies.[41] Because ego-fixation is therefore doomed to frustration, we will continue to experience dissatisfaction, anxiety, and lack of fulfilment until we realize unconditioned awareness as "our" true nature. Because ego-fixation is the ultimate root of aggression, greed, indifference, and denial, there will be no end to conflict so long as we continue to identify so strongly with the characters we create in the stories of who we are.

With regard to moral education, I predict that programs restricted to the development of justice-reasoning skills or facility in dialectical argument will not succeed in producing people committed to justice at the level of practice (much less people who love justice for justice's own sake). Further, I propose that we should not think of moral education primarily as something that we should be doing to students in schools. We are all already inseparable from unconditioned insight and compassion, which is obscured only by our ingrained, now instinctual reluctance to surrender to that wisdom. No one but ourselves can work with that resistance. On this view, the most important form of moral education we can undertake is to cultivate our own true nature so that we can be of genuine benefit to others.

> If I am not for myself, who shall be for me?
> If I am only for myself, then who am I?
> If not now, when?

> —Hillel

Abbreviations

The following title abbreviations have been used in citing works by Alasdair MacIntyre.

AET Does applied ethics rest on a mistake? 1984b. *Monist* 67, 498–513.

AV *After virtue: A study in moral theory.* 2d ed. 1984a. Notre Dame: University of Notre Dame Press.

EC Epistemological crises, dramatic narrative, and the philosophy of science. 1977. *Monist* 60, 453–472.

EP The idea of an educated public. 1987a. In G. Haydon, ed., *Education and values: The Richard Peters Lectures*, 15–36. London: Institute of Education.

FG The form of the good, tradition and enquiry. 1990b. In R. Gaita, ed., *Value and understanding*, 242–262. London: Routledge.

FP *First principles, final ends and contemporary philosophical issues.* 1990a. Milwaukee: Marquette University Press.

GH How moral agents become ghosts. 1982. *Synthese* 53, 292–312.

ITC Incommensurability, truth, and the conversation between Confucians and Aristotelians about the virtues. 1991. In E. Deutsch, ed., *Culture and modernity: East-West philosophic perspectives*, 104–122. Honolulu: University of Hawaii Press.

MA Moral arguments and social contexts: A response to Rorty. 1985. In R. Hollinger, ed., *Hermeneutics and praxis*, 222–223. Notre Dame: University of Notre Dame Press.

MD Moral dilemmas. 1990c. *Philosophy and Phenomenological Research* 50 supplement, 367–382.

MP Moral philosophy: What next? 1983. In S. Hauerwas and A. MacIntyre, eds., *Revisions: Changing perspectives in moral philosophy*, 1–15. Notre Dame: University of Notre Dame Press.

PC   Philosophy: Past conflict and future direction. 1987b. *American Philo-sophical Association Proceedings and Addresses* 61, 81–87.

PPI   *Philosophical imagination and cultural memory: Appropriating historical tra-ditions.* 1993. Durham: Duke University Press.

PRC   A partial response to my critics. 1994. In J. Horton and S. Mendus, eds., *After MacIntyre,* 283–304. Cambridge: Polity Press; Notre Dame: University of Notre Dame Press.

RPP   Relativism, power, and philosophy. 1989. In M. Krausz, ed., *Relativism: Interpretation and confrontation,* 182–204. Notre Dame: University of Notre Dame Press.

RVG   Plain persons and moral philosophy: Rules, virtues and goods. 1992. *American Catholic Philosophical Quarterly* 66(1), 3–19.

SH   *A short history of ethics.* 1966. London: Macmillan. 2nd ed. London: Routledge, 1997; Notre Dame: University of Notre Dame Press, 1998.

TC   Traditions and conflicts. 1987c. *Liberal Education* 73, 6–13.

TRV   *Three rival versions of moral inquiry: Encyclopaedia, genealogy, and tradition.* 1990d. Notre Dame: University of Notre Dame Press.

VSD   *Sophrosune:* How a virtue can become socially disruptive. 1988a. In A. French, T. E. Uehling, Jr., and H. K. Wettstein, eds., *Ethical theory: Character and virtue,* 1–11. Notre Dame: University of Notre Dame Press.

WJ   *Whose justice? Which rationality?* 1988b. Notre Dame: University of Notre Dame Press.

Notes

Introduction

1. When using *we* and *our* and *us* I am referring either to myself plus you, my readers, or to all people. Which sense I intend is, I hope, clear from context when it makes a difference. I should add that I am not assuming that what makes us similar is more important than what makes us different.

2. As I use the term, a heuristic definition specifies some unknown by (a) describing either a question to which that unknown will be the answer or a problem to which it will be the solution, (b) specifying the procedure through which the answer or solution could be determined, and/or (c) identifying the criteria or features by which the answer or solution will be recognized. Such definitions assist enquiry by clarifying what is presupposed in the very asking of particular kinds of questions or the posing of particular kinds of problems. I owe my appreciation of the importance of heuristic definitions to the writings of Bernard Lonergan (1958; 1973).

3. For example, a newspaper article on Paul Hill (Toronto Star, Dec. 7, 1994, A3), who was convicted of first degree murder in the shooting of Dr. John Britton and James Barrett outside the Ladies Centre abortion clinic in Pensacola, reports that from one point of view Hill's action was seen as murder (he was sentenced to die in Florida's electric chair), but from a competing point of view it was seen as "justifiable homicide" that "saved human lives by killing two murderers."

4. MacIntyre (*WJ*, 5–6). See also MacIntyre's (*AV*, 6–8) examples of how the different points of view of rival moral traditions can lead not only to incompatible courses of action but also to interminable debate. (The list of abbreviations I use to refer to the titles of MacIntyre's publications immediately precedes these notes.)

5. I am using the term *moral scepticism* here broadly; compare Mackie (1977, 15, 18). For an alternative definition of ethical scepticism, see Williams (1985, 24–26).

6. *AV*, 23; see also *WJ*, 51–52, 86; *RPP*, 191–192. Laudan (1990, 162–163) and Allen (1989, 362–363) raise similar concerns about the moral-political implications of cognitive relativism.

7. For a summary of the conditions that I am referring to as the "global context of oppression" see Maxwell (1984, 1–2).

8. This has been argued by Freire (1970, esp. 30–31, 40–45, 73, 130, 150–156, 162–163; 1985, 50, 67–91, 122).

9. For a discussion of the immanent relation of legitimation and truth, see Habermas (1975, 95ff.).

10. Horkheimer (1974, 23–25) spoke eloquently of the impotence of "subjective reason" to oppose oppression; see also Meiland and Krausz's (1982, 4–6) references to authors concerned with the negative consequences of cognitive and moral relativism. Similar concerns have been raised about the nihilistic potential of postmodern epistemologies, e.g., by Lather (1991a, 153–154; 1991b, 36–39), and by McGowan (1991).

11. Morgan (1988, 151–153) makes a similar point in her discussion of the exclusion of women from the public domain.

12. The application of epistemology to political theory is illustrated by Nagel (1987, especially 230–233; cf. Elshtain 1981, 184), who differentiates on epistemological grounds the kinds of moral commitments that should and should not be a basis for government policies. See also Raz (1990) for a comparison of Nagel and Rawls in this regard.

13. For example, the Values Clarification (Raths, Harmin, and Simon 1978) and Reflective (Beck 1976) moral education programs incorporate a relativistic metaethics in the sense that their theoretical frameworks provide no grounds for the rational evaluation of competing moral points of view. For critical analyses of Values Clarification, see Boyd and Bogdan (1984, 1985), Carter (1984, 49–53), Lockwood (1975), and Stewart (1975). For critical analyses of the Reflective approach, see Falikowski (1984) and Varga (1976). The Cognitive-Developmental program formulated by Lawrence Kohlberg and his associates (Kohlberg 1971, 1973, 1975, 1976, 1978, 1980, 1981, 1984, 1985; Kohlberg, Levine, and Hewer 1983; Kohlberg, Boyd, and Levine 1990) is usually tied to a Kantian, liberal, formalistic metaethics, as evidenced by Kohlberg's use of Rawls, Habermas, and others (Boyd 1980; Kohlberg 1985, 506–542). For critical analyses of the Cognitive-Developmental approach, see Broughton (1985), Carter (1985, 19), Gilligan (1982), and Locke (1980, 1985). The Just Community approach to moral education has also been associated with Kohlberg's moral Cognitive-Developmental framework, but the relationships between the Just Community's educational practices and Kohlberg's theoretical scheme have yet

to be adequately elaborated. Approaches to moral education that place emphasis on character or virtue and on community (O'Leary 1981, 1983; Sichel 1988) are generally contemporary versions of an Aristotelian metaethics. Finally, there have been attempts to develop the educational implications of the Ethic of Care (Brabeck 1989) associated with the psychological studies of Carol Gilligan (1982, 1988) and the moral philosophy of Nel Noddings (1984, 1985, 1987a, 1987b). Not all moral education programs, of course, have an explicitly formulated theoretical framework—their assumptions may be embedded in their practices (Vokey 1987, especially 8).

14. For a similar argument that affirming the value of personal autonomy is *not* incompatible with ethical cognitivism and may in fact require it, see Callan (1993).

15. The *Toronto Star*, February 19, 1994, reported that sixteen people, describing themselves as "Christians upholding the Bible as the only route to the 'one true God,'" told the trustees of the Perth County Board of Education in Stratford, Ontario, that they were opposed to the use of texts from a variety of religions in the schools. One person was quoted as saying, "We do not want or appreciate other religious beliefs." The group was referred by the trustees to the Ministry of Education, whose directive initiated the practice of using a variety of religious texts. If the ideals of multiculturalism are to be respected, defensible grounds are required to refuse to accommodate the requests of such groups.

16. Mackie (1977, 17–18) suggests that subjectivism as a "second order" ethical position is equivalent to emotivism.

17. See, for example, MacIntyre (*AV*, 12–14; *TRV*, 11, 28), Mackie (1977, 32–35), and Wong (1984, 5, 10–12).

18. In addition to the differences in moral language across moral traditions, there are those that Kohlberg's research observes among people at different developmental stages and those that Gilligan's (1982; 1988; Gilligan and Attanucci 1987) research observes among people with distinct moral orientations.

19. For similar arguments, see MacIntyre (*SH*, 3–4); also Barrow (1993, 9), Frankena (1973a, 96), Mackie (1977), Rawls (1974/75, 10–14), and Williams (1985, 127–131). Linguistic analysis can settle questions about how moral terms *are* being used, but not about how moral terms are *correctly* used, unless "correct" is defined as being grammatically correct, or as being consistent with the usage of some particular moral community.

20. Harman (1991, 16). Recent surveys of epistemological and moral relativism consulted for my summary include Arrington (1989), Krausz (1989), Meiland and Krausz (1982), Odegard and Stewart (1991), and Wong (1984).

21. Regarding the possible compatibility of belief in both the objectivity and the relativity of moral judgments, see also Wong (1984, 1–5).

22. This initial characterization of framework relativism is based on the following discussions of moral and cognitive relativism: Aiken (1963), Bernstein

(1983, 8, 11–12), Burbules (1991, 235), Devine (1984, 405–409), Doppelt (1983, 111), Meiland and Krausz (1982, 8), Krausz (1989, 1–3), and Weinert (1984, 376–377).

23. For examples of these arguments, see Mackie (1977, esp. 36–38) and Snare (1984).

24. For a comprehensive bibliography of MacIntyre's publications, see Horton and Mendus (1994, 305–318). Although I will draw from texts published over almost thirty years, I will present what I understand to be MacIntyre's current position, taking into account his remarks on the relationships between his later and his earlier works (e.g., *FG*, 257; *ITC*, 104). For a summary of the relationships among his three major works, *AV*, *WJ*, and *TRV*, see Horton and Mendus (1994, 1–5; cf. 298). Wherever possible I will cite more than one of MacIntyre's publications to support my interpretation of his views.

Chapter One. The Rationalism-Relativism Debate

1. Bernstein (1983, 18; cf. *TRV*, 58). For an example of at least a mild form of the Cartesian anxiety, see Salmon (1967, 55). See also the remarks by Carter (1985, 9). Wilfred Cantwell Smith's (1988, 15) remarks are instructive here: "Ineluctable variety has become conspicuous, in virtually every area of life, including the moral and the religious; so that there is no firm ground on which to stand. This can be terrifying for those who see nothing higher than the ground."

2. Bernstein (1983, 4–5, 62), also Barnes and Bloor (1982, 46–47), Beyer and Liston (1992, 373–374), Davis (1990, 160–161), Geertz (1989, 14–19), Margolis (1991, xi), Meiland and Krausz (1982, 4–5).

3. See, for example, Bernstein (1983, 3, 12), Geertz (1989, 32), Laudan (1977, 129; 1990, 134–135), Margolis (1984a, 310), Nola (1988, 1–2), and Simpson (1987, 1–3). Mandelbaum (1982, 45) attributes the "widespread acceptance" that relativism enjoys today to three "convergent streams of influence." "The first stems from developments within the philosophy of science; the second from problems of method in the *Geistes-wissenschaften*; the third from the ways in which certain perceptual phenomena, and also data drawn from comparative linguistics, have often been interpreted." Krausz (1984, 395–397) differentiates the logical thesis of absolutism from the epistemological thesis of foundationalism; and while he seems to allow that an absolutist view of truth might be coherently formulated, he categorically rejects any foundationalist claim to universal, ahistorical truths.

4. Although not all of the following theorists talk about going beyond objectivism and relativism in precisely those terms, they are engaged in essentially that project as the cited pages attest: Allen (1989, 360–363), Beck (1995, 127–129),

Dewey (Rockefeller 1992, 178–179), Doppelt (1982, 134; 1983, 107–108), Haraway (1988, 576–580), Kekes (1980, 96–98), Keller (1989, 149), Krausz (1984, 402–403), Laudan (1990, 134–135), Mandelbaum (1982, 55), Matilal (1989), Maxwell (1984, 254–258), McKinney (1987, 97), Meynell (1993, 3–8), Mohanty (1989), Seller (1988), and Weinert (1984, 382). This is not an exhaustive list. See Hollis and Lukes (1982, 14–20) for a characterization of other theorists intent upon formulating epistemological positions which are neither objectivist nor relativist. Note also that Komesaroff (1986, 12) reports of the theorists of the early Frankfurt School that "all these thinkers accepted that in some sense knowledge must be regarded as historically conditioned; however they insisted that an independent moment of criticism was nevertheless a possibility," which suggests that they too had to be committed to the possibility of a non-foundational justification for the norms implicit in critique.

   5. For example, Feyerabend (1978, esp. 10), Haraway (1988, 592), King (1989), and Ruddick (1993, 140, 143, 145).

   6. Edwards (1990, 5–31) reviews the taxonomy of relativisms provided by Hollis and Lukes (1982, 5–12) and concludes that they boil down to either (a) "relativism of truth," which relativizes truth to individuals or to commensurable linguistic communities; or (b) "cognitive relativism," which relativizes truth to incommensurable conceptual frameworks. According to Edwards (20), this distinction corresponds to Swoyer's (1982, 92ff.) distinction between "strong" and "weak" versions of relativism. The arguments against versions of "strong" relativism are summarized by Edwards (1990); my concern in this chapter is primarily with versions of "weak" relativism, which Edwards believes are more plausible. Margolis (1991) defends a form of relativism quite different from either version considered by Edwards. How Margolis' version of relativism is related to my position will be explained in chapter four.

   7. Laudan (1990, viii) remarks that, although neither Quine nor Kuhn wish to be considered relativists, their work has "unmistakable relativist implications."

   8. For example, Allen (1989, 359–361), Bernstein (1983, 37, 48–49, 52, 59), Doppelt (1983, 108), Kekes (1980, 99), Laudan (1990, 86, 134–135; 1984, 3–4), and MacIntyre (*WJ*, 353; *TRV*, 59). For a related endeavour in a more practical context, see Winograd and Flores (1987, 8).

   9. Bernstein (1983, 9), also Margolis (1991, 160).

   10. Laudan (1984, 5–6) attributes this view of science to philosophers between the 1930s and the 1950s, and refers to it as the "Leibnizian ideal." Compare Salmon's (1967, 112–118) contrasting account of twentieth-century science: "Not since Francis Bacon has any empiricist regarded the logic of science as an algorithm that would yield all scientific truth."

   11. For a characterization of method that does not equate it with following rules, see the discussion by Lonergan (1973, 3–6).

12. On this point, see Bernstein (1983, 23, 53–59, 71–73), Brown (1983, 4), Doppelt (1983, 108), and Laudan (1990, 134–135).

13. Compare, for example, Allen (1989), Bernstein (1983, esp. 38–40, 47–48, 54–55, 146–148), Nussbaum (1986a), and Nussbaum and Sen (1989). Bernstein contends that Gadamer's critical appropriation of Aristotle's work is itself an excellent example—a *paradigm* in its original sense—of the exercise of *phronēsis*.

14. For a discussion of the social, political, and moral as well as epistemological dimensions of the contrast between *phronēsis* and technical rationality, see Bernstein (1983, 39–40, 43, 148–150), Fay (1975), and Schön (1983).

15. Bernstein (1983, 156–158). Nussbaum and Sen (1989, 317) note that the utility of *phronēsis* seems to presuppose a prior commitment to at least two regulative ideals: "to live in a community with others and to share with others a conception of value" and "rational argumentation—especially to standards of consistency and clarity."

16. Bernstein (1983, 156–158) makes a similar point in his discussion of Gadamer. See also MacIntyre's (*WJ*, 320–321; cf. Owens 1981, 277) discussion of Aristotle and Hume.

17. I am presenting what I believe to be the best case that can be made for framework relativism using arguments based upon the incommensurability of meaning. I do not consider versions that other reviewers (for example, Edwards 1990, 116–117) have judged weak or implausible.

18. When *language* is used interchangeably with *conceptual scheme*, it usually refers to a set of technical or specialized framework-specific terms. It is worth noting that speakers of the same natural language can use different conceptual schemes, and the same conceptual scheme can be expressed in different natural languages (Edwards 1990, 22, cf. 34–39).

19. When saying that people within different conceptual schemes live in "different worlds," some relativists mean it more literally that others. Compare Goodman (1982) and Sperber (1982, 154–155).

20. Weinert (1984, 383–384) distinguishes between perceptual and conceptual versions of incommensurability of meaning: Perceptual incommensurabilists claim that "theories have such a strong impact on their proponents that they begin to see the world differently according to their different world-views," while conceptual incommensurabilists claim that "arguments and propositions are embedded in epistemological structures or complex problem-situations and cannot be apprehended in isolation from these structures."

21. This way of putting it was inspired by reading Edwards (1990, 45) on the "inextricability thesis" regarding the truth values and truth conditions of sentences along with Okrent (1984, 348–351) on the conditions for avoiding incoherent versions of relativism. As Okrent observes, to collapse "true" into "true for someone" or to equate "true" with "believed to be true" is the same thing as

not being able to distinguish between a position being held and it being held truly.

22. See, for example, Hacking's (1982, 62–64) argument that at least some statements are only candidates for truth or falsehood because of the existence of certain "styles of reasoning," which are roughly equivalent to conceptual schemes.

23. Nola (1988, 15) makes this point: "Clearly not all relational notions of truth need commit one to any substantial doctrine of relativism." See also Okrent (1984, 342–343) and Bernstein's (1983, 76) discussion of the remark by Donald Davidson: "Truth of sentences remains relative to a language, but that is as objective as can be."

24. A "domain of human experience" may be roughly defined as a range of phenomena, including at least sights and sounds, that can be ostensibly delimited. On the point that rival frameworks necessarily interpret what could be ostensibly identified as the same "thing," see Laudan (1977, 143; 1990, 123, 140), MacIntyre (*RPP*, 189–190), Mandelbaum (1982, 49–50), Halweg and Hooker (1988, 111–113), and Swoyer (1982, 100–101). That they must be about the same thing in order to be rivals suggests an instrumentalist as opposed to a realist (or *representational* in the foundationalist sense) understanding of conceptual schemes, including scientific theories. See Komesaroff's (1986, 65) discussion of Feyerabend's comments in this regard. As MacIntyre points out, although rivalry requires that two traditions of enquiry are concerned about the same "thing," the perception that two traditions are rivals is only made from within a tradition according to its own criteria. Thus two traditions may agree that they are rivals without necessarily agreeing on how to characterize that rivalry.

25. Edwards (1990, 5–31) argues at length that a diversity of conceptual schemes does not entail relativism, although he characterizes the "extra step" required in a different way.

26. This list was compiled from the lists provided by Devine (1984, 418, n. 1), Edwards (1990, 40), Krausz (1989, 2–30), and Nola (1988, 10).

27. For an argument that Kohlberg's theoretical framework is properly located within a mechanistic view of the world, see Vokey (1987, 59–64). The topic of world views will be taken up in chapter five.

28. Regarding the historical development of mechanistic narratives and metaphors, see Cantor (1995). Regarding the association of science with the expectation of progress, see MacIntyre (*TRV*, 20–24). Regarding the relationships between world view and social context, see Schön's (1983) illustration of how the priority of theory over practice follows from mechanistic ontological assumptions, and how that priority is institutionalized in such things as educational hierarchies, wages, and the definition of what it means to be a "professional."

29. For an analysis of the different kinds and roles of assumptions "governing" a research paradigm, see Strike (1989, 5–8).

30. For this formulation of the argument for indeterminacy, and for the rationalist objections to it, I am following Laudan (1990, 127–134). Newton-Smith (1982, 116–120) provides a more detailed case for the same conclusion. Note that my concern here is not with theories which claim only that the translation of *certain kinds* of utterances are indeterminate.

31. "It is, as Aristotle remarked, difficult to know that one knows" (*WJ*, 175). Laudan points out that the issue of indeterminacy of translation is essentially the same as the issue of the underdetermination of choice among competing paradigms. In other words, arguments for indeterminacy of translation based on holistic theories of meaning or justification are special cases of similar arguments that choice among competing theories or paradigms is underdetermined. See also Newton-Smith (1982, 116–120). Because the issues are the same, I will not discuss relativist arguments directed specifically against the possibility of justified accurate translations, but will assume that, if the general arguments for framework relativism fail, the specific applications to translation also fail.

32. Margolis (1991, 35; cf. Bernstein 1983, 71, 90–92): "Contrary to what Bernstein suggests, it is extremely difficult to find a mainstream relativist who denies cross-cultural, cross-paradigmatic, cross-linguistic, cross-theoretical intelligibility or comparability. *It is also difficult to show that the defence of incommensurability is equivalent to the denial of cross-cultural comparability.*" Other theorists who have made this point include Brown (1983), Edwards (1990, 116), Gellner (1982, 183–185), Swoyer (1982, 89), and Weinert (1984, 387–88).

33. For this point, see Mandelbaum (1982, 49); also Davidson (1982, 167) and MacIntyre (*WJ*, 370–375; *RPP*, 189; *TRV*, 113). Amélie Rorty (1989, 420–421) makes similar claims that the inability to translate exactly, and the inability to be *certain* that translations are correct, does not foreclose the possibility of understanding and evaluation across frameworks: "The poignant sense of untranslatability—of lost meaning—does not argue for incomprehensibility: a translator might be able to fabricate a 'missing verse' good enough to fool a discerning native literary critic."

34. In speaking of the "original" way of conceiving the content out of which human sense-making constructs the objects of belief, I am following Okrent (1984, 347–348) and Richard Rorty (Bernstein 1983, 75–76) in understanding modern "schemers" as descendants of Kant.

35. Swoyer (1982, 97); also Edwards (1990, 40–43, 86–102) and Bernstein (1983, 75–77).

36. Komesaroff (1986, 71, n. 55) claims that there is now agreement that observation is "theory-laden": the term was coined by Gilbert Ryle (1949) in *The Concept of Mind*. However, to accept that (a) all human experience is the outcome of human sense-making activities and (b) all *linguistic* descriptions of experience are conceptually and hence theoretically mediated is *not* to grant that all meaningful experience is linguistically mediated. For example, see Merlin Donald

(1993) for an account of human mimetic sense-making activities which predate, and which remain distinct from, the use of language.

37. For example, Okrent (1984, 349–353), Edwards (1990, 88–93), and Hacking (1982, 64).

38. E.g., Kekes (1980, 209–210), Amélie Rorty (1989, 419), and Wikan (1989). Mandelbaum (1982, 49) argues that translation is possible precisely because language functions in part to represent the "real" world, hence the possibility of ostensive definitions: "If it were the case that every statement in a language received its meaning solely through other expressions used within that language, each language would be self-enclosed, and no equivalence of meaning between statements in any two languages could be established." According to Newton-Smith (1982, 118), even Quine holds that "observational language always admits of determinate translation." For a discussion of how human sensory-motor capabilities shape the basic categories of thought and action, see Varela (1992, 102–108).

39. Horton (1982, 230). There are parallels between Horton's notion of secondary theories and Laudan's (1977, 78–81) notion of research traditions.

40. For relevant examples and converging views, see Doppelt (1982, 125–126), Hacking (1982, 61), MacIntyre (*TRV*, 17–18, 111–112; *ITC*, 110), and Laudan (1977, 143–144).

41. W. Newton-Smith (1982, 121–122) comes to a similar conclusion in his evaluation of relativisms based on Hacking's notion of different styles of reasoning. See also Brown's (1983, 3–5) comments on Kuhn and Feyerabend.

42. The assessment of the relative merits of alternative conceptual schemes will always involve truth claims even if the conceptual schemes in question are developed in traditions of enquiry that do not aim at producing true descriptions of the natural or social environment. For example, even if scientific theories are to be evaluated, not as more or less true, but as more or less adequate to solving problems, assessing the relative merits of rival scientific theories and associated conceptual schemes or research traditions will involve truth claims about which set of assumptions is actually more adequate to solving problems.

43. Edwards (1990, 30–31; cf. Swoyer 1982, 97). Okrent (1984, 342, 349–350) argues that this form of framework relativism does not necessarily entail a coherence theory of truth, although it is often confused with it. However, even those relativists who allow some form of truth-as-correspondence allow it only within different frameworks or "versions" of the world and maintain that it is not in principle possible to say that a particular framework or version is true.

44. Hacking (1982, 64–65) makes this point in relation to *styles of reasoning*, and his notion of styles of reasoning seems roughly equivalent to the notion of conceptual schemes. Hacking himself remarks that "Perhaps I am proposing a version of the conceptual scheme idea."

45. For a critical look at Quine's alternative theory of meaning, see W. Newton-Smith (1982, 116ff). See also Lyons (1982) and Swoyer (1982, 101–103) for

arguments that it is incoherent to interpret relativism as meaning the same claim can be both true and false at the same time.

46. Okrent (1984, 348): "A position is incoherently relativistic if on that position it is impossible to distinguish what is the case from what seems to be the case given some opinion, language, or whatever." Similarly (351): "Relativism is self-refuting only if that in virtue of which propositions are true is dependent upon mind, context, language, etc. in such a way that it is impossible to distinguish between the mere assertion of such dependence and the truth of such dependence." For other discussions of self-defeating forms of relativism, see Horton (1982, 256–258), Margolis (1991, 8–9, 67, 84), and Swoyer (1982, 96).

47. According to Brown (1983, 20), Kuhn makes a similar distinction between "the world" and "the environment," "with the latter term serving to designate entities which exist quite apart from our theories, frameworks, or paradigms, and which scientific research is always ultimately concerned with." For a discussion of the sense in which the behaviour of an organism's nervous system can be said to function to "represent" information from the environment, see Maturana and Varela (1988, 129–137).

48. The languages in which truth claims are formulated are a pervasive aspect of human living, and as such are the objects as well as the products of human attempts to make sense of experience. Both written and spoken languages illustrate the general point that the "output" of one sense-making activity (e.g., sensation) can become the "input" for another (e.g., linguistic description). Hence it is possible to have—this chapter being an example—a conceptual scheme of conceptual schemes of conceptual schemes.

49. For other arguments against collapsing truth into warranted assertability, see McCarthy (1989, 259–260) and MacIntyre (*RPP*, 201, 357–359, 363–367; *TRV*, 120–122).

50. Incoherency results from collapsing truth and belief in asserting frameworks as well as particular claims. See Okrent's discussion (1984, 348–349), MacIntyre (*WJ*, 169–170), and also Edwards (1990, 37–39) on Carnap's distinction between "internal" and "external" questions.

51. In the linguistically mediated practices of assigning truth values to propositions, "no ultimate recourse is possible to an unshakeable underlying foundation of intuitive givenness" (Komesaroff 1986, 346).

52. I speak of correspondence *theories* of truth because to accept that the sentence "X is true if it really is the case that X" captures something important about the meaning of truth does not settle all philosophical disputes over rival theories of truth. See, for example, Margolis' (1989, 241–245) discussion of Davidson's position. I do not claim to raise, much less address, these disputes. For a more elaborate defence of a correspondence theory of truth, see Zemach (1989). My point is simply that, as Krausz (1984, 396) observes, to reject foundationalism

or objectivism does not entail the logical position that truth is relative in all senses of the term.

53. Swoyer (1982, 86; cf. Nola 1988, 10–14) summarizes the two basic stages of the "ontological relativist" argument: "a defence of a constructivist epistemology according to which the knower somehow organizes or constitutes what is known, and second, an argument that there is no uniquely correct way of doing this." Thus "there are no neutral facts, for the facts as we know them are correlative with the set of concepts that we employ." Thus while Swoyer (1982, 97) argues that the relativist requires the concept of a framework-independent world, "such a notion is nearly empty, for, by the relativist's own lights, it can not be experienced or described in a neutral way."

54. Haraway (1988, 591–593) proposes that the world be seen not as a passive object of scientific theorizing, but as an agent, actor, or subject.

55. Edwards (1990, 105), Gellner (1982), W. Newton-Smith (1982, 113–114), Sperber (1982, 154–155). I should acknowledge that Laudan (1984, 103ff.) presents telling arguments against traditional scientific realism. I do not claim here to be addressing the issues of contention among different realist positions (e.g., Nola, 1988, 3–10). I am committed only to the minimal claim that the beliefs formulated in the terms of our conceptual schemes are properly constrained by what is prior to and independent of those schemes. For arguments against contemporary forms of idealism and for a "naturalistic realism," see Cashman (1992, 7–17), cf. Varela (1992, 102–104).

56. Meiland and Krausz (1982, 110). For a more extended discussion of the ways in which classical and relativistic mechanics are incommensurable in this sense but still comparable, see Brown (1983, 12–18).

57. Okrent (1984, 357). See also Edwards (1990, 43–46) and Laudan (1977, 42–44; 1990, 71ff.).

58. Bernstein (1983, 138). McCarthy (1989, 261) emphasizes the importance of recognizing that our current practices of warranting truth claims are fallible and may be superseded by those of another tradition or point of view.

59. Wong (1989, 142). MacIntyre emphasizes that untranslatability or incommensurability of meaning is not overcome by translation, for if two frameworks could be adequately translated into each other's terms then they would not be incommensurable. Untranslatability is overcome by learning to speak the language and adopt the perspective of the other standpoint.

60. Bernstein (1983, 24–25, see also 77–79). Although Komesaroff (1986, 338) uses a different conceptual framework than Bernstein or Kuhn to describe the commitments shared within communities of enquiry, he arrives at a similar conclusion that understanding science requires understanding how traditions of enquiry develop: "our problem of the evolution of object domains is seen to be embedded in a larger problem: how can we give an account of the emergence

of the stable discursive unities within which objectivity is formed?" For a description of this shift to a "traditions" perspective in the philosophy of education, see Hirst (1992).

61. Kuhn (1977, xviii–xix) developed the notion of a *paradigm* to explain how scientific research traditions formed the consensus necessary for the practice of "normal" science. He took the term from the study of language instruction where it originally meant *exemplary solution to a concrete problem.* The meaning of the concept expanded to include "the classic books in which these accepted examples initially appeared and, finally, the entire global set of commitments shared by members of a particular scientific community." Thus, in Kuhn's terms, a *paradigm* is a set of shared meanings, commitments, and values "that constitutes a scientific community of a group of otherwise disparate men."

62. Carr and Kemmis (1986, 74) make a similar point. Of course, there may be conflicts between the implicit and explicit commitments of a community of enquiry: discrepancies between what they do and what they say they do.

63. MacIntyre (*RPP*, 187–188). See also Bernstein (1983, 57) for otherwise unpublished remarks by MacIntyre on the role of case histories in teaching and learning judgment.

64. The notion that enquiry is shaped by assumptions is at least as old as Francis Bacon's discussion of the "Idols of the Mind" in his *Novum Organum,* Book I (Flew 1984, 36–37, 162). MacIntyre (*EC*, 458–459) argues that Descartes was "blind" to the assumptions he had inherited from his tradition of enquiry and, in particular, blind to the very fact that this tradition "sees" knowledge as analogous to vision.

65. Doppelt (1982, 121); see also MacIntyre (*EC*, 465; *WJ*, 350–352).

66. On this point, see Komesaroff's (1986, 76–85) discussion of Popper, Kuhn, and Habermas regarding the role of the scientific community.

67. I am drawing here on the discussion of speech act theory in Winograd and Flores (1987, 54–69).

Chapter Two. The Rationality of Traditions

1. *WJ* (327); *RPP* (201); *TRV* (116). Although MacIntyre does not consider this possibility, a *degenerate* tradition would be one that was once mature, but had inadvertently forgotten or systematically repressed the memories of earlier stages of its history, and had come to mistake a particular formulation of its commitments for eternal, unchanging truth.

2. Lukes (1982, 301–305) makes a similar point in his discussion of perspectivism and relativism, as does Brown (1983, 20–23) in his discussion of comparing incommensurable alternatives in scientific and other forms of enquiry.

3. Louis Mink, cited in Krausz (1984, 401). See also Bernstein (1983, 74) and Laudan (1977, 164–165).

4. MacIntyre (*WJ*, 144, 166, 175–176, 398–399). In another context, Barnes and Bloor (1982, 46) argue that "The rationalist goal of producing pieces of knowledge that are both universal in their credibility *and* justified in context-independent terms is unattainable."

Chapter Three.   The Search for Wide Reflective Equilibrium

1. This raises the interesting possibility that a tradition could, through successive reformulations of its constitutive agreements, arrive at a conceptual scheme radically at odds with its earliest beliefs.

2. See Elgin (1989, 86–89) for an account of how classificatory schemes are neither absolute nor arbitrary: "Rightness of categorization . . . depends on suitability to a purpose". The interests, values, and assumptions implicit in judgments about which differences are important enough to form the basis of classificatory schemes are themselves open to critical assessment, as the literature on the politics of difference attests, e.g., Minow (1990, 50–55), Pratt (1988), and Rothenberg (1990).

3. For a discussion of the differences between traditional and modern societies concerning the extent to which they are characterized by conflict among rival conceptual schemes, see Horton (1982, 239). See Laudan (1977, 104–105) for examples of people "picking and choosing from among the assumptions of two incompatible research traditions".

4. This point was inspired, in part, by Minow's (1990) discussion of the "dilemma of difference".

5. Lonergan (1973, 236–237) suggests that horizons are related complementarily, genetically, or dialectically. I have reformulated his original categories and added four more. Even this list may not be exhaustive.

6. For arguments that, in justification, the criterion of success in practice takes precedence over the criterion of logical consistency, see Kekes (1980, 112–115).

7. Often, solving a paradox or dilemma involves surfacing and rejecting some mistaken assumption shared by both sides: "In such cases it is a heuristic maxim that truth lies not in one of the two disputed views but in some third possibility which has not yet been thought of, which we can only discover by rejecting something assumed as obvious by both the disputants" (Kekes 1980, 99).

8. For arguments that the rule of the excluded middle cannot be assumed to apply to all domains of human experience, see Margolis (1989, 1991, esp. 52–53). Indeed, Margolis (1991, 17; cf. Lather 1991b, 155) stipulates that: "Any doctrine counts as a form of relativism if it abandons the principle of excluded

middle or bivalence (and *tertium non datur*), or restricts its use, so that, in particular sectors of inquiry, incongruent claims may be validated".

9. Brown (1983) provides some excellent examples of how the "same" object, when viewed from different perspectives corresponding to different interests, is characterized in incommensurable terms. The examples also illustrate how there can be incompatible right answers to the "same" question according to distinct interests. Elgin (1989, 88) provides examples of how different systems of classification, even when concerned with the same domain of experience, may "complement one another or be indifferent to one another." This category also provides room for Williams' characterization of "notional confrontation" between two cultural or moral systems in which neither is a "real" option for the other (Matilal 1989, 342–343).

10. Kaplan (1984, 3): "Different interpretations of reality may be equally valid, provided their uses are not inconsistent. Wave and particle interpretations of the photon, for instance, are not inconsistent, because the investigations proceed within incompatible, but not contradictory, frameworks of inquiry". See also Schön (1983) and Tarnas (1991, 406–407).

11. MacIntyre (*AV*, 153–154, 253) himself provides relevant examples. In another context, Rawls (1971, 41) argues that, because of the complexities of concrete situations, it would not be possible to capture our firm convictions about justice in a single set of ordered principles.

12. Kohlberg (1984, 238) defines a "hard" cognitive stage as "a distinction or qualitative difference in structures (modes of thinking) that still serve the *same basic function* (for example, intelligence) at various points in development" (emphasis added; see also his remarks on 239).

13. For an account of intentionality that is compatible with MacIntyre's notion of continuity through change in a person's or a tradition's understanding of its final goal, see Lonergan (1973, 34–36), cf. MacIntyre on Aquinas (*WJ*, 173–174; *TRV*, 133–134).

14. Compare, for example, *AV* (10, 128–129) and *WJ* (349) with *WJ* (169–170, 328–329, 362, 371, 393), *TRV* (43–44, 99, 113, 120–121, 230–231), and *ITC* (109–110). MacIntyre's tendency to equate a tradition's point of view with its scheme of beliefs is also evident in his exclusive focus on *epistemological* crises.

15. MacIntyre (*EC*, 465): "What Polanyi has shown is that all justification takes place within a social tradition and that the pressures of such a tradition enforce often unrecognized rules by means of which discrepant pieces of evidence or difficult questions are often put on one side with the tacit assent of the scientific community." For MacIntyre's recognition that different traditions of enquiry represent different ways of "seeing as" and of imagining, see *ITC* (110).

16. MacIntyre himself (*TRV*, 158–159) mentions the role played in contemporary academic philosophy of "informal agreements on what kind of thesis or argument is to be taken seriously, what disregarded or scorned." See also his remarks (*FG*, 259–260) on the "unacknowledged expulsion of certain subject-matters from the realm of serious enquiry" in philosophy; and Davis (1990, 161): "While Habermas would seem to be clinging to a universalistic philosophy to save liberal politics, his French critics are prepared to give up liberal politics in order to avoid a universalistic philosophy."

17. See, for example, Greene (1981, esp. 11, 194).

18. In distinguishing world views from ways of life, I am following Kearney (1984) and other authors (e.g., Greene 1981, 3) who use *world view* to refer only to beliefs and images about the fundamental nature of things as opposed to those authors (e.g., Kekes 1980, 59) who define world views as including, and not just associated with, certain sets of attitudes, interests, norms, priorities, and practices. I will talk about the relationship between world views and ways of life in more detail when I examine the interconnections between world views and moral perspectives.

19. This summary of mechanistic assumptions is my own synthesis, based in large part on Pepper's (1942) analysis of the mechanistic "world hypothesis," especially discrete mechanism (195–205). It draws also from Capra (1983, 53–74), Cantor (1995, Chapter Three), Greene (1981, 12–14, 128–157), Kilbourn (1980, 38–39), Kubrin (1989, 154–156), Polanyi (1962, 3–18, 134–141), and Tarnas (1991, 277–279; 284–290). Of course, it is too simplistic to speak of *the* mechanistic world view, for it has undergone significant changes during its long history. This summary can be considered a snapshot of the mechanistic view at the zenith of its development during the eighteenth and nineteenth centuries.

20. In Descartes' dualism only the body, and not the mind, was conceived as a machine. It was Paul Heinrich Dietrich d'Holbach who extended mechanistic explanations to consciousness and thought (Cantor 1995, 50; cf. Greene 1981, 130–131).

21. For a discussion of how the clock came to symbolize cosmic order, see Cantor (1995, chapter 3).

22. "'By convention coloured, by convention sweet, by convention bitter; in reality only atoms and the void'" (attributed to Democritus, cited by Polanyi 1962, 8). See also Berlin (1956, 17–21), and Roszak (1972, 179) vs. Pepper (1942, 193–195). Cantor (1995) says that the distinction between primary and secondary qualities was revived by Descartes and subsequently emphasized by Locke.

23. Kilbourn (1980, 38–39). For a contemporary advocate of this view, see Monod (1971, 172–173, 180). The belief that the order of nature is contingent was not a component of early European mechanistic views, but emerges after the

decline of confidence in Divine providence, in part due to the uneasy relation between mechanistic and theistic assumptions. However, even when the mechanistic order of the world was attributed to a Creator its value was instrumental: the purpose of the world was to provide an appropriate stage for human activity. See Greene (1981, 12–14, 16–17).

24. On this point, see Fay (1975, 18–20) and Havel (1992, 2).

25. Agassi (1964) and Komesaroff (1986, 26) make a similar points. For more detailed examples, see Shweder (1989, 120–124) for arguments concerning how modern anthropology has been shaped by ontological assumptions associated with the Enlightenment. See Greene (1981, e.g., 34–36) for an analysis of the interrelation of world view and the practice of "natural history." See Blackman (1980, 99–112) concerning the connections between mechanistic assumptions and behaviouristic psychology. This is not to say that world views are always developed first and then applied to scientific problems. Rather, the ascendence of mechanism (for example) was first initiated and supported by interconnected scientific, technological, mathematical, economic, political, psychological, social, and cultural developments which in turn were given legitimacy by their coherence within a deterministic, materialistic, reductionistic, and atomistic view of the world (Cantor 1995, chapter 3). For a discussion of the theological motivation for welcoming mechanism, see Taylor (1994, 18–19).

26. Like any tradition of inquiry, the positivistic approach to science has changed over time, and was characterized by disagreements as well as by consensus. This characterization of the positivistic paradigm of science and objectivity is my own synthesis of certain common elements among the varieties of positivism, based on the voluminous literature on "positivistic paradigm" research (compare Hollis 1977, 47). For historical accounts and philosophical analyses of the varieties of positivism, see Bernstein (1976, 5–14) and Phillips (1987, 37–42).

27. See Leatherdale (1974, 223ff.) for an account of the historical development of the demand for precise language.

28. Fay (1975, 34–41); also Carr and Kemmis (1986, 51–81) and Roszak (1972, 194). This is the view of science presented in at least some popular introductory texts to educational research, e.g., Mouley (1978, 26–29) and Travers (1969, 5).

29. I am not claiming that holding mechanistic assumptions necessarily leads to adopting the positivist paradigm, or vice versa, because either or both may be adopted for other, e.g., ideological reasons. At the same time there is both a conceptual and a historical connection: positivism originated and developed when the mechanistic world view was dominant. Indeed, Comte, in his introduction to *The Positive Philosophy*, states that "the first characteristic of the

Positive Philosophy is that it regards all phenomena as subjected to invariable natural laws" (Queen's University Department of History, 228).

30. Compare MacIntyre (*TRV*, 116), Nielsen (1987, 146). In this characterization of non-foundational justification I am integrating and extending the work of authors from a wide variety of contexts who have themselves adapted elements of each other's work (Nielsen 1987, 144, n. 2). For a conception of wide reflective equilibrium as including dialectical argument I am indebted to Rawls (1974/75, 8), also Daniels (1979, 258). I encountered the distinction between internal and external coherence in Laudan (1984, 47–66, 73–87). Laudan (1984, 71–80) also provides an analysis of how the assumptions and commitments of a scientific research paradigm must form a mutually supportive whole with the ontological assumptions of its corresponding world view (cf. Doppelt 1983, 136). For support for the idea that the sets of agreements guiding inquiry are properly justified with reference to their success in furthering the intentions for which they were developed—intentions which themselves are assessed dialectically—see Feyerabend (1978, 25), Hahlweg and Hooker (1988, 93–115), Kearney (1984, 52–56), Komesaroff (1986, 377), Laudan (1988, 126–138; 1990, 18–19, 101–105, 135–136), and Margolis (1984a, 313–316; 1991, 196).

31. I use "Rationalists" (upper-case *R*) to differentiate this group, who might look to Descartes as exemplar, from the larger collection of "rationalists" who affirm one or another form of non-foundational justification.

32. See Schön (1983, esp. 184–187) for other examples of how new ways of "seeing-as" can function as "generative metaphors"; that is, as innovate perspectives inspiring solutions to problems that proved intractable within previous points of view.

33. For more on this point, see Bernstein (1983, 56–57); cf. MacIntyre (*WJ*, 110; *TRV*, 95–96, 120, 133).

34. For an allusion to this distinction in MacIntyre's later work, see *FP* (36).

35. This is not to say that science cannot also be understood as intending to represent features of the environment. Rather, it is to say that the intention of solving problems is primary, which makes it reasonable for scientists to accept conceptual constructs which they know are not "true" in a correspondence sense. Nor is it to say that justification can dispense with a correspondence notion of truth. On the contrary, comparing rival scientific frameworks as Laudan describes requires that claims about their relative problem-solving ability are *true*.

36. MacIntyre's (*EC*, 466–467) early characterization of the rationality of traditions also included a rejection of this aspect of Kuhn's work.

37. For an alternative interpretation of Kuhn which supports Laudan's point (if not his interpretation), see Bernstein (1983, 84–85).

38. In the same way that the terms of rival conceptual schemes exhibit partial incommensurability of meaning, their distinct interests could represent only partial evaluative incommensurability. Doppelt (1983, 137, italics added) makes a related point: "my argument here is that Laudan needs to develop some philosophical conception of that partial cumulativity at the level of the empirical and (possibly) conceptual problems presupposed by the unity of scientific discipline. This would involve a reconstruction of that *minimal set of concepts, assumptions, and interests necessarily shared by all research traditions in any given scientific discipline.*"

39. For example, see Goleman (1991, 89–102) for a comparison between American and Tibetan models of mental health.

40. Kearney (1984, 52–56; 58–64); see also Greene (1981, 42–43).

41. Greene (1981, 2); see also Laudan (1977, 55–57, 61–64).

42. According to Nola (1988, 4–6), the belief that "something" exists in a mind-independent way is common to all forms of ontological realism.

43. Compare with the discussion of "the mirror of nature" in *The Embodied Mind* (Varela, Thompson, and Rosch 1991).

44. Conn (1976, 198) makes a similar point in his discussion of the related senses of "being objective."

45. On these definitions, it is possible to have objective knowledge (true belief) about something which only exists in a mind-dependent way, for example, something that is a product of human imagination.

46. One problem with the search for the "view from nowhere" is that it equates objective knowledge with that which is most context-free, without defending the world view in light of which this equation would be intelligible. For a discussion of the difficulties involved in a "view from nowhere" approach to conceiving *moral* objectivity, see Aiken (1963, esp. 90) and Robertson (1989, 105).

47. Ronald de Sousa (1987, 145–148) identifies four clearly distinct senses of the term "subjective," which he labels *phenomenology, projection, relativity,* and *perspective. Phenomenology* refers to the qualitative aspect of subjective experience, e.g., pain as *felt. Projection* refers to the mistaken attribution of a property to an object, typically a property which is more properly attributed to the subject in question. *Relativity* refers to the belief that some contents of experiencing result from the *interaction* between a subject and its environment. In such cases, e.g., perception, variation in either the subject or the environment would be expected to affect the nature of the experience. *Perspective,* finally, refers to the individual nature of subjective experience, that is, what makes an experience "mine" and not "yours." This observes that, regardless of the particular felt quality of an experience, or the ontological status of its stimulus, experiences are always something had by particular subjects. As de Sousa is quick to point out, and as Kuhn

(1977, 337; cf. Bernstein 1983, 56) implies, it is only when being *subjective* means indulging in *projection* that it is incompatible with being objective.

48. See, for example, Conn (1976), Deutscher (1983), Nielsen (1987, 145–146), Nussbaum and Sen (1989, 308–312).

Chapter Four.   Moral Tradition and Dialectical Debate

1. *AV* (187–203), cf. *WJ* (30–33). In *After Virtue* (273), MacIntyre clearly outlines the first three stages of his account of the ethics of virtue. He claims that his account will in some sense unify the various and competing conceptions of the virtues that were developed within the Aristotelian tradition (*AV*, 186). He also notes that *After Virtue* should be understood as a work in progress (278). I have reconstructed further stages that I discern in MacIntyre's account after the first three in order to integrate work from his texts that follow *After Virtue*. In this chapter, I will summarize what I understand to be the key points of MacIntyre's account; in the next chapter I will return to some of those that require clarification or correction.

2. MacIntyre's distinction between internal and external goods is reminiscent of Plato's (*Republic*, Book I, chapter 3; I. 336B–347E) argument that the benefit specific to each craft or *technē* is distinct from the earning of wages, which is common to all crafts.

3. MacIntyre (*SH*, 85; cf. *WJ*, 183–184). Searle (1983, 57) makes the same point.

4. *AV* (206–208, 215), cf. *RVG* (14). MacIntyre's arguments here reinforce my earlier point that particular claims are embedded within progressively broader sets of assumptions—including theories, paradigms, and world views—that develop or decline over time.

5. Although I cannot develop the point here, I think it would also be correct to say that narratives presuppose actions, i.e., that actions and narratives are constructed together through the same sense-making process.

6. *AV* (207, 213, 218), cf. *RVG* (8). In this context, I will use *histories* to refer to the sequences of events that comprise individual and collective enacted narratives, and *stories* to refer to the reconstructions of those events.

7. This claim is supported by the comparative study of religious traditions. See Slater (1978, 3–4, 7–9).

8. See Rom Harré (1989, 387–393) for a careful elaboration of this point. Wilfred Cantwell Smith (1984, 264) expresses the corroborating view that "an individual can become a person only in community. To be a person is to be involved in the polarity between the social and the individual."

9. *AV* (218, cf. 205), *TRV* (197). As I will discuss in more detail below, MacIntyre (e.g., *TRV*, 94) understands each individual life to have a narrative unity

even before the story of that life is told—either by the individual herself or himself or by someone else—because he understands the universe to have a teleological, and hence narrative, structure.

10. *AV* (218, cf. 208; *WJ*, 291; *TRV*, 196–203). For a different way of arriving at a similar view, see Neville (1981, 93).

11. *AV* (216), cf. *WJ* (25), *RVG* (8–9). This would suggest that understanding one's own or another person's specific actions and intentions would be enhanced through familiarity with the cultural resources available for the construction of the personal identity in question, which is part of the story that forms the context for those actions and intentions.

12. MacIntyre remarks in *After Virtue* (197, cf. 271; *PRC*, 298) that his account of the virtues in that text "requires for its completion a cogent elaboration of just those distinctions and concepts which Aristotle's account requires: voluntariness, the distinction between the intellectual virtues and the virtues of character, the relationship of both to natural abilities and to the passions and the structure of practical reasoning." I will follow MacIntyre in presenting Aquinas' views on practical rationality as building upon, modifying, and correcting Aristotle's account.

13. *AV* (149), cf. *VSD* (4–5), *WJ* (109, 126–130); also *NE* 1103a20–25. See *WJ* (128) for a summary of Aristotle's distinctions between *akratic, enkratic,* and fully virtuous persons on the basis of the degree to which their passions have been first controlled and then transformed.

14. On MacIntyre's (*WJ*, 117–118) interpretation, Aristotle understood dialectic as a mode of enquiry comprised both of *epagōgē* and of debate between opposing conceptual schemes (*elenchus*). I use *dialectical debate* to refer only to the latter part of dialectical enquiry.

15. *WJ* (213–214), cf. *SH* (167, 266–268), *GH* (305), *AV* (43–49), and *RVG* (12–13). Elsewhere, MacIntyre briefly considers two additional alternatives. The third, represented by Kierkegaard, is that of basing moral principles on choice (*SH*, 215–218; *AV*, 39–43, 47; *FG*, 256–257). The fourth alternative, represented by Stoicism and certain forms of Christianity, is to base moral principles on some conception of absolute law (*AV*, 168–170, cf. *SH*, 148).

16. For other examples of attempts to base social norms and priorities upon untutored human desires, see MacIntyre's contrast (*WJ*, esp. 45, 74–76) between the goods of excellence and the goods of effectiveness.

17. *Tradition* is MacIntyre's shorthand term for the understanding of rational enquiry he expounds as *the rationality of traditions,* an understanding he believes to be implicit within the Thomistic practice of dialectic. For questions about the accuracy of MacIntyre's interpretation of Aquinas, a topic outside my present concerns, see Coleman (1994) and Haldane (1994). To avoid confusion, I itali-

cize the term *tradition* when it refers to Thomistic dialectics, and not to traditions in MacIntyre's more usual sense of a set of fundamental agreements. Similarly, I italicize *encyclopaedia* when it is used to refer to the point of view of the authors of the Ninth Edition, and not to the actual texts themselves.

18. MacIntyre seems to understand *encyclopaedia* as naively assuming the validity of their distinctions between what is "savage" and what is "civilized" (*TRV*, 182).

19. *SH* (148, cf. 268; *ITC*, 104). For MacIntyre's other examples of how moral facts are theory-dependent, see *MD* (371–372) and *PPI* (68–69). For an excellent depiction of a conflict between moral perspectives in which rival world views render incommensurable interpretations of "the facts," see the confrontation between priest and humanist social worker in Miller's *A Canticle for Leibowitz* (1959, 239–246).

20. In saying this, I am interpreting MacIntyre (*TRV*, 101–102, 173) in light of how he characterizes the failings of those moral traditions which either have a mistaken conception of the human *telos* or reject the notion of an overriding human good altogether. See, for example, his arguments for the goods of excellence against the goods of effectiveness (*WJ*, 52–54, 67–70, 108–109, 143–144).

21. For MacIntyre's recommended response to such situations, see his remarks on constructing "a cogent theoretical explanation of ideological blindness" (*TRV*, 147–148).

22. This is implicit in MacIntyre's claim that theoretical enquiry proceeds by way of an appropriation of past debates. See also *TRV* (77) and Lonergan's (1973, 125–151) proposed functional specialties within theological method.

23. *PRC* (289). MacIntyre suggests that while such dialectical endeavours are primarily undertaken to maintain and vindicate the confidence of those already committed to the ethics of virtue, they might also serve, under favourable conditions, to bring new faithful into the fold.

24. For MacIntyre's identification of the key contemporary contenders to the ethics of virtue, see *AV* (256–259; cf. *TRV*, 194–195). Utilitarianism might also be considered a current contender, but since MacIntyre considers utilitarianism one version of the Enlightenment project of finding a tradition-independent basis for morality, his general argument that the Enlightenment project was doomed to failure applies to utilitarianism as much as liberalism. For a critical review of MacIntyre's arguments that deal specifically with utilitarianism, see Kelly (1994).

25. On September 26, 1995, I attended a lecture by Shri A. Parthasarathy at the Ontario Institute for Studies in Education (Toronto, Ontario). Parthasarathy was giving the second of four talks on the Bhagavad Gita's answer to the

question "Who is an ideal person?" During the course of his lecture, he explicitly stated that no one would ever experience lasting peace or happiness until she or he had realized their true nature, and thereby achieved the highest human potential. For a Christian version of this teleological view, see Lonergan (1973, 36, 39, 242–243).

26. In MacIntyre's narrative, Kant is a transitional figure in the shift from traditional to modern ethics, because although his ethics was deontological, Kant also believed that a theistic teleological framework was required for the project of morality to be intelligible (*AV*, 56; cf. *MP*, 7–8).

27. Elizabeth Anscombe presented a similar characterization of modern moral concepts and practices as "survivals" as early as 1958, as MacIntyre acknowledges (*MP*, 7; *AV*, 53).

Chapter Five.   The Intellectualist Bias

1. On this point, see Hirst (1992, 41).

2. I have already given some indication of how valorization of the intellect, and corresponding disparagement of the qualitative and affective aspects of human experience, forms part of a coherent and mutually supportive whole with a mechanistic world view and positivistic epistemology. A more complete narrative reconstruction of the emergence of the intellectualist bias in its current forms would link the priority of control or domination with the emergence of the technical view of rationality and the desacrilization of the cosmos. For elements of that narrative, see Bernstein (1983, 46–48), Greene (1994, 423–433), Habermas (1975, 80–91), Horkheimer and Adorno (1972, 4–17), Keller (1985, 120–126), Komesaroff (1986, 14–16, 146–147), MacIntyre (MP, 2–3), and Wilber (1985, 35–37).

3. I am not claiming that the failure to formulate an adequate account of intrinsic moral value simply *results from* an intellectualist bias because it could equally be the case that the failure to appreciate the nature of intrinsic value *contributes to* the tendency to privilege theoretical knowledge.

4. *AV* (149); compare to *VSD* (10), *WJ* (262), and Aristotle (*NE* 1106b15–28).

5. The tendency to privilege theoretical over practical knowledge would fit with an epistemology that equated practical learning with learning through repetition reinforced by praise or rewards. On such a view, the person of virtuous character has learned which course of action is genuinely virtuous as a well-trained rat has learned which path through a maze will result in a food pellet. In each case, the learning has been a kind of blind conditioning, in which the subject has become disposed to select a particular kind of action as the "right" action without knowing *why* it is right. On such a view, then, true knowledge of the

rightness or goodness of actions is provided only by theoretical enquiry, which supplies explanations in the form of general principles that summarize cause-effect relationships: as such and such a path results in a food pellet because the scientist designed the experiment in such and such a way, acting honestly or justly results in the final human good because God designed the cosmos to that effect. The full significance of this point will become evident in the context of a later discussion of whether or not the quality of human experience exercises a cognitive as well as motivating function.

6. I suspect that theoretical enquiry more often serves to systematize the implications of innovations originally introduced in an ad hoc way to meet the practical difficulties of epistemological crises. To my best recollection, MacIntyre does not explicitly entertain such a possibility.

7. For an anthropologist's endorsement of this point, see Wikan (1989, esp. 469–470).

8. WJ (130–134, 185); cf. Bourke's (1966, 121–136) reconstruction of a Thomistic model of deductive practical rationality.

9. WJ (92); cf. Aristotle's remarks that "some who do not know [theoretically], and especially those who have experience, are more practical than others who know" (NE 1141b16–17) and that "arguments about matters concerned with feelings and actions are less reliable than facts; so when they clash with the facts of perception they are despised" (NE 1172a35).

10. "When a final cause is thought of as the object of desire, it is called a good. When it is considered as the terminus of an act, it is called an end. Thus, though minor formal differences of meaning distinguish the terms, the same thing, in the same relationship, is a good, an end, and a final cause" (Bourke 1966, 28). The claim that all ends are goods is not purely analytic: Aquinas defends the statement that all actions aim at a good on the basis of a psychological claim that no intellectual agent desires anything unless in some way he or she holds it to be some form of good (Copleston 1955, 180–185; Summa Contra Gentiles III, 3 and 16: all my references to Aquinas' texts are to Pegis 1948). The question of what good might mean beyond being that which intellectual agents believe to be desirable will be taken up below.

11. Compare Aristotle (NE 1094a1–16) and Aquinas (Summa Contra Gentiles III, 2). It is potentially confusing that, in these terms, an action can be an end or good in the sense that it is chosen for a specific purpose, and, at the same time, be a means in the sense that it is chosen to accomplish a result that is distinct from the action itself. An action can also be both an internal and external good: I might practice T'ai chi both for its own sake and for its effects in promoting good health.

12. On the view that not all the ends desired for their own sake are correctly desired, to observe that certain activities pursued as ends-in-themselves are the

internal goods of a practice does *not* warrant the conclusion that those activities are intrinsically good.

13. "The good life for a human being consists, Aristotle argues, in activity according to the excellences; repeatedly he insists that it is these activities, not either their consequences or the states of soul that produce them, which are the ultimate bearers of values, the ends for which we pursue everything else that we pursue" (Nussbaum 1986a, 158; cf. *NE* 1176b1–9). Because a behaviour is only a virtuous action if performed with the right motivation or inspiration (Kosman 1980, 103–105, 108–109), I use the term *virtuous activity* to refer to the combination of virtuous feeling and conduct.

14. For example, the player with the opportunity to pass might believe that his or her team had earlier been allowed a goal by the referee that should have been disallowed and conclude that playing fairly (cf. *WJ*, 33) requires that he or she forego the opportunity to score. That it is thus questionable that MacIntyre can show how an action is justifiable by a single practical syllogism even within his highly contrived example suggests that his Thomistic, deductive model of practical rationality would have difficulty applying to the complex contexts of actual practice.

15. MacIntyre's reference (*AV*, 175; *WJ*, 142) is to J. L. Ackrill's *Aristotle on Eudaimonia* reprinted in Amélie Rorty (1980, 15–33). According to Ackrill, Aristotle is not at all clear on two issues that are central to his ethics. The *second* of these is "what is the best life for a man to lead?"

16. *WJ* (107–108, 132–133, 143, 165–166), *FG* (254–255). MacIntyre provides some indications that he is following Aquinas in his preference for one among the possible readings of Aristotle's position. However, MacIntyre (*WJ*, 192; cf. *TRV*, 137) is not clear whether he understands Aquinas' arguments that the life of moral virtue cannot be the human *telos* to be *amending* and *extending* or to be *recapitulating* Aristotle's own arguments.

17. That the structure of Aquinas' narrative of human life results in a consequentialist ethics is supported by Bourke's (1966, 7) presentation of Thomistic ethics as "an acquired habit of the human intellect enabling its possessor to reason to true conclusions about the kind of human actions which are calculated to bring man to the attainment of true happiness."

18. MacIntyre (*WJ*, 192, 331). Of course, this problem could be solved from the point of view of the narratives that would understand human confusion about what is good to be a consequence of Adam's original sin (*WJ*, 231–233; Bourke 1966, 42). However, if he wishes to make human knowledge of the intrinsic goodness of virtuous actions wholly dependent upon ecclesiastically mediated revelation, MacIntyre must shoulder a number of other commitments that he hardly begins to enumerate, much less defend (in this connection, see *TRV*, 91–94; 140–141; *RVG*, 19).

19. On Aristotle's notion of *nature*, see Jacobs (1995, 24–25).

20. *NE* 1097b15–23. I have used Ross's (McKeon 1947, 317) translation here except in substituting *eudaimonia* where he prefers *happiness*, a practice I will continue in subsequent references to translations of Aristotle because it is widely acknowledged that what Aristotle means by *eudaimonia* is not what modern speakers of English generally mean by *happiness*.

21. *SH* (118–119), *WJ* (74, 107–108), *TRV* (62, 66–67, 134, 138). To the best of my recollection, MacIntyre makes no explicit reference to anything beyond these first two senses of *good* when arguing for the superiority of teleological over liberal deontological ethical schemes.

22. In my interpretation of the significance of what is *kalon* (χαλόν) in Aristotle's ethics, I am following Owens (1981), except by using Ross's translation *noble* or *fine* instead of *right*, the term Owens prefers, with *seemly* a close second. It appears that there is no one English word that has the same range of correct applications as *kalon*.

23. *NE* 1099a10–251. Aristotle later qualifies this rather rosy picture by observing that the pleasure that is an inseparable part of noble action is sometimes only chosen at the cost of other pleasures (*NE* 1117b6–15).

24. On this point, see Gilson (1979, 339); also Lonergan (1973, 35–36); cf. Jacobs (1995, 26–27).

25. That Aristotle held the supreme good to be that which is most *kalon* is argued by Owens (1981, 268–269).

26. *WJ* (173–174), *TRV* (26, 122); cf. Bourke (1966, 37), Gilson (1979, 340, 344).

27. On Plato's reticence, see Cornford (1941, 212). According to the Ackrill article (1980, 15) that MacIntyre cites with approval, the *first* of the two central issues "as to which it is not even quite clear what Aristotle's view really is" is "what is the criterion of right action and of moral virtue?" See also Owens (1981, 277).

28. MacIntyre states that the *Republic* "tells us what structure and content a theory which could rationally warrant its account of justice would possess. But it does not itself provide such a theory" (*WJ*, 82).

29. *WJ* (191–192), cf. Bourke (1966, 32–34, 37–38), also Aquinas' (*S.T.* Ia, 5,6) distinctions among the *befitting*, the *pleasant*, and the *useful*. Similarly, MacIntyre argues that it is a mistake to confuse pursuit of internal goods with pursuit of pleasure, even though realization of the goods internal to practices is accompanied by various kinds of enjoyment (*AV*, 160, 197; cf. 62–64).

Chapter Six.　Reasons of the Heart

1. Ziff (1960, chapter 6, esp. 247).

2. For an argument that answers to such questions as "Is chocolate good?" *are* open to disputation, see Stanley Godlovitch, "A matter of taste" (1981).

3. My distinction between contingent and necessary relations between the quality of a response and the nature of what is responded to was inspired by a distinction within religious studies between *signs* and *symbols*. See Slater (1978, 17); also Lonergan (1973, 64–67).

4. Thomas (1989, 60–63); Wallace and Walker (1970, introduction). This is not, of course, to say that this distinction is drawn universally.

5. Turiel's and Nucci's research on the distinctions people draw between conventional and moral norms lends support to this point. For a summary of research on that distinction, see Nucci (1989, 184–186).

6. As Wallace and Walker (1970, introduction) suggest, it is part of something being a valid reason for me to do something that it would also be a reason for anyone else in a similar situation. I should add that, because religious values are sometimes understood to trump moral values, I will take up the issue of the relation of religion to morality in my last chapter.

7. On moral language as prescriptive, see R. M. Hare (1952). It is worth noting that, having taken a formalistic approach to differentiating the moral from non-moral domains, Hare is only able to support his way of drawing the distinction with a circular argument (144).

8. Owens (1981, 261–262, 268).

9. For more on this point, and a look at the ontological assumptions corresponding to Aristotle's cognitive view of the emotions, see L. A. Kosman (1980).

10. See Matthew Fox (1979, chapter one) for a discussion of *compassion* in biblical use. Indeed, the word compassion derives (so my Concise Oxford dictionary tells me) from the Latin *pati/passi* meaning "suffer," and *com*, a prefix meaning "with, together, altogether, completely." Thus, in its most basic sense, to be compassionate means to identify with others in their suffering. Compare Abraham Heschel's words in *The Prophets:* "Justice . . . is not an abstraction, a value. Justice exists in relation to a person, and is something done by a person. An act of injustice is condemned, not because the law is broken, but because a person has been hurt" (I am grateful for this quote to Claudia Eppert and Roger Simon).

11. On the role of personal experience in interpretation across difference, a process which requires "feeling-thought" or *resonance*, see the narratives by anthropologists Wikan (1989), Rosaldo (1989, introduction, esp. 11), and Ellis (1993, esp. 725–726). Of course, the link between the experiences that shape a person's enacted values on the one hand and the values they espouse on the other is by no means always clear, even to the person in question. And, as Wikan warns and Rosaldo's narrative illustrates, it cannot be naively assumed that our experiences are actually (as opposed to potentially) comparable to those of other people. For these references I am grateful to Pamela Cushing of McMaster University.

12. For examples of these objections, see Coburn (1982, 664) and MacIntyre's (*WJ*, 271–278) discussion of Hutcheson's "moral sense."

13. Williams (1989, 9) notes that some historians would place the death of the Buddha more than a century later, at approximately 370–368 B.C.E.

14. For a classic presentation and elaboration of the foundational Buddhist teachings, see Walpola Rahula (1974). Entries in the *Shambhala Dictionary of Buddhism and Zen* (Fischer-Schreiber, Ehrhard, and Diener 1991) such as those under "Siddhartha," "Buddha," "Buddhism," "Theravāda," "Hīnayāna," and "Mahāyāna," provide excellent, concise descriptions both of the historical development and geographical expansion of Gautama's teachings and of technical Buddhist terms. Williams (1989, introduction) also provides a good overview. I should note that I do not use the term *Hīnayāna* in any pejorative sense (on this see Varela, Thompson, and Rosch 1991, 219; cf. Williams 1989, 4, 32–33), but follow Trungpa in using it to refer to the teachings and practices that form the basis of the Buddhist spiritual path.

15. Trungpa was authorized to represent both the Karma Kagyü and the Nyingma lineages, two of the main lineages of Tibetan Buddhism. A list of Trungpa's principle publications is provided in my references. The Mahāyāna teachings and practices to which I will refer represent one of a variety of heterogeneous developments out of the earlier Indian texts, and thus represents a, not the, Mahāyāna point of view (Williams 1989, 275–276).

16. Williams' (1989, xi) cautions and disclaimers apply here *fortissimo*.

17. Epstein (1973). Our self-absorption is delightfully portrayed in Tom Dicillo's (1994) film *Living in Oblivion*.

18. For a detailed explanation and defence of the claims that (a) our usual dualistic, subject-object experiencing results from the habitual superimposition of conceptual frameworks upon nondual percepts; and (b) this multi-layered process of superimposition can be unlearned, resulting in "pure," unmediated perception, see Loy (1988, 39–95, 138–150), particularly on the distinction between *sa-vikalpa* and *nir-vikalpa* and on the critique of *prapañca-nāmarūpa*; cf. Williams (1989, 82–85, 90). To appreciate how quickly we usually move from percepts to concepts, consider the contrast between listening to people speaking a familiar language and listening to people speaking one that is unfamiliar.

19. Williams (1989, 66–67) provides an excellent summary of Buddhist dialectical arguments against inferences to belief in a permanent Self or Soul.

20. The Buddhist psychology of the *Abhidharma* literature describes the multi-layered process of self-creation under five categories: "form, feeling, perception, mental constructions, and consciousness" (Gyamtso 1988, 21–32). For a phenomenological characterization of these processes and their self-perpetuating interrelationship, see Trungpa (1975); also Kongtrül (1992, 30–35).

21. Like most western non-specialists, I am familiar with this literature primarily in the form of translations of and commentaries upon the Heart Sūtra and the Diamond (*Vajracchedika*) Sūtra, e.g., Conze (1958), Hanh (1992), and Price and Wong (1990). Williams (1989, 13–15) claims that the earliest known text proclaiming the egolessness of objects as well as subjects, the *Lokānuvartana Sūtra*, was associated with a non-Mahāyāna group, and only subsequently adopted by Mahāyāna traditions.

22. Loy (1988, 50). For discussion of the philosophical and meditative route to the realization of emptiness, see Gyamtso (1988) and Williams (1989, 60–74).

23. On this doctrine, see Varela, Thompson, and Rosch (1991, esp. 221–224).

24. Compare Bertrand Russell's (1967, 72) observations: "The mental continuity of a person is a continuity of habit and memory: there was yesterday one person whose feelings I can remember, and that person I regard as myself of yesterday; but in fact, myself of yesterday was only certain mental occurrences which are now remembered, and are regarded as part of the person who now recollects them. All that constitutes a person is a series of experiences connected by memory and by certain similarities of the sort we call habit."

25. For one attempt to be more specific about this limited kind of continuity, see Williams (1989, 90–92) on the Mahāyāna *Cittamātra* theory of consciousness.

26. Tarnas (1991, 101–103, 144). I am grateful to Charles Davis, then chair of the Department of Religious Studies at Concordia University in Montréal, for first pointing out to me that the belief in the immortality of the soul found in many Christian liturgies and theologies is not easily made compatible with belief in resurrection of the body.

27. For the "no boundaries" argument, see Wilber (1985, esp. 15–29). For arguments against the commonsense view that objects or "things" composed of matter exist, see Gyamtso (1988, 40) and Loy (1988, 74–79).

28. See Williams (1989, 96–109) on the historical roots and development of the concept of *tathāgata-garbha*. In my description, I am following those who equate Buddha-nature with the luminous *dharmakaya* and ultimate *bodhicitta*, e.g., Kongtrül (1992, 27).

29. This follows from the inseparability of experiencer, experiencing, and experienced. See Shunryu Suzuki (1970), also Loy (1988, 24) and Williams (1989, 114–115).

30. On unconditioned awareness, see Trungpa (1976, 119–120). On how affirming the inseparable, "primordial" qualities of Buddha-nature is not attributing qualities to an object with self-nature, see Gyamtso (1986, 81–85).

31. For a discussion of the dispute between the Tibetan Rangtong (*rang stong*) and Shentong (*ghzan stong*) schools over the senses in which it is and is not accurate to say that Buddha-nature is already enlightened, see Williams (1989, 105–109, 179–180); cf. Kongtrül (1992, 20, 29, 75) and Gyamtso (1986, 75–86).

32. Like many Buddhist teachings—for example, those related to the connections among *body, speech,* and *mind*—the distinction between absolute and relative occurs in a number of contexts and has a correspondingly rich variety of meanings, only one of which I touch upon here.

33. On non-dualistic and hence non-conceptual insight, see Loy's (1988, 135–138) analysis of *prajñā;* cf. Ames's (1991, 227–244) discussion of the Confucian/Taoist *chih.* On the historical development of the meaning of *prajñā,* see Williams (1989, 42–45). For more on the doctrine of the two truths, see Gyamtso (1988, 14–15, 58–59); Kongtrül (1992, 27–28); Loy (1988, 69); Thurman (1991, 60–61); Varela, Thompson, and Rosch (1991, 226–228); and Williams (1989, 69–72).

34. From this perspective, because propositional truth claims are formulated "as if" subjects and objects had separate, independent existence, *all* relative truth, including science and analytic philosophy, is metaphorical. Crossan (1975, 38) cites Robert Frost as making a similar point in his essay "The Constant Symbol."

35. Those within the Prāsangika Mādhyamaka tradition take the limitations of relative truth so seriously that they decline to defend any substantive metaphysical position. When they do use discursive reasoning, it is only to show that any substantive claim is vulnerable to dialectical critique. On the tradition of dialectical deconstruction beginning with Nāgārjuna, which employs *reductio ad absurdum* arguments similar to those used by Zeno of Elea, see Gyamtso (1986, 65–70), Williams (1989, 67–72), and Loy (1988, 28–29, 55). For a discussion of the senses in which the Prāsangika Madhyamaka view it is and is not compatible with the apparently substantive claims of the Yogācāra-Svatantrika or Cittamātra (Mind only) tradition, see Gyamtso (1986 59ff.), Kongtrül (1992, 29), Loy (1988, 192–197), and Williams (1989, 82–86). For a historical perspective on debate over the value of relative truth, see Williams (1989, esp. 193–197); also Loy (1988, 20–21).

36. For a development of the dream analogy, see the relevant sections in each chapter of Gyamtso (1986).

37. See Williams (1989, 30–32, cf. 99, 106, 143–144) on the historical development within Buddhism of the understanding that whatever is "well-spoken" (i.e., whatever conduces to enlightenment) is genuine *dharma,* equivalent to the words of the Buddha. See Loy's (1988, 120–122) remarks on Wittgenstein and Heidegger in this connection; cf. Wikan's (1989, 464) remarks on Davidson and Rorty's theory of language. I put "pragmatic" in quotes because I intend no claims about the relation of Buddhist epistemology and notions of truth to the pragmatism of Dewey or James.

38. "Those who believe in substantiality are like cows; those who believe in emptiness are worse" (Saraha, ca. ninth century C.E.; cited by Varela, Thompson,

320 NOTES TO PAGES 221–224

and Rosch 1991). See also Kongtrül (1992, 49–51), Williams (1989, 75), and Loy (1988, 19–20).

39. *TRV* (49); I am here recalling MacIntyre's reference to Nietzsche's "final standpoint." Compare Trungpa (1973, 194–195). I will comment upon the implications of the Mahāyāna distinction between relative and absolute truth for genealogy later in this chapter.

40. Paul Warwick, talk given during meditation retreat, Karmê Chöling, Vermont, August 1989. Ames (1991, 229–230) makes comparable remarks on the ultimate dispensability of words and images within Confucian epistemology.

41. For an elaboration of this viewpoint, see Shunryu Suzuki (1970, 29–31, 133–135) on the distinction between *little mind* and *big mind*; cf. Tarnas' (1991, 335–336) remarks on Berkeley's critique of Locke's distinction between primary and secondary qualities.

42. See Williams (1989, 85; cf. Loy 1988, 66); also Gyamtso (1988, 57–58). To quote the *Sūtra of the Heart of Transcendent Knowledge* again: "Form is emptiness; emptiness also is form. Emptiness is no other than form; form is no other than emptiness" (on this, see Trungpa 1973, 187–190). Similarly, lineage holders of the Tibetan Mahamudra tradition report that the *emptiness* of unconditioned awareness—its lack of fixed, determinate natures or boundaries—is inseparable from its *luminosity*, the self-cognizing manifestation of phenomena in all its rich variety. On this, see Gyamtso (1988, 77–78) and Kongtrül (1992, esp. 4, 21–27, 34–35, 66–69, 71–73, 85–86) on the three *kayas*.

43. For a succinct description of grasping and fixation, see Kongtrül (1992, 32–34); cf. Loy (1988, 36–50) and Trungpa (1976, 150).

44. I am adapting an answer provided by Jeremy Hayward to a similar question raised during a lecture at Rocky Mountain Shambhala Center, Colorado, August 1990.

45. Williams (1989, 25, 47–48, 198). In Hanh's (1992, 32) words: "*Bodhi* means awake. *Satva* means living being. A bodhisattva is an awakened being who helps other beings to wake up."

46. I am here drawing upon Buddhist teachings on *karma* and on the *bardos*.

47. I should also note that, Buddhism's understanding of how actions condition subsequent actions notwithstanding, it does not (to the best of my knowledge) explain why some people do and others do not undertake the process of "waking up," or even why our confusion occurred in the first place.

48. See, for example, Gyatso (1995b) and McKenna (1995).

49. Kongtrül (1992, 48–49, 80–81); also Gyamtso (1988, 11–12, 23).

50. For an introduction to the "mind-training" (Tib. *lojong*) practices originating with Atisha, see Trungpa (1993) and Chödrön (1994). Mahāyāna post-mediation disciplines have a dualistic flavour because, in reversing our usual tendency to put self before others, they presuppose the *self* and *other* frame of

reference. There is therefore some danger that, if recommended or applied indiscriminately, such disciplines could reinforce neuroses rooted in subject-object fixation. For this reason, they are properly introduced only to those who have developed some personal understanding of egolessness and *śūnyatā* (Trungpa 1993, xvi).

51. *Bodhicitta* is usually translated "Awakened mind," but it would be accurate to render *citta* as "heart/mind." Like the Chinese *hsin*, *citta* does not presuppose a duality of reason and emotion, the cognitive and the affective: "It is not that this *hsin* sometimes means one thing, and sometimes the other, but rather that it always means both. Mental events do not simply evoke an emotion—they are not attended by an emotion. Rather, the cognitive and the affective are integrally and inextricably intertwined: one "feels" one's thoughts (Ames 1991, 238).

52. Krishnamurti (1973, 69, 477–507) emphasizes this point; see also Loy (1988, 30–31).

53. See, for example, Gyamtso (1988, 71–72) and Kongtrül (1992, 38–39, 41–42) on the Two Accumulations.

54. Kongtrül (1992, 61, 68); cf. Frye (1990d, 17). This description is, of course, from the relative point of view; from the absolute point of view there was never any confusion to arise.

55. Loy (1988, 10; cf. 96–112); see also Kongtrül (1992, 56–57, 75), Buber (1970, 62), and Murdoch (1970, 40).

56. Although I cannot pursue the idea here, I expect that understanding the awakened state as beyond the distinction between meditation and non-meditation could provide an answer to the long-standing question within the Thomistic tradition of how the proper relation between contemplative and political activity should be conceived.

57. See Williams (1989, 44–45); cf. Kongtrül (1992, 64–65) on *Three-Fold Purity* and on the *Six Perfections* (pāramitās).

58. On spontaneous beneficial action, see Williams (1989, 180), also Thrangu (1996, 50–51); on wisdom as the joining of insight and compassion, see Trungpa (1973, 208–210; 1976, 123, 154).

59. I do not wish, by adopting Pascal's phrase, to signal approval of or even familiarity with his overall point of view.

60. In such examples I am drawing not only upon my own experience, but also Loy (1988, 70), and presentations by John McQuade on the *Miksang* (lit. "Good Eye") Society for Contemplative Photography, Toronto, Ontario. For another example, if you have ever absent-mindedly walked down a flight of stairs and reached the bottom one step earlier than you expected, try to recall the "gap" that occurred between your thinking before the last step and your figuring out what happened after. Reading Buber's (1970) characterization of the

differences between "I-Thou" and "I-It" might be another way to make the notion of nondual experiencing more familiar.

61. For example, see Mullet's (1987, 333–338) description of Charles Taylor's proposals that "imports" are directly intuited through feelings, and that it is important to distinguish between "self-referring" and "other-referring" emotions.

62. Loy (1988, 1–2, 8–9) makes this claim while recognizing exceptions, notably Berkeley and Hume. For his discussion of these philosophers in relation to Eastern nondualism, see Loy's chapter on non-dual perception (esp. 75–76).

63. Loy (1988, 298–302); cf. Bernstein's (1983, 118–123) discussion of Gadamer on "Truth and the Experience of Art"; also Buber (1970, 60–61).

64. Keller (1985, 117–120), cf. Noddings' (1984, 33–37) characterization of *engrossment.*

65. For recent discussions of this debate from a variety of perspectives, see Odegard and Stewart (1991).

66. *TRV* (136–137), Lonergan (1973, 240–241). This point is similar to the argument that contemplatives from different traditions sometimes express their insights in conflicting terms because of their different metaphysical convictions and because of the limits of subject-object languages (Loy 1988, 202–260, 292–295).

67. Nielsen (1987, 150–152) elaborates a very similar point in connection with his appeal to "considered convictions" in the search for wide reflective equilibrium.

68. Murdoch (1970, 23, cf. 59, 64–68) comes to mind in this regard: "Freedom is not the sudden jumping of the isolated will in and out of an impersonal logical complex, it is a function of the progressive attempt to see a particular object clearly."

69. *NE* 1139b15–1141a6. In this connection, I find it puzzling that MacIntyre (*WJ*, 99, cf. 277) cites with apparent approval Aristotle's claim that *nous* grasps particulars as instantiating universals but considers Hutcheson incoherent in making what seems to be an equivalent claim about the moral sense.

70. For an extended analysis of the objectivity and rationality of emotions, see de Sousa (1987).

71. Trungpa (1976, 114–116). MacIntyre (*AV*, 202, 234) characterizes the medieval Christian virtue of patience similarly as "waiting attentively without complaint."

72. *De Anima*, 433a24 (hereafter *DA*, trans. W. D. Ross, in McKeon 1941); cf. *DA* 432b5–9; *NE* 1139a35–1139b; *TRV*, 62. A related point is that what distinguishes Aquinas from Aristotle is not that Aquinas has a conception of the "rational" appetite and Aristotle does not, but that Aquinas understands the will as *corrupted* by original sin.

73. Voegelin (1978, 95–96; cited in Davis 1979, 19). See Davis (1983, 41–46) for more on this interpretation of *nous*.

74. For a positive view of surrender, see Murdoch (1970, 40) on *obedience*. I suspect that the intellectualist bias and corresponding absence of appreciation for experiential learning has contributed to the extremely unfortunate split between "religion" (conceived as assent to dogma) and "philosophy" (conceived as the exercise of formalized reason).

75. For an excellent overview of that history, see Tarnas (1991, e.g., 138–148).

76. Bourke (1966, 93). From this view, it is a short step to the deontological position that MacIntyre (*WJ*, 265) finds unsatisfactory: "it is just insofar as actions are explicable by interests or advantages that they cease to have moral worth."

77. *WJ* (170–171, 356–357), *FP* (13), *TRV* (66–67); cf. Coleman (1994, 68–71).

78. A similar relation between the absolute and the relative is suggested by Aquinas' own view that being, truth, and goodness are predicated of God only *analogically* (*TRV*, 166). As Loy (1988, 78) remarks, "It is difficult indeed to distinguish between pure being and pure non-being as a category."

79. Tarnas (1991, 483, n. 6; cf. *WJ*, 193). Haldane (1994, 102) is worth citing in this context: "The conclusion of this study is a thesis about what lies at the heart of Aquinas' work: 'Behind the discursive arguments, the conceptual distinctions, the whole impressive display of *ratio* . . . there lies the experience of Being . . . a profound, if implicit mysticism. In the end, St. Thomas is properly understood only by converting the coin of his metaphysical theology into its religious and alethiological equivalent'."

80. Williams (1989, 38) compares the scholar who would write on Buddhist texts without considering the traditional context of meditation practice in which they are employed to the art historian "who would study architecture by ignoring the building and looking only at the bricks."

81. Regarding this concern, see Davis (1973) and Crowe (1977).

82. Ames (1991, 227–228, 238–239) lists similar dualisms as related to a notion of *transcendence* that "in various guises has been a recurrent and dominant feature since the inception of classical Western philosophy."

83. Griffin (1992), Havel (1992, 2), Keller (1985, esp. 95–97, 123–124), Komesaroff (1986, esp. 12–17), Taylor (1994, 19–20), Vokey (1987, 61–62).

84. For an excellent discussion of the fear of death, see Wilber (1985, e.g., 75–78).

Chapter Seven.   Moral Discourse

1. The distinction between moral traditions and moral points of view is similar to that between religious traditions and religious faiths, where *faith* refers to a personal way of life, e.g., Slater (1978, 13–14).

2. On this point, see Gaon (1996) for a critique of Habermas' recent efforts to rescue the Kantian project by shifting from a philosophy of the transcendental subject to a philosophy of language.

3. For arguments that Kantian procedural or formalistic moralities presuppose commitment to substantive "goods," see Benhabib (1987), Strike (1995), and Taylor (1994, esp. 20–28).

4. For an argument that an attitude of respect for persons as ends-in-themselves arising from sympathy or compassion is the "motivational heart" of both Rawl's and Kohlberg's liberalism, see Boyd (1980, 195–198). For a characterization of the liberal ideal of rational autonomy and associated assumptions about human nature, see Boyd (1979). Purely political (in the modern sense) versions of liberalism seem to be driven more by a vision of a stable political society, e.g., Allen (1987, 189–190).

5. My questioning was initially prompted by studying Lonergan's *Insight* (Vokey 1980), and subsequently by Habermas' early efforts to rationally ground the moral commitments implicit in critical social theory and by Alison Jagger's search in the Jerome S. Simon Memorial Lectures (March 11–12 and 18–19, 1992, University of Toronto, Toronto, Ontario) for a theoretical basis for the moral commitments implicit within feminist politics.

6. I take this example from the editorial "Of man, mind and machine" in *The Globe and Mail*, February 23, 1996; A16.

7. For a similar view expressed in different terms, see Brandt's (1959, 244–251) arguments for the "Qualified Attitude Method" as the "standard" method in ethics.

8. *WJ* (57, 88). Elsewhere, MacIntyre states, "Notice that the move from myth to philosophy is itself the Platonic movement from picture to concept" (*FG*, 245). This move is necessary because, according to Plato, the forms cannot be expressed by or grasped in images or diagrams (*FG*, 250). "So Socrates' companions, who are being introduced to the good only by images are thereby informed that they are asleep, not awake; and so are we, the readers of the *Republic*" (*FG*, 251).

9. *WJ* (63). For an opposing view that dramatic poetry was precisely what Plato was against, see Bogdan (1983).

10. *WJ* (70). Elsewhere, MacIntyre (*TC*, 11) refers to "both discursive and poetic reason" without explaining their similarities (as reason) and their differences (as distinct). See also his discussion of the different senses corresponding to different genres (*TRV*, 85–86).

11. Haldane (1994, 102–103) makes a similar point: Justification cannot be purely historical because there is a difference between showing that the reasoning behind the changes in a tradition's fundamental agreements made sense

at the time and showing that those agreements are still defensible in light of present knowledge.

12. See, for example, *AV* (263), *WJ* (87); cf. Frye's (1963, 55, 63–64, 67) references to "a hare-and-tortoise race between mob rule and education." Of course, as the Jedi knights of Star Wars fame illustrate, there are countless variations upon the theme of the light versus the "dark side," the fair-haired hero versus the swarthy villain.

13. I depart from Crossan's (1975, 58–59) definitions of *apologue* and *action* by not limiting them to fictional narratives, for on his own account there is no strict boundary between fact and fiction.

14. For an elaboration of this claim, see MacIntyre (1984, 239–243).

15. Crossan (1975, 68). For more recent examples of parables, see Crossan's (1975, 77–85) analysis of short stories by Franz Kafka and by Jorge Luis Borges.

16. This is true both for individual and collective sense-making. For a discussion of the analogies between the selective/constructive nature of individual acts of perception, and the enactment/selection processes of group sense-making, see Weick (1979, esp. 147–153, 174–187). In both cases, "What is going on here?" comes before "What should I/we do?"

17. See Schön (1983, 14–20, 40–42, 63, 309–310) and Benner (1984, 6–10).

18. Peters and Waterman (1982, esp. 266) provide a wealth of examples of how "war stories" are important to developing good judgment in business contexts.

19. See Nussbaum (1987). Psychological research testifies to the power of folk tales to help us make difficult decisions by engaging our unconscious processes, although *how* such archetypal narratives are understood to condition our subliminal interpretation of events will vary according to different assumptions about the nature and functions of the psyche. See von Franz (1977, 1980) for a Jungian perspective; Bettelheim (1986) for a Freudian. Although the bulk of this work focuses on folk or fairy tales (e.g., Dieckmann 1986), Joseph Campbell (1949) has interpreted the heroic journey motifs found in sacred legends, romances, epics, novels, folk-tales, comics, and films as an extended allegory of the Jungian quest for individuation.

20. I am here presupposing that *symbols* are objects within the natural or social environment that communicate or evoke or allude to something other than themselves because of their no-longer-contingent association with certain emotions, ideas, or other images. In this sense, symbols are part of the "language" of the imagination (Frye 1963, 25–26). Images can be "stand-ins" for the symbolic objects they represent, e.g., a picture of a national flag or of a person can evoke the same response as the original. For discussions of how stories serve to clarify and enhance symbolic meaning, see Slater (1978, 29–63), Lonergan (1973, 64–69), and Vokey (1980, 172–178). Deanne Bogdan reminded me, after

reading this note, that it is part of the power of symbols that they are never exhausted by any one interpretation.

21. On the role of imagination in deliberation, and the function of deliberation in the search for wide reflective equilibrium in the moral context, see Nussbaum and Sen (1989, 312–316).

22. Adventure-based experiential education involves providing opportunities and support for participants to adopt new patterns of behaviour. It also involves facilitating their reflection upon what can be learned from those experiences that is relevant to their post-program lives. Encouraging participants to share stories of their exploits and to keep both group and individual journals have been effective methods of facilitating such reflection. I should add that *The Outward Bound Story Project* (Clarkson 1988; see also Beale 1984) is an exploration of the potential for certain carefully chosen stories, when told or read at strategic moments during a wilderness program, to help participants access the archetypal significance of their "heroic" journeys.

23. I am here thinking particularly of gossip, which in my experience is a universal feature of human communities.

24. According to Benjamin (1968, 89–90), it is just this feature of the story of the Egyptian king Psammenitus as told by Herodotus that accounts for its longevity.

25. Waley (1958, e.g., chapter 2). For a less literal, more poetic rendering, see Mitchell (1988).

26. For an outline of a way of life with the Rational Individual at its core, see Hirst (1992, 41–43).

27. The same point has been made by those warning against too quick a marriage between Buddhist ethics and quantum mechanics: what would/should happen to those ethical commitments if quantum mechanics was eventually replaced by another theoretical framework?

28. On "tightly coupled," see Weick (1979). The danger is illustrated by the inflexible conservatism of those communities that allow only literal interpretations of authoritative texts.

29. My use of quotation marks here reflects my belief that equating a particular moral theory with *the* truth reflects a loss, not an affirmation, of true faith. On the other hand, as MacIntyre observes, affirming the provisional nature of our conclusions is not inconsistent with defending them as the most adequate so far to a given intention.

30. In Crossan's (1975) interpretation, Jesus' most powerful parables were the ones he enacted, most centrally his submission to crucifixion.

31. For a discussion of the potential for understanding across such differences as race, class, and gender, see Burbules and Rice (1991, 393–416) and responses by Leach (1992) and by Garrison and Kimball (1994).

32. Shared periods of silence has been an important part of establishing the "ground" for productive dialogue among contemplatives from different traditions. See Walker (1987, Introduction).

33. Goulet (1994) describes how arriving at even a partial understanding of the Dene Tha was possible only when his participation in their way of life opened up new forms of experiencing, and a corresponding shift in his standpoint and horizon.

34. On the need for educated and re-educated imaginations, see Bogdan (1992); on the importance of a "critical poetics," see Davis (1975).

35. On this point, see Wilshire (1990, xx, 39–40, 46, 87, 207).

36. On this point, see Aristotle (*Posterior Analytics* 71a1, trans. G. R. G. Mure, in McKeon, 1947), Aquinas (*Summa Theologica* I, I,8, in Pegis, 1948), Bernstein (1983, 2; 161–162), MacIntyre (*TRV*, 88–89, 223), Nielsen (1987, 147), and Rawls (1971, 580).

37. This observation is supported by Carter (1987) and Fernhout (1989), who expand Kohlberg's own attempts to ground his moral theory in "Stage Seven" ethical and cosmological beliefs.

38. This point is very well illustrated by Vehmas' (1999) survey of competing positions on the moral status of infants with intellectual disabilities.

39. *EP* (25, cf. 30–33; also *TRV*, 216–217). TV talk shows and radio call-in commentaries come to mind as forums lacking "the constraints of disciplined exchange." Wilshire (1990) raises similar concerns to MacIntyre in speaking of the "moral collapse" of the university.

40. As he himself acknowledges, in some cases MacIntyre only sketches what Thomistic arguments *would* look like *if* they were developed in sufficient detail to demonstrate the explanatory power of its overall conceptual scheme and corresponding narrative of human life (*TRV*, 147, 194; see also *AV*, 278; *WJ*, 10–11; *FP*, 65, 67–68; *RVG*, 13; *PRC*, 298).

41. In saying this, I am drawing upon my reading of Young (1976); also Capra (1983), Hayward (1995), and Zukav (1979).

References

Ackrill, J. L. 1980. Aristotle on *eudaimonia*. In A. O. Rorty, ed., *Essays on Aristotle's ethics*, 15–33. Berkeley: University of California Press.

Agassi, Joseph. 1964. The nature of scientific problems and their roots in metaphysics. In M. Bunge, ed., *The critical approach to science and philosophy*, 189–211. New York: Macmillan.

Aiken, Henry D. 1963. The concept of moral objectivity. In H. Castandea and G. Makhnikian, eds., *Morality and the language of conduct*, 69–105. Detroit: Wayne State University Press.

Alcoff, Linda, and Elizabeth Potter, eds. 1993. *Feminist epistemologies*. New York: Routledge.

Allen, Barry G. 1987. Groundless goodness. In E. Simpson, ed., *Antifoundationalism and practical reasoning*, 183–192. Edmonton: Academic Printing and Publishing.

Allen, Charles W. 1989. The primacy of *phronesis*: A proposal for avoiding frustrating tendencies in our conceptions of rationality. *Journal of Religion* 69, 359–374.

Altieri, Charles. 1987. From expressivist aesthetics to expressivist ethics. In A. J. Cascardi, ed., *Literature and the question of philosophy*, 132–166. Baltimore: Johns Hopkins University Press.

Ames, Roger T. 1991. Meaning as imaging: Prolegomena to a Confucian epistemology. In E. Deutsch, ed., *Culture and modernity: East-West philosophic perspectives*, 227–244. Honolulu: University of Hawaii Press.

Anscombe, G. E. M. 1958. Modern moral philosophy. *Philosophy* 33, 1–19.

Arrington, Robert L. 1989. *Rationalism, realism, and relativism: Perspectives in contemporary moral epistemology*. Ithaca: Cornell University Press.

Bai, Heesoon, and Daniel Vokey. 1995. *Beyond foundationalism and relativism: An ethical re-visioning for the twenty-first century*. Paper presented at the 21st Annual Meeting of the Association for Moral Education, New York, N.Y., November 16–18, 1995.

Barnes, Barry, and David Bloor. 1982. Relativism, rationalism, and the sociology of knowledge. In M. Hollis and S. Lukes, eds., *Rationality and relativism*, 21–47. Cambridge, Mass.: MIT Press.

Barnes, Jonathan. 1976. Introduction and bibliography. In B. Radice, ed., *Nicomachean ethics*, 9–52. London: Penguin Books.

Barrow, Robin. 1986. Socrates was a human being: A plea for transcultural moral education. *Journal of Moral Education* 15(1), 50–57.

———. 1993. *Language, intelligence, and thought*. Brookfield, Ver.: Edward Elgar.

Beale, Valerie. 1984. *The heroic journey and other metaphors in Outward Bound*. Paper presented at the Educators' Seminar, Canadian Outward Bound Wilderness School, Ontario, August 21–22, 1984.

Beck, Clive. 1976. *The reflective approach*. Toronto: OISE Press.

———. 1995. Postmodernism, ethics, and moral education. In W. Kohli, ed., *Critical conversations in philosophy of education*, 127–136. New York: Routledge.

Begley, Shirley S. 1994. Tibetan Buddhist medicine: A transcultural nursing experience. *Journal of Holistic Nursing* 12, 323–342.

Benhabib, Seyla. 1987. The generalized and the concrete other: The Kohlberg-Gilligan controversy and moral theory. In E. F. Kittay and D. T. Meyers, eds., *Women and moral theory*, 154–177. Totowa, N.J.: Rowman and Littlefield.

Benjamin, Walter. 1968. The storyteller. In H. Arendt, ed., *Illuminations: Essays and reflections*, 83–109, trans. H. Zohn. New York: Schocken.

Benner, Patricia. 1984. *From novice to expert: Excellence and power in clinical nursing practice*. Don Mills, Ont.: Addison-Wesley.

Berlin, Isaiah, Sir. 1956. *The age of enlightenment: The eighteenth-century philosophers*. New York: New American Library.

Bernstein, Richard J. 1976. *The restructuring of social and political theory*. New York: Harcourt Brace Jovanovich.

———. 1983. *Beyond objectivism and relativism: Science, hermeneutics, and praxis*. Philadelphia: University of Pennsylvania Press.

Bettelheim, Bruno. 1976. *The uses of enchantment*. New York: Alfred A. Knopf.

Beyer, Landon E., and Daniel Liston. 1992. Discourse or moral action? A critique of Postmodernism. *Educational Theory* 42, 371–393.

Blackman, D. E. 1980. Images of man in contemporary behaviourism. In A. J. Chapman and D. M. Jones, eds., *Models of man*, 99–112. Leicester: The British Psychological Society.

Bogdan, Deanne. 1983. Censorship of literature texts and Plato's banishment of the poets. *Interchange* 14(3), 1–16.

———. 1992. *Re-educating the imagination: Toward a poetics, politics, and pedagogy of literary engagement*. Portsmouth, N.H.: Heinemann Educational Books.

Bourke, Vernon J. 1966. *Ethics: A textbook in moral philosophy*. New York: Macmillan.

Boyd, Dwight. 1979. An interpretation of principled morality. *Journal of Moral Education* 8, 110–123.

———. 1980. The Rawls connection. In B. Munsey, ed., *Moral development, moral education, and Kohlberg: Basic issues in philosophy, psychology, religion, and education,* 185–213. Birmingham, Ala.: Religious Education Press.

———. 1984. The principle of principles. In W. Kurtines and J. Gewirtz, eds., *Morality, moral behaviour, and moral development,* 365–380. New York: John Wiley and Sons.

———. 1989a. Moral education, objectively speaking. In J. Giarelli, ed., *Philosophy of Education 1988: Proceedings of the Forty-Fourth Annual Meeting of the Philosophy of Education Society,* 83–100. Normal, Ill.: Philosophy of Education Society.

———. 1989b. *Cross-cultural concerns in philosophical perspective.* Paper presented at the International and Interdisciplinary Conference on "Cross-cultural Comparability and Applicability of Primary and Secondary Socialization: Personal, Societal, and Political Perspectives" at Jagiellonian University, Cracow, Poland, September 5–9.

———. 1991. One man's reflection on a masculine role in feminist ethics: Epistemic vs. political privilege. In D. Ericson, ed., *Philosophy of Education 1990: Proceedings of the Forty-Sixth Annual Meeting of the Philosophy of Education Society,* 286–299. Normal, Ill.: Philosophy of Education Society.

———. 1996. Dominance concealed through diversity: Implications of inadequate perspectives on cultural pluralism. *Harvard Educational Review* 66, 609–630.

Boyd, Dwight, and Deanne Bogdan. 1984. "Something" clarified, nothing of "value": A rhetorical critique of values clarification. *Educational Theory* 34, 287–300.

———. 1985. Rhetorical realities: A response to McAnich's interpretation of *Values and Teaching. Educational Theory* 35, 327–330.

Brabeck, Mary M., ed. 1989. *Who cares? Theory, research, and educational implications of the ethic of care.* New York: Prager.

Brandt, Richard B. 1959. *Ethical theory: The problems of normative and critical ethics.* Englewood Cliffs, N.J.: Prentice-Hall.

Broughton, John M. 1985. The genesis of moral domination. In S. Modgil and C. Modgil, eds., *Lawrence Kohlberg: Concensus and controversy,* 363–385. London: Falmer Press.

Brown, Harold I. 1983. Incommensurability. *Inquiry* 26(1), 3–29.

Buber, Martin. 1970. *I and Thou.* 2d ed., trans. R. G. Smith. New York: Charles Scribner's Sons.

Burbules, Nicholas C. 1991. Rationality and reasonableness: A discussion of Harvey Siegel's *Relativism refuted* and *Educating reason. Educational Theory* 41, 235–252.

Burbules, Nicholas C., and Suzanne Rice. 1991. Dialogue across differences: Continuing the conversation. *Harvard Educational Review* 61, 393–416.

Callan, Eamonn. 1993. Noncognitivism and autonomy. *Paideusis* 7(1), 15–29.

Campbell, Joseph. 1949. *The hero with a thousand faces.* New York: Pantheon Books.

Cantor, Alan. 1995. Crafted bodies: Interpretations of corporeal knowledge in light of the technological imagination in antiquity, the Renaissance, and the present. Unpublished master's thesis, University of Toronto, Toronto, Ontario.

Capra, Fritjof. 1983. *The Tao of physics: An exploration of the parallels between modern physics and Eastern mysticism.* Boston: New Science Library.

Caputo, John D. 1986. *The mystical element in Heidegger's thought.* New York: Fordham University Press.

Carr, Wilfred, and Stephen Kemmis. 1986. *Becoming critical: Education, knowledge, and action research.* Philadelphia: Falmer Press.

Carter, Robert E. 1984. *Dimensions of moral education.* Toronto: University of Toronto Press.

———. 1985. Does Kohlberg avoid relativism? In S. Modgil and C. Modgil, eds., *Lawrence Kohlberg: Consensus and controversy,* 9–20. London: Falmer Press.

———. 1987. Beyond justice. *Journal of Moral Education* 16, 88–97.

Cascardi, Anthony J. 1988. *Narration and totality.* Paper presented at the Eleventh International Congress of Aesthetics, University of Nottingham, England, Aug. 28–Sept. 2, 1988.

Cashman, Tyrone. 1992. Epistemology and the extinction of the species. In J. Ogilvy, ed., *Revisioning philosophy,* 1–18. Albany: State University of New York Press.

Cassirer, Ernst. 1955. *The philosophy of the Enlightenment.* Trans. Fritz C. A. Koelin and James Pettegrove. Boston: Beacon Press.

Chödrön, Pema. 1994. *Start where you are.* Boston: Shambhala.

Clarkson, Austin. 1988. *Stories for Outward Bound: Themes and interpretations.* Toronto: Soundway Press.

Coburn, Robert C. 1982. Morality, truth, and relativism. *Ethics* 92, 661–669.

Coleman, Janet. 1994. MacIntyre and Aquinas. In J. Horton and S. Mendus, eds., *After MacIntyre,* 65–90. Notre Dame: University of Notre Dame Press.

Conn, Walter E. 1976. Objectivity—A developmental and structural analysis: The epistemologies of Jean Piaget and Bernard Lonergan. *Dialectica* 30, 197–221.

———. 1981. *Conscience: Development and self-transcendence.* Birmingham, Ala: Religious Education Press.

Conze, Edward. 1958. *Buddhist wisdom books: The Diamond Sutra and the Heart Sutra.* New York: Harper and Row.

Coombs, Jerrold. 1987. Education and practical rationality. In N. Burbules, ed., *Philosophy of Education 1986: Proceedings of the Forty-Second Annual Meeting of the Philosophy of Education Society,* 3–20. Normal, Ill.: Philosophy of Education Society.

Copleston, Frederick C. 1955. *Aquinas.* Harmondsworth, Middlesex: Penguin Books.

Cornford, Francis M., ed. 1941. *The Republic of Plato.* London: Oxford University Press.

Crossan, John D. 1975. *The dark interval: Towards a theology of story.* Niles, Ill.: Argus Communications.

Crowe, Frederick E. (S.J.) 1977. Doctrines and historicity in the context of Lonergan's *Method. Theological Studies* 38, 115–124.

Daniels, Norman. 1979. Wide reflective equilibrium and theory acceptance in ethics. *Journal of Philosophy* 76, 256–282.

———. 1980. Reflective equilibrium and Archimedean Points. *Canadian Journal of Philosophy* 10, 83–103.

Davidson, Donald. 1982. On the very idea of a conceptual scheme. In J. Meiland and M. Krausz, eds., *Relativism: Cognitive and moral,* 66–80. Notre Dame: University of Notre Dame Press.

———. 1989. The myth of the subjective. In M. Krausz, ed., *Relativism: Interpretation and confrontation,* 159–172. Notre Dame: University of Notre Dame Press.

Davis, Charles. 1973. Theology and *praxis. Cross Currents* 2, 154–168.

———. 1975. Towards a critical theology. In J. W. McClendon, Jr., ed., *Philosophy of religion and theology 1975: Proceedings of the American Academy of Religion,* 213–229. Missoula, Mont.: Scholars Press.

———. 1976. *Body as spirit: The nature of religious feeling.* New York: Seabury Press.

———. 1979. *Tradition and reason in ethical discourse.* Paper presented to the Canadian Society for the Study of Religion, London, Ontario, 1979.

———. 1983. Reason, tradition, community: The search for ethical foundations. In L. S. Rouner, ed., *Foundations of ethics,* 37–56. Notre Dame: University of Notre Dame Press.

———. 1986. *What is living, what is dead in Christianity today?* San Francisco: Harper and Row.

———. 1990. Our modern identity: The formation of the self. *Modern Theology* 6(2), 159–171.

Denham, Robert D., ed. 1990. *Northrop Frye: Myth and metaphor* selected essays 1974–1988. Charlottesville: University Press of Virginia.

de Sousa, Ronald. 1987. *The rationality of emotion.* Cambridge, Mass.: MIT Press.

Deutscher, Max. 1983. *Subjecting and objecting.* Oxford: Blackwell.

Devine, Philip E. 1984. Relativism. *The Monist* 67, 405–418.

Dicillo, Tom, director. 1994. *Living in oblivion* [film]. JDI Productions and Lemon Sky Productions.

Dieckmann, H. 1986. *Twice-told tales: The psychological meaning of fairy tales.* Wilmett, Ill.: Chiron Press.

Dijksterhuis, Eduard J. 1961. *The mechanization of the world picture.* Trans. C. Diks-
hoorn. London: Oxford University Press.

Donald, Merlin. 1993. Précis of *Origins of the modern mind: Three stages in the evolution of culture and cognition. Behavioural and Brain Sciences* 16, 737–791.

Doppelt, Gerald. 1982. Kuhn's epistemological relativism: An interpretation and
defense. In J. Meiland and M. Krausz, ed., *Relativism: Cognitive and moral,*
113–147. Notre Dame: University of Notre Dame Press.

———. 1983. Relativism and recent pragmatic conceptions of scientific rationality. In N. Rescher, ed., *Scientific explanation and understanding: Essays on reasoning and rationality in science,* 107–142. Lanham, Md.: University Press of
America.

Edwards, Stephen D. 1990. *Relativism, conceptual schemes, and categorical frameworks.* Brookfield, Vt.: Gower Publishing.

Elgin, Catherine Z. 1989. The relativity of fact and the objectivity of value. In
M. Krausz, ed., *Relativism: Interpretation and confrontation,* 86–98. Notre Dame:
University of Notre Dame Press.

Ellis, Carolyn. 1993. "There are survivors": Telling a story of sudden death. *The
Sociological Quarterly* 34(4), 711–730.

Elshtain, Jean B. 1981. *Public man, private woman: Women in social and political
thought.* Princeton, N.J.: Princeton University Press.

Epstein, Seymour. 1973. The self-concept revisited, or, the theory of a theory.
American Psychologist (May), 404–416.

Falikowski, Anthony. 1984. Clive Beck's Reflective Ultimate Life Goals' approach
to values education: A philosophical appraisal. *Journal of Educational Thought*
18, 12–20.

Fay, Brian. 1975. *Social theory and political practice.* London: George Allen and
Unwin.

Feinberg, Walter. 1990. A role for Philosophy of Education in intercultural re-
search: A reexamination of the relativism-absolutism debate. In R. Page, ed.,
*Philosophy of Education 1989: Proceedings of the Forty-Fifth Annual Meeting of the
Philosophy of Education Society,* 2–19. Urbana-Champaign, Ill.: Philosophy of
Education Society.

Fernhout, Harry. 1989. Moral theory as grounded in faith. *Journal of Moral Education* 18, 186–198.

Feyerabend, Paul. 1975. *Against method.* London: New Left Books.

———. 1978. *Science in a free society.* London: Lowe and Brydone.

Fiskin, James S. 1984. *Beyond subjective morality: Ethical reasoning and political philosophy.* New Haven: Yale University Press.

Flanagan, Owen, and Kathryn Jackson. 1987. Justice, care, and gender: The
Kohlberg-Gilligan debate revisited. *Ethics* 97, 622–637.

Flanagan, Owen, and Amélie O. Rorty, eds. 1990. *Identity, character, and morality.*
Cambridge, Mass.: MIT Press.

Flew, Anthony. 1984. *A dictionary of philosophy*. New York: Macmillan.

Foot, Philippa. 1978. *Virtues and vices: And other essays in moral philosophy*. Berkeley: University of California Press.

———. ed. 1967. *Theories of ethics*. Oxford: Oxford University Press.

Fowler, James W. 1976. Faith development theory and the aims of religious socialization. In G. Durka and J. M. Smith, eds., *Emerging issues in religious education*, 187–208. New York: Paulist Press.

———. 1981. *Stages of faith: The psychology of human development and the quest for meaning*. New York: Harper and Row.

Fox, Matthew. 1979. *A spirituality named compassion and the healing of the global village, Humpty Dumpty, and us*. Minneapolis: Winston Press.

Fox, Richard M., and Joseph DeMarco, eds. 1986. *New directions in ethics*. New York: Routledge and Kegan Paul.

Frankena, William. 1973a. *Ethics*. 2d ed. Englewood Cliffs, N.J.: Prentice-Hall.

———. 1973b. The principles of morality. In C. Carter, ed., *Skepticism and moral principles*, 43–76. Evanston, Ill.: New University Press.

———. 1980. *Thinking about morality*. Ann Arbor: University of Michigan Press.

———. 1986. Moral philosophy and the future. In R. M. Fox and J. DeMarco, eds., *New directions in ethics*, 299–316. New York: Routledge and Kegan Paul.

Fraser, Nancy. 1986. Toward a discourse ethic of solidarity. *Praxis International* 5, 425–429.

Freire, Paulo. 1970. *Pedagogy of the oppressed*. Trans. M. B. Ramos. New York: Continuum.

———. 1985. *The politics of education: Culture, power, and liberation*. Trans. D. Macedo. South Hadley, Mass.: Bergin and Garvey.

French, A., T. E. Uehling, Jr., and H. K. Wettstein, eds. 1988. *Ethical theory: Character and virtue*. Notre Dame: University of Notre Dame Press.

Freudenthal, Gideon. 1986. *Atom and individual in the age of Newton: On the genesis of the mechanical world view*. Dordrecht, The Netherlands: D. Reidel Publishing.

Frye, Northrop. 1963. *The educated imagination*. Toronto: CBC Publications.

———. 1990a. Literature as critique of pure reason. In R. D. Denham, ed., *Northrop Frye: Myth and metaphor*, 168–182. Charlottesville: University Press of Virginia.

———. 1990b. The expanding world of metaphor. In R. D. Denham, ed., *Northrop Frye: Myth and metaphor*, 108–123. Charlottesville: University Press of Virginia.

———. 1990c. The journey as metaphor. In R. D. Denham, ed., *Northrop Frye: Myth and metaphor*, 212–226. Charlottesville: University Press of Virginia.

———. 1990d. The *Koine* of myth: Myth as a universally intelligible language. In R. D. Denham, ed., *Northrop Frye: Myth and metaphor*, 3–17. Charlottesville: University Press of Virginia.

————. 1990e. The view from here. In R. D. Denham, ed., *Northrop Frye: Myth and metaphor,* 63–78. Charlottesville: University Press of Virginia.

Gaon, Stella. 1996. *Ethics at issue: Critical political theory and the modernism/post-modernism debate.* Paper presented at the LXVIII Annual Meeting of the Canadian Political Science Association, Brock University, St. Catharines, Ontario, June 2–4, 1996.

Garrison, James W., and Stephanie L. Kimball. 1994. Dialoging across differences: Three hidden barriers. In A. Thompson, ed., *Philosophy of Education 1993: Proceedings of the Forty-Ninth Annual Meeting of the Philosophy of Education Society,* 177–185. Urbana, Ill.: Philosophy of Education Society.

Geertz, Clifford. 1989. Anti anti-relativism. In M. Krausz, ed., *Relativism: Interpretation and confrontation,* 12–34. Notre Dame: University of Notre Dame Press.

Gellner, Ernest. 1982. Relativism and universals. In M. Hollis and S. Lukes, eds., *Rationality and relativism,* 181–200. Cambridge, Mass.: MIT Press.

————. 1985. *Relativism and the social sciences.* Cambridge: Cambridge University Press.

Gilligan, Carol. 1982. *In a different voice.* Cambridge, Mass.: Harvard University Press.

————. 1988. *The moral domain.* Cambridge, Mass.: Harvard University Press.

Gilligan, Carol, and Jane Attanucci. 1987. Two moral orientations: Gender differences and similarities. *Merrill-Palmer Quarterly* 34, 223–237.

Gilson, Etienne. 1979. *The philosophy of Saint Thomas Aquinas.* New York: Arno Press.

Godlovitch, Stanley. 1981. A matter of taste. *Dialogue* 20, 530–547.

Goleman, Daniel. 1991. Tibetan and Western models of mental health. In D. Goleman and R. A. F. Thurman, eds., *MindScience: An East-West dialogue,* 89–102. Boston: Wisdom Publications.

Goodman, Nelson. 1982. The fabrication of facts. In J. Meiland and M. Krausz, eds., *Relativism: Cognitive and moral,* 18–29. Notre Dame: University of Notre Dame Press.

————. 1989. "Just the facts, Ma'am!" In M. Krausz, ed., *Relativism: Interpretation and confrontation,* 80–85. Notre Dame: University of Notre Dame Press.

Goulet, Jean-Guy A. 1994. Ways of knowing: Towards a narrative ethnography of experiences among the Dene Tha. *Journal of Anthropological Research* 50, 113–139.

Green, Thomas F. 1973. Judging. In C. J. Troost, ed., *Radical school reform: Critique and alternatives,* 196–215. Boston: Little, Brown, and Company.

————. 1982. On transcendental arguments. In D. R. DeNicola, ed., *Philosophy of Education 1981: Proceedings of the Thirty-Seventh Annual Meeting of the Philosophy of Education Society,* 334–339. Normal, Ill.: Philosophy of Education Society.

Greene, John C. 1981. *Science, ideology, and world view: Essays in the history of evolutionary world views.* Berkeley: University of California Press.

Greene, Maxine. 1994. Epistemology and educational research: The influence of recent approaches to knowledge. *Review of Research in Education* 20, 423–464.

Griffin, Susan. 1992. Daring witness: The recovery of female time. In J. Ogilvy, ed., *Revisioning philosophy*, 49–60. Albany: State University of New York Press.

Gross, Rita M. 1993. *Buddhism after patriarchy: A feminist history, analysis, and reconstruction of Buddhism.* Albany: State University of New York Press.

Gyamtso, Tsultrim. 1988. *Progressive stages of meditation on emptiness.* 2d ed. Oxford: Longchen Foundation.

Gyatso, Tenzin. 1995a. *The good heart summary: The John Main Seminar 1994* [videotape]. Medio Media, 23 Kensington Square, London, W8 5HN.

———. 1995b. Buddhism and Christianity. *Shambhala Sun* (May), 14–21.

Habermas, Jürgen. 1975. *Legitimation crisis.* Trans. T. McCarthy. Boston: Beacon Press.

Hacking, Ian. 1982. Language, truth, and reason. In M. Hollis and S. Lukes, eds., *Rationality and relativism*, 52–66. Oxford: Basil Blackwell.

Hahlweg, Kai, and Clifford A. Hooker. 1988. Evolutionary epistemology and relativism. In R. Nola, ed., *Relativism and realism in science*, 93–115. Dordrecht, The Netherlands: Kluwer Academic Publishers.

Haldane, John. 1994. MacIntyre's Thomist revival: What next? In J. Horton and S. Mendus, eds., *After MacIntyre*, 91–107. Notre Dame: University of Notre Dame Press.

Hanen, Marsha, and Kai Nielsen, eds. 1987. *Science, morality, and feminist theory: Canadian Journal of Philosophy* 13 supplement. Calgary: Unversity of Calgary Press.

Hanh, Thich Nhat, ed. 1992. *The diamond that cuts through illusion: Commentaries on the Prajnaparamita Diamond Sutra.* Berkeley: Parallax Press.

Haraway, Donna. 1988. Situated knowledges: The science question in feminism and the privilege of partial perspective. *Feminist Studies* 14(3), 575–599.

Hare, R. M. 1952. *The language of morals.* Oxford: Oxford University Press.

———. 1981. *Moral thinking: Its levels, method, and point.* Oxford: Clarendon Press.

Harman, Gil. 1991. Moral diversity as an argument for moral relativism. In D. Odegard and C. Stewart, eds., *Perspectives on moral relativism*, 13–31. Milliken, Ont.: Agathon Books.

Harré, Rom. 1989. The "self" as a theoretical concept. In M. Krausz, ed., *Relativism: Interpretation and confrontation*, 387–417. Notre Dame: University of Notre Dame Press.

Havel, Václav. 1992. (Untitled). Address to the Annual Meeting of the World Economic Forum unofficial translation, February 4, 1992.

Hayward, Jeremy. 1995. *A guide to sacred world.* Toronto: Bantam Books.

Herman, Edward S., and Noam Chomsky. 1988. *Manufacturing consent: The political economy of the mass media.* New York: Pantheon Books.

Higgins, Ann. 1991. The just community approach to moral education: Evolution of the idea and recent findings. In W. M. Kurtines and J. L. Gewirtz, eds., *Handbook of moral behavior and development, Volume I: Theory,* 111–142. Hillsdale, N.J.: Lawrence Erlbaum Associates.

Hirst, Paul H. 1992. Educational aims: Their nature and content. In M. Buchmann and R. E. Floden, eds., *Philosophy of Education 1991: Proceedings of the Forty-Seventh Annual Meeting of the Philosophy of Education Society,* 40–53. Normal, Ill.: Philosophy of Education Society.

Hollis, Martin. 1977. *Models of man: Philosophical thoughts on social action.* Cambridge: Cambridge University Press.

Hollis, Martin, and Stephen Lukes, eds. 1982. *Rationality and relativism.* Cambridge, Mass.: MIT Press.

Honderich, Ted, ed. 1985. *Morality and objectivity: A tribute to J. L. Mackie.* London: Routledge and Kegan Paul.

Horkheimer, Max. 1974. *Eclipse of reason.* New York: Seabury Press.

Horkheimer, Max and Theodor W. Adorno. 1972. *The dialectic of the enlightenment.* New York: Herder and Herder.

Horton, John, and Susan Mendus. 1994. Alasdair MacIntyre: *After Virtue* and after. In J. Horton and S. Mendus, eds., *After MacIntyre,* 1–15. Notre Dame: University of Notre Dame Press.

———. eds. 1994. *After MacIntyre: Critical perspectives on the work of Alasdair MacIntyre.* Notre Dame: University of Notre Dame Press.

Horton, Robin. 1982. Tradition and modernity revisited. In M. Hollis and S. Lukes, eds., *Rationality and relativism,* 201–266. Cambridge, Mass.: MIT Press.

Horwood, Robert H. 1993. Humpty Dumpty reconsidered: Seeing things whole in Outward Bound. *Journal of COBWS Education* 6, 13–21.

Hurley, S. L. 1985. Objectivity and disagreement. In T. Honderich, ed., *Morality and objectivity: A tribute to J. L. Mackie.* London: Routledge and Kegan Paul.

Huxley, Aldous. 1994. *The perennial philosophy.* London: HarperCollins.

Irwin, John. 1989. The liberation of males. In J. Irwin, ed., *Men,* 1–12. Seattle: Rational Island Publishers.

Jacobs, Jonathan. 1995. Why is virtue naturally pleasing? *The Review of Metaphysics* 49(1), 21–48.

Jaggar, Alison M. 1992. *Towards a feminist conception of practical reason.* Jerome S. Simon Memorial Lecture, University of Toronto, Toronto, Ontario, March 11–12, 18–19, 1992.

Kaplan, Morton A. 1984. *Science, language, and the human condition.* New York: Paragon House.

Kearney, Michael. 1984. *World view.* Novato, Calif.: Chandler and Sharp.

Kekes, John. 1980. *The nature of philosophy.* Oxford: Basil Blackwell.

Keller, Evelyn F. 1985. *Reflections on gender and science.* New Haven: Yale University Press.

———. 1989. The gender/science system: Response to Kelly Oliver. *Hypatia* 3, 149–152.

Kelly, Paul. 1994. MacIntyre's critique of utilitarianism. In J. Horton and S. Mendus, eds., *After MacIntyre,* 127–145. Notre Dame: University of Notre Dame Press..

Kilbourn, Brent. 1980. World views and science teaching. In H. Munby, G. Orpwood, and T. Russell, eds., *Seeing curriculum in a new light,* 34–43. Toronto: OISE Press.

King, Ynestra. 1989. Healing the wounds: Feminism, ecology, and nature/culture dualism. In A. M. Jaggar and S. R. Bordo, eds., *Gender/body/knowledge: Feminist reconstructions of being and knowing,* 115–141. New Brunswick: Rutgers University Press.

Kohák, Erazim. 1984. *The embers and the stars: A philosophical inquiry into the moral sense of nature.* Chicago: University of Chicago Press.

Kohlberg, Lawrence. 1971. From is to ought: How to commit the naturalistic fallacy and get away with it in the study of moral development. In T. Mischel, ed., *Cognitive development and epistemology,* 151–235. New York: Academic Press.

———. 1973. The claim to moral adequacy of a highest stage of moral judgment. *Journal of Philosophy* 70, 630–646.

———. 1974. Education, moral development and faith. *Journal of Moral Education* 4, 5–16.

———. 1975. The cognitive-developmental approach to moral education. *Phi Delta Kappan* 56, 670–676.

———. 1976. Moral stages and moralization: The cognitive-developmental approach. In T. Lickona, ed., *Moral development and behaviour,* 31–53. New York: Holt, Rinehart, and Winston.

———. 1978. Revisions in the theory and practice of moral development. In W. Damon, ed., *Moral development,* 83–87. San Francisco: Josey-Bass.

———. 1980. Stages of moral development as a basis for moral education. In B. Munsey, ed., *Moral development, moral education, and Kohlberg,* 15–98. Birmingham, Ala.: Religious Education Press.

———. 1981. *Essays on moral development. Volume I: Philosophy of moral development.* San Francisco: Harper and Row.

———. 1984. *Essays on moral development. Volume II: Psychology of moral development.* San Francisco: Harper and Row.

————. 1985. A current statement on some theoretical issues. In S. Modgil and C. Modgil, eds., *Lawrence Kohlberg: Consensus and controversy*, 485–546. Philadelphia: Falmer Press.

Kohlberg, Lawrence, and Ann Higgins. 1987. School democracy and social interaction. In W. M. Kurtines and J. J. Gewirtz, eds., *Moral development through social interaction*, 102–128. New York: John Wiley and Sons.

Kohlberg, Lawrence, and Thomas Lickona. 1986. *The stages of ethical development: From childhood through old age*. San Francisco: Harper and Row.

Kohlberg, Lawrence, Dwight Boyd, and Charles Levine. 1990. The return of Stage Six: Its principle and moral point of view. In T. E. Wren, ed., *The moral domain: Essays in the on-going debate between philosophy and the social sciences*, 151–181. Cambridge, Mass.: MIT Press.

Kohlberg, Lawrence, K. Kauffman, P. Scharf, and J. Hickey. 1975. The Just Community approach to corrections: A theory. *Journal of Moral Education* 4, 243–260.

Kohlberg, Lawrence, Charles Levine, and Alexandra Hewer. 1983. *Moral stages: A current formulation and a response to critics*. New York: Karger.

Komesaroff, Paul A. 1986. *Objectivity, science, and society: Interpreting nature and society in the age of the crisis of science*. London: Routledge and Kegan Paul.

Kongtrül, Jamgon the Third. 1992. *Cloudless sky: The mahamudra path of the Tibetan Buddhist Kagyu School*. Trans. R. Gravel. Boston: Shambhala.

Kosman, L. A. 1980. Being properly affected: Virtues and feelings in Aristotle's ethics. In A. O. Rorty, ed., *Essays on Aristotle's ethics*, 103–116. Berkeley: University of California Press.

Krausz, Michael. 1984. Relativism and foundationalism. *The Monist* 67, 395–404.

————. ed. 1989. *Relativism: Interpretation and confrontation*. Notre Dame: University of Notre Dame Press.

Krishnamurti, J. 1973. *The awakening of intelligence*. New York: Harper and Row.

Kubrin, David. 1989. Review of Gideon Freudenthal's *Atom and individual in the age of Newton: On the genesis of the mechanistic world view*. *Journal of the History of Philosophy* 27, 154–156.

Kuhn, Thomas S. 1962. *The structure of scientific revolutions*. Chicago: University of Chicago Press.

————. 1977. *The essential tension: Selected studies in scientific tradition and change*. Chicago: University of Chicago Press.

Lather, Patti. 1989. Postmodernism and the politics of enlightenment. *Educational Foundations* 3(3), 7–28.

————. 1991a. Deconstructing/deconstructive inquiry: The politics of knowing and being known. *Educational Theory* 41, 153–173.

————. 1991b. *Getting smart: Feminist research and pedagogy with/in the classroom*. New York: Routledge.

Laudan, Larry. 1977. *Progress and its problems: Toward a theory of scientific growth.* Berkeley: University of California Press.

———. 1984. *Science and values: The aims of science and their role in scientific debate.* Berkeley: University of California Press.

———. 1988. Are all theories equally good? A dialogue. In R. Nola, ed., *Relativism and realism in science,* 117–140. Dordrecht, The Netherlands: Kluwer Academic Publishing.

———. 1990. *Science and relativism: Some key controversies in the philosophy of science.* Chicago: University of Chicago Press.

Leach, Mary. 1992. Can we talk? A response to Burbules and Rice. *Harvard Educational Review* 62, 257–263.

Lear, Jonathan. 1985. Moral objectivity. In S. C. Brown, ed., *Objectivity and cultural divergence,* 135–170. Cambridge: Cambridge University Press.

Leatherdale, W. H. 1974. *The role of analogy, model, and metaphor in science.* New York: American Elsevier Publishing.

Levin, Malcom A. 1986. Ways of life, citizenship education, and the culture of schooling. In D. Nyborg, ed., *Philosophy of Education 1985: Proceedings of the Forty-First Annual Meeting of the Philosophy of Education Society,* 279–283. Normal, Ill.: Philosophy of Education Society.

Lewis, C. S. 1960. *The four loves.* London: Collins.

Lickona, Thomas. 1991. *Educating for character: How our schools can teach respect and responsibility.* New York: Bantam Books.

Lincoln, Yvonna S. 1983. *The substance of the emergent paradigm.* Paper presented at the conference on Linking New Concepts of Organizations to New Paradigms for Inquiry: Fruitful Partnerships in Administrative Studies, Overland Park, Kansas, November 4–5, 1983.

Locke, Don. 1980. The illusion of Stage Six. *Journal of Moral Education* 9, 103–109.

———. 1985. A psychologist among the philosophers: Philosophical aspects of Kohlberg's theories. In S. Modgil and C. Modgil, eds., *Lawrence Kohlberg: Consensus and controversy,* 21–38. London: Falmer Press.

Lockwood, Alan L. 1975. A critical view of Values Clarification. *Teachers College Record* 76, 35–50.

Lonergan, Bernard J. F. 1958. *Insight: A study in human understanding.* Revised student edition. San Francisco: Harper and Row.

———. 1973. *Method in theology.* 2d ed. London: Dartman, Longman, and Todd.

Loy, David. 1988. *Nonduality: A study in comparative philosophy.* New Haven: Yale University Press.

Lukes, Steven. 1982. Relativism in its place. In M. Hollis and S. Lukes, eds., *Rationality and relativism,* 261–305. Cambridge, Mass.: MIT Press.

Lyons, David. 1982. Ethical relativism and the problem of incoherence. In J. Meiland and M. Krausz, eds., *Relativism: Cognitive and moral*, 209–225. Notre
Dame: University of Notre Dame Press.

MacIntyre, Alasdair. 1966 *SH. A short history of ethics*. New York: MacMillan.

———. 1977 *EC.* Epistemological crises, dramatic narrative, and the philosophy
of science. *Monist* 60, 453–472.

———. 1982 *GH.* How moral agents become ghosts. *Synthese* 53, 292–312.

———. 1983 *MP.* Moral philosophy: What next? In S. Hauerwas and A. MacIntyre, eds., *Revisions: Changing perspectives in moral philosophy*, 1–15. Notre Dame:
University of Notre Dame Press.

———. 1984a *AV. After virtue: A study in moral theory*. 2d ed. Notre Dame: University of Notre Dame Press.

———. 1984b *AET.* Does applied ethics rest on a mistake? *Monist* 67, 498–513.

———. 1985 *MA.* Moral arguments and social contexts: A response to Rorty. In
R. Hollinger, ed., *Hermeneutics and praxis*, 222–223. Notre Dame: University
of Notre Dame Press.

———. 1987a *EP.* The idea of an educated public. In G. Haydon, ed., *Education
and values: The Richard Peters Lectures*, 15–36. London: Institute of Education.

———. 1987b *PC.* Philosophy: Past conflict and future direction. *American Philosophical Association Proceedings and Addresses* 61, 81–87.

———. 1987c *TC.* Traditions and conflicts. *Liberal Education* 73, 6–13.

———. 1988a *VSD. Sophrosune*: How a virtue can become socially disruptive. In
A. French, T. E. Uehling, Jr., and H. K. Wettstein, eds., *Ethical theory: Character and virtue*, 1–11. Notre Dame: University of Notre Dame Press.

———. 1988b *WJ. Whose justice? Which rationality?* Notre Dame: University of
Notre Dame Press.

———. 1989 *RPP.* Relativism, power, and philosophy. In M. Krausz, ed., *Relativism: Interpretation and confrontation*, 182–204. Notre Dame: University of
Notre Dame Press.

———. 1990a *FP. First principles, final ends and contemporary philosophical issues*.
Milwaukee: Marquette University Press.

———. 1990b *FG.* The form of the good, tradition, and enquiry. In R. Gaita, ed.,
Value and understanding, 242–262. London: Routledge.

———. 1990c *MD.* Moral dilemmas. *Philosophy and Phenomenological Research* 50
Supplement, 367–382.

———. 1990d *TRV. Three rival versions of moral inquiry: Encyclopaedia, genealogy,
and tradition*. Notre Dame: University of Notre Dame Press.

———. 1991 *ITC.* Incommensurability, truth, and the conversation between
Confucians and Aristotelians about the virtues. In E. Deutsch, ed., *Culture and
modernity: East-West philosophic perspectives*, 104–122. Honolulu: University of
Hawaii Press.

——. 1992 *RVG*. Plain persons and moral philosophy: Rules, virtues and goods. *American Catholic Philosophical Quarterly* 66(1), 3–19.

——. 1993 *PPI*. *Philosophical imagination and cultural memory: Appropriating historical traditions*. Durham: Duke University Press.

——. 1994 *PRC*. A partial response to my critics. In J. Horton and S. Mendus, eds., *After MacIntyre*, 283–304. Notre Dame: University of Notre Dame Press.

Mackie, John L. 1977. *Ethics: Inventing right and wrong*. New York: Penguin Books.

Mandelbaum, Maurice. 1982. Subjective, objective, and conceptual relativisms. In J. Meiland and M. Krausz, eds., *Relativism: Cognitive and moral*, 34–61. Notre Dame: University of Notre Dame Press.

Margolis, Joseph. 1984a. Historicism, universalism, and the threat of relativism. *The Monist* 67, 308–326.

——. 1984b. Relativism, history, and objectivity in the human sciences. *Journal for the Theory of Social Behaviour* 14, 1–23.

——. 1989. The truth about relativism. In M. Krausz, ed., *Relativism: Interpretation and confrontation*, 232–255. Notre Dame: University of Notre Dame Press.

——. 1991. *The truth about relativism*. Cambridge, Mass.: Basil Blackwell.

Matilal, Bimal K. 1989. Ethical relativism and the confrontation of cultures. In M. Krausz, ed., *Relativism: Interpretation and confrontation*, 339–362. Notre Dame: University of Notre Dame Press.

Maturana, Humberto R., and Francisco J. Varela. 1988. *The tree of knowledge: The biological roots of human understanding*. Boston: Shambhala Publications.

Maxwell, Nicholas. 1984. *From knowledge to wisdom: A revolution in the aims and methods of science*. Oxford: Basil Blackwell.

McAninch, Amy R. 1985. A response to Boyd and Bogdan on *Values and Teaching*. *Educational Theory* 35, 321–325.

McCarthy, Thomas A. 1989. Contra relativism: A thought-experiment. In M. Krausz, ed., *Relativism: Interpretation and confrontation*, 256–271. Notre Dame: University of Notre Dame Press.

McGowan, John. 1991. *Postmodernism and its critics*. Ithaca: Cornell University Press.

McKenna, Paul. 1995. Christians can learn from Buddha's Way. *Compass* (March/April), 40–43.

McKeon, Richard, ed. 1941. *The basic works of Aristotle*. New York: Random House.

——. ed. 1947. *Introduction to Aristotle*. New York: Random House.

McKinney, R. H. 1987. Beyond objectivism and relativism. *Modern Schoolman* 64, 97–110.

Meiland, Jack, and Michael Krausz. 1982. *Relativism: Cognitive and moral*. Notre Dame: University of Notre Dame Press.

Meynell, Hugo. 1993. Bernard Lonergan and education. *Paideusis* 7(1), 3–13.

Miller, John. 1988. *The holistic curriculum*. Toronto: OISE Press.

Miller, Walter M. Jr. 1959. *A canticle for Leibowitz*. Toronto: Bantam Books.

Mink, Louis O. 1978. Narrative form as a cognitive instrument. In R. H. Canary and H. Kozicki, eds., *The writing of history: Literary form and historical understanding*, 129–149. Madison: University of Wisconsin Press.

Minow, Martha. 1990. *Making all the difference: Inclusion, exclusion, and American law*. Ithaca: Cornell University Press.

Misgeld, Dieter. 1987. The limits of a theory of practice: How pragmatic can a critical theory be? In E. Simpson, ed., *Antifoundationalism and practical reasoning*, 165–181. Edmonton: Academic Printing and Publishing.

Misgeld, Dieter. 1990. *A global context of repression: Possibilities of community response.* Paper presented at the 15th Annual Meeting of the Association for Moral Education, Notre Dame, Ind., November 7–10, 1990.

———. 1992. Pedagogy and politics: Some reflections on the critical pedagogy of Henry Giroux and its postmodern turn. *Phenomenology and Pedagogy* 10, 124–142.

Mitchell, Stephen. 1988. *Tao te ching*. New York: Harper & Row.

Mohanty, Jitendra N. 1989. Phenomenological rationality and the overcoming of relativism. In M. Krausz, ed., *Relativism: Interpretation and confrontation*, 326–338. Notre Dame: University of Notre Dame Press.

Monod, Jacques. 1971. *Chance and necessity*. New York: Alfred A. Knopf.

Moon, J. Donald. 1993. *Constructing community: Moral pluralism and tragic conflicts*. Princeton, N.J.: Princeton University Press.

Morgan, Kathryn. 1988. Women and moral madness. In L. Code, S. Mullett, and C. Overall, eds., *Feminist perspectives: Philosophical essays on method and morals*, 146–165. Toronto: University of Toronto Press.

———. 1991. Strangers in a strange land. In D. Odegard and C. Stewart, eds., *Perspectives on moral relativism*, 33–60. Milliken, Ont.: Agathon Books.

Morowitz, Harold J. 1989. Biology of a cosmological science. In J. B. Callicott and R. T. Ames, eds., *Nature in Asian traditions of thought: Essays in environmental philosophy*, 37–49. Albany: State University of New York Press.

Mouley, George J. 1978. *Educational research: The art and science of investigation*. 2d ed. Boston: Allyn and Bacon.

Mullett, Sheila. 1987. Only connect: the place of self-knowledge in ethics. In M. Hanen and K. Nielsen, eds., *Science, morality, and feminist theory*, 309–338. Calgary: University of Calgary Press.

Murdoch, Iris. 1970. *The sovereignty of good*. London: Routledge and Kegan Paul.

Nagel, Thomas. 1986. *The view from nowhere*. New York: Oxford University Press.

———. 1987. Moral conflict and political legitimacy. *Philosophy and Public Affairs* 16, 215–240.

Narayan, Uma. 1988. Working together across difference: Some considerations on emotions and political practice. *Hypatia* 3 (2), 31–47.

Neville, Robert C. 1981. *Reconstruction of thinking*. Albany: State University of New York Press.

Newton-Smith, William. 1982. Relativism and the possibility of interpretation. In
M. Hollis and S. Lukes, eds., *Rationality and relativism*, 106–122. Cambridge,
Mass.: MIT Press.

Nielsen, Kai. 1987. Searching for an emancipatory perspective: Wide reflective
equilibrium and the hermeneutical circle. In E. Simpson, ed., *Antifoundationalism and practical reasoning*, 143–163. Edmonton: Academic Printing and
Publishing.

———. 1988. In defense of wide reflective equilibrium. In D. Odegard, ed.,
Ethics and justification, 19–38. Edmonton: Academic Printing and Publishing.

Noddings, Nel. 1984. *Caring: A feminine approach to ethics and moral education.*
Berkeley: University of California Press.

———. 1985. *Some answers to questions on ethics of caring.* Paper presented at the
10th Annual Meeting of the Association for Moral Education, Toronto, Ontario, November 8–9, 1985.

———. 1987a. Do we really want to produce good people? *Journal of Moral Education* 16, 177–188.

———. 1987b. Doubts about radical proposals on caring. In N. C. Burbules, ed.,
*Philosophy of Education 1986: Proceedings of the Forty-Second Annual Meeting of the
Philosophy of Education Society*, 83–86. Normal, Ill.: Philosophy of Education
Society.

Nola, Robert, ed. 1988. *Relativism and realism in science.* Boston: Kluwer Academic
Publications.

Nucci, Larry. 1989. Challenging conventional wisdom about morality: The domain approach to values education. In L. Nucci, ed., *Moral development and
character education: A dialogue*, 183–203. Berkeley, Calif.: McCutchan.

———, ed. 1989. *Moral development and character education: A dialogue.* Berkeley,
Calif.: McCutchan.

Nussbaum, Martha C. 1986a. The discernment of perception: An Aristotelean
conception of private and public rationality. In J. C. Cleary, ed., *Boston Area
Colloquium in Ancient Philosophy*, 155–201. Lanham, Md.: University Press of
America.

———. 1986b. *The fragility of goodness: Luck and ethics in Greek tragedy and philosophy.* Cambridge: Cambridge University Press.

———. 1987. Finely aware and richly responsible: Literature and the moral
imagination. In A. J. Cascardi, ed., *Literature and the question of philosophy*,
167–191. Baltimore: John Hopkins University Press.

———. 1988. Non-relative virtues: An Aristotelean approach. In A. French,
T. E. Uehling, Jr. and H. K. Wettstein, eds., *Ethical theory: Character and virtue.*
Notre Dame: University of Notre Dame Press.

Nussbaum, Martha C., and Amartya Sen. 1989. Internal criticism and Indian rationalist traditions. In M. Krausz, ed., *Relativism: Interpretation and confrontation*, 299–325. Notre Dame: University of Notre Dame Press.

Oddie, Graham. 1988. On a dogma concerning realism and incommensurability. In R. Nola, ed., *Relativism and realism in science,* 169–204. Dordrecht, The Netherlands: Kluwer Academic Publishing.

Odegard, Douglas. 1987. Introduction. In E. Simpson, ed., *Antifoundationalism and practical reasoning,* 137–142. Edmonton: Academic Printing and Publishing.

———. 1991. Introduction: Challenges to moral relativism. In D. Odegard and C. Stewart, eds., *Perspectives on moral relativism,* 1–12. Milliken, Ont.: Agathon Publishing.

Odegard, Douglas, and Carole Stewart, eds. 1991. *Perspectives on moral relativism.* Milliken, Ont.: Agathon Books.

O'Donohoe, James A. 1980. Moral and faith development theory. In J. W. Fowler and A. Vergote, eds., *Toward moral and religious maturity: The First International Conference on Moral and Religious Development,* 373–401. Morristown, N.J.: Silver Burdett.

Okin, Susan M. 1989. Reason and feeling in thinking about justice. *Ethics* 99, 229–249.

Okrent, Mark B. 1984. Relativism, context, and truth. *The Monist* 67, 341–358.

O'Leary, Paul T. 1981. Moral education, moral character, and the virtues. *Journal of Educational Thought* 15, 42–46.

———. 1983. Moral education, character traits, and reasons for action. *Canadian Journal of Education* 8, 217–231.

Owens, Joseph. 1981. The KALON in Aristotelean Ethics. In D. J. O'Meara, ed., *Studies in Aristotle,* 261–277. Washington, D.C.: The Catholic University Press of America.

Pascal, Blaise. 1910. *Pensées.* Trans. W. F. Trotter. New York: F. Collier and Sons.

Pegis, Anton C., ed. 1948. *Introduction to St. Thomas Aquinas.* Toronto: Random House of Canada.

Pepper, Stephen C. 1942. *World hypotheses: A study in evidence.* London: University of California Press.

Peters, Tom J., and Robert H. Waterman, Jr. 1982. *In search of excellence.* New York: Harper and Row.

Phillips, Denis C. 1987. *Philosophy, science, and social inquiry: Contemporary methodological controversies in social science and related applied fields of research.* New York: Pergamon Press.

Polanyi, Michael. 1962. *Personal knowledge: Towards a post-critical philosophy.* Chicago: University of Chicago Press.

Power, F. Clark. 1981a. The just community approach to moral education. *Journal of Moral Education* 17, 195–208.

———. 1981b. Moral education through the development of the moral atmosphere of the school. *Journal of Educational Thought* 15(1), 4–19.

Power, F. Clark, Ann Higgins, and Lawrence Kohlberg. 1989. The habit of the common life: Building character through democratic community schools. In

L. Nucci, ed., *Moral development and character education: A dialogue*, 125–144. Berkeley, Calif.: McCutchan.

Pratt, Minnie B. 1988. Identity: Skin blood heart. In E. Bulkin, M. B. Pratt, and B. Smith, eds., *Yours in struggle: Three feminist perspectives on anti-semitism and racism*, 11–61. Ithaca: Firebrand Books.

Price, A. F., and Mou-lam Wong, eds. 1990. *The Diamond Sutra and the Sutra of Hui-neng*. Boston: Shambhala.

Putnam, Hilary. 1989. Truth and convention: On Davidson's refutation of conceptual relativism. In M. Krausz, ed., *Relativism: Interpretation and confrontation*, 173–181. Notre Dame: University of Notre Dame Press.

Queen's University Department of History. *Intellectual origins of the contemporary world*. Queen's University, Kingston: Author.

Rahula, Walpola. 1974. *What the Buddha taught*. Rev. ed. New York: Grove Press.

Raths, Louis E., Merrill Harmin, and Sidney B. Simon. 1978. *Values and teaching: Working with values in the classroom*. 2d ed. Columbus: Charles E. Merrill.

Rawls, John. 1971. *A theory of justice*. Cambridge, Mass.: Harvard University Press.

———. 1974/75. The independence of moral theory. *Proceedings and Addresses of the American Philosophical Association* 48, 5–22.

———. 1980. Kantian constructivism in moral theory. *Journal of Philosophy* 77, 515–572.

———. 1985. Justice as fairness: Political, not metaphysical. *Philosophy and Public Affairs*, 14, 239.

———. 1987. The idea of an overlapping consensus. *Oxford Journal of Legal Studies* 7, 1–25.

———. 1988. The priority of right and ideas of the good. *Philosophy and Public Affairs* 17, 251–276.

Ray, G. Thomas. 1995. *Ecological consciousness, moral imperative, and the double bind of local thinking*. Paper presented at the 21st Annual Meeting of the Association for Moral Education, New York, N.Y., November 16–18, 1995.

———. 1996. *Implications of closure for moral thinking*. Paper presented at the 22nd Annual Meeting of the Association for Moral Education, Ottawa, Ontario, November 14–16, 1996.

Raz, Joseph. 1990. Facing diversity: The case of epistemic abstinence. *Philosophy and Public Affairs* 19, 3–46.

Rice, Suzanne, and Nicholas C. Burbules. 1994. Communicative virtues and educational relations. In H. A. Alexander, ed., *Philosophy of Education 1993: Proceedings of the Forty- Ninth Annual Meeting of the Philosophy of Education Society*, 33–44. Normal, Ill.: Philosophy of Education Society.

Rigali, Norbert J. 1974. Human experience and moral meaning. *Chicago Studies* 13, 88–104.

Robertson, Emily. 1989. Moral education: Subjectively speaking. In J. Giarilli, ed., *Philosophy of Education 1988: Proceedings of the Forty-Fourth Annual Meeting of the Philosophy of Education Society*, 101–108. Normal, Ill.: Philosophy of Education Society.

Rockefeller, Steven C. 1992. John Dewey, spiritual democracy, and the human future. In J. Ogilvy, ed., *Revisioning philosophy*, 165–190. Albany: State University of New York Press.

Rorty, Amélie O. 1989. Relativism, persons, and practices. In M. Krausz, ed., *Relativism: Intrepretation and confrontation*, 418–440. Notre Dame: University of Notre Dame Press.

———. 1992. The advantages of moral diversity. *Social Philosophy and Policy* 9(2), 38–62.

———. ed. 1980. *Essays on Aristotle's ethics.* Berkeley: University of California Press.

Rorty, Richard. 1980. Pragmatism, relativism, and irrationalism. *Proceedings and Addresses of the American Philosophical Association* 53, 719–738.

———. 1989. Solidarity or objectivity? In M. Krausz, ed., *Relativism: Interpretation and confrontation*, 35–50. Notre Dame: University of Notre Dame Press.

Rosaldo, Renato. 1989. Introduction: Grief and a headhunter's rage. In R. Rosaldo, ed., *Culture and truth: The remaking of social analysis*, 1–21. Boston: Beacon Press.

Roszak, Theodore. 1972. *Where the wasteland ends.* New York: Doubleday.

Rothenberg, Paula. 1990. The construction, deconstruction, and reconstruction of difference. *Hypatia* 5(1), 42–57.

Ruddick, Sara 1993. New feminist work on knowledge, reason, and objectivity. *Hypatia* 8(4), 140–148.

Russell, Bertrand. 1967. *Why I am not a Christian.* London: Unwin Books.

Ryle, Gilbert. 1949. *The concept of mind.* London: Hutchinson.

———. 1966. Knowing how and knowing that. In I. Scheffler, ed., *Philosophy and education: Modern readings*, 2d ed., 140–162. Boston: Allyn and Bacon.

Saint-Exupéry, Marie-Antoine-Roger de. 1943. *The little prince.* Trans. Katherine Woods. New York: Harcourt, Brace, and World.

Salmon, Wesley C. 1967. *The foundations of scientific inference.* Pittsburgh: University of Pittsburgh Press.

Sandel, Michael J. 1982. *Liberalism and the limits of justice.* New York: Cambridge University Press.

Saunders, Trevor J., ed. 1981. *Aristotle: The Politics.* Markham, Ont.: Penguin Books.

Scholes, Robert. 1981. Language, narrative, and anti-narrative. In W. J. T. Mitchell, ed., *On narrative*, 200–208. Chicago: University of Chicago Press.

Scholes, Robert, and Robert Kellogg. 1966. *The nature of narrative.* New York: Oxford University Press.

Schön, Donald A. 1983. *The reflective practitioner: How professionals think in action.* New York: Basic Books.

Searle, John R. 1983. *Intentionality: An essay in the philosophy of mind.* Cambridge: Cambridge University Press.

Seller, Anne. 1988. Realism vs. relativism: Towards a politically adequate epistemology. In M. Griffiths and M. Whitford, eds., *Feminist perspectives in philosophy,* 169–186. Bloomington: Indiana University Press.

Shah, Indries. 1971. *Thinkers of the East.* Baltimore: Penguin Books.

Sherman, Nancy. 1989. *The fabric of character: Aristotle's theory of virtue.* Oxford: Clarendon Press.

Shweder, Richard A. 1986. Storytelling among the anthropologists. *The New York Times Book Review,* September 21, 1, 38–39.

————. 1989. Post-Nietzschian anthropology: The idea of multiple objective worlds. In M. Krausz, ed., *Relativism: Interpretation and confrontation,* 99–139. Notre Dame: University of Notre Dame Press.

Sichel, Betty A. 1988. *Moral education: Character, community, and ideals.* Philadelphia: Temple University Press.

Siegel, Harvey. 1987. *Relativism refuted: A critique of contemporary epistemological relativism.* Boston: Riedel Publishing.

Simpson, Evan. 1987. Colloquimur, ergo sumus. In E. Simpson, ed., *Antifoundationalism and practical reasoning: Conversations between hermeneutics and analysis,* 1–12. Edmonton: Academic Printing and Publishing.

Slater, Peter. 1978. *The dynamics of religion.* San Francisco: Harper and Row.

Smith, Huston. 1989. *Beyond the post-modern mind.* 2d ed. Wheaton, Ill.: The Theosophical Publishing House.

————. 1992. Is there a perennial philosophy? In J. Ogilvy, ed., *Revisioning philosophy,* 19–48. Albany: State University of New York Press.

Smith, Wilfred Cantwell. 1984. *Philosophia* as one of the religious traditions of humankind. In J. Galey, ed., *Différences, Valeurs, Hiérarchie: Textes offerts à Louis Dumant,* 253–279. Paris: Editions de l'École des Hautes Études.

————. 1988. Transcendence. *Harvard Divinity Bulletin* (fall), 10–15.

Snare, Francis. 1984. The empirical bases of moral scepticism. *American Philosophical Quarterly* 21, 215–225.

Sperber, Dan. 1982. Apparently irrational beliefs. In M. Hollis and S. Lukes, eds., *Rationality and relativism,* 149–180. Cambridge, Mass.: MIT Press.

Sprigge, Timothy. 1985. *Theories of existence.* Markham, Ont.: Penguin.

Stewart, J. 1975. Clarifying Values Clarification: A critique. *Phi Delta Kappan,* June, 684–688.

Streng, Frederick J. 1972. Studying religion: Possibilities and limitations of different definitions. *Journal of the American Academy of Religion* 40, 219–237.

Streng, Frederick, Charles Lloyd, and Jay Allen. 1973. *Ways of being religious.* Englewood Cliffs, N.J.: Prentice-Hall.

Strike, Kenneth A. 1987. Marxist and Liberal views of education: Some differences in moral epistemology. In N. Burbules, ed., *Philosophy of Education 1986:*

Proceedings of the Forty-Second Annual Meeting of the Philosophy of Eduation Society, 121–132. Normal, Ill.: Philosophy of Education Society.

———. 1989. *Liberal justice and the Marxist critique of education: A study of conflicting research programs*. New York: Routledge and Kegan Paul.

———. 1995. Discourse ethics and restructuring. In M. Katz, ed., *Philosophy of education 1994: Proceedings of the Fiftieth Annual Meeting of the Philosophy of Education Society*, 1–14. Urbana, Ill.: Philosophy of Education Society.

Suzuki, Shunryu. 1970. *Zen mind, beginner's mind.* New York: Weatherhill.

Swimme, Brian, and Thomas Berry. (1994). *The universe story: From the primordial flaring forth to the Ecozoic era.* San Francisco: Harper Collins.

Swoyer, Chris. 1982. True for. In J. Meiland and M. Krausz, eds., *Relativism: Cognitive and moral*, 84–108. Notre Dame: University of Notre Dame Press.

Tarnas, Richard. 1991. *The passion of the Western mind: Understanding the ideas that have shaped our world view.* New York: Ballantine.

Taylor, Charles. 1994. Justice after virtue. In J. Horton and S. Mendus, eds., *After MacIntyre*, 16–43. Notre Dame: University of Notre Dame Press.

Thomas, Laurence. 1993. Moral flourishing in an unjust world. *Journal of Moral Education* 22, 83–96.

Thomas, R. Murray. 1989. A proposed taxonomy of moral values. *Journal of Moral Education* 18, 60–75.

Thrangu, Khenchen. 1996. *The Uttara Tantra: A treatise on Buddha nature.* Rev. ed. Boulder, Colo.: Namo Buddha Seminar.

Thurman, Robert A. F. 1991. Tibetan psychology. In D. Goleman and R. Thurman, eds., *MindScience: An East-West dialogue*, 53–73. Boston: Wisdom Publications.

Travers, Robert M. 1969. *An introduction to educational research* 3d ed. New York: MacMillan.

Trigg, Roger. 1973. *Reason and commitment.* Cambridge: Cambridge University Press.

Trungpa, Chögyam. 1966. *Born in Tibet.* London: George Allen and Unwin.

———. 1973. *Cutting through spiritual materialism.* Boston: Shambhala.

———. 1975. *Glimpses of abhidharma.* Boston: Shambhala.

———. 1976. *The myth of freedom and the way of meditation.* Boston: Shambhala.

———. 1988. *Shambhala: The sacred path of the warrior.* Boston: Shambhala.

———. 1991. *The heart of the Buddha.* Boston: Shambhala.

———. 1993. *Training the mind and cultivating loving-kindness.* Boston: Shambhala.

Varela, Francisco J. 1992. Making it concrete: Before, during, and after breakdowns. In J. Ogilvy, ed., *Revisioning philosophy*, 97–110. Albany: State University of New York Press.

Varela, Francisco J., Evan Thompson, and Eleanor Rosch. 1991. *The embodied mind: Cognitive science and human experience.* Cambridge, Mass.: MIT Press.

Varga, Andrew, S. J. 1976. Reaction to Beck: Can moral values be excluded? In T. C. Hennessey, ed., *Values and moral development*, 23–28. New York: Paulist Press.

Vehmas, Simo. 1999. Newborn infants and the moral significance of intellectual disabilities. *JASH* 24, 111–121.

Vokey, Daniel. 1980. *Bernard J. F. Lonergan on the objectivity of judgments of value.* Unpublished master's thesis, Carleton University, Ottawa, Ontario.

———. 1987. *Outward Bound: In search of foundations.* Unpublished master's thesis, Queen's University, Kingston, Ontario.

———. 1990. Objectivity and moral judgment: Towards agreement on a moral education theory. *Journal of Moral Education* 19, 14–23.

———. 1993. MacIntyre and Rawls: Two complementary communitarians? In A. Thompson, ed., *Philosophy of Education 1992: Proceedings of the Forty-Eighth Annual Meeting of the Philosophy of Education Society,* 336–341. Normal, Ill.: Philosophy of Education Society.

———. 1994. *Meditation and moral development: A Buddhist view.* Paper presented at the 20th Annual Meeting of the Association for Moral Education, Banff, Alberta, November 11–12, 1994.

von Franz, Marie-Louise. 1977. *An introduction to the psychology of fairy-tales.* Zurich: Spring Publications.

———. 1980. *The psychological meaning of redemption motifs in fairy-tales.* Toronto: Inner City Books.

Waley, Arthur. 1958. *The way and its power: A study of the Tao Tê Ching and its place in Chinese thought.* New York: Grove Press.

Walker, Susan, ed. 1987. *Speaking of silence: Christians and Buddhists on the contemplative way.* New York: Paulist Press.

Wallace, Gerald, and A. D. M. Walker, eds. 1970. *The definition of morality.* London: Methuen.

Wallwork, Ernest. 1985. Sentiment and structure: A Durkheimian critique of Kohlberg's moral theory. *Journal of Moral Education* 14, 87–101.

Walsh, Roger, and Frances Vaughan. 1993. The art of transcendence: An introduction to common elements of transpersonal practices. *Journal of Transpersonal Psychology* 25, 1–9.

Weick, Karl E. 1979. *The social psychology of organizing.* 2d ed. Reading, Mass.: Addison-Wesley.

Weinert, Friedel. 1984. Contra res sempiternas. *The Monist* 67, 376–394.

Wellman, Carl. 1975a. Ethical disagreement and objective truth. *American Philosophical Quarterly* 12, 211–221.

———. 1975b. *Morals and ethics.* Glenview, Ill.: Scott, Foresman.

Wikan, Unni. 1989. Beyond the words: The power of resonance. *American Ethnologist* 19, 460–478.

Wilber, Ken. 1985. *No boundary: Eastern and western approaches to personal growth.* Boston: Shambhala.

Williams, Bernard. 1985. *Ethics and the limits of philosophy.* Cambridge, Mass.: Harvard University Press.

Williams, Paul. 1989. *Mahayana Buddhism: The doctrinal foundations.* London: Routledge.

Wilshire, Bruce. 1990. *The moral collapse of the university: Professionalism, purity, and alienation.* Albany: State University of New York Press.

Wilson, John. 1990. *A new introduction to moral education.* London: Cassell Educational Limited.

Winograd, Terry and Fernando Flores. 1987. *Understanding computers and cognition: A new foundation for design.* Reading, Mass.: Addison-Wesley Publishing.

Wong, David B. 1984. *Moral relativity.* Berkeley: University of California Press.

———. 1989. Three kinds of incommensurability. In M. Krausz, ed., *Relativism: Interpretation and confrontation,* 140–158. Notre Dame: University of Notre Dame Press.

Worsfold, Victor L. 1993. MacIntyre and Bloom: Two complementary communitarians. In H. A. Alexander, ed., *Philosophy of Education 1992: Proceedings of the Forth-Eighth Annual Meeting of the Philosophy of Education Society,* 328–335. Urbana, Ill.: Philosophy of Education Society.

Young, Arthur M. 1976. *The reflexive universe: Evolution of consciousness.* San Francisco: Delacorte Press.

Zemach, Eddy M. 1989. On meaning and reality. In M. Krausz, ed., *Relativism: Interpretation and confrontation,* 51–79. Notre Dame: University of Notre Dame Press.

Ziff, Paul. 1960. *Semantic analysis.* Ithaca: Cornell University Press.

Zukav, Gary. 1979. *The dancing Wu Li masters: An overview of the new physics.* New York: Morrow.

Zukier, Henri. 1986. The paradigmatic and narrative modes in goal-guided inference. In R. M. Sorrentino and E. T. Higgins, eds., *Motivation and cognition,* 465–502. New York: Guilford Press.

Index